Gardening with Native Plants of the Pacific Northwest

Gardening

of the

Second Edition, Revised and Enlarged

with Native Plants

Pacific Northwest

Arthur R. Kruckeberg

University of Washington Press *Seattle & London*

Copyright © 1982, 1996 by the University of Washington Press
First paperback edition, 1989
Fourth printing, 1993
Second edition, revised and enlarged, 1996
Third printing, 2003
Printed in the United States of America

The Library of Congress Cataloging-in-Publication Data can be found at the
end of this book.

The paper used in this publication meets the minimum requirements of
American National Standard for Information Sciences—Permanence
of Paper for Printed Library Materials, ANSI Z39.48-1984. ⊗

To my father, Arthur Woodbury Kruckeberg,

who early inspired in me a love of native plants

and an appreciation of their garden value

And to my wife, Mareen,

who conceived the idea of this book

and who contributed to its consummation in many ways

Credits (photographs not listed were taken by the author)

Contents

Preface to the Second Edition   ix

Preface to the Original Edition   xi

Acknowledgments   xii

Introduction   3   *Chapter 1*

Natural Environments in the Pacific Northwest   7

Garden and Landscape Uses of Native Plants   14

Propagation of Native Plants   21

Native Ornamental Trees   25   *Chapter 2*

Conifers   25

Broad-leaved Evergreens   57

Broad-leaved Deciduous Trees   66

Native Ornamental Shrubs   80   *Chapter 3*

Broad-leaved Evergreens and Ground Covers   81

Deciduous Shrubs   107

Native Ornamental Herbaceous Perennials   129   *Chapter 4*

Ferns   131

Ground Orchids   142

Lilies, Irises, and Their Kin   143

Other Herbaceous Perennials   158

Tall Herbs (3 to 10 feet)   158

Medium-sized Herbs (1 to 3 feet)   163

Small Herbs (less than 1 foot)   181

Chapter 5   220   Grasses and Grasslike Plants

222   Grasses for Woodland Settings

223   Grasses and Their Kin for Wetlands

224   Meadow Grasses

224   Grasses at the Seashore

225   Alpine and Low-growing Grasses for the Rock Garden

225   Grasses for East of the Cascades

Chapter 6   227   *Supplement*: More Native Plants
for Garden and Habitat Reclamation

227   Annuals

229   Herbaceous Perennials

236   Trees

239   Shrubs

243   *Appendix A.* Collecting in the Wild

244   *Appendix B.* Lists of Native Plants for Particular Settings

251   *Appendix C.* Sources of Information on Native Plants

255   *Appendix D.* Native Grasses and Their Kin

257   Glossary of Botanical, Horticultural, and Gardening Terms

261   Derivations and Meanings of Genus and Species Names

271   Selected Bibliography

275   Index

Preface to the Second Edition

At the time of the first edition, in 1982, the use of native plants as garden subjects was still a pioneering effort, with only a scattering of devotees. Fifteen years later a minor garden cult has become a major focus in American gardening. With *Time Magazine* featuring natives for the garden in a 1993 issue, the groundswell in popularity of native plants must have crested! Vastly more natives are now available and being planted, and gardeners may be becoming a bit smug in their successes with water-saving natives. The great surge of interest and fascination in growing native species has come from several quarters. Certainly, nationwide environmental concern, water-saving consciousness, and the intrinsic appeal of one's nearby wild flora have helped create the demand. Native plant societies provide additional motivation; nearly every state in the Union has one. Most western states have active societies, whose similar aims are the conservation and enjoyment of native flora, as well as education about native plants and plant life. Since 1982, the Canadian Wildflower Society's colorful magazine *Wildflower* has gained popularity on both sides of the border.

Two conservation efforts have also helped raise the visibility of native plants. One is the national recognition that certain native species—and their associated plant communities—are in trouble. Preservation of endangered species, as well as their habitats, has been the major thrust of the Rare and Endangered Species Act. Efforts at the state and national levels to preserve rare and endangered plants have elevated the public's level of awareness of our native floras. A second impetus for appreciating and using native species has been the dramatic upswing in applying ecological ideas to restoring degraded habitats. Northwest natives can heal ravaged landscapes. Wetlands have been the prime target of habitat or landscape restoration.

Habitat restoration has finally come into its own as a flourishing field of applied ecology. In the 1982 edition of this book, a section on this subject (pp. 14-17) was tentative, yet promising and provocative for the future. The future is now! In little more than a decade, landscape reclamation has become mainstream in the practice of theory. The literature on ecological reclamation is burgeoning and now formal college-level programs of instruction are available. Yet, much still needs to be done in reclaiming wetlands, wastelands, and other degraded habitats here in the Pacific Northwest and elsewhere. A prime objective in restoration work is the use of durable native plants—trees, shrubs, and herbaceous perennials—for pioneer sites. Currently the demand still exceeds the supply, even as more and more nurseries stock natives for restoration projects (see Appendix C and "Hortus West" for current sources). The "Useful References" section of the bibliography includes sources that will help the novice restorer or the established practitioner undertake reclamation work.

What else could be added to an already rather sumptuous reference on Pacific Northwest natives for the garden? Not much, a self-satisfied author might opine. But I now see several omissions in that first edition, which I rectify here with supplements to the original text. I have added a fifth chapter to take account of the very important native grasses and grasslike plants, and, in addition, more than forty grasses and their kin are listed in Appendix D. Grasses and similar herbs have come into their own as integral elements in the garden. Most now used are exotics; why not add some natives?

A few woody plants (trees and shrubs) also escaped the first edition. They appear alphabetically by genus in chapter 6. In 1982, I was rash enough to avoid mention of native annuals. There are, indeed, a few that merit the gardener's palette. They, along with a surprisingly ample list of more herbaceous perennials, are discussed in chapter 6. The roster of useful references inevitably has needed revision; new works or more recent editions of old favorites have been added to the Selected Bibliography.

The demand for natives in the coming century will surely exceed the supply. The number of nurseries and seed houses that stock natives, exclusively or partially, has escalated, though some last only a few years. Appendix C is an updated roster of sources, mostly of those that have persisted—and even thrived. But the best and last stop for those seeking retail sources of live plants or seed is "Hortus West—A Western North American Native Plant Directory and Journal," P.O. Box 2870, Wilsonville, OR 97070-2870. Look for revisions of "Hortus West" twice a year; issue no. 6 (1995) lists sources for nearly nine hundred species of natives. (I should caution enthusiasts about so-called "wildflower mixes," packets of seed purported to be native wildflowers. Some are genuine, but many others are liberally laced with the seed of roadside weeds. Beware!)

Pacific Northwest natives can satisfy aesthetically, practically, and ecologically; grow and enjoy them. Whether you "go native" all the way or mix natives with plants from other lands, you can expect pleasure from the beauty that natives can bring to your garden.

A.R.K.
June 1996

Preface to the Original Edition

As living ornaments in our culture and as the essential life-stuff on our planet, plants are today grown indoors and out in ever-increasing profusion. This reawakened popularity of the plant world includes wildlings, as well as lush indoor greenery from the tropics—witness the multitude of wildflower handbooks, mushroom guides, and pocketbooks on wild edibles. With this lively fascination with plants has come a rebirth of gardening, long a Western tradition and now, more than ever, a source of pleasure for people of all ages. The love of gardens has focused mostly on the colorful and the exotic, kindled by showy plants from other lands that grow with ease in outdoor and indoor gardens. But around the country, the urge to grow native plants in one's own garden or at the summer cabin is very much on the upswing. There are only a few books that satisfy this gardening-with-natives interest. In North America, it is only California and the East Coast that have a modest literature on natives for the garden. It is time that such a book on native plants of the Pacific Northwest catered to the large gardening public in that region and in other temperate climates. That is the object of this book.

More than 250 kinds of plants native to the Pacific Northwest claim a place here as ornamentals for gardens and other civilized places. I deal with each in this book, describing the plant's key features and commenting on its natural habitat, distribution, uses in the garden, and methods of propagation. Both common and botanical names are used throughout. Botanical names can take on added meaning or interest if one knows something of their derivation. The user of this manual will find derivations and meanings of the binomial or botanical names in a glossary at the end of the book.

The use of native plants as living ornaments in our built environment (cities, suburbia, rural communities) is a logical extension of our concern for preserving some of the Northwest's natural features. This book's prime audience is the gardening public, from the casual weekend gardener to the serious amateur with self-taught horticultural skills. Beyond the home gardener, others who traffic in plants, such as retail and wholesale nursery people, can profit from this book. Landscape architects, professional gardeners, and gardening contractors can add awareness of the appeal and beauty of native plants to their horticultural knowledge. Parks, building complexes, open spaces, reclaimable land, highway roadsides, and other public places get the professional attention of planners, landscapers, and other specialists. Native plants can become a part of their efforts, too. The largely untapped potential of gardening with Northwest natives needs to become a way of life for those who look to the plant world for beauty and serenity.

A.R.K.
Seattle, Washington
June 1981

Acknowledgments

Many persons have made contributions to this labor of love. Roy Davidson and Brian Mulligan gave early drafts critical readings and made valuable suggestions for additions to the text. Joe Witt of the University of Washington Arboretum was consulted on many facets of the writing. And, of course, a book on the garden values of Pacific Northwest plants inevitably utilizes the published accounts of the flora of our region by C. Leo Hitchcock and Arthur Cronquist. Hitchcock's frequent comments on garden value in his two major works on Northwest plants reflect the interest and firsthand experience that "Hitchy" has had in using natives in the garden; for his keen insight, I owe him a great debt of gratitude.

The many illustrations in the book come from the collections of several different artists, photographers, and naturalists. Though each contributor is acknowledged in the list of picture credits, I want to thank all of them for generously sharing their work. Special recognition is given the late Sigurd Olson of Seattle, whose photographic artistry adorns many a species description in the book. The line drawings are the work of Mareen S. Kruckeberg, Phyllis Woolwine, and Jeanne R. Janish. Mrs. Janish originally prepared her drawings for the five-volume *Vascular Plants of the Pacific Northwest*, and I am very grateful to her and, again, to C. Leo Hitchcock for permission to use them here. The two maps were executed with great skill by David Woo, University of Washington Department of Geography (Cartography).

I am also indebted to the University of Washington Arboretum Foundation and to the University of Washington Graduate School Research Fund for their generous support of this book in its prepublication phases; and to Sylvia Duryee, the Stanley Smith Horticultural Trust of Scotland, and the Bloedel Foundation of Washington for publication grants.

Naomi Pascal of the University of Washington Press gave me continued encouragement to complete the manuscript. She and her colleagues at the Press applied their many and singular talents to see the book through to publication. To them I am most grateful.

Gardening with
Native Plants
of the Pacific
Northwest

Chapter 1

Introduction

Any plant untainted by artificial breeding or selection grows as a native somewhere in the world. Red oak *(Quercus rubra)* ranges throughout the eastern United States; the strawberry tree *(Arbutus unedo)* grows wild in southern Europe and North Africa; and there are *Rhododendron* species galore growing wild in eastern Asia. A "native," in our sense of the word here, is a plant under cultivation that grows wild in the same local region.* Peoples around the world have for centuries cultivated plants that grow close by, raising them for food, for ornament, and for cultural symbols. They are truly gardening with natives.

The Pacific Northwest, with its abundant and enchantingly varied native plantlife, is the scope of this book. The Northwest region is broadly taken to include southern British Columbia and the territory south through Washington and Oregon to the northern counties of California; its eastern boundaries are the northern Rocky Mountains and the Great Basin. This huge area covers a great diversity of terrain, climate, and vegetation types. The mild oceanic climate of the western part is separated from the more extremes of heat, cold, and low moisture in the eastern sector by the Cascade Range, a near continuous rampart cleaving in two the north–south sweep of the Northwest country.

It will be necessary to look more closely at the diversity of this vast region as a source of native plants and of gardens where natives can flourish. Simply dividing the territory into the "wet side" and the "dry side" of the mountains is not enough. Within each of these broad subdivisions are local conditions of microclimate, soil, and vegetation that accommodate plants of particular temperament as natives in a garden setting.

What kinds of Northwest natives make good garden plants? Aesthetic appeal is primary, but the visual qualities of a plant are largely matters of individual taste. My chief goal is to present those natives that can satisfy the majority, yet, I cannot resist including some plants that will appeal to a minority of gardeners. Garden suitability includes the quality of plant form, its foliage, flowering, fruit, wildlife attraction, erosion control, and reclamation potential. Appropriate size, good garden temperament, and ease of propagation are further desirable traits. Plants with some mix of these traits abound in the Pacific Northwest.

Yellow pine *(Pinus ponderosa)*

Elmera *(Elmera racemosa)*

* Removed from its native setting to gardens elsewhere in the world, a plant is then called an "exotic."

3

They can be trees (evergreen and deciduous), shrubs (evergreen and deciduous), and ground covers and herbaceous perennials. Annuals, those plants of but a year's duration, are excluded. Unlike in California and the Southwest, there are few native annuals in the Northwest, and even fewer with any exceptional garden potential. So we will stick to long-lived plants, woody and herbaceous. Here, the herbaceous perennial includes ferns, bulbs, and those flowering plants that may die back to rest underground or at ground level through fall and winter, after a season's growth. The persisting parts of herbaceous perennials can be bulbs, root-crowns, leaf rosettes, stems, runners, and rhizomes, all devices rooted in the soil to bridge the seasons with their ongoing life.

In the following pages I discuss natural environments in the Pacific Northwest and the successful propagation and use in gardens and open spaces of plants from these natural environments. Beginning with chapter 2, every native plant of proven or potential value in cultivation is presented. For each species the common name(s), botanical name, and plant family are given, followed by a brief description of the plant, its habitat and geographic range, its garden uses and methods of propagation. Where appropriate, special attributes—such as wildlife values, edibility, and uses in land reclamation, open spaces, and conservation—are featured. Some native plants have accumulated their own folklore, and I have recounted these stories, as well as other anecdotal tidbits.

Following the descriptions of individual native trees, shrubs, and herbaceous perennials are appendixes which give practical information for the gardener: regulations on collecting in the wild, nursery sources, lists of natives suitable for planting in particular settings. Also provided are two glossaries: one for common garden and botanical terms, and one for genus and species names.

Plant Names

The authority for botanical names used in this book is Hitchcock and Cronquist, *Flora of the Pacific Northwest* (1973). Sources for plants growing outside the range of the Hitchcock book are Munz and Keck, *A California Flora* (1959) and Peck, *Manual of Higher Plants of Oregon* (1961). Many trees and shrubs have good, reliable common names, and I encourage their use, along with the correct botanical name. Some common names used in the Northwest, however, will not be recognized elsewhere. *Amelanchier* is called serviceberry by Northwesterners, but Saskatoon berry in parts of Canada, shadberry or shadbush in the East, and even snowy mespilus in England. The botanical name, with its universality and relative stability, is more reliable. After the initial stagefright of using them, persistent gardeners will learn and apply the botanical names with ease.

For botanical names in this book, I use the two-word term (binomial) for a particular species or kind of plant. Thus *Quercus garryana* is the full name of our deciduous white oak, the Garry oak. When discussing

Family: Liliaceae

Genus: *Fritillaria*

species: *lanceolata*

variety: *montana*

forma: *alba*

cultivar: 'Tom Thumb'

Common name: checker lily

a group of allied plants, I use the genus name only, or its equivalent common name. Thus, in speaking of the oaks, we can use the genus name, *Quercus;* for all wild buckwheats, we can use *Eriogonum;* for blue-eyed grasses, *Sisyrinchium;* and so on. After a genus name first appears in the text, subsequent reference to species in that genus may use the first letter of the genus followed by the species name. Thus, *Q. garryana* and *Q. chrysolepis* appear in abbreviated form immediately after the appearance of the genus name, *Quercus.*

Family names, in English and Latin, appear after each new species listing. Their utility to the user comes with time. The gardener will come to sense the affinity of one genus to another—their family allegiance. Knowing the features shared by salal, madrone, heather, and kinnikinnik confirms their placement in the heather family (Ericaceae). Since most books on plant identification use the family as the focal grouping, familiarity with the family's attributes will make botanical exploring for other members of that family easier.

Gardening with native plants can be a natural outcome of close association with the plants in the wild. There is no better way to gain this familiarity than to learn to identify plants. The indispensable reference for our area is *Flora of the Pacific Northwest* by C. Leo Hitchcock and Arthur Cronquist (1973), a one-volume condensed version of the five-volume *Vascular Plants of the Pacific Northwest;* the many quotes from Hitchcock on gardening qualities of natives are taken from this latter, unabridged, work.

History of Gardening with Natives in the Northwest

In nearly every epoch of discovery and exploration in the Pacific Northwest, naturalists collected plant material for introduction to gardens. José Moziño of the Malaspina expedition at Nootka Sound, Vancouver Island, undoubtedly was the first to send back seeds of a Northwest plant to the Old World in 1791. His introduction to Spain of the Cascade Oregon grape (*Berberis,* or *Mahonia aquifolium*) marks the first of a select number of introductions of live plants to Europe by early explorers, naturalists, and itinerant horticulturists.

Most early collecting, however, was not of seeds or live plants, but took the form of pressed specimens, eventually identified and shelved in the world's museums. From these specimens came the information in the botanical publications (called floras) describing the region's plant life. These dried collections were studied by gardeners and horticulturists whose appetites were whetted by what they saw, and who contrived to have some of the Northwest's floral treasure brought to European gardens. In 1824 the London Horticultural Society, for example, sent the young Scotsman David Douglas to the Pacific Northwest as their plant explorer. Douglas was charged with collecting dried specimens of the region's flora and with harvesting seeds for propagation back in Britain. In his journal, Douglas, for whom the Douglas fir is named, describes his mission: ". . . the Horticultural Society of London,

David Douglas (1799–1834), outstanding plant collector in the Pacific Northwest

desirous of disseminating among the gardens of Britain the vegetable treasures of those widely extended and highly diversified countries, resolved on sending a person experienced in the modes of collecting and preserving botanical subjects and of transmitting seeds to England." Besides his own valuable and extensive botanical collecting, Douglas' many introductions of plants to British gardening earn him the highest praise. Nearly every important tree and shrub in this book was either introduced or called attention to by him. And what a price he paid for all this treasure! Accounts of Douglas' travels and travail in the Pacific Northwest read like John Bunyan's *Pilgrim's Progress.* Hardship, disaster, mental anguish, loneliness, and difficulties with Indians were his almost continual lot; yet he succeeded beyond all expectations. No one since has made a greater contribution to the use of Northwest plants in the gardens of the world.

Between the Douglas period and the beginnings of the twentieth century, hardly any concerted efforts were made to introduce plants of the Northwest to the gardening public. Settlement and exploitation of the rich Northwest country were the major preoccupations. For most of that period, field botany for botanists—not for gardeners—was the custom. Railroad and geological surveys, exploring expeditions, and those solitary botanical correspondents of eastern "closet" botanists were still sending back only dried specimens.

By the 1920s, the region's plant life was reasonably well recorded, though publicized only through floras and scientific articles. Enough was known to encourage Northwest plantsmen to tap the rich garden potential in the nearby wilds. Carl Purdy of Ukiah, California, made trips into the Oregon Siskiyous in search of plants for his nursery and bulb business. Later in the 1930s and 1940s, Carl S. English, Jr., began to make his name known locally and internationally as a plantsman with a keen eye for natives with garden value. English's home nursery as well as his display of many natives at the Government Locks in Seattle provided the first real focus on natives for Northwest gardens. His many introductions include silk-tassel bush *(Garrya elliptica),* evergreen oaks, such as *Quercus vaccinifolia, Q. chrysolepis,* and *Q. sadleriana,* not to mention many choice herbaceous plants. During this same period, Elsa Frye of Seattle did much to further interest in natives through her writings, her garden, and her rare plant nursery.

Among the several outstanding native plantsmen in Oregon, Marcel LePiniec and the team of Lawrence Crocker and Boyd Kline are preeminent. They developed a thorough knowledge of the plants of southwestern Oregon and have shown a fine sense of what plants to grow and how to cultivate them. The work of another outstanding Oregon plantsman, Rae Berry of Portland, lives on in her garden, now endowed as the Berry Botanical Garden.

Natives as rock garden subjects have been a special passion of Ed Lohbrunner of Victoria, British Columbia. For years his nursery provided superb specimens of natives as well as exotics for the rock gardener.

The quest for fine native plants still goes on. An increasing number of specialty plantsmen (nursery managers and seed dealers) offer the public the fruits of their searches for good forms of old favorites and the rare, unusual, and untried plants in our flora. Appendix C lists some of these dealers. Several horticultural and native plant societies in the Pacific Northwest foster the use of natives in the garden; some carry on seed exchanges for members and conduct annual plant sales (Appendix C).

Natural Environments in the Pacific Northwest

The vast territory of the Pacific Northwest embraces a diversity of climates, terrain, and natural vegetation. Towering coastal forests, open coastal prairies and bogs, montane forests, timberline and alpine tundra in the high country, yellow-pine forests, sagebrush and bunchgrass hills and plains, all are attuned to particular mixes of climate and other

A subalpine habitat near Mt. Stuart, Washington, rich in herbs and conifers

defining features of habitat. Some appreciation of this rich variety of growing conditions is needed for gardening with natives, as with exotics. First, having information on the natural habitats of desirable natives for the garden can make their cultivation elsewhere more successful. Knowing that the blueblossom or wild lilac *(Ceanothus thyrsiflorus)* is restricted to coastal Oregon tells us where it is liable to do best in the Pacific Northwest. Second, the garden habitat itself has to be appreciated. The growing conditions in a garden in Spokane, Bend, or Omak will be far different from those in Tacoma, Coos Bay, or Victoria. While it is true that a garden is a less demanding habitat than the nearby natural environment, the local and regional setting of a garden does place restraints on the adaptability of a plant.

Ecologists recognize over sixteen natural provinces in the Northwest (Map 1). Each is characterized by relatively uniform climate, geology, and vegetation. Table 1 gives some of the major attributes of those provinces where gardening is practiced.

Particular climates and topography produce characteristic responses in the life they support. In the ecological view, each province supports a unique biota; the native flora is then a measure of garden plant potential. The major vegetation types in the Northwest correspond roughly to the physiographic provinces. Forested regions, though they occur on either side of the Cascades, are more extensive on the west side. The several major forest types (after Franklin and Dyrness 1973) can be separated by altitude and proximity to the ocean.

Weather bureau records are valuable guides for the gardener. Records of rainfall, temperature, winds, killing frosts, and amount of sunshine can help define the character of a regional setting in which the garden occurs. Table 3 gives some selected data useful to gardeners (see also, regional weather data, anon. 1941).

Plant Hardiness Zones

The United States Department of Agriculture has provided a practical conversion of low temperatures to a scale of hardiness. "Hardiness" is a plant's ability to withstand cold. Hardiness Zone 1 has the lowest temperatures, while Zone 9 is the mildest in the Northwest. The hardiness-zone map for the Pacific Northwest (Map 2) may seem to be of limited value in the use of native plants, as their hardiness ratings are not always known. But the gardener can be sure that a plant native in Zone 8 or milder habitats will have trouble surviving in colder zones. Conversely, a plant native to a colder zone can be grown successfully in a milder zone, if other factors, especially moisture, are compatible. Several books and pamphlets on ornamental plants that include some natives, give the hardiness zone for each plant. Rehder's *Manual of Cultivated Plants* (1956) and the Washington–Oregon Cooperative Extension Bulletin No. 592, *Plant Materials for Landscape* (1969), should be consulted. A new hardiness-zone system appears in the *Sunset New Western Garden Book.*

TABLE 1. Gardening Potential for Regions of the Pacific Northwest

Province	Climate	Geology and Soils	Gardening Conditions
Puget Trough: Lower Fraser River, San Juan Islands, Puget Sound and south to the Columbia River	Winters mild, wet; summers mild to warm, wet to dry	Mostly alluvial soils from rivers and glacial action; all but river-bottom soils rather infertile	Year-round growing conditions for evergreen trees and shrubs. Optimal hardiness for all Pacific Northwest natives and mild temperate exotics
Willamette Valley: Portland to Roseburg	Winters mild, wet; summers warm, dry	Alluvial soils in valleys, mostly lava soils in foothills; moderate fertility	Similar to Puget Trough, but milder. Excellent for all natives and temperate exotics; summer watering
Olympic Peninsula: Lowlands, including Vancouver Island	Winters mild, very wet; summers mild, wet to dry; "rain shadow" areas with less moisture	Mostly alluvial soils from rivers and glacial deposits; soils mostly infertile	Optimal for mild temperate species, natives and exotics. Summer watering in "rain shadow" areas
Coast Ranges: Chehalis–Grays Harbor area south to Coos Bay	Winters mild, very wet, colder in mountains back of coast; summers mild, wet to dry in interior sections	Fertile alluvial soils in coastal valleys, infertile dune sand often in coastal areas; lava soils in foothills	Optimal for mild temperate species, natives and exotics. Wind protection, salt tolerance, and fertilizer needed in some coastal sites
Klamath Mountains: Coastal southwest Oregon and adjacent northwest California; Rogue River valley (mountains excluded)	Winters moderate to cool, wet; summers cool, dry on coast and hot, dry inland	Alluvial soils in valleys, lava soils upland; infertile serpentines in many upland sections	With summer watering, optimal for mild-temperate species. Coastal and serpentine areas pose special problems of protection and fertility
Okanogan Highlands and Cascades: Canada to northern California (mid- and upper-montane excluded)	West side: winters moderate to cool, wet; summers warm and dryish. East side: winters cold, heavy to light snowfall; summers hot, dry	Alluvial soils in mountain valleys; diverse rock types weathering to shallow stony soils in upland areas; fairly infertile	Westside lower montane with moderate hardiness; mountain valleys suffer frost (zone 6). East side: only the hardier natives/exotics survive (zones 4, 5, 6)
Columbia Basin: Wenatchee–Ephrata–Spokane to Redmond–Bend	Winters cold, dry with little snow cover; summers hot, dry	Fertile lava soils in valleys and upland	Hardier natives should be tried. Winter protection, summer water needed
Blue Mountains: Oregon–Washington, Idaho uplands and montane valleys (excludes mid- to upper-montane), Prineville–La Grande–Baker, N.E. to Walla Walla–Lewiston	Winters cold, moderate to heavy snow cover; summers hot, dry, with thunder showers	Fertile lava soils in valleys and foothills	Hardier natives should be tried. Winter snow protection; summer water needed

(The remaining provinces of south-central and southeastern Oregon and adjacent Idaho are the High Lava Plains, Basin and Range, and Owyhee Upland. Though the climate is as severe as in the Columbia Basin, or more so, hardier natives merit trial here.)

TABLE 2. Natural Vegetation Zones and Their Gardening Potential

Zone/Vegetation Type	Location	Associated Natives	Garden Growing Conditions
Westside Forest Regions			
Sitka Spruce Zone	Pacific coastal strip: Vancouver Island to northwest California	Sitka spruce, western hemlock, swordfern, salal, other ericads	Optimal for evergreen trees, shrubs, ericads, mild temperate species
Western Hemlock Zone	Southwest British Columbia, western Washington, western Oregon, northwest California	Western hemlock, western red cedar, red alder, Douglas fir	Same as above
Puget Sound Area	San Juan and Gulf Islands, Puget Sound to Chehalis, Washington	Same as for Western Hemlock Zone, plus Garry oak and madrone	Same as above
Mixed Conifer/Mixed Evergreen	Klamath–Siskiyou Mountains, southwest Oregon, northwest California	Douglas fir, sugar pine, white fir, black oak, bay laurel, Garry oak, tan oak	Lower elevations, mild, warm; optimal for many garden plants
Subalpine	Cascades, Olympics	Mountain hemlock, subalpine fir, silver fir	Short growing season; little garden potential
Interior Valleys of Western Oregon			
Willamette	Portland to Eugene	Garry oak, Douglas fir, hazel, swordfern	Ideal for mild temperature plants and drought-tolerant species
Rogue/Umpqua	Roseburg to Ashland	Same as Willamette Zone, plus yellow pine and black oak	Same as above, but warmer and drier
Eastside Forest Regions			
Yellow Pine Zone	Okanogan Highlands to northern California	Yellow pine, sagebrush, bitterbrush	Severe winters; hot summers; low rainfall. Hardier natives
Pumice Area	Central Oregon	Lodgepole pine, bitterbrush	Same as Yellow-Pine Zone
Grand Fir–Douglas Fir Zone	Lower to mid east slope uplands	Grand fir, Douglas fir, larch, lodgepole pine, buckbrush	Cold, heavy snowpack; hot summers. Hardy natives
Non-forested Regions			
Timberline and Alpine Zones	Cascades, Olympics	Limited to hardy natives or exotics of similar zone type	
Steppe ("Desert") Regions: including sagebrush steppe, grass-shrub steppe, desert shrub, and western juniper zones	Plains and foothills of eastern British Columbia, Oregon, and Washington	Sagebrush, bitterbrush, rabbitbrush, many grasses, herbaceous perennials	All steppe/desert regions have cold winters with high wind-chill factor; low rainfall, scant snow cover; summers hot and dry. Only drought- and cold-tolerant natives

TABLE 3. Some Weather Records for the Pacific Northwest

Location	Annual Rainfall (inches)	Normal Temperatures °F January			Normal Temperatures °F July			Last Spring Frost	First Fall Frost	Growing Season (days)
		Min.	Ave.	Max.	Min.	Ave.	Max.			
British Columbia										
Vancouver	58.7		36			63				
Victoria	27.7		37			62				
Kelowna	11.6		25			68				
Washington										
Bellingham	33.6		37			63		5/10	10/05	148
Port Angeles	24.6		37			57		3/26	11/19	238
Seattle (Airport)	38.9	33	38	44	54	65	76	4/06	11/04	212
Olympia	52.4	31	38	45	48	64	80	5/08	10/15	160
Aberdeen	84.5		39			60		4/16	10/30	197
Vancouver	39.0		39			67		3/25	11/13	233
Omak	10.4		23			74		5/07	10/03	149
Wenatchee	9.0		26			73		4/14	10/19	188
Spokane	17.2	19	25	31	55	71	86	4/25	10/11	169
Ephrata	8.4		26			77		4/13	10/15	185
Yakima	7.9	19	27	37	53	71	89	4/21	10/15	177
Tri-cities*	7.5		30			75		4/13	10/22	192
Walla Walla	15.5	27	33	39	63	76	89	4/09	10/28	202
Pullman	20.5		29			68		4/26	10/10	167
Oregon										
Astoria	77.5		40			61		3/08	12/06	273
Portland	39.4		39			67		3/06	11/24	263
Salem	37.2		40			67		4/01	10/31	213
Corvallis	40.1		39			66		4/15	10/23	191
Eugene	37.9		40			66		4/13	11/04	205
Roseburg	30.5		41			67		3/30	11/19	234
Grants Pass	29.2		39			70		5/09	9/28	142
Medford	16.5		38			72		5/06	10/14	161
Ashland	19.8		38			69		4/23	10/22	182
Newport	66.2		44			57		3/23	11/26	248
Brookings	73.6		46			58		3/15	12/09	269
The Dalles	13.7		32			73		5/11	10/24	166
Pendleton	13.7		33			72		5/03	10/05	155
Bend	12.6		31			65		6/08	9/07	91
La Grande	19.5		30			70		4/26	10/03	160
Klamath Falls	12.4		29			68		5/18	9/26	131
Baker	10.7		25			66		5/12	10/03	144

* Pasco, Kennewick, Richland

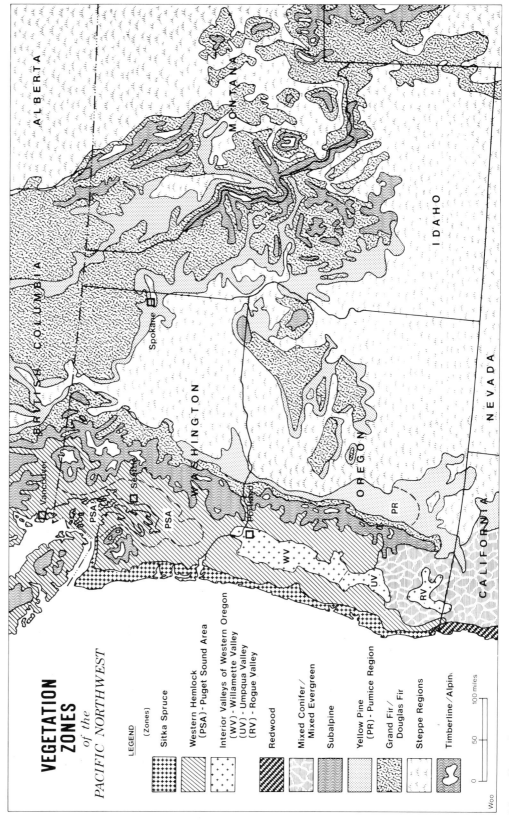

Map 1. Vegetation zones

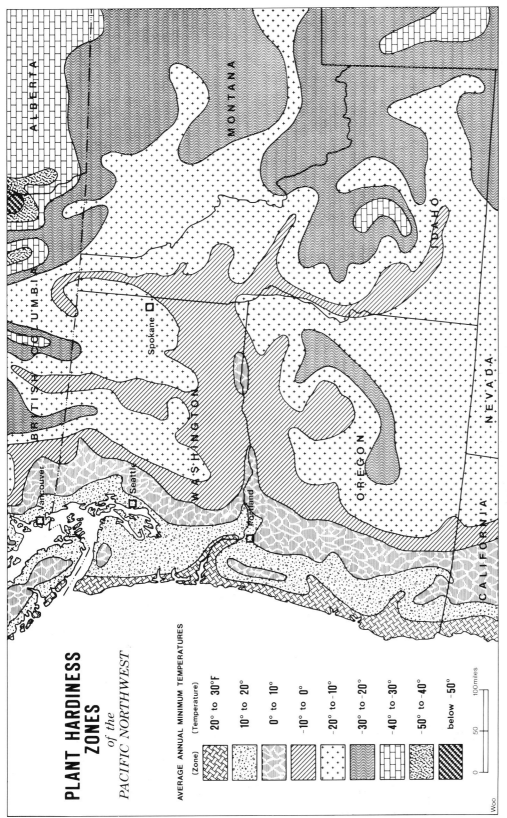

Map 2. Plant hardiness zones

Garden and Landscape Uses of Native Plants

There is no real difference between the requirements for growing natives and those for growing exotics in the garden. Once introduced to the garden setting, natives and exotics are on equal footing: their success in every sense, from aesthetic to practical, is the result of good judgment, garden skill, and luck.

The key to garden success is the compatibility of a plant to its place in the garden. This means that natives can easily coexist with exotics in the garden as long as the requirements of the plant—and the desires of the creator of the plantings—are met. Of course, some purists may wish to "go all native." A garden entirely made up of native plants may be most appropriate in a woodland or semi-wild setting in suburbia, in rural areas, or at the vacation cabin by the sea or in the mountains. And there is often good reason to emphasize natives in such places. The site likely will already be stocked with wild trees, shrubs, or herbs that remain after development. Why not add those natives that are suited to the surrounding natural vegetation? Planting salal, oceanspray, madrone, and huckleberry in a westside scene that contains Douglas fir can restore the beauty of a natural woodland setting. Once established, the native garden becomes a nearly self-sustaining, low-maintenance setting.

Good taste and an ecological eye should be the prime arbiters in growing native plants in people-oriented environments and landscapes. Herbert Durand in his North American classic, *Taming the Wildlings,* gives a list of the varied uses for natives that is as valid today as it was in 1923. Though his gardening public was on the East Coast, his

Deer fern *(Blechnum spicant)* in a garden setting

vision of how natives could be used is broad and timeless. Well worth paraphrasing are his categories of uses to which natives can be put:

1. *The Small Home Garden.* Natives can be used to define boundaries, in borders and shrubbery groups, and in sites adjacent to the house and outbuildings. Natives for the small garden need to be chosen with special care; matters of scale, quality of color and texture, and habitat preference are particularly important.

2. *Suburban and Rural Places.* "For restoring the original charm of neglected woodlands and developing the latent beauty of any forested area." With these words, Durand makes an appeal that is even more urgent today. Many pockets of land in our countryside can regain some of their natural beauty by the judicious use of native plants. Larger homesites in suburbia that include a remnant of the former native vegetation can be enhanced with natives. Farm buildings, pastures, and hedgerows are other places for beautification with natives.

3. *The Seashore, Woodland, or Mountain Retreat.* Vacation cabins and summer homes now dot much of the landscape that was once wild shoreline, forest, even farmland and tree farms. The very purpose of a house in the wilds cries out for restoring its surroundings with wildlings. Rather than put in reluctant and unsuited exotics that will do poorly and look out of place, make the summer place more a part of the surroundings with the planting of compatible natives.

4. *Parks, Open Spaces, and Estates.* Nearly every community in the Pacific Northwest has tracts of land set aside for public and private recreation. City and county parks, small vest-pocket (triangle) open spaces, or the grander open spaces and buffer lands are the community amenities that must coexist with the built environment for psychic and physical well-being of the human occupants. Large private acreages still exist where their owners can afford such luxuries. Native trees and shrubs are especially suited to all such large tracts of land. Not only do the natives blend in well with the regional landscape, they are usually self-perpetuating. Alder, maples, willows, Oregon grape, madrone, salal, the lowland conifers, these and many more take to naturalizing with ease. Once established, they mature and spread their well-adjusted progeny nearby.

5. *Wildlife Sanctuaries.* The choice of natives for birds and other wildlife is a common-sense one. Plants from the surrounding wilds for use in the re-created wildlife sanctuary should emphasize the attributes of shelter, nesting sites, and food. Most native trees and shrubs qualify without question; even though some may not have edible fruits or seed, they surely harbor insects and the like. Some conservation groups can start their own wildflower preserves, especially as sanctuaries for rare or unusual species whose existence in the nearby wilds is threatened. A native plant section in a community arboretum or park adds a wild flavor to the setting, demonstrates the uses of natives in cultivation, and serves as a living outdoor classroom for students of our native plant heritage.

6. *Highway Plantings.* Some natives, like salal, Oregon grape, vine ma-

ple, Douglas fir, and kinnikinnik, have already proved their worth in plantings along freeways and other roadside places. Others merit trial, particularly shrubs of proven durability in stressful habitats. The highway rest area is a particularly apt proving ground for durable natives. Most rest areas are abused bits of wild nature that can be best reclaimed by planting natives.

7. *Commercial, Industrial, and Public Sites.* There should come a time when the harsh and the ugly around our areas of public and private commerce will be screened or buffered from view by amenity plantings. Even a railyard, garbage pit, sawmill, or steel plant can look less stark after tree and shrub plantings have begun to mature. The more durable species of pines, Douglas fir, incense cedar, or tougher hardwoods like alder, birch, and big-leaf maple could do wonders in industrial and waste areas around our towns and cities.

8. *Ecological Restoration with Natives.* Hardly new to the ecologist who is accustomed to seeing land reclaimed by vegetation following disturbance, this natural process of succession has yet to be exploited by the land planner and kindred professionals. Only in recent years have ecological principles been applied to the practical functions of revegetating despoiled landscapes. The strip mines of the East offered the initial challenge. Though the successes are modest yet, land managers are learning how to apply living green to desecrated landscapes.

Blighted landscapes are nearly everywhere in the Northwest where human activity or natural catastrophe has visited the land. Most often the blights are near sea level, where the human enterprise is concentrated. Seaports, with their attendant assault on the shoreline (land fills, dumps, spoil heaps, and debris-strewn wasteland) are all too often left alone. In their neglect, aggressive weeds of European origin come in with rank vigor. But most weeds die back after the season's growth, leaving their own desolation. Woody natives, especially trees and shrubs with urban durability, should be given a chance to soften or erase the neglected squalor.

Other lowland waste places come to mind: community sanitary fills, old gravel quarries, abandoned farm and industrial land, mine heaps— the list goes on and on. The need for restoration of these abused habitats is there. But the effort to restore them with plants is yet to become an accepted part of urban responsibility. Even with the best of intentions and financial commitment, communities would be hard-pressed to start projects of restoring the habitat. The major stumbling blocks are the short supply of two resources: native plants and trained personnel. There is as yet no substantial enterprise devoted to harvesting the seeds of natives or to growing them as nursery stock. The forest industry and public forestry agencies grow commercial tree species and a number of seed companies carry seeds of timber species. But the simple practice of producing large quantities of vine maple, salal, big-leaf maple, and even alder is lacking. Collecting the seeds, processing the harvest, and storing, propagating, and disseminating the seed stocks need a modest technology and financial support.

The skills required to put the native plants to work restoring landscapes are a bit more exacting. A new breed of "ecological engineers" will have to be trained. A product of this training will have combined the rudiments of plant ecology, plant identification, landscape design, soils-hydrology, and urban forestry. The two goals—meeting the need for native plant materials and for trained personnel—are readily attainable, once the private and public sectors of our society see the value of such an enterprise.

The Right Place for the Right Plant

It is rather remarkable that there are as many successes as failures for those who garden in ignorance of the right habitat for a plant. With exotic species, we only have access to secondary cues as to where a plant should be placed: in sun or shade, in wet or dry sites, etc. For such plants from faraway places, the very limited information on habitat requirements in books, nursery catalogs, or gained by hearsay may work, but further insurance can come from learning a plant's own cues: small gray leaves suggest sun; large, dark green leaves signify tolerance to shade. For natives, the best cues are right at hand. The practiced eye can observe the native plant in its nearby natural surroundings to learn the conditions that suit it best. The serious gardener will study firsthand (or vicariously from books on local floras) the ecological requirements of his chosen natives. Some species have wide environmental tolerances in nature: salal, Douglas fir, and tall Oregon grape are broad-gauge species; but the little salal (Gaultheria ovatifolia), Brewer's spruce, and low Oregon grape are more fastidious.

In the largest section of this book (chapters 2 through 4) on particular native species for cultivation, specific habitat preferences are given for each plant. Here I will only note some of the general precautions one should take in choosing a particular garden place for a plant. Each distinct garden habitat is its own mix of temperature, moisture, light, soil (texture, acidity, fertility), and terrain. Those gardens that have the advantage of a variety of exposures and terrain have several small-scale environments (microclimates), each suited to certain kinds of plants.

Temperature. Within the confines of a regional climate, a particular locality can have areas of exceptional warmth or cold, depending on terrain. Cold air may drain away from or collect in a given spot. A south-facing aspect can be warmer in the summer and winter on the west side of the Cascades, but can be more severe in winter on the east side, due to loss of protective snow cover.

Moisture. A 35-inch annual rainfall may give seasonal aridity in one place and a water-logged condition year-round in another. Such wide variation in soil moisture results from differing degrees of drainage; some soils are well-drained, tending to be arid in the summer, while others hold water longer. Most natives like well-drained soils; those few that like their feet wet can be pampered. Good drainage comes from coarse-textured, loose sandy soil with free drainage (no hardpan) in the subsoil. Gardens on sloping terrain are usually well drained, while those on flat land may have problems.

Soil Fertility. Rarely are garden soils anything like original native soil prior to modification of the site. The original soils in our built environment have usually been altered, reclaimed, or wholly replaced by a variety of mixtures, good and bad. Hence soil texture, water-holding capacity, and fertility of the garden soil can vary widely from one place to another and are usually less than optimal. One can depend on a newly established garden to have fertility problems. Books on gardening for our region (Grant and Grant, *Trees and Shrubs for Pacific Northwest Gardens;* Willis, *The Pacific Gardener*) give the essentials for improving soil fertility. Amounts of available nutrients in soils can affect the growth of natives; like exotics, they do better with adequate soil nutrients. But it is safe to say that most natives will thrive on levels of fertility below those of the intensively cultivated vegetable garden or flower bed. Most often, one needs to fertilize only at the time of planting; once established the natives will usually perform well.

Most westside soils are acid (soil acidity or pH levels less than 7.0, often as low as 4.5–5.0), which usually means that nutrients like calcium and potassium are in short supply. Plants known to be tolerant of strongly acid soils, like most ericads (salal, huckleberry, kinnikinnik, madrone, and other members of the heather family), do well in acid soils, if they get sufficient nitrogen and phosphorus. Growth of other species not tolerant of acid conditions can be improved by adding lime to the soil. By judicious and sparing use of both compost and organic or chemical fertilizers, native plantings can be made to thrive as well as or better than in their wild homes. A consolation to eastside gardeners, who are often limited in their choices by hardiness problems, is that fertility of soils is higher on the more arid east side of the Cascades.

Special infertility problems are encountered in some soils. Peaty soils are usually strongly acid and sterile. Sandy soils will need the addition of organic matter and nutrients. Soils of dune areas may have a high salt content from ocean sprays, and therefore call for salt-tolerant natives. In southwestern Oregon and adjacent northern California, great tracts of serpentine soils nearly always have fertility problems. One solution is to use natives with their own inborn tolerance, plants that grow naturally on serpentines. For those natives or exotics not tolerant to serpentine soils, heavy application of lime, nitrogen, phosphate, and potassium is usually necessary.

Light. All green plants require light, but they can differ sharply in the amount they need. And thereby does the essence of a garden with rich textures and form come into being. The plants that require full sun dominate in one part of the garden, and those needing partial to full shade are happiest in other garden microclimates. Northwest native plants are no different. In a westside forest, Douglas fir is the sun-lover, while many of the shrubs and herbs under the forest canopy tolerate partial to full shade. The forest ecologist expresses the light requirement as levels of shade tolerance, or just plain tolerance. To say that Douglas fir is intolerant of shade, while western hemlock and western red cedar are tolerant, is to recognize that at the crucial seedling stage, Douglas fir cannot thrive in shade, while hemlock and cedar can. Shrubs and herbs of the forest floor are shade tolerant. Who would think of growing wild ginger *(Asarum caudatum)*, devil's club *(Oplopanax horridum)*, or oak fern *(Gymnocarpium dryopteris)* in full sun? Most natives that come from open habitats (yellow-pine forest, oak woodlands, rock outcrops, or sagebrush "desert") demand full sun.

Topography. In even the most level garden site, the terrain can be molded into pleasing irregularities. Rock walls, mounds, and depressions, humanly contrived, not only relieve the eye of flat monotony, but can provide, with miniature hills, valleys, and slopes, those varied environments on a micro-scale for the garden. For the property owner blessed with natural topography of slope, rock outcrop, depression, or hillock, the prospects are wide open for exploiting habitat variations. And there is a good native for nearly every kind of terrain. Remember: it is variations in topography that produce highly local climatic variations. One side of a rock gives full sun; the other, full shade.

Plant Interactions. Plants respond to one another, often more noticeably than they do to the non-living features of their environments. The ecologist recognizes this potent source of influence of one life on another as "biotic interaction." Plants make shade, extract moisture and nutrients, and control local temperatures to dramatically effect responses in their neighbors. For the gardener, the prospect of plant-to-plant interactions should stimulate skillful and artistic manipulation of the plantings, native and exotic. A state of instant maturity in a garden can be achieved only at a cost of undesired plant competition. Youngish plants placed too close to one another will soon become overcrowded. And this can lead to the suppression of growth, one plant by another. It pays to plan the spacing and vertical stratification of plants in the garden at the time of planting. This means "elbow room" for the trees and shrubs, and a suitable ground-level habitat for the shade-tolerant herbaceous plants and ground covers.

Sometimes the effect of an overtopping mature shrub or tree can adversely affect the understory plantings in all respects, robbing the groundlings of light, moisture, and nutrient. Madrone and western red cedar can have this adverse effect, to be overcome only by seeing what nature provides as the compatible ground cover.

Practical gardening is hardly aware of still another, more subtle, control of plant growth. The new word "allelopathy" has a firm place in the ecologist's vocabulary, and it will certainly make its way into ornamental horticulture. Allelopathy is the adverse effect of one plant's chemistry on another plant's growth. Roots, stems, and leaves are continuously giving off substances, presumably waste products, manufac-

Successful use of shade-tolerant exotics under native Douglas fir and vine maple

tured by the plant. In moist climates, most such chemicals are washed out and off into the soil. If the exudates are toxic, they can inhibit the growth of adjacent plants, especially when they are still juvenile. Recent research on allelopathy of Northwest natives discloses that vine maple, western yew, western red cedar, and madrone produce inhibitory chemicals under experimental conditions. From this we can infer that under natural or garden conditions, these species *may* alter the growth potential of other plants growing under the inhibitory species.

Garden Attributes of Northwest Natives

What makes a good garden plant is compounded of both aesthetic and cultural attributes. Good quality of form, foliage, flower, or fruit will appeal to the aesthetic sense. Where these qualities are combined with ease of propagation and cultivation, a Northwest native is sure to be a winner.

Evergreen foliage is a highly prized feature. Besides the many cone-bearing evergreens (pines, firs, hemlocks, cedars, etc.) there are a few broad-leaved evergreen trees and many evergreen shrubs. The madrone, Oregon myrtle, and two oaks (tan oak and canyon live oak) are trees with superb evergreen foliage. Among the best evergreen shrubs, look to manzanitas, wild lilacs (species of *Ceanothus*), Oregon box, shrubby oaks (Sadler's oak, huckleberry oak, and leather oak), California wax myrtle, and evergreen huckleberry for exceptional quality. Deciduous trees and shrubs parade their best foliage attributes in spring and fall. Newly emerging leaves of hazel, vine maple, red huckleberry, western azalea, and Sitka mountain ash are some of the deciduous delights of early spring. For fall color, open slopes around the Northwest advertise a riot of color, especially east of the Cascades. Leaves of deciduous plants go out in a blaze of fall glory against the somber dark greens of needle-leaved evergreens. For reds and yellows, seek out big-leaf maple, vine maple, the water and paper birches, serviceberry, creek dogwood, willows, mountain ash, squashberry *(Viburnum edule)*, and the several kinds of huckleberry.

Gardening with natives has not always had a merited popularity. Native plants have tended to be hard to locate in the nursery trade. Moreover, landscape architects as well as do-it-yourself gardeners have not been educated to their great ornamental value. Further impediments to their more widespread use were recognized by Herbert Durand, writing so eloquently of American natives back in the 1920s. He saw that there were two misapprehensions that stifled the use of wildlings in gardens. First, he said, "it is a common but mistaken impression that wild plants are inherently scraggly and unattractive in form. The fact is that if they are relieved of the intense competition that prevails in the wild and given room to develop in a congenial location, they quickly make luxurious growth, become compact and shapely and produce larger and better flowers in greater profusion." He goes on to say:

There is another widespread but erroneous notion that the cultivation of wild plants is a complicated process which usually results in failure. On the contrary, it is a very simple undertaking, particularly when compared with ordinary gardening. The main thing is to provide the plants with comfortable quarters, in which the conditions of soil, exposure, moisture and environment shall duplicate those of their natural haunts as closely as possible. This done, the only after-care necessary to insure vigorous growth, bountiful bloom and normal reproduction is to keep out undesirable intruders (weeds and vandals) and to prevent overcrowding by an occasional judicious thinning out of the plants. [1923: 6–7]

It is my hope that this book may redress some misapprehensions and ignorance about growing natives. Only when more and more places of human activity are decorated with some of the green treasure of the Northwest, will their rightful place in ornamenting gardens become assured.

Propagation of Native Plants

On first thought, propagating natives for one's own garden may not appeal to most gardeners. Yet, once tried and found to work, it can become a rewarding pursuit. Since do-it-yourself propagation may be the only way some natives can be obtained, the serious gardener will want to acquire the simple skills of plant propagation. This chapter has yet another audience besides those who garden for pleasure. The retail nursery manager, to meet the growing demand for natives, will have to stock native plants largely by propagating them himself, since only a few wholesale nurseries produce natives in quantity.

As with exotics, native plants are propagated vegetatively and from seed. Vegetative propagation mainly employs cuttings (or "slips"), although layering, dividing the root or underground stem, and grafting are also commonly used methods. Transplanting whole plants from the wild *should not be done* except under particular circumstances, as explained below. Materials for propagation can come from wild sources or from a fellow gardener's plant.

In the past it was common practice to dig plants in the wild for transplanting to the garden. What harm could come from taking a few samples of nature's seemingly unlimited bounty? Harm indeed did come, and these former ravagings of the wild have made some rare beauties nearly extinct. The chance of successfully establishing in the garden plants dug in the wild turns out to be dismally low. Insufficient root ball, wilting of new growth, and other mishaps spelled a high probability of failure. The conservation ethic that has surfaced in recent years is now championed by those who grow native plants. Only under permissible circumstances should the seeker of wildlings collect whole live plants in the wild.* There are sites where digging

* Rarity and endangerment of some native plants is becoming more "official" with the passage of laws protecting them. Native plant societies or the Nature Conservancy's Natural Heritage programs in each state should be contacted for further information.

Fruits of the hairy manzanita *(Arctostaphylos columbiana)*

Columbine seeds *(Aquilegia formosa)*

wild plants may be condoned. Some natives of ornamental value grow on road cuts or in other disturbed places. When the disturbance is recurrent or about to eradicate a colony of plants, it is agreed that the natives dug are natives saved. But these are the exceptional circumstances. The better practice is to take only seeds or cuttings, leaving the whole plant to survive in the wild. Of course, collecting of any kind is prohibited in state and national parks, as well as in certain other public and private preserves. On other public lands, the managing agencies—the U.S. Forest Service, state departments of natural resources, and the like—have regulations governing the collection of natives (see Appendix A). District and local officers can be contacted for information. There is no restriction on collecting seeds or taking cuttings on state or national forest lands.

Propagation by Seeds

Most seeds ripen during the summer and are ready for harvest in late summer and fall. Seeds of fleshy-fruited species like serviceberry, huckleberry, and mountain ash are easily harvested, but the seeds should be separated from the skin and pulp. With large quantities of fleshy fruit, cleaning can be done with a home blender fitted with rubber paddles to replace the cutting blades. The fruits once macerated in water by this device release their seeds, which usually sink so that the water pulp can be discarded. Seeds of dry-fruited species often easily separate from the capsule or cluster. Sometimes fruit with dry seeds can be stripped from the dry stalks; if not, it may be easier to cut the dry-fruit cluster with scissors or a razor blade. The seeds of ripe fruits should be collected and stored in paper bags or envelopes; they usually mold if stored in plastic bags.

After harvest, seeds are cleaned to remove most of the chaff. Seeds of dry-fruited species (mostly in capsules) can be easily winnowed from the chaff in flat trays by gently blowing. If seeds are to be saved for later sowing they should be stored in a cool, dry place, usually in coin envelopes, stoppered bottles, or other containers. Many gardeners put seeds in the home refrigerator; cold preserves seeds and can assist germination by breaking dormancy, a natural feature of some seeds. Ideally, most seeds should be sown soon after harvest, in the fall. Most plants germinate well in a loamy garden soil, mixed with peat and sand (1:1:1), screened to remove rocks and debris. Species with short-lived large seeds, like oaks, Oregon myrtle, and maples, should be planted soon after harvesting in deep boxes filled with a peat/soil mix (3:1).

Seeds planted in the fall do best outdoors. A cold temperature regime (stratification) is often sufficient to trigger germination (actually, break dormancy) of many native species. Containers (pots, flats, seed trays) should be plunged in moist soil, pea gravel, or sand and covered with glass or plastic to keep out excessive rain and to guard against removal of seeds by animals. Direct sun should be avoided to prevent heating and drying. The garden cold frame with glass or plastic covers is ideal for fostering outdoor germination and for protection against rain and animals.

Some species require special treatment to induce germination. Two procedures are commonly used: scarification (mechanical abrasion of a hard seed coat) and stratification (cold or heat treatment of seeds) to break inherent dormancy. Scarification can be done by filing, sandpapering, or nicking the seed coats. Legumes are often treated by this method. Placing seeds in a motorized rock polisher, with moist sand, works well for scarifying large quantities of seeds. Hot water also is used to scarify seeds, especially of the *Ceanothus* species, of legumes, and of other species with hard seed coats.

Stratification usually involves putting seeds in moist sand or peat and storing them for a prescribed period of time at a given temperature. Following stratification, the seeds are sown in the usual manner: in pots, containers, or seed beds with screened loam, sand, and peat (1:1:1).

Special treatments are described for each species in question in the appropriate chapter of this book. Even for those seeds requiring special treatment, it is usually possible to get some germination without the treatment if a large quantity of seed is sown.

Natives that are easy to germinate might best be tried first, in order to gain familiarity with and confidence in the art of seed propagation. Ones to begin with are spirea, maple, and oak (when fresh), Douglas fir, pines, salal, penstemons, mock-orange, birch, *Campanula*, *Heuchera*, *Aquilegia*, *Erysimum* (wallflower), *Sedum*, and *Tellima*.

Cutting dipped in rooting powder

Vegetative Propagation

Starting new plants from cuttings works well for many natives. Moreover, having to wait for ripe seeds or deal with problems of germination is avoided. Vigorous vegetative shoots, cut from mid-summer on (July through August), can be collected in plastic bags or moist toweling. Then within hours the twigs should be prepared for rooting. Twigs collected should be larger than the intended cutting to prevent early wilting. Short branches of the cut twig are firmly pulled off at their base. This gives a "heel" cutting, which, when trimmed with a sharp knife or razorblade, roots best. If heel cuttings cannot be made, then the unbranched shoot should be cut slant-wise at the junction of stem and leaf. Often it helps to trim away a little of the bark above the cut, so as to allow for more rooting surface. Wetted cuttings are then dipped in some commercial root-stimulating chemical (e.g., Rootone, Hormodin); these preparations contain a plant hormone like indole-3-butyric acid (IBA) or napthalene acetic acid (NAA). This pre-treatment hastens the formation of callus tissue at the cut surface. Once callus tissue forms, roots will usually develop.

Good rooting mixtures are sand and peat, vermiculite and peat, or perlite and peat (all 1:1). Flats or apple boxes with one of these mixes,

A well-rooted cutting

well moistened beforehand, are now ready for the fresh, treated cuttings. Make a groove or punch holes in the moistened mixture and place cuttings at a slant in the furrow or hole. Water with a fine spray periodically. The box with the cuttings should have a plastic "tent" over it, placed in a greenhouse, or in a glass-covered cold frame to maintain high air humidity. Avoid direct sun, and water when needed. Some propagators use an overhead mist system. Pots, especially plastic ones, can also be conveniently used for small amounts of seed. They can be covered with a plastic bag and should be kept out of direct sunshine.

Some native plants root quickly. Try any of the woody penstemons (*Penstemon fruticosus, P. rupicola,* or *P. cardwellii*), junipers, kinnikinnik, Alaska cedar, Port Orford cedar, coast redwood, or yew for initial successes.

Layering is a successful method of propagation for those plants with branches that can easily be bent to the ground. Guide a length of the attached branch into a shallow soil trench, cover and hold down the branch with a rock, forked stick, or bent wire. In layering, it is advantageous to bend up the layered branch until it just cracks at the bend; the upright portion can be supported by a small stake. It usually takes two year's growth to produce a well-rooted plant. This method works especially well for plants with horizontal, ground-hugging stems like kinnikinnik, salal (underground stems), twinflower *(Linnaea borealis),* and trailing honeysuckle; but many others can be layered too, as long as their branches can be easily bent to the ground. Snowberry, Indian plum, and Oregon box are good examples of the latter. Layering is most often done in the garden to increase the already established plant. It should work in the wild if done during the rainy season and if one is able to get back to the expectant mother plant in the next season. When rooted, the section of branch between layer and main plant clump is cut; the layered piece is then dug and potted or transplanted to the garden site.

Natives with creeping runners (wild strawberry) or underground stems (salal, Oregon grape, wild rose) can be increased by planting sections of stem or root after carefully removing small rooted sections and replacing the divot. Similarly, herbaceous perennials that produce several rosettes are increased by rooting the rosettes. Potentillas, penstemons, campanulas, and violets are some of the many rosette-perennials that can be increased in this manner.

Vegetative propagation is the only way a particular selected form of a species can be propagated. Wild or garden mutants (deviant forms of species) usually do not breed true. To perpetuate such distinctive *cultivars* as the western hemlock 'Iron Springs', or other dwarf forms of conifers, vegetative methods must be used.

There is a special pleasure gained from increasing your own native plant collection by seeds or by vegetative propagation: first, the fun of exploring in the wild for choice native plants, and then the later delight of seeing one's efforts at propagation yield new plants.

Chapter 2

Coast redwood *(Sequoia sempervirens)*

Native Ornamental Trees

Trees are the mainstay of most man-created landscapes. Perhaps we bring them from the wilds to the civilized scene out of some inner primeval urge that survives in us from ancient times. Northwest gardens have traditionally utilized trees mostly from other regions, except when the native species, already at hand, have been spared—and even nurtured—after development of the landscaped scene. But with over fifty native species to choose from there are strong arguments for using them as ornamentals. Many are highly prized in other temperate landscapes. Our native trees come in three groupings: (1) the needle-leaved (or scaled-leaved) cone-bearing trees (mostly evergreen), with thirty species; (2) the broad-leaved evergreens, with only five species; and (3) the broad-leaved deciduous trees, with twenty-six species. These trees are a rich inventory that has yet to be fully utilized in our civilized places.

Conifers

Cone-bearing trees dominate natural landscapes in the Pacific Northwest from the Cascades west to the sea. So familiar are the needle-leaved evergreens in the natural setting that their garden potential is often overlooked. Most of our pines, firs, spruces, hemlocks, and others of their clan have graced gardens elsewhere in the world. Why not our own?

Conifers

DOUGLAS FIR *(Pseudotsuga menziesii).* This magnificent evergreen hardly needs an introduction. No other member of the plant world is so thoroughly a part of the cultural fabric of the Pacific Northwest. Not only is it the most important lumber tree of North America, Douglas fir is *the* evergreen that persists in suburbia as urbanization creeps over the landscape. So common and so successfully self-perpetuating is the tree that scarcely anyone thinks of propagating it intentionally for ornamental use. Yet the gardener, arborist, nursery manager, and parks supervisor should take steps to ensure the persistence of Douglas fir in the urban scene. Since it has been so easily and extensively propagated for commercial reforestation, the know-how of growing it is readily available.

Douglas fir grows wild nearly everywhere that forest vegetation can thrive. On the west side of the Cascades it is nearly continuous from sea level to the subalpine, especially in less moist situations. Then eastward from the Cascade crest, Douglas firs cohabit with all the other major coniferous species east to the Rocky Mountains. Only where treeless sagebrush, bunchgrass, or scabland vegetation takes over on the east side, is the Douglas fir absent. It is largely missing from the Columbia Basin in Washington and on the lava plains of southeastern Oregon. But in the more mountainous terrain of eastern Oregon and Washington, it thrives in coexistence with the yellow pine, western larch, grand fir, and lodgepole pine.

Distinguishing Features. The ever-present cone is the hallmark of recognition for the Douglas fir, distinguishing it from true firs or spruce, its nearest relatives. Between each of the broad, leathery seed scales, a three-pronged ribbony bract protrudes a good ½ inch beyond the tip of the seed scale. The oval cone, bristling with the three-pronged (trident) bracts reaches up to 4 inches in length. The foliage is a dark lusterless green, the needles either flat or in bottle-brush array on the twigs; the lower branchlets of older trees are often pendant. Foliage buds at the tips of branchlets are sharply-pointed and narrow, and are dark reddish brown, without resin.

Douglas fir *(Pseudotsuga menziesii)*

Douglas fir is a fast-growing tree, with amazingly high reproductive capacity. Seedlings establish well on bare mineral soil and the young saplings thrive in the open, free from shading by other trees. Although specimens up to 200 feet tall are known, the average old-growth trees are from 75 to 125 feet in height. When mature, the symmetrically tapered and massive trunks are free of branches for the first 40 to 60 feet. Older trees have thick, deeply fissured bark, reddish brown and fibrous in texture. The trunks of young trees are smooth, often with pitch blisters, and soft gray green in color.

Garden Uses. Every new residential tract in Douglas fir country captures prospective homeowners with the allure of a forested landscape. So often the new tract has simply opened up a dense second-growth stand of thin-stemmed trees, leaving a few for "decoration." The remaining trees are often unsightly sticks with a tuft of foliage in the crown, more susceptible to windthrow now that the dense stand has been thinned. Only if the trees were well spaced to begin with would they stand a chance of survival after the homes are built; such open-grown trees are often most decorative for the larger garden.

Douglas fir is either grown as a specimen tree, or as a screen in rows or drifts. Since it responds well to shearing, it can be made into a large and broadly shaped hedge. For the spacious garden, Douglas fir makes a handsome ornamental conifer. And, for gardens with still more room in suburbia, a small woodlot of Douglas fir has many rewards: a source of Christmas trees, fir boughs, and firewood, a wildlife habitat, and a protective greenbelt buffer for privacy and quiet.

In eastern Washington and Oregon, the nearby native stands of Douglas fir furnish the hardiest stock. Even more than ponderosa pine, Douglas fir could become much more widely planted in communities on the east side. There is considerable variation in foliage color, limbiness, and growth habit throughout its natural range. The fir with the blue green (glaucous) foliage, so common east of the Cascades and on to the Rocky Mountains, is called var. *glauca.* Yet individuals of this glaucous form occur everywhere throughout the range of the species. Particularly fine forms with graceful broadly pyramidal stature, limby to the ground, are seen on the gravelly prairies of western Washington and Oregon.

Propagation. Douglas fir easily seeds itself even in urban habitats. It is also easily transplanted when young, however, so that spontaneous seedlings out of place can be safely moved to a desired location. Unusual garden varieties with dwarf or drooping stature are known. Since these are the product of mutations and are unlikely to reproduce their kind, they must be propagated by grafting. Over fifteen varieties, with such cultivar names as 'Fletcheri' and 'Brevifolia', are known. Besides dwarf cultivars, forms with variegated or yellow green foliage, cultivars with pendant branches, and those with compact stature are in the trade, mostly available in Europe. Like pines and true firs, Douglas fir does not take well to propagation by cuttings. Seeds and spontaneous seedlings are the best source of these trees.

Douglas fir (var. *glauca*)

True Firs (species of *Abies*)

Stately and symmetrical trees of mostly formal habit, these evergreens are best distinguished by their foliage and cones. Needles of true firs leave a smooth round scar when detached from the twig, and are often notched at the tip. Their needle leaves are arranged with geometrical symmetry on the branchlet, either in flat sprays (in one plane) or in circular array like the bristles of a bottle brush. Cones of true firs are always borne erect on the uppermost branches of the tree, and do not fall to the ground when mature. Instead, they fall apart, shattering into cone scales and winged seeds to leave only a peg-like stalk on the twig. Of the six species of *Abies* in the Northwest, four are to be commended for their value as ornamentals. All species are most easily propagated by seeds.

WHITE FIR *(Abies concolor).* This widespread native of Oregon and California is one of the West's largest and finest ornamental evergreens. Its steely blue gray foliage, like that of Colorado blue spruce, is a most appealing attribute. White fir is common in the Cascades of southern Oregon, especially on the east slopes. It gets into Washington in the southeastern corner where it is easily confused with grand fir *(Abies grandis).*

Distinguishing Features. Older specimens become stately trees of broadly pyramidal habit, with symmetrical branching, and may reach 75 to 100 feet in cultivation. Its leaves are the longest of any true fir, up to 2 inches in flat (two-ranked) arrays, and are usually glaucous. The bark is grayish and smooth when young, but rough at maturity, the latter a rarely realized condition in gardens.

Garden Uses. White fir, though potentially a large tree, is slow-growing and may be accommodated in a fairly large garden. It is a superb tree for parks and other public locations, and thrives in an open sunny position with good drainage. As with many conifers, white fir is not too tolerant of pollution and thus is best grown in the suburbs or in rural areas.

GRAND FIR *(Abies grandis).* This stately evergreen is much more common in the Pacific Northwest than is white fir, especially in Washington and northern Oregon. On the west side of the Cascades, it grows from sea level to about 1,500 feet in elevation. It is often intermixed with Douglas fir on the bluffs and headlands bordering Puget Sound and the Strait of Juan de Fuca. It reappears in fine stands on the east side of the Cascades, through the Okanogan Highlands as well as into the Blue Mountains and Palouse country, again in association with Douglas fir.

Distinguishing Features. This fir resembles the white fir, but differs in its green rather than glaucous foliage and its shorter needles of about 1½ inches.

Garden uses. Its needs are identical to the white fir. For gardeners in

Grand fir *(Abies grandis)*

eastern Washington and Oregon, it is essential that garden plants originate from the nearby mixed coniferous forests and not from the west side; the east slope trees are hardier. Grand fir should be much more widely planted in gardens on the colder side of the mountains.

SUBALPINE FIR *(Abies lasiocarpa)*. More than any other native conifer, subalpine fir has become a popular landscape feature of gardens in the Northwest. Yet at what a price! Nearly all specimens are dug in the wild and in quantity by commercial collectors. Moreover, this extensive harvesting is usually done in areas near timberline where growth is slow and soil disturbance is substantial. The dilemma of how to secure this fine tree without disturbing a high montane habit can be resolved.

Subalpine fir is a common tree in the drier areas of the Cascades and Olympics, occurring often in the subalpine parklands as clumps of narrowly tapering spires—evergreen islands—here and there throughout the mountain meadows. The mountain-dug plant is usually taken in drifts; several artfully dwarfed saplings are dug in one huge sod for placement in a rock garden or simulated subalpine setting. Though such a clump is truly beautiful, its removal to a garden focus has been at an unreckoned cost to the place it once grew. What is the alternative? Try nursery-grown plants from seedlings or seeds, though they may not have the form of collected trees.

Distinguishing Features. At maturity, this fir is a small, 30- to 50-foot, tree with a narrowly conical shape. Its spiky, cathedral-like spires form the most familiar silhouette on the upper montane slopes and ridge tops in the Northwest. The foliage, unlike the lowland species of *Abies,* is stiffly upturned along the branchlets, and has a bluish gray green cast. At timberline, the specimens are usually much dwarfed, often with broad skirts of low spreading branches. Clusters of such hardy specimens form impenetrable shrub-like thickets near tree line. Like other firs, its 2- to 4-inch-long cones are in erect clusters on the uppermost branches of a mature tree. The smooth, upright cones are a brilliant dark purple until maturity when they turn a glistening resinous brown.

Garden Uses. Though the practice is to be frowned upon, collected clumps of specimens dwarfed by the rigors of a severe high-montane environment will undoubtedly continue to make their way into gardens. Individuals of subalpine fir are striking showpieces in a rockery or a tussock plant setting. Single specimens from carefully collected seedlings (the smaller the better, both from a conservation and a survival standpoint) or as nursery-grown trees from seeds will grow slowly into fine specimens of symmetrical shape. The tendency toward an "exclamation-point" shape is considerably lessened in trees started from seeds or seedlings under cultivation. Garden-grown plants are more broadly tapering if they have lived out their lives in a garden or nursery row.

Propagation. Conservation ethics should dictate that this tree be grown from seeds or from *small* seedlings carefully dug in the wild. For plants

Subalpine fir *(Abies lasiocarpa)*

Subalpine fir in cultivation

from seeds, cones can be harvested in areas where avalanches have downed specimens, or from squirrel caches (but take only a few). As yet, subalpine fir is not extensively grown from seeds by nurserymen. It is a slow process, with return on the investment several years down the road from seed harvest. Yet trees from seeds must eventually replace the rape of mountain meadows.

Abies lasiocarpa has been called "alpine fir" for so long that it is probably an uphill battle to bring about a change in the common name. Yet, "alpine fir" is definitely a misnomer. The true alpine region is a *treeless* landscape, ever above timberline. Both Hitchcock et al. (1973) and the U.S. Forest Service *Handbook on Trees of the United States* (Agriculture Handbook No. 271) use the more appropriate name *subalpine* fir.

NOBLE FIR *(Abies procera)*. The noble fir truly lives up to its distinguished name. Noble it is, from sapling to stately 200-foot tree. It can be seen abundantly on Mount Rainier, between Christine Falls and Ricksecker Point on the slopes of the upper Nisqually River canyon where it occurs in company with Douglas firs, western hemlocks, and occasional Pacific silver firs. In Oregon, the noble fir is abundant on Larch Mountain near the Columbia River and into the Clackamas River drainage nearby; it is also common at Crater Lake where it thrives from the lake's edge to the crater's rim. Its total range is from Stevens Pass in Washington, south to the Siskiyou–Klamath mountains of the California–Oregon border country. Noble fir is largely restricted to the west slopes of the Cascades, and claims that it occurs in the Olympic Mountains have not been substantiated.

Distinguishing Features. Mature trees have an impressive form: straight and massive trunks, clear of branches for up to 100 feet from the ground; then, a disproportionately small and rounded crown with branches reaching out at right angles from the uppermost taper of the bole (or trunk). These stiffly horizontal branches bear equally stiff fingerlike branchlets. Hand specimens of foliage can be distinguished from the look-alike branches of subalpine fir by the shape of the needles. The leaves of noble fir have a "hockey-stick" twist to the base of the needles, while those of subalpine fir are stiff but straight. As with subalpine fir, the needles of noble fir turn upward from the twig rather than lying horizontal, as do the flat sprays of white fir or grand fir foliage. Noble fir cones are large, up to 7 inches long, and are beset with bristle-tipped bracts that recurve or point downward on the cone surface.

Garden Uses. Noble fir is the best-tempered of our native firs for the garden. It is highly ornamental, easily adapted to garden culture and not overly fast in growth. Like Douglas fir, it is intolerant of shade, especially when young. Open sunny situations with good drainage suit it well.

Propagation. Abies procera is propagated from seeds; as with all true firs, the cones must be harvested intact. Since many Christmas tree farms are now growing this species for premium-cut trees, some of the seedling stock has made its way into the nursery trade. Noble fir makes an ideal specimen for a living Christmas tree. Kept in a container, it can be moved into the house for the holidays, or, after a single use at Christmas, the living plant can be transplanted from its container to the garden. Specimens of a particularly intense, glaucous hue are in the trade (*A. procera* forma *glauca*), as is a low and spreading type (forma *prostrata*).

PACIFIC SILVER FIR *(Abies amabilis)*. Mention should be made of at least one other native true fir, the Pacific silver fir (or, lovely fir). It is rarely grown in Northwest gardens, perhaps because it is not of easy culture, despite its graceful though formal habit. In British gardens, the traditional trial grounds for most temperate-zone ornamentals, it has been only moderately successful. Pacific silver fir is easy to distinguish from all other firs: it has a unique "ruff" of shorter needles flattened and projecting forward on the tops of the leafy twigs (this "hair-on-a-dog's-back" ruff of needles is in addition to the horizontally placed longer needles). It should be tried more often in gardens, for it is certain to find a suitable habitat. In the wild, it is a fir of mid-elevations in all Northwest mountains, sandwiched between subalpine firs and grand firs along the altitudinal transect from sea level to timberline.

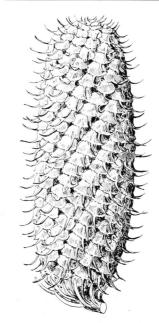

Noble fir *(Abies procera)*

Pines (species of *Pinus*)

To many people, all cone-bearing evergreens are "pines," so broad is the layman's view of conifers. Though the genus *Pinus* is a large clan of over eighty species worldwide, the word "pine" botanically speaking encompasses much less than the total inventory of cone-bearing trees. Pines are easily told by their foliage: the needle leaves are clustered in definite numbers. Of the eight or nine species in the Pacific Northwest, there are four five-needled pines (also called white pines), three three-needled species, and one two-needled species. Although their cones vary in size from the little 2-inch-long cone of the lodgepole pine to the mammoth 16-inch sugarpine cone, the basic pattern of relatively large and woody seed cones that retain their scales at maturity is another hallmark of pines.

Every one of the eight species of pines in the Northwest has been tested in cultivation and a good case can be made for each as an ornamental. However, only two or three species are sufficiently versatile for garden culture to merit a detailed account here. All are grown from seeds or from small seedlings collected in the wild.

FIVE-NEEDLED PINES *(Pinus monticola, P. albicaulis,* and other species). The western white pine *(Pinus monticola)* is the most widely encountered native in Northwest gardens, despite its rather easy susceptibility to white pine blister-rust disease. The risk of losing a specimen to the fungus is freely taken by many gardeners, especially as the tree is so

Western white pine *(Pinus monticola)*

easily grown. When the forest geneticists finally develop a blister-rust resistant strain of western white pine, specimens for ornamental use can be assured of a safer existence.

Distinguishing Features. The soft-textured, glaucous needles are borne in stiffly horizontal branches, widely spaced in symmetrical whorls along the stem. Mature trees in the wild may reach a height of 80 to 100 feet, and older garden-grown plants may get up to 50 feet high. These trees are best for large gardens, parks, and public open spaces. Old trees have a tell-tale bark pattern, a checkerboard or alligator-hide texture of raised squarish scales.

Garden Uses. Western white pine responds well to shearing and thus can be kept small and symmetrical. Another dwarfing procedure is to pinch back, when half-grown in early spring, the young elongating shoots (called "candles"). *Pinus monticola* can easily be mistaken for its eastern counterpart, *P. strobus* (eastern white pine), although the latter has softer foliage and shorter (4 to 6 inches long) cones.

Western white pine is common through the Northwest from nearly sea level in the Puget Sound region to nearly timberline in the Blue Mountains. Just north of Seattle, it vies with Douglas fir and western hemlock as the dominant evergreen, easily spotted from the freeway (just south of the Edmonds turnoff) by its open symmetrical silhouette and the large, 8- to 10-inch pendant cones at the ends of branches in the crown of the tree. East of the Cascades it is likewise frequently encountered in the mixed conifer stands of the Inland Empire around Spokane, the Wallowa Mountains, and other Great Basin mountain ranges to the south.

Two close relatives of the western white pine merit the gardener's attention. The sugar pine *(Pinus lambertiana)* of Oregon and California is occasionally encountered in cultivation. It has nearly the same attributes as *P. monticola,* though it grows more slowly in the Puget Sound area. One specimen on the University of Washington campus, now about fifty years old, cones freely, its magnificent "sugar loaves" pendant at the tips of upper branches. In vain, though, have I waited for cones to drop to the ground. Unlike the trees in the wild, the cultivated specimen tenaciously retains its cones. This is a good pine for parks and the community arboretum. It, too, is susceptible to blister-rust.

The other five-needled pine is *Pinus flexilis,* the limber pine. Although native of the dry interior mountain ranges of the West, limber pine does well west of the Cascades. It is of slower growth and maintains a more dense habit than the western white pine or the sugar pine.

Though just outside the Pacific Northwest boundaries, two other five-needled pines of the West surely deserve brief mention. The bristle-cone pine *(Pinus aristata)* is a rugged dweller in the highest timbered reaches of desert mountain ranges in Colorado and Arizona.* Yet it

* The form in eastern California, Nevada, and Utah is now called Great Basin bristle-cone pine *(Pinus longaeva).*

seems perfectly at home in the landscaped grounds of lowland Oregon and Washington. Its short needles, coated with white dots of resin, are densely set on closeknit branches. It makes a perfect slow-growing, compact pine for the small garden and is rapidly gaining in popularity. The foxtail pine *(P. balfouriana)* can easily be mistaken for a bristle-cone pine, save for the absence of the white flecks of resin. Foxtail pine is native to the upper montane of the Salmon–Trinity mountains of northern California and a widely separated second area in the Sierras (the headwaters of the Kings River).

The last five-needled pine that has garden potential is the timberline species, *Pinus albicaulis* (whitebark pine). Just east of the Cascade crest and in the highest of our intermountain ranges, the rugged grandeur of dwarfed whitebark pine is sure to goad the gardener into trying the plant. But it is hardly possible to transplant the elfinwood scene created by this pine to the lowland garden. Only with the sculpting tools of cold wind and snow can the stark beauty of a timberline specimen be achieved. Yet *P. albicaulis* is well worth trying in the garden even if it will not behave as it does on the high summits of our mountains. Whitebark pine is only moderately successful as a garden specimen. Since it is so very slow of growth, perhaps its best use is in a bonsai container or in a miniature rock garden. We have had some success with small seedlings taken in the wild. Seeds from mature cones are hard to come by since they are the major food source for such birds as Clark's nutcracker and the gray jay, as well as for tree squirrels. Seeds from cones that escape bird or squirrel foraging have low germinability (20 percent), but it still is a tree worth the effort to propagate.

Whitebark pine *(Pinus albicaulis)*

Whitebark pine dwarfed at timberline, Mt. Adams

Conifers

Yellow pine *(Pinus ponderosa)* in the wild, eastern Washington

THREE-NEEDLED PINES *(Pinus ponderosa, P. jeffreyi, P. attenuata).* The yellow pine, or ponderosa pine *(Pinus ponderosa),* is the most familiar of the three-needled pines in the Northwest. On any eastward descent from the crest of the Cascades, the bold form of this tree catches the traveler's eye.

Distinguishing Features. In pure stands or intermixed with Douglas fir, lodgepole pine, or western larch, it is an easy conifer to recognize. Stout, dark green, 5-inch-long needles in threes, bristly brown cones up to 6 inches long, and, in mature specimens, that tell-tale fissured and platey buff-colored bark, shed as jigsaw puzzle pieces, are easy identifying features. Yellow pine is a massive, fast-growing tree, reaching heights of up to 200 feet and with maximum girths of 15 to 20 feet.

Garden Uses. So ponderous a tree is hardly suitable for a small garden. Yet it surely deserves planting in parks, arboreta, and other public places, especially in drier areas of the Northwest. Cities and towns in eastern Washington and Oregon still have native populations of yellow pine persisting at least in the suburbs. But as human activity continues to reduce these urban remnant stands, it would be wise to replace them with individuals from nearby native stocks. Ponderosa pine could well be used in towns that have sprung up in the sagebrush and bunchgrass country. After all, these treeless stretches of land are never far from ponderosa pine country. The yellow pine propagates readily from seeds; young seedlings tolerate transplanting with fair success.

Ponderosa pine is no stranger west of the Cascades. In Oregon it is common in the western valleys of the Willamette, Umpqua, and Rogue rivers. The only known westside colony in Washington is at Fort Lewis, just south of Tacoma; early botanists recorded an isolated stand on drier slopes of the upper Skagit River basin. These outlier colonies west of the Cascades suggest that it should do well in the well-drained alluvial soils of the Tacoma prairies and in the oak woodland country of western Oregon. In extreme southwestern Oregon, one can expect to find a near relative of ponderosa pine, *Pinus jeffreyi.* It is not uncommon on serpentine soils southwest of Grants Pass. Jeffrey pine may be distinguished from ponderosa pine by its larger cones, more massive, thickly tapering bole, and small bark plates. Specimens of Jeffrey pine are occasionally grown in conifer collections and public places west and east of the Cascades.

The knobcone pine *(Pinus attenuata)* occurs on serpentine soils in southwestern Oregon, where it is rather common. Although the country around Cave Junction seems to be the northern limit of its extensive growth, isolated occurrences of knobcone pine are known a bit further to the north in the drainages of the Rogue, Umpqua, and Willamette rivers. South of Oregon, its distribution is again patchy but tenacious all the way to the San Bernardino Mountains of southern California.

Distinguishing Features. Knobcone pine is rarely a tree of impressive stature. Even in the best of habitats, trees are not more than 30 feet high, with a broadly pyramidal crown. Lower branches usually persist in open stands to give the small tree a stately, fulsome aspect. Needles in threes and tenaciously closed cones hugging the main trunk and branches are the key recognition features. Even young saplings produce the longish, tapered, and buff-colored cones in quantity. The cones persist, tightly closed, for years—in fact, for life—on the main trunk and branches of the growing tree, releasing their seeds only after fire.

Garden Uses. The knobcone pine has been used occasionally as a fast-growing but rather short-lived and drought-resistant ornamental conifer. Its persistent and precocious cones in dense clusters are an added attraction to the good form and light green foliage of the young trees. In the Puget Sound area it is grown either as a single specimen tree or in rows and drifts to serve as screened plantings, space dividers, or path definers. It could take to shearing and thus have some value as an evergreen hedge.

Propagation. Pinus attenuata is easily propagated from seeds. Young seedling plants from the wild establish well in cultivation. Cones can be induced to open by keeping them in a warm place for a few weeks. Gloves and shears are essential for harvesting the easily reached, but tenacious, bristly and resinous cones.

TWO-NEEDLED PINES *(Pinus contorta).* The shore pine or lodgepole pine is our only native two-needled member of the pine clan. It is widespread and common throughout the Northwest, from sea level to timberline, and can be found on either side of the Cascades. So widespread a species is bound to have distinctive varieties. Botanists recognize two geographic races. The lowland variety (*Pinus contorta* var. *contorta*) is the shore pine, so frequently encountered in the San Juan Islands, more sporadically in the Willamette–Puget trough, and with fair frequency along the outer coasts of Oregon and Washington. The other, more montane form is the familiar lodgepole pine (*P. contorta* var. *latifolia*), often forming pure "matchstick" stands after fire or other disturbance. Witness the vast expanses of lodgepole pine in the lava and volcanic ash areas south of Bend, Oregon, and on up to Crater Lake.

Distinguishing Features. Open-grown specimens of shore pine may reach 50 feet in height, but are more often of a lower, almost bushy stature. The short, dark green needles in twos are mostly at the end of the twigs, giving the plant an open character. Cones are small, numerous, and slow to open; they may persist for years on the twigs and branches, and even on the main trunk. Fire usually triggers the opening of cones, although very old ones eventually open to shed viable seeds. *Pinus contorta* can be easily separated from the jack pine *(P. banksiana)* of western Canada by the position of the cones. In jack pines the cones are twisted so that their ends point toward the tips of the branchlets; in lodgepole pines the basal twist makes the cones point in the opposite direction, back toward the trunk.

Garden Uses. The shore pine form of *Pinus contorta* is a valuable conifer

Shore pine *(Pinus contorta)*

for seaside plantings where salt spray, wind, and sterile dune soils prevail. Both lodgepole pines and shore pines are of rapid growth and easily trained to produce unusual, even striking shapes. Under conditions of dwarfing (little soil in shallow pans or troughs, scant fertilizer, and judicious root pruning), both varieties of *P. contorta* make admirable bonsai specimens. When not subject to dwarfing techniques, this pine grows rapidly into an open, intricately branched small tree. It is useful as an evergreen for boundary screening in rows or in drifts. As a single specimen tree, it is probably not as effective as Scots pine or Japanese red pine, two Old World relatives of our two-needled pine.

Propagation. Pinus contorta is easily grown from seeds or started as collected seedlings. Older, unopened cones will release their seeds if stored in a dry place; they germinate copiously about thirty days from sowing.

DISEASES AND PESTS OF NATIVE PINES. Pines, as with other conifers, are susceptible to a wide variety of fungus and insect pests, both in cultivation and in the wild. The five-needled pines are uniquely attacked by white pine blister-rusts, and an infected tree simply has to be destroyed. The source of infection is undoubtedly the alternate host of the fungus, almost any one of our currants or gooseberries (species of *Ribes*). Most other fungus diseases are not severe problems in cultivation. Of the many insects that may attack pines, the most serious is the pine-shoot moth. This pest is of fairly recent introduction to the Pacific Northwest. So far it is restricted to ornamental plantings in urban areas. Foresters are naturally apprehensive of its possible spread to native stands of pines, especially the two-needled species. Larvae hatch from eggs deposited in terminal buds, to devour the young growing shoot tips in the spring. Infected shoots should be removed and destroyed in mid-summer.

An unnatural affliction of conifers is urban and industrial pollution. No doubt their exceptional sensitivity to noxious fumes is partly due to the persistence of their foliage. Coniferous evergreens do not shed the pollutants with their leaves as readily as do deciduous trees. Sulfur dioxide and fluorides can severely retard the growth and affect the vitality of several Northwest native conifers.

Hemlocks (species of *Tsuga*)

Our two native hemlocks are superb ornamentals, each with distinctive habit, foliage character, and garden value. Species of the genus *Tsuga* are evergreen trees, usually with horizontal branches and slender, more delicate branchlets than in firs. The tips of horizontal branches and the terminal leader tend to droop. The linear leaves, when detached, leave a slightly elevated peglike scar. Seed cones are small and papery, and at maturity detach intact from the tree.

WESTERN HEMLOCK *(Tsuga heterophylla)*. Western hemlock is a tall, graceful evergreen with a drooping leader and pendant lateral branches. Mature trees reach up to 225 feet in height under the ideal growing conditions of high rainfall and deep alluvial soils near the coast. Western hemlock may form nearly pure stands under optimal conditions where it is almost self-perpetuating, generation after generation. Its best development in forests is from 2,000 feet down to sea level on the western slopes of the Cascades. It can be found growing with nearly every other westside conifer. On the east side, it is restricted to the more mountainous extreme northeast corner of Washington and adjacent northern Idaho.

Distinguishing Features. The graceful droop of the terminal leader and the tips of the lateral branchlets, as well as the ferny texture and lustrous green color of the foliage is further marked by the short, linear needles of unequal length (from ¼ to ¾ of an inch long) set in flat (two-ranked) arrays on the twigs. The lower surface of the leaves has two broad whitish bands. The abundantly produced seed cones are small (¾ to 1 inch long), falling intact to the ground.

Garden Uses. So ornamental an evergreen as western hemlock should be more widely used. Its rapid growth and eventual towering height deter its use for the small garden. Special treatment can dwarf it, however, either by pruning the roots, or starving the tree (as often occurs

Western hemlock *(Tsuga heterophylla)* in University of Washington Arboretum

naturally in bogs.) Also there are two or three cultivars that are dwarfs. Cultivar 'Conica' is a dense compact, broadly conical bush, and cv. 'Iron Springs' is a miniature gem for the planter box, trough garden, or rockery. Young hemlock saplings can be sheared to make excellent hedging plants. For larger areas, the species can be grown for its impressive landscape attributes as single show specimens, in drifts or as a tall screen. Western hemlock already has a solid reputation as an ornamental in Britain, where it is widely planted on estates and in public open spaces. It deserves much more use in urban areas of the Pacific Northwest.

Propagation. Propagation is best from seed or small seedlings collected in the wild. The latter are ever-present in lowland hemlock forests where the seedlings grow commonly on the decaying trunks of fallen trees—the so-called nurse-log effect. Seeds or young plants from native habitats in the colder portions of its range are best for ornamental plantings east of the Cascades. Larger specimens are difficult to transplant. Some success can be had with cuttings: the cultivar 'Iron Springs' has been propagated by treated cuttings under mist.

MOUNTAIN HEMLOCK *(Tsuga mertensiana).* Nearly all upper-montane reaches of the Cascades and Olympics, in what is called the subalpine or Hudsonian zone, support pure or mixed stands of this elegant conifer. Ranging from 4,000 to 7,000 feet, mountain hemlock grows in both the upper fringes of continuous forest or out in the subalpine parkland where isolated drifts of conifers are surrounded by the flowery mountain meadows. When in mixed stands, it usually coexists with subalpine fir, Pacific silver fir, or Alaska cedar. Despite its natural preference for the rugged high country, it is elegantly at home in cultivation at sea level. There are isolated pockets of mountain hemlock east of the Cascades, in the Rocky Mountains of northern Idaho; eastside gardeners should seek such hardier stock for cultivation.

Distinguishing Features. In gardens, it is a small to medium-sized tree of irregular, though handsome, habit. It has dense, often gray green foliage. Its branchlets are of unequal length, the longer ones overtopping the shorter ones to give the branch a tufted habit. The needle leaves are densely set all over the twig (like a bottle-brush), and are often entirely glaucous. Seed cones are narrowly cylindrical, tapered at each end, and up to 2½ inches long (the largest of any hemlock species). Trees in nature may vary in height from the timberline dwarfs of not more than 6 to 10 feet up to 80 to 100 feet in the lower border of the mountain hemlock zone.

Garden Uses. If asked to choose the very best native conifer for the small garden, mountain hemlock would be my first choice. Its dense compact foliage form, handsomely displayed on an informally irregular branching pattern, coupled with its slow growth, make it ideal as a garden evergreen. The best forms are often multi-stemmed from the base (like Mugo pine) and have a fine, soft-textured, bluish-gray green foliage. It is most often planted as a single specimen tree, but is even

Mountain hemlock *(Tsuga mertensiana)*

more striking in clumps or drifts of three to five individuals of uneven height. It works well as accent or focal points in border plantings or in contoured rockeries.

Mountain hemlock is an unparalleled conifer for container plantings. Its singular beauty of form and texture and its slow growth make it an object of great ornament in containers where it thrives with its roots intermingled with those of salal, low manzanita, or evergreen huckleberry; the contrasting green hues of these broad-leaved native evergreens harmonize well with the hemlock.

Mountain hemlock, like its lowland cousin western hemlock, is susceptible to several forest tree diseases and pests but in cultivation it is remarkably free of pests. Only woolly aphids can sometimes be a problem. But, alas, the tree is not very tolerant of urban pollution. Dallimore and Jackson, in their *Handbook of* Coniferae *and* Ginkoaceae, ruefully speak of its success in Britain: "It is more at home in the hills of Wales and Scotland than on low ground near smoky towns." However, it seems perfectly happy grown in suburban gardens in the Northwest. Given its wide range along the West Coast, from south-eastern Alaska to the central Sierra Nevada of California, it should be possible to secure individuals to match a particular geographic location where it is to be grown ornamentally. Moreover, it is known from restricted regions of the northern Rockies (southern British Columbia to northern Idaho and western Montana); plants from these more continental climates merit trial in gardens east of the Cascades.

Only two varietal forms are known, each accenting to a superb degree the glaucous hue to the foliage: cv. 'Argentea' and cv. 'Glauca.'* A natural hybrid between western hemlock and mountain hemlock, called

* There are in cultivation several clones so slow of growth that it is nearly immeasurable; in time they should become available to the nursery trade, and might prove of value as small specimens of "bonsai" quality.

Mountain hemlock

Tsuga X *jeffreyi,* is reported to do well in Britain, mostly in collections of cultivated conifers. It is possibly of fairly common occurrence in the north Cascades of Washington (Mt. Rainier, Mt. Baker) and on Vancouver Island.

Propagation. Mountain hemlock can be propagated by seeds, seedlings collected in nature, or by layering of garden plants; in addition, cuttings under mist have succeeded. It is a prolific seeder in nature, but seeds are of short viability. Growth of seedlings is slow at first.

As with so many of our garden-worthy natives, mountain hemlock had an early start in cultivation, thousands of miles from its native home. William Murray, British forester, is credited with introducing the tree to Britain in 1854. He found it on Scotts Mountain in British Columbia. Specimens, presumably from this early introduction are over 80 feet high at Murthley Castle, Perth, in Scotland. Credit is also given John Jeffrey for its introduction in 1851, from seeds collected in British Columbia. It is from this earlier collection that the first hybrid hemlock was presumed to have come. These, however, turned out to be only a glaucous form of *Tsuga heterophylla.* It was only much later that conifer specialist Hornibrook introduced *T.* X *jeffreyi* to Irish gardens from collected seedlings taken in the mountains back of Cowichan Lake on Vancouver Island. Recent studies on the presumed hybridity between *T. heterophylla* and *T. mertensiana* by Ron Taylor, Western Washington State University, Bellingham, show that the hybrid is of much rarer occurrence than previously believed. Some supposed "hybrids" are in his opinion only extreme variants of one or the other parent species.

So distinctive from all the other hemlock species is mountain hemlock that some botanists, mostly in Europe, have sought its origin by hybridization. Sitka spruce *(Picea sitchensis)* and western hemlock are often taken as the probable parents, but not all botanists and foresters of our region agree with this intriguing hypothesis.

The slowness of establishing and growing seedlings may deter nurserymen and gardeners from trying mountain hemlock. Having sung its praises here, I hope that propagators will persevere with patience and ingenuity, for the reward is great. Possibly one aspect of its culture can be improved. Like all other conifers, the roots of mountain hemlock require the intimate association of certain fungi. Such associations, called mycorhizae, are nearly universal in nature, but may be missing in the artificial soil or rooting media often used in gardens, especially sterilized potting soil. Without the mycorhizal fungi, nutrition of the conifer host is severely impaired. Inoculation of potting soil with some humus from a conifer forest soil could provide the mycorhizal boost for better growth of young seedlings.

Beware of hemlocks as cut Christmas trees. Though ever so appealing when fresh, within hours needles begin to drop and after two or three days in a dry place, the cut tree will be bare of foliage. The same caution applies to all spruces, native as well as exotic species. Live container-grown plants might be tried for the indoor tree at holiday time.

Spruces (species of *Picea*)

All three species of spruce in the Northwest have value as ornamentals, but only one, weeping spruce *(Picea breweriana),* is of outstanding quality. Spruces are easily recognized by their sharp-pointed needles and the stout quadrangular leaf-pegs elevated perpendicularly from the twig. Spruce cones are 3 to 6 inches long, with tough but papery texture, and remain intact through to maturity. All are trees, attaining impressive dimensions in the wild and in cultivation.

BREWER'S or WEEPING SPRUCE *(Picea breweriana).* This is one of the most restricted conifers in western North America, found only in the Klamath–Siskiyou mountains of southwestern Oregon and adjacent northwestern California, usually in isolated groves at 4,000 to 8,000 feet. In its native haunts it prefers the most moist, north-facing slopes, as well as canyons. It is commonly associated with Port Orford cedar, Shasta red fir, Douglas fir, and western white pine.

Distinguishing Features. Its most striking characteristic is the drooping, almost perpendicular secondary branches from the slender crown to the base of the trunk. Average heights for trees in the wild are from 50 to 75 feet. Add to the weeping habit, the 4- to 6-inch-long cones and this spruce stands apart from its two other Northwest relatives.

Garden Uses. Brewer's spruce is a fine evergreen for the small garden. Not only is it of handsome habit, its growth is slower than that of most conifers so that it would rarely outstrip its garden location. In fact, so slow is the growth that the gardener may despair of ever seeing the singular drooping habit of a young tree. Though seedlings and small saplings are slow to achieve stature, the wait is worth it. A specimen at Kew Gardens, England, was 2½ feet high in 1905 and only 36 feet high in 1963; it first produced cones in 1920. But, after all, it is just this slow growth rate that is desired in cone-bearing evergreens, since so many of them do outstrip their garden site in a short time.

Propagation. Plants should be obtained from specialty nurseries, or as seeds or seedlings collected judiciously in the wild. As this is a rare species, cultivation from seeds is much to be urged.

SITKA SPRUCE *(Picea sitchensis)* and ENGELMANN SPRUCE *(P. engelmannii).* The other two native spruces in the Northwest are occasionally used as ornamentals. Sitka spruce is a coastal and lowland species, so much at home in the rain forests of the Olympic Peninsula. Here the tree reaches grand proportions of height and girth, simply overwhelming in bulk and stature. Certainly it is much too large and fast-growing a tree for the small garden. Moreover, it is easy victim of a variety of insect pests, especially those that attack buds; the abnormalities from such infection even assume the shape of a cone-like structure.

Distinguishing Features. Sitka spruce is easily recognized, for it is the only spruce of our westside lowland forests. It has stiff, sharp-pointed, pale green needles, papery cones up to 4 inches long, and the ends

Brewer's spruce *(Picea breweriana)* in the wild, northern California

of its branches tend to droop. Mature trees have trunks with a buttressed and swollen base and shallow flakey bark.

Engelmann spruce is a tree of the upper montane valleys and slopes on the east side of the Cascades. Though having much of the character of Sitka spruce, its young branchlets are pubescent, its cones are longer, and the mature trees are smaller and without the pronounced buttress.

Both Sitka and Engelmann spruce are grown in conifer collections and in public places. Glaucous forms of *Picea engelmannii* are similar to Colorado blue spruce *(P. pungens);* this and other cultivars should be tried in the colder areas of the Northwest.

It is worth mentioning that Sitka spruce is the most widely grown exotic conifer in Britain. Since its natural range from southern Alaska to northern California is so wide, British foresters can select appropriate seed sources from the wild to match the climates of mild west coast Scotland to the more severe heathlands of the Scottish Highlands.

Engelmann spruce *(Picea engelmannii)*

Larches or Tamaracks (species of *Larix*)

There are two species of deciduous conifers in western North America; both are larches and occur in the Pacific Northwest. In early summer, larches are easily distinguished from other native cone-bearing trees by their tufts of soft green needles on tiny peglike short shoots. The needle leaves turn a soft golden yellow in the fall, before they are shed. Cones of larches are smaller than those of Douglas firs, only 1 to 1½ inches long, but with similar exserted bracts below the scales. Larch cones are held upright on branches, not pendulous as in the Douglas fir, and they often persist on branchlets for several years.

WESTERN LARCH, TAMARACK *(Larix occidentalis).* Often seen in gardens and parks, western larch is easily and rapidly grown. Though likely to become too tall for many gardens, it seems not too intrusive or overwhelming, perhaps because it has a slender profile. Why does larch, so thoroughly deciduous in winter, seem any more dead to the beholder than deciduous oaks or maples? Yet unkind souls are known to have questioned its being alive when seen in winter. True, it is disconcerting to watch a conifer so like a pine or fir in summer turn yellow in the fall, then lose its leaves altogether. The winter habit of larch, with starkly naked branches, stiffly horizontal from the single straight bole, is perhaps less appealing than the irregular tracery of broad-leaved trees like the big-leaf maple or Garry oak in winter. But, because the tips of larch branches are usually pendulous, this winter aspect does have its own grace—and the tree is only sleeping until the coming spring. Then, its grass-green new foliage emerging from the stubby short shoots is exquisite and of delicate grace.

Western larch is wholly a tree of eastside forests, from the eastern slopes of the Cascades to the northern Rocky Mountains. It usually cohabits with yellow pine, Douglas fir, and grand fir, but can occur

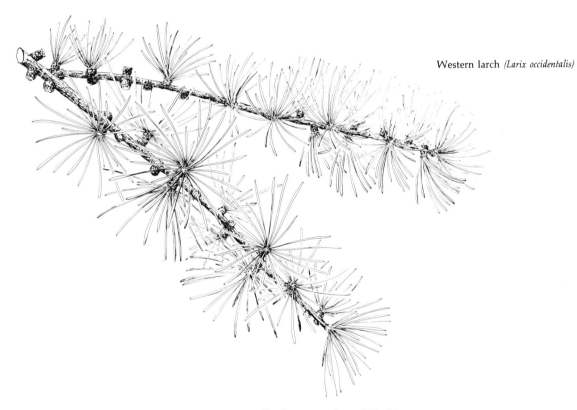

Western larch *(Larix occidentalis)*

in pure stands, often following fire. Especially fine stands in Washington are just east of Chinook Pass, Loup Loup Pass in Okanogan County, and in the Blewett Pass–Swauk Pass country of the central Cascades. In Oregon, it is plentiful in the Ochoco, Blue, and Wallowa mountains. So prolific a seeder, the young seedlings can be found in great numbers, especially following the usual human disturbances of logging, fire, and roads. They transplant easily when dug in fall after the first rains. Juvenile plants without too much leader growth can be treated as bonsai trees, in place of the less accessible Asiatic larches (e.g., *Larix gmelinii*).

LYALL LARCH *(Larix lyallii).* When seen in its craggy, rock-strewn haunts near timberline, Lyall larch is a thing of rugged beauty. Yet no one has really brought it into cultivation with success. Perhaps it will have to be enjoyed where it grows, high in the rocky rims of alpine lakes and on timberline talus and avalanche tracks. In Washington, it can be seen in the Mount Stuart area, especially high up in the Enchantment Lakes country where it is the dominant living thing in this austerely grand place. The easiest place to see Lyall larch is just off the North Cascades highway at the foot of Liberty Bell Mountain. Another locality of easy access in Washington is at Hart's Pass, Chelan County.

Lyall larch differs more in its habitat and stature from western larch than in its features of leaf and cone. While western larch is a forest tree, Lyall larch ekes out survival in thin, park-like stands (called "larchparks" in western Montana) near timberline. Of the several timberline conifers, Lyall larch takes the greatest punishment from the alpine elements, and, perhaps as a consequence, is the least successful in seed output and regeneration. Seedlings are rarely found and small saplings are usually much older than they appear. I collected a quantity of seed on Tiffany Mountain (Okanogan County, Washington) a few years ago; none germinated.

Perhaps the best recommendation for this tantalizing conifer is to let it be, to perpetuate itself in the alpine wilderness where it is truly at home. Only if a plant can be secured without disturbing the alpine scene, should it be tried back home. It may prove useful as an outdoor container conifer in colder areas. Bonsai devotees could well experiment with specimens of Lyall larch, which should be well suited to that art form, if it can somehow be grown away from its home. *But,* any trials of Lyall larch should be judged on the effect the removal of its seeds or seedlings might have on areas where it is collected. Attempts to experiment with the tree as a cultivated conifer must be done with the best of conservation practices. Take seeds only when plentifully available in good seed years; collect only those seedlings that are threatened by extermination by other causes.

Cedars (species of *Thuja, Calocedrus, Chamaecyparis*)

The word "cedar" can mislead the unwary. Many different conifers—and even some flowering plants—masquerade under the name of cedar. Our native cedars, though all conifers, are not related to the true cedar (species of *Cedrus*) of the Old World; rather, they are placed in three genera: *Thuja, Calocedrus,* and *Chamaecyparis.*

While most Northwest conifers have the needle leaves of pine and fir, the native cedars have minute scale leaves set snugly on the branchlets. The tiny scale leaves are either attached in opposing (cedars) or whorled (junipers) ranks. The three cedars of the Northwest all have seeds in small woody cones.

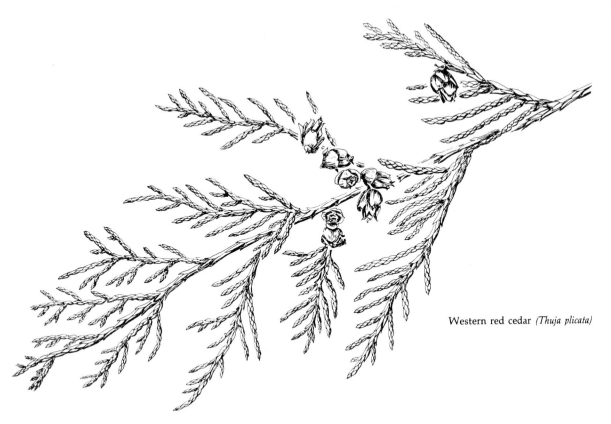

Western red cedar *(Thuja plicata)*

WESTERN RED CEDAR *(Thuja plicata)*. The most common cedar of Northwest forests is the giant canoe or western red cedar, with massive buttressed trunks and tapered boles (stems).

Distinguishing Features. The typical mature tree is rather squat of stature, less imposing in form than the taller western hemlocks and Douglas firs with which it so commonly grows. Lower limbs often trace a graceful s-shaped curve. Western red cedar can easily be told from other native cedars by the sweet (chamomile or tansy) odor of its foliage when crushed. The small elongated cones are also trustworthy marks of recognition.

Garden Uses. Even considering its eventual huge size, western red cedar is a versatile and valuable ornamental evergreen, suitable for a variety of garden uses and planting conditions. Young saplings can be planted close together (3 to 5 feet centered) and when the foliage of adjacent plants is sufficiently interwoven, the young trees can be sheared to form a tall hedge. With similar spacing, but topping only the terminal leaders, this cedar can make a beautiful screen, a use for which it is famous in Britain. Young trees planted singly or in clumps make handsome ornaments in the settings of parks and large gardens. The lower branches, gracefully curved, persist for years, clothing the stem with foliage to the ground.

Conifers

Western red cedar as garden hedge

Over ten cultivars are known: among them, good dwarfs (cv. 'Pumilio' and cv. 'Cuprea') or those with distinctive foliage character (cv. 'Aurea' with yellow foliage, cv. 'Aureovariegata' with variegated foliage, and cv. 'Atrovirens' with glossy foliage). These unusual horticultural varieties, mostly originating as mutants ("sports") from seeds, are available from nurseries specializing in conifers. For the adventuresome gardener, a search for unusual foliage and habit forms of any conifer can be rewarding. The western red cedar cultivar, 'Hogan,' a particularly fine compact, fastigiate form, was just such a reward. It has been found in the Kelso–Woodland area of Cowlitz County, Washington, and in northern Oregon. In some instances such unusual forms may occur as seedlings or saplings in the wild, especially in areas where there are many young plants, as in a burn or logged area. Or, one can collect seeds in the wild, sow them in the nursery bed, and watch for rare mutants for further propagation.

Propagation. Western red cedar is easily grown from seeds or cuttings, or from layered branches. Young seedlings, dug in nature, transplant well. Plants originating in the colder districts east of the Cascades should be hardy in gardens on the east side. Western red cedar, though most common on the west side, does occur in the forests of northern Idaho and adjacent northeastern Washington. A good stand of the interior form, the Bernard de Voto Memorial Grove, is to be seen near the Powell campground along Highway 12 on the Lochsa River, Idaho County, northern Idaho.

LAWSON CYPRESS or PORT ORFORD CEDAR *(Chamaecyparis lawsoniana)*. Port Orford cedar is the most versatile and widely used ornamental of all our native Northwestern conifers. Over two hundred cultivars are known, providing an unending variety of sizes, shapes, and foliage colors. Yet it is a remarkably uniform tree in its restricted native habitats of southwestern Oregon and adjacent northwestern California. Mature stands with trees from 125 to 185 feet in height are rarely seen now, so severe have been the inroads on the natural stands by logging and fire.

Distinguishing Features. Lawson cypress has a more delicate habit than that of western red cedar; its foliage is lacy and fernlike in texture. Ultimate branchlets are clothed with scale leaves, bright green above and dull green with whitish streaks beneath. The x-shaped design of the scale leaf pattern as seen on the underside of branchlets is a good recognition feature. Foliage of many cultivars varies enormously in color, streaking, and texture. Seed cones are rounded, ⅓ of an inch in diameter, glaucous green before ripening and reddish brown when mature. These pea-sized cones, so plentifully produced in cultivation and in the wild, are easy recognition marks for Lawson cypress (and other species of *Chamaecyparis*).

Lawson cypress rarely occurs in pure stands; it can be found with all the other native conifers common to the lowland country near the sea. The best stands have been north of the Rogue River, from sea level to 5,000 feet, in the more coastal mountains. Other good stands grow in more interior habitats, as around Oregon Caves and south into the Siskiyou Mountains. It takes the name Lawson from the nurseryman of Edinburgh, Scotland, who in 1854 first raised plants of the species in Europe.

Garden Uses. There is a cultivar of Lawson cypress for every garden situation, from dwarfs for the rock garden to tall narrowly pyramidal to cylindrical tree specimens. In color, the cultivated forms vary from bright green and yellow green to gray green (glaucous); golden and variegated forms are also available. Columnar, globose, spreading, and tiny mounds encompass the diversity of shapes. All are hardy, well-tempered plants, happy in almost any soil, thriving best in partial to full sun. The columnar forms (like cv. 'Allumii') are widely used in screen or hedge plantings. For large gardens and open-space plantings, the tree form found in the wild is most desirable.

Propagation. These stately graceful evergreens come easily from seeds

Lawson cypress *(Chamaecyparis lawsoniana)*

and cuttings, or from young plants in the wild. Unfortunately many young stands of second-growth in the wild are fighting a stand-off battle with a debilitating fungus disease (*Phytophthora lateralis,* a root pathogen). Lawson cypress should not be planted in moist soils because of the fungus problem. It would be best to start wild-collected material from seeds or from cuttings of a healthy tree in disease-free stands, to avoid this killing fungus. All the named cultivars are easily propagated from cuttings.

ALASKA or YELLOW CEDAR *(Chamaecyparis nootkatensis).* The hallmark feature of this remarkable and graceful conifer is its drooping habit: its terminal leader and lateral sprays of scale leaves hang vertically from the horizontal limbs. Though it may appear funereally somber to some, the many gardens graced with its presence—here and in Europe—signify the high popularity of this evergreen.

Alaska cedar is a common tree of the upper-montane zone in Washington, mainly keeping to the west of the Cascade crest. Here it is a common associate near timberline with mountain hemlock and subalpine fir. It is also a frequent member of the Pacific silver fir forest type, usually in the upper fringes, from 2,500 to 4,000 feet elevation. In the Oregon Cascades and Coastal Mountains it is a less common tree of the upper montane, occurring sporadically from Mount Hood to the California border. An abundant tree in the more coastal mountains of British Columbia, it reaches sea level at the northern limits of its range in southeastern Alaska. Its rare occurrences in the Blue Mountains of Oregon are significant as a likely source of a strain more tolerant to the colder areas east of the Cascades. A good stand of Alaska cedars can be seen beside the road to Hurricane Ridge, in Olympic National Park, above most Douglas firs and below or among the lower subalpine firs.

Distinguishing Features. Alaska cedar (also called yellow cedar or cypress, Alaska cypress, Sitka cypress, or Nootka cedar) is a tree of medium height (80 feet) when it occurs as a member of the closed upper-montane forest. At higher elevations, especially in the open mountain parklands and near timberline, specimens are dwarfed, not over 8 to 15 feet high. Mature trees have white stringy bark and often buttressed trunk. The sulphur-yellow wood is an unmistakable clue to identification. Beyond the sapling stage, the characteristic weeping aspect of the branches becomes evident. Its foliage, in flat drooping sprays, is of a dull, dark green hue, smelling pungent and acrid when crushed. The small round cones, woody at maturity, resemble closely those of the Lawson cypress in size and shape.

Garden Uses. Alaska cedar fits well in urban settings, large or small. Its narrow profile and slow growth make it suitable for the average-sized garden. Its striking profile serves admirably as a pliant accent-point when standing free or planted against a building. In more spacious settings, young trees planted in drifts of three, five, or more (the uneven number is traditional) make a grandly impressive scene. Alaska cedars

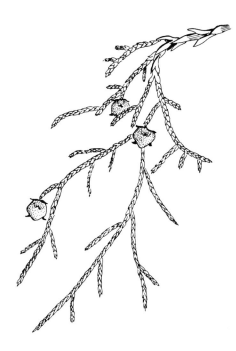

Alaska cedar *(Chamaecyparis nootkatensis)*

are suitable as border or accent plants in large rockeries, which are, after all, one of their typical habitats in our mountains. Unlike Lawson cypress, with its many garden forms, there are only a few desirable cultivars of Alaska cedar. The cultivar 'Compacta' is a dwarf of dense growth; cv. 'Lutea' is a handsome tree with yellowish young shoots; cv. 'Pendula' accentuates to the extreme the weeping habit, with the leafy branchlets vertically pendant from horizontal primary branches. Given its occurrence in upper-montane habitats where snowfall is heavy and temperatures are low, as well as the isolated populations from the Blue Mountains of Oregon, it should be possible to select cold-hardy types for gardens east of the Cascades.

It likes to be located in moderately moist situations and can tolerate soils of rather low fertility and coarse texture. Open sites with partial to full exposure to sun are preferred, although it is probably more shade-tolerant than most native conifers.

Propagation. Propagation is by seeds or cuttings. Cultivars can be easily perpetuated by rooted cuttings, though some nurserymen prefer grafting the cultivar on understock of the wild type. Often in the wild, seedlings may be encountered in abundance. With discretion, these may be collected, 4 to 8 inches high, for transplanting into the garden or nursery holding-bed. Seed germination is not high.

LEYLAND CYPRESS (X *Cupressocyparis leylandii*). Natural hybrids are next to unknown amongst our Northwest conifers. Yet an occasional garden hybrid can be expected when two or more species of close kinship are grown in ornamental collections. One such hybrid involving Alaska cedar and Monterey cypress *(Cupressus macrocarpa)* has proved to be an exceptional garden plant. Named Leyland cypress, it is an intergeneric hybrid, a cross between two species belonging to different genera.

Leyland cypress originated first in England in the late nineteenth century. A seed lot from an Alaska cedar growing in the vicinity of *Cupressus macrocarpa* gave six hybrid progeny. These were planted on the property of C. J. Leyland. The same hybrid was later obtained with *C. macrocarpa* as the seed parent. From these original sources, countless thousands of offspring as cuttings have been distributed around the world. This chance hybrid has given the horticultural world one of its most useful new evergreens. The high promise of the Leyland cypress is particularly noteworthy, as unintentional hybrids typically are either inferior to the parents or usually escape detection. In the eighth edition of W. J. Bean's *Trees and Shrubs Hardy in the British Isles,* a strong case is made for this unusual hybrid conifer:

> The Leyland cypress is one of the most important tree introductions of recent times, having all the virtues for which *Cupressus macrocarpa* has been so widely planted and none of its vices. It is, in the first place, of very rapid growth, capable of making a fine specimen 55 to 60 feet high in twenty-five years. Like the Monterey cypress, it is resistant to sea-winds, but whereas the use of that species is restricted to the milder parts, the Leyland cypress

Conifers

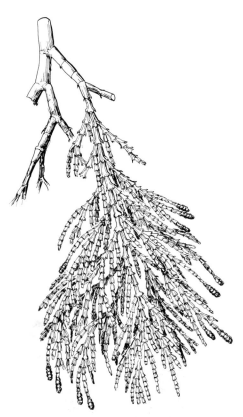

Incense cedar *(Calocedrus decurrens)*

inherits from its other parent the ability to resist the worst of our [British] winters without damage and is likely to prove a reliable and fast-growing shelter-belt tree over much of the country. It also makes an excellent hedge plant; its ability to withstand restriction is shown by the flourishing dwarf hedges in the Arboretum nursery at Kew, planted in 1947, which have been kept by mechanical trimming to a height of four feet and show no resentment at such drastic treatment. Finally, it makes a fine specimen tree of columnar habit but it is to be hoped that gardeners will not be tempted by its rapid growth into using it to excess.* [1:797–98]

INCENSE CEDAR *(Calocedrus decurrens* or *Libocedrus decurrens)*. Oregonians will be familiar with this handsome evergreen tree. Its distinctive columnar to pyramidal form, its widespread coexistence with Douglas fir or yellow pine in Oregon and California, and its highly successful adaptability to garden conditions make it a much-prized ornamental conifer for both mild and more demanding environments.

Though more common throughout montane California, incense cedar is well represented in Oregon in a variety of coniferous forest habitats. It is continuous in southwestern Oregon on both sides of the Cascades, throughout the Siskiyou Mountains and portions of the Coast Range. The best stands are in the country of the Umpqua and Rogue River divide. In northern Oregon, its distribution is more interrupted, with stands in the foothills along the southeast sectors of Mount Hood, then at the head of Breitenbush River in the eastern Marion County, and in scattered but always mixed stands within the Ochoco National Forest in central Oregon. Occurrences on the upper Klamath Basin and in the Warm Springs Indian Reservation are also known.

Distinguishing Features. Like the other native conifers that are called cedars or cypress, incense cedar has small scale-leaves densely clothing the ultimate branchlets. The flat sprays of foliage resemble those of western red cedar, but the older and lowermost scale leaves on the branchlets of incense cedar are much longer. A useful recognition feature of the foliage concerns the placement of the scale leaves. In incense cedar the free tips of adjacent scale leaves are equal in length, thus appearing as groups of four at a node. In western red cedar the adjacent scale leaves appear in groups of two at a node. Seed cones of incense cedar are elongate, up to an inch long, and of a pale straw color. Those of western red cedar are also elongate, but usually not more than ½ to ⅓ of an inch long.

Mature trees in nature are mostly between 75 and 90 feet tall, though exceptional specimens may reach 125 feet. They have open, irregular crowns and rapidly tapering trunks, widely buttressed at the base. Young trees take on a narrowly columnar stature when about 15 to 25 feet tall; this distinctive form is not to be seen in our other native cedars. The name incense, as applied to this cedar, describes the pleasant odor of both foliage and wood.†

---

* A yellow-foliage form is a highly popular new introduction in Britain.
† "The famous planting at Westonbirt Arboretum is among the most admired conifer plantings in all of Britain" (Roy Davidson).

Garden Uses. The narrow columnar to pyramidal form gives incense cedar a special niche in urban gardening. Though vigorous and fast-growing, the tree has minimal lateral spread and is densely bushy to the base. These traits make it ideal as a screening evergreen, planted in rows or drifts to define walkways, roads, or boundaries. Indeed, it is, in its stature, the evergreen counterpart of the Lombardy poplar. It can be used with good effect as a single specimen tree, for focal point value or to soften the angular emphasis of buildings. It is most useful in highway plantings where screening or boundary definitions are needed.

Incense cedar, though probably more tolerant of drought and cold than western red cedar, appears to do well in a wide range of moisture and temperature conditions. Plants originating from colder localities should do well in gardens east of the Cascades. Despite its being limited to Oregon and California, incense cedar is perfectly hardy in the Puget Sound Basin and adjacent British Columbia and has been widely planted there. Three or four cultivars are known, providing variegated or glaucous hues, as well as a more narrowly columnar habit, and in one cultivar (cv. 'Compacta'), a dwarf stature.

Propagation. As with other native cedars, progeny come well from seeds or cuttings. Small plants collected in the wild transplant with ease. Four-inch seedlings, collected in the Sierra Nevada of California in 1955 are now 35 feet high in my own garden. And plants grown from seeds collected in 1967 near Mount Shasta were 6 to 8 feet tall in 1975.

Other Attributes. Incense cedar was discovered in northern California by the famous adventurer-explorer General John C. Fremont. The tree has been in cultivation in England since 1853, when John Jeffrey collected seeds for the Scottish plantsmen's syndicate, the Oregon Association of Edinburgh. This group typified the strategy of early British plant enthusiasts who pooled funds and resources to send collectors to other parts of the world on their behalf with specific requests for plants. Jeffrey's initial successes in collecting in western North America amply rewarded his patrons. He provided the Association with the first sources of many choice western natives, but his third year in the West was a fateful one. He gave up his efforts on behalf of the Oregon Association, joined an expedition to explore the Colorado and Gila rivers of Arizona, and thereafter mysteriously disappeared.

Incense cedar might possibly occur in the wild in southern Washington, most likely in the Mount Adams–Glenbrook–Trout Lake country, since its present northernmost station is just across the Columbia on the east side of Mount Hood. Wilhelm Suksdorf, pioneer plant collector of Klickitat County, should surely have encountered it if it were actually there. It may yet turn up on the north side of the Columbia, so collectors in the area should be on the alert.

And as a final footnote to this grand tree, Carl B. Wolf, former director of the Rancho Santa Ana Botanic Garden, who in the 1940s did so much to bring natives to western gardens, states: "I suggest

Incense cedar *(Calocedrus decurrens)* in University of Washington Arboretum

the planting of Incense-Cedars in California gardens, parks, parkways and roadsides because they are not only beautiful evergreens, but are also able to thrive under so many different conditions of soils, moisture, and exposure. Equally fine specimens can be grown in a lawn or on a comparatively dry hillside. Because of their fairly narrow growth habit they are suited to small gardens where such popular, but often misplaced, trees such as Deodar Cedars are far too large." [1941:2]. So, try one, you'll like it.

Note that we give two alternative botanical names for incense cedar, *Calocedrus decurrens* and *Libocedrus decurrens*. The thirteen species of *Libocedrus* do not constitute a homogeneous group. Only three species are in north temperate localities; these appear to have closer affinities to *Thuja* than to the other species of *Libocedrus*. Thus the northern species are segregated out of *Libocedrus* and placed in *Calocedrus*, to include our native *C. decurrens*. The other ten species are placed in a more narrowly defined *Libocedrus*. These latter occur in Chile, New Zealand, New Caledonia, and New Guinea. Either name is thus correct, and a choice of one or the other depends on taking a narrow or broad interpretation of these cedars.

Junipers (species of *Juniperus*)

All three species of juniper native to the Pacific Northwest are of garden value. Two are small trees and one is a low shrub. The common recognition feature for *Juniperus* is the distinctive fruit: a round, firm berry, usually gray from its glaucous "bloom." In fact, to call these evergreens "conifers" is a bit of a misnomer since none produces a woody seed cone. All three species bear their seeds in pea-sized, glaucous berries. Yet technically, *Juniperus* species are conifers, for not only does the fleshy berry start out as a tiny cone, but the pollen is produced in small conelets. Juniper foliage varies around two constant themes: the leaves are either short, sharp, and linear needles, or are tiny overlapping scales, just like our native cedars and cypresses. Often, both types of leaves can occur on the same individual; the needle leaves are considered juvenile, the scale leaves adult. Though usually in pairs, either kind of leaf can occur in clusters of three.

ROCKY MOUNTAIN JUNIPER, ROCKY MOUNTAIN RED CEDAR *(Juniperus scopulorum)*. Next to the Douglas fir and shore pine, this juniper is the most common conifer of the drier exposed habitats in the San Juan Islands of western Washington. Its presence in the islands was first noticed in 1792 by the Vancouver Expedition; Cypress Island in the eastern San Juans probably got its name from this early encounter. It is sporadic elsewhere in the Northwest and an isolated colony is supposed to exist at the mouth of the Snohomish River. Colonies of the species are known from along the Columbia River between Chelan and Wenatchee and on north into the Kettle Falls area. Rocky Mountain juniper dominates the dunes just north of the Tri-cities area of Washington. It is also found in the Wallowas of eastern Oregon. The largest known specimen (8½ feet in circumference) has been sighted near Lostine, Wallowa County, Oregon. In British Columbia, the species is encountered in the Gulf Islands and in the dry interior of the province.

Distinguishing Features. In its coastal, island habitats, Rocky Mountain juniper is a small evergreen tree, up to 25 feet in height, with a somewhat rounded to columnar habit. The trunk of mature specimens is usually fibrous or stringy. Inland, it tends to be of a more shrubby stature. Foliage is of two types, often on the same specimens. Juvenile foliage consists of short pointed needles, in threes, often glaucous. The juvenile foliage can occur in mature specimens, especially when branches grow back after injury. The adult foliage is gray green and consists of scale-like opposite leaves, in pairs. Foliage is usually sparse giving an airy, open aspect to older specimens. The seeds are in pea-sized, berry-like fruits. These so-called juniper berries are bluish purple (glaucous).

Garden Uses. This juniper is not commonly grown here or abroad. Yet its tolerance to drought and salt spray should make it most useful in coastal or island plantings in northwestern Washington and adjacent British Columbia. It can be grown as a specimen shrub or small tree. In dense plantings it can serve well as an evergreen hedging plant. Several cultivars have been described: representative are cv. 'Argentea' (conical, with silvery foliage); cv. 'Columnaris' (columnar habit); cv. 'Horizontalis' (upright, but horizontally spreading branches); and cv. 'Viridiflora' (conical habit with bright green foliage). Some fifteen cultivars of Rocky Mountain juniper can be seen in the University of Washington Arboretum, near the office or in the Pinetum.

Propagation. Nearly all junipers root well, as nodal (heel) cuttings. Less reliable is propagation from seeds, due to inhibitory (dormancy) substances in seeds and surrounding pulp. To clean seeds, soak dried berries in water, then macerate and wash to separate plump from seeds. Seeds retain viability for several years, when stored at 20° to 40° under slightly moist conditions. Uncleaned seeds of *Juniperus scopulorum* stored at room temperature showed only 30 percent germination after 3½

Rocky Mountain juniper *(Juniperus scopulorum)*

years. Untreated seeds may require 14 to 16 months to germinate. Warm stratification at 60°F for 45 to 90 days followed by cold stratification will hasten germination.

WESTERN or SIERRA JUNIPER *(Juniperus occidentalis)*. Ancient specimens of this tree in the Sierra Nevada of California or through much of the arid sagebrush country of central Oregon are truly magnificent to behold.

Distinguishing Features. Massive, squat trunks with many branches in intricate patterns, silhouetted against a sere landscape make spectacular images. Such trees are undoubtedly hundreds of years old, hardly a time span for a garden. Yet the younger specimens are handsome in their own right. They are trim, erect trees of vigorous growth and pleasingly informal in their branching pattern. Their pale green foliage is made up of scale leaves set in threes, the twiglet thus rounded in form.

Western juniper reaches Washington in its southern and southeastern extremities in Kittitas, Yakima, Klickitat, Asotin, and Whitman counties, but only in scattered stands. It is much more widespread in eastern Oregon where it is the dominant tall shrub or small tree in the vegetation zone between the yellow-pine forest and the sagebrush "desert" (or steppe, as it is called by ecologists). Superb stands of this tree can be seen just northwest of Bend, Oregon. It, like sagebrush, is disappearing, as agriculture and other human disturbance modify the native steppe-desert landscape.

Garden Uses. Western juniper should do exceptionally well as a garden shrub or small tree in urban plantings in the Columbia Basin and other east Cascades environments.

Propagation. The same method as for propagating the Rocky Mountain juniper can be used successfully.

COMMON or DWARF JUNIPER *(Juniperus communis)*. *Distinguishing features.* In the high north latitudes of every continent, one juniper is nearly always found. Its steely blue gray foliage, prickly to the touch, and its low-to-prostrate habit make it the most unusual conifer of our mountains. Most often dwarf juniper lives at the upper edges of the subalpine fir forest zone and on into the true alpine (treeless) zone. Under these conditions it is either a low shrub or at very high elevations for plant life, such as on Burroughs Mountain in Mount Rainier National Park, it is wholly prostrate. In other parts of the world, as in northern Europe, forms of *Juniperus communis* can become small trees with many branches from the base, while in the upper Fraser River country of British Columbia, the plant is a shrub of from 6 to 8 feet tall. It is the dwarf forms, of course, that are highly prized for the garden.

Garden Uses. This is a choice conifer for the low border or rock garden. The low shrubby (var. *depressa*) or even prostrate (var. *montana*) forms of the plant and the fine glaucous foliage give it excellent garden charac-

Common juniper (*Juniperus communis* var. *jackii*), local form from southwest Oregon

ter. It should thrive in almost any of our region's climates so long as the plant is not shaded and is given ample root-run and good drainage. Though probably not as drought-tolerant as *Juniperus sabina* var. *tamarisci-folia* (the popular juniper "Tam" of Europe), our dwarf native juniper should fare well in even the coldest sectors of the Northwest.

Native varietal forms and cultivars abound in this extremely variable species. Though many natural variants are known in other parts of its vast north temperate range, only a few forms are recognized from our region. The most remarkable is *Juniperus communis* var. *jackii,* of the Siskiyou Mountains in Oregon. The variety *jackii* is prostrate, producing long relatively unbranched trailing stems, adorned with silvery gray foliage, the hallmark of the species. Long streamer-like stems of this form may be seen on serpentine (low calcium–high magnesium) soils in the Takilma–O'Brien area of Josephine County, Oregon. The compact alpine form on Burroughs Mountain, adjacent to Mount Rainier, is especially attractive. Since true alpine tundra is rare in the Cascades and Olympics, however, this good dwarf form may be rare outside the Park. Brian Mulligan has seen this form on Hurricane Ridge in the Olympic Mountains of Washington.

Propagation. Juniperus communis propagates readily from heel cuttings. Fruits, ripening the second or third year after pollination, will require the special treatments for germination described in chapter 1.

Other Conifers

WESTERN YEW *(Taxus brevifolia).* Native yew is a shrub or small ever-green tree, infrequently encountered throughout all mountains and forested lowlands of the Northwest. Though classed as a conifer, the only cone the yew produces is the tiny, short-lived pollen cone. Seeds of the yew are borne singly, surrounded by a scarlet fleshy cup, called an aril.

Distinguishing Features. Foliage of western yew is easily mistaken for that of Douglas fir, true fir, or even hemlock. But on closer inspection, the distinctive leaf attachment—the decurrent leaf base—serves to sin-

Conifers

Western yew *(Taxus brevifolia)*

gle out the yew from most other needle-leaved evergreens. The pointed leaves have two prominent but dull grayish green bands between the midrib and leaf margin.

Garden Uses. Only the best foliage forms of western yew can compete as ornamental shrubs with the much more widely planted English yew *(Taxus baccata)*. We have found the western yew of the Wenatchee Mountains in Washington well worth using in the garden. The plant is rather common in the upper reaches of the Teanaway and Cle Elum river drainages. They form compact bushes with foliage more glaucous than the rather scraggly forms of the species growing in the understory of westside forests.

Propagation. Yew is easily propagated from cuttings, hence a particularly fine wildling can be perpetuated in the garden with ease. When well established on its own roots, such plants from cuttings do well in partial to full sun, in well-drained soil.

COAST REDWOOD *(Sequoia sempervirens)*. This magnificent evergreen tree barely gets into our Northwest domain. The northern limits of its geographical range are in the coastal mountains just east of Brookings, Oregon. Coast redwood foliage resembles the flat spray of needles of the western yew, even down to the decurrent leaf base. Redwood leaves, however, drop with entire twiglets, rather than singly. Also, redwood seeds are produced in small cones, about the size of western hemlock cones, bearing no similarity to the red, berry-like fruits of the yew.

Though not presently native north of southwestern Oregon, the coast redwood is perfectly hardy west of the Cascades, north to British Columbia. It makes a handsome large evergreen for plantings in spacious settings. The typical tree form is too rapid a grower for the small garden. But there are some desirable cultivars with more compact habit. The cultivars 'Nana Pendula' and 'Prostrata' are good examples of plants with reduced stature; however, even they may occasionally produce erect shoots.*

Propagation. Coast redwood is easily propagated from cuttings, layering, or from sucker shoots, as well as from seeds although seeds have low germinability.

Broad-leaved Trees

Though ours is a land of conifers, there is a surprisingly large number of evergreen and deciduous broad-leaved trees in the Pacific Northwest. Botanically, these are all members of that vast clan, the flowering plants (angiosperms), in contrast to the distinct group of seed plants (gymnosperms) to which the cone-bearing plants belong. In nature, broad-leaved trees in our needle-leaf country are subordinate threads in the fabric of evergreen landscapes. They are found either as scattered individuals amongst the vast conifer forests, or in more populous stands under special habitat conditions. The most usual circumstance is the disturbed habitat areas where logging, fire, or other clearing activities promote the more gregarious growth of deciduous tree seedlings. Special habitats such as swamps, shorelines of lakes, streamsides, or the dry and exposed headlands near saltwater, and even the porous, cobbly soils of the "prairies," all foster the growth of hardwood trees.

Every one of our native hardwoods belongs to a genus that includes other species of great garden value elsewhere in the world. Thus, maple, alder, willow, ash, birch, and oak have their Northwest representatives: all are of ornamental value, some outstandingly so. Only five of our Northwest hardwoods are evergreen; the vast majority (twenty-six species) are deciduous.

Evergreen Broad-leaved Trees

PACIFIC MADRONE *(Arbutus menziesii)* (Other Names: Coast Madroño, Madrone-tree, Arbute-tree, Tree Arbutus, Strawberry Tree, and Madroña). Heather Family (Ericaceae). So common, yet so distinctive, is this elegant broad-leaved evergreen tree. Throughout the lowlands and foothills of Puget Sound and beyond in the coastal Pacific Northwest, one is sure to encounter the madrone in dry, exposed sites, as isolated trees or in gregarious stands.

Distinguishing Features. Madrone is best known for its satiny smooth, reddish brown trunk, its large evergreen leaves, and its small, dull red berries that follow the clusters of small white flowers of spring. Though the bark of the main trunk is best known when sleekly smooth

---

* 'Cantabrica' is handsome for its broader needles; there are glaucous forms of special attraction to those who admire their foliage.

Broad-leaved Evergreens

and red, it may be irregularly flakey on young trees or on upper branches. And there lies the gardener's dilemma: how to live with this gorgeous ornament amidst its continual rain of bark fragments, leaves, flowers, and fruit! Madrone leaves are broadly oblong, up to 5 or 6 inches long and 3 inches wide. They are of leathery texture, shiny green above and gray green beneath; the leaf margin is usually without teeth. The smallish white, goblet- or urn-shaped flowers so characteristic of many members of the heather family are borne in showy terminal clusters in mid-spring. The orange to dull red fruits about ½ inch in diameter have a warty or glandular exterior and contain several small seeds.

Though the average young specimen may have the upright stature of a rhododendron or bull bay, the madrone can assume elegant posture as it matures. The main trunk in time often bends or leans at an artful angle.

Garden Uses. A bold and massive tree that in the wild may reach from 30 to 75 feet in height at maturity seems not for the smaller town garden. Yet, there are those who so worship the madrone that they are willing to see it grow slowly in their gardens until it must come down. The daring gardener with little space should chance a smallish specimen in a starved sunny corner where it will not make too rampant a growth. Indeed, the madrone thrives on neglect. Give it a dryish, exposed piece of the garden and it will take care of itself, once established. For the larger garden or public planting, there is no grander broad-leaved evergreen, especially when planted in clumps, groves, or drifts. The older specimens with their smooth cinnamon upper trunks and platey-barked lower boles, bearing aloft great spreading branches to form a broad canopy of the shiny leathery leaves, give the setting as bold a contrast as one could want with coniferous evergreens and other trees in a large setting.

As in nature, the madrone in cultivation does best in a west- or south-facing exposure on a well-drained site, where it both catches sun most of the year and can keep its "feet" dry. It thrives in proximity with Douglas fir or grand fir where these conifers do not shade the madrone. Does such a paragon of regal beauty have any defects? Alas, there are not a few. First, there is the litter problem: peeling bark raining down all the time and the almost incessant drop of leaves (greatest in late summer), for evergreens do lose their leaves—in fact all year around, not just once in the fall. Twigs, flowers, and berries make up the rest of the durable compost. So much litter does it produce that, coupled with the shading effect and the local aridity of its understory, it seems hardly worth attempting special plantings under the tree. Then there is the sufferance of certain pests and diseases: leaf miner for one, plus a nasty fungal or bacterial leaf-spotting blight that does its worst when the tree is pampered by over-watering and cultivation. But only the most timid gardener will be frightened away from madrone by these drawbacks. Ingenuity or studied neglect can give a tree tremendous aesthetic worth. For a solution to planting under

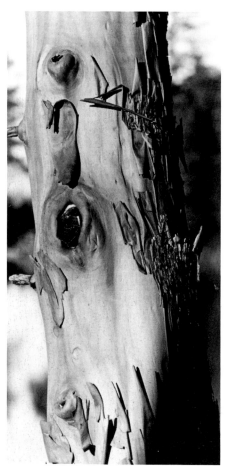

Madrone *(Arbutus menziesii)*

a madrone, try drought-resistant native shrubs like salal, Oregon grape, snowberry, or exotics, such as cotoneaster, Pfitzer juniper, or rock-roses *(Cistus)*.

Propagation. The surest way to have madrone in the garden is to wait for seedlings from bird-disseminated seeds to establish in just the right spot. Barring that stroke of luck, stray seedlings, not over a foot or so high, can be dug and moved to the chosen spot. Better put in three or so seedlings in the same site to ensure that one survives transplanting. Though difficult to move, the seedlings are so plentiful in gardens, waste places, and in the wild that generous transplantings do no disservice to the survival of the species. Growing madrone from seeds can be easy. The fresh berries have several tiny seeds that germinate well when planted in fall; half peat and loam lightly covering the seeds makes a good seed mix. Some authorities recommend three months' cold stratification. Occasionally nurseries handle madrone in cans; they too should be planted when only a foot or so high, as older plants may not survive transplanting.

Other Attributes. The orange red, mealy berries are prime food for birds, and fruiting madrones are a bird-watcher's paradise. The surrounding garden will grow bird-dispersed seedlings in ample supply for friends.

Madrone in its natural setting consorts with Douglas fir or grand fir in the more open and exposed bluffs, promontories, and sunlit slopes of Puget country and other lowland Northwest settings, usually back of the open coastline. Impressive stands in the Seattle area are on the University of Washington campus west of Parrington Hall, on the steep west-facing slopes of Innis Arden, and on the Magnolia bluffs above Elliott Bay where they were taken by early explorers as magnolias. Magnificent specimens of truly oriental form rim rocky bluffs throughout the San Juan and Gulf Islands, the east coast of Vancouver Island, and the Chuckanut country south of Bellingham.

In only the most stressful urban situations does madrone show the effects of pollution; its evergreen leaves have to endure atmospheric fallout longer than do their deciduous counterparts. Like needle-leaved evergreens, the madrone cannot handle a heavy load of urban airborne pollution.

Though *Arbutus menziesii* ranges from southern California (isolated colonies in the mountains of San Diego and Los Angeles counties) to southern British Columbia, the tree reaches the zenith of its magnificence in size and conformation in the drier inner Coast Ranges of northern California. Yet it was in upper Puget Sound that the madrone was first brought to the attention of European botanists. Archibald Menzies, surgeon-naturalist with Captain Vancouver, came upon it first at Port Discovery on the Olympic Peninsula in 1792. Later, in 1827, it was David Douglas, that intrepid collector-naturalist, who sent seed back to England for the horticultural world. In Europe it is one of the most highly prized evergreen trees.

And finally should we not ponder on the derivation of that lovely

Madrone in flower

Broad-leaved Evergreens

common name, madrone? It was another explorer, Father Juan Crespí, who aptly applied the Spanish name, madroño, to our *Arbutus menziesii,* a close relative of the European *Arbutus unedo* (strawberry tree). Since Archibald Menzies' collection at Port Discovery was the basis for the formal publication, Father Crespí's earlier find at Monterey Bay is now only of historical interest. Both Menzies and Crespí were astute enough botanists to recognize the kinship of madrone to the European relative, *A. unedo.* Menzies refers to his discovery as the Oriental Strawberry Tree and relates that "it [the tree] was at this time [May 2, 1792] a peculiar ornament to the Forest by its large clusters of whitish flowers and evergreen leaves, but its peculiar smooth bark of a reddish brown colour will at all times attract the Notice of the most superficial observer."

GOLDEN CHINQUAPIN *(Chrysolepis* chrysophylla).* Oak Family (Fagaceae). *Distinguishing Features.* This evergreen relative of oaks and chestnuts has two distinctive features. Its small, dark green leathery leaves have a soft golden sheen on their lower surfaces, made by countless tiny golden scales. Then, in fruit, the chinquapin bur resembles closely the spiny husk of the edible chestnut: the three-angled, shiny, light brown nut is enclosed by a spiny, four-valved bur. Male flowers are tiny, but showy, clustered in erect spike-like catkins. Spectacular in full bloom, the creamy white male spikes boldly contrast with the dark green foliage. The somewhat musky odor of the flowers may be slightly offensive to some—but, then, nature is not always mild. The equally tiny female flowers, taking fully two years before reaching the massive bur stage at maturity, are at the base of the male spikes. However, some male spikes may be devoid of female florets.

Under optimal conditions in nature, mature specimens may reach heights of over 100 feet. But wild plants in the northern limit of the range in northern Oregon and southern Washington habitats tend to be smaller, even shrubby in habit.

The heart of the chinquapin's geographic range is in the coastal redwood belt of northern California. But it is rather common northward along the west-facing slopes of the Oregon Cascades, the Siskiyous, and intermittent in the coastal mountains of Oregon. It reaches its northern limit in Washington at two widely separate localities, one in the Hood Canal country, and the other near Willard, in Skamania County just north of the Columbia River Gorge. These are small populations, outliers at the edges of their tolerance to climate. Moreover, these northernmost localities are increasingly under human pressure; they should be set aside as preserves, dedicated to the survival of the hardiest individuals of the species.

Garden Uses. Chinquapin is best grown as a specimen tree in filtered sunlight, matching its natural habit as a member of the open conifer understory. It is slow-growing and of rather dense, bushy habit. Only

Golden chinquapin *(Chrysolepis chrysophylla)* in cultivation

* *Castanopsis* is the older generic name, still found in many books.

very old trees in cultivation attain tree stature. In England where it is occasionally grown, specimens of 20 to 50 feet in height are recorded. It is admirably suited for Northwest gardens where it can be a companion to rhododendrons, coniferous evergreens, holly, and camellias.

The tree is only seldom found in nurseries. The most likely sources are the few native plant nurseries in the Northwest. At least three shrubby forms of chinquapin are known: *Chrysolepis chrysophylla* var. *minor,* the cultivar 'Obovata', and a distinctive shrubby species, *C. sempervirens* (see p. 94 for the bush chinquapin).

Propagation. As with most of the oak family, vegetative propagation by cuttings is difficult. Even with mist and rooting hormone, rooted cuttings seldom are obtained. Propagation by layering, grafting, or budding has been reported to be successful. These more exacting methods of propagation reduce the availability of the plant commercially. Seeds are the grower's only salvation. Freshly collected seeds have a germination capacity of 14 percent to 53 percent; seedlings take from 16 to 24 days to emerge. Cold stratification is not necessary. Extraction of seeds from the spiny burs is a bit tricky. After being spread out and dried, the burred fruits may open to release their seeds spontaneously, or they may require mechanical separation. If the collector is lucky enough to come upon a good supply of burs, then after drying, they could be spread between thick canvas sheets and trampled on. Once cleaned, seeds are sown in leafy or peaty loam in deep boxes, and when germination begins, the smell of success is sweet—for then, the prospect of growing a superb evergreen is within the gardener's grasp. A word of further caution: chinquapin, like other members of the oak family, has very robust and deep-growing roots even as seedlings. The young seedlings should be set out in large containers or in the garden as soon as possible, to prevent coiling of this aggressive root system.

TAN OAK *(Lithocarpus densiflorus).* Oak Family (Fagaceae). Though this exquisite broad-leaved evergreen barely gets into the Northwest, it must be included as one of our most desirable ornamentals. Its superb foliage and bold specimen profile lend unique character to any garden.

Most oaks are in the genus *Quercus.* But tan oak, or tanbark oak, is placed in a separate but related genus in the family (Fagaceae) of oaks, beeches, and chinquapins. Unlike typical oaks with their pendant male-flowered catkins borne back from the tips of twigs, *Lithocarpus* has stiffly erect male catkins that emerge in clusters from the tips of branches. Sudworth (1908) calls it "the connecting link between oaks and chestnuts." Tan oak ranges northward in the Coast Range from central California to the Umpqua River drainage of Oregon. In our province it is mostly associated with Douglas fir and mixed conifer-hardwood forest, along major river drainages.

Distinguishing Features. In the wild, tan oak can reach 50 to 80 feet; garden specimens rarely get over 25 or 30 feet tall. The slender trunk is seldom straight, and may often be buttressed with a flaring base.

Tan oak *(Lithocarpus densiflorus)*

Broad-leaved Evergreens

Single, open-grown trees have a broad crown with large, horizontal limbs. The trunks have a smooth bark, often broken into large plates by thin deep seams.

Tan oak foliage has unexcelled character. Mature leaves are thick and leathery, with shallowly toothed margins and bold, straight lateral veins. When young, the leaves (and twigs) are coated with a fine down of starshaped hairs. Male flowers grow in erect spikes, clustered at ends of twigs, and are creamy white in bloom. The 1 to 2-inch-long acorns come singly or in pairs at the base of the male catkins, and are in shallow cups beset with recurved, pointed scales.

Garden Uses. Tan oak is such a strikingly beautiful evergreen that it will command admiration in any choice garden spot. As it is shade-tolerant in nature it will take to partial shade in the garden setting. For the small garden it should be planted to give it room as a single specimen tree, where its tannish, gray green foliage can lend contrast to the darks of conifers, rhododendrons, and camellias. For larger spaces, a grand effect can be developed by planting groves or drifts of the tree rather widely spaced (10 to 15 feet apart) in groups of uneven number.

Though only reaching southern Oregon in the wild, the trees have proved hardy as far as Seattle. Only the 1955 freeze cut it back. Like most other broad-leaved evergreens, it cannot take the winters east of the Cascades. A robust tree with ample, dense foliage, it thus is a permanent source of decorator greenery. Every time there is a festive occasion at our house, in come the sprays of this bright and bold foliage. It is a perfect foil for cut conifer evergreens.

There are two choice varietal forms of tan oak, both originating in the wild. *Lithocarpus densiflorus* var. *echinoides* is a spreading shrub 6 to

Cut-leaved tan oak (*Lithocarpus densiflorus* f. *attenuato-dentatus*)

10 feet tall, with soft gray green foliage (see p. 98). The other variant is almost unknown in cultivation as yet, and is rare in nature. It is so unlike the species that it took oak specialist John Tucker to place it with the tan oaks. This small tree has deeply dentate, almost dissected, narrow leaves, and the marginal teeth bear slender spines. Dr. Tucker calls the plant forma *attenuato-dentatus*. We were fortunate in getting cuttings established from cut specimens sent from the type locality in northern California. It will be a collector's item once it is further propagated.

Propagation. Tan oaks usually produce bumper crops of acorns. When ripe in the fall, they are ready for collecting. The acorns need to be sown soon after harvest, in a light compost or pure peat in deep containers; they can also be sown directly outside, with protection against animals. One source recommends delay in collecting until the earliest acorns fall; these are usually ones infested with insect larvae. Germination may take up to two months and yield from 20 to 80 percent seedlings under average conditions. Better results—more seedlings and faster germination—are obtained under greenhouse conditions and by sowing fungicide-treated acorns in a vermiculite-perlite mixture. Propagation by cutting, layering, or grafting is resorted to only when a particular form of the species is desired, though the "take" will be poor. Older trees in cultivation often set viable seeds. It is useful to remember with all oaks: young container-grown plants transplant better than field-grown specimens. Avoid potbound plants.

Other Attributes. Tan oak has figured prominently in the cultural history of the Far West. Before the coming of white men, Indians used the acorns as a principal food source. The large acorns were prepared by grinding and leaching, and then made into a soup, a cooked mush, or a kind of bread. Livestock, especially hogs and cattle, fattened themselves on the acorns, as did wild game-birds and mammals. Pioneer whites found the bark to be a premium source of material for the tanning of leather. Unfortunately, great quantities of bark were taken but the wood was left behind to rot or to become fuel for wildfires. This practice has essentially vanished, as other sources of tannage have come into use. Although now principally used as firewood, the trees also serve as a specialty lumber.

To David Douglas goes the honor of having discovered this magnificent tree. On an exploring trip into central California he encountered the tan oak, and sent dried specimens back to England. It was Professor Sargent of Harvard University who introduced tan oak to the garden; plants of his introduction of 1874 are still in the oak collection at the Royal Botanical Gardens, Kew, England.

CANYON LIVE OAK *(Quercus chrysolepis).* Oak Family (Fagaceae). Of the three evergreen broad-leaved trees with oak affinity in the Pacific Northwest, only canyon live oak is a member of the oak genus *Quercus.* This magnificent evergreen reaches its northern limit in southwestern Oregon. It thrives in open woods and canyons of the major drainages

Broad-leaved Evergreens

Canyon live oak *(Quercus chrysolepis)*

of the coastal mountains in Douglas, Josephine, and Curry counties. Southward, it reaches across the entire length of California and just beyond into Baja California. No one description will suffice for such a variable tree. In habit it may be no more than a tallish shrub in the drier portions of its range, while in moist canyons and lower wooded slopes it can reach nearly 100 feet in height. The foliage is equally varied in texture, color, and toothing of leaf margin. Despite the variety of forms taken by canyon live oak, the gardener can depend on the leathery-textured foliage of contrasting hue on a framework of exquisitely branching form.

Distinguishing Features. Canyon live oak is a small-to-large evergreen tree, accommodating in form to a variety of habitats. Color, texture, and toothing of leaves vary widely. Young leaves are yellow green with a soft golden fuzz beneath. Older leaves may be bluish green (glaucous "bloom") or glossy dark green and dull white beneath. Leaves are 1 to 2 inches long and ¾ of an inch wide, broadly lance-shaped, and usually pointed at the tip. The leaf margin is bewilderingly variable. Some trees have leaves with entire margins throughout; others are wholly spine-toothed like holly leaves; and still other individual specimens have both entire margins and toothed leaves. Such variability of leaf margin—entire to toothed—is reminiscent of English holly. The acorns, copious in good seed years, are ½ to 1 inch long, buff colored, and set in golden brown cups.

Garden Uses. Canyon live oak can be grown singly as a show specimen or in groups widely spaced. As a hedge plant, trimmed specimens tend to produce spiny-margined leaves. It will take to almost any garden exposure except extreme shade and wet. In the Puget Sound area and other coastal localities, it grows best in sunny exposures, retaining a dense rounded form of medium height. It is best to use plants that come from the northern portion of its natural range in order to ensure hardiness in the Northwest. In colder areas west of the Cascades, the tree takes well to planting against a warm wall, its foliage blending with fine effect against brick, rock, or natural wood. Of all our native broad-leaved evergreens, this is the most likely to be available in nurseries, especially those specializing in native plants.

Propagation. As with other oaks, plants of *Quercus chrysolepis* are best raised from acorns sown shortly after harvesting in the fall. Acorns planted in peat and loam in deep boxes and covered with an inch of firmed soil will germinate in about 60 days. Germination capacity ranges from 50 to 75 percent. Seedlings should be transplanted to gallon containers or nursery beds when they have two or three leaves. Propagation by cuttings is next to impossible, even with hormone treatment and under constant mist conditions.

CALIFORNIA BAY LAUREL *(Umbellularia californica).* Laurel Family (Lauraceae). No other broad-leaved evergreen of our north coast country leaves such an indelible memory. Once the foliage of laurel is crushed and lightly whiffed, its overpowering but spicy-sweet pun-

Broad-leaved Evergreens

California bay laurel *(Umbellularia californica)*

gency will linger on. The aroma from the long and narrow lance-shaped leaves is the hallmark of this stately tree with oak-like proportions. The native bay laurel first appears southward in Coos County, Oregon, along the south fork of the Umpqua River. From Oregon, the tree in many forms (even shrub-like) extends all the way to the Mexican border; it can be found in both Coast Ranges and the Sierra Nevada. Mostly it keeps to moister sites: stream banks, flood plains, and lower mountain slopes, where it coexists with maple and alder, and even appears in mixed conifer forests.

Distinguishing Features. The habit of this evergreen is so variable in response to different habitats, that no single description will suffice. Under the most favorable conditions of moisture, shade, and minimal slope, the species may reach up to 80 feet in height, with trunks 2 to 3 feet in diameter. In dense forest, its stems are straight and slender, with a narrow crown of upright leafy branches. In drier, more open sites it may be a shrub only 3 to 5 feet tall, or a closely cropped, windswept bush or small tree in exposed headlands near the sea. The long-persistent leaves grow densely on the branchlets; they can be up to 6 inches long and 1½ inches wide. The usual leaf shape is lanceo-late (long-tapered and narrow); they are dark, shiny green above and yellowish green beneath. The flowers, borne in little umbellate clusters, are greenish yellow—rather unprepossessing. But from insignificant flowers come large fruits, olive-like with a leathery hull, and single, large thin-shelled seeds.

Garden Uses. Because it is so tolerant of shade, bay laurel can be grown beneath the canopy of larger trees, both coniferous and hard-wood. As long as it has its feet wet, though, laurel will do well in full sun, where it tends to remain shrubby. It has not been grown much in Northwest gardens, probably because it is so common in adja-cent wildlands, in Oregon at least. Several fine specimens can be seen at the University of Washington Arboretum in Seattle, midway along the upper (east) road. As single specimens or planted in drifts, the dark evergreen foliage serves as a bold contrast with deciduous shrubs and trees. Like its Old World counterpart, the laurel of ancient classic cultures, *Laurus nobilis, Umbellularia* can be shaped by clipping into hedge plants or boxwood form. Although it is ordinarily slow-growing, its growth can be accelerated on moist and rich soils. Particularly desirable for the small garden or even container plantings are specimens of the unnamed shrub form that grows on serpentine (high magnesium) habitats in southwestern Oregon.

Propagation. Bay laurel is easily started from seeds, sown soon after harvest in the late fall. Removal of the leathery fruit coat will shorten germination time to about two months. Seeds are produced copiously in the wild. Bay laurel should be planted, much like oaks, shortly after harvest, in deep (8 to 12 inches) containers in peat, oak leaf mold, or a light loamy soil. It can also be propagated by cuttings. In the wild it easily sprouts from stumps and fallen trunks.

Other Attributes. The long list of common names for *Umbellularia* is testimony to the role it has played in the course of human affairs in the Far West. Besides Oregon myrtle, it has been known as spice tree, California or green bay tree, California olive, mountain laurel, California sassafras, and pepperwood. Besides familiarity through its unique odor and its conspicuous position in coastal forests, bay laurel has been adopted by man for a variety of Indian and pioneer uses, from cookery and medicine to lumber in specialty cabinetry. The widespread use of the burls (knobby outgrowths of the trunk) for myrtlewood novelty items is still practiced in Oregon, although sources of the burls are vanishing. The chemical basis of the spicy aroma comes from two aromatic oils, menthol and exumbelluline. The latter is known to have toxic properties. Despite the possible danger from over-exposure to the aromatic and volatile oils (dizziness, sneezing, headaches, etc.), the leaves and bark, in cautious moderation, can be used as a kitchen spice and beverage. Indians baked the seeds, then cracked them to eat (Clarke 1977). It would be safest not to eat them raw.

Umbellularia californica was discovered by Archibald Menzies of the Vancouver expedition in 1790 and subsequently introduced to the gardening world by David Douglas in 1829. It is a popular tree in California, is grown in Britain, and should be more widely tried in the Pacific Northwest. It is perfectly hardy on the west side of the Cascades, north into southern British Columbia, though young shoots and flower buds may get nipped by late spring frosts.

Broad-leaved Deciduous Trees

The great expanses of coniferous forest in the Pacific Northwest overshadow the presence of a considerable variety of native deciduous hardwood trees. Twenty-six species of broad-leaved deciduous trees occur within the dominant coniferous forest types. The basic kinds are the familiar genera of Old and New World temperate forests: maples, alder, oak, ash, cherry, and cottonwood, to name a few. Some can be singled out for their known ornamental value or for their promise as garden plants. Several of our native trees share the feature of producing male or female flowers separately in tassels (called catkins or aments). They are all deciduous trees of forest and parkland; some are of considerable ornamental value, such as alder, birch, and oak.

PACIFIC or WESTERN FLOWERING DOGWOOD *(Cornus nuttallii)*. Dogwood Family (Cornaceae). The queen of our native hardwoods surely must be the flowering dogwood. While other broad-leaved trees may blend with coniferous evergreens, the dogwood in bloom glows brilliantly—a beacon in the forest. Never abundant, the scattered individuals appear with a frequency that charms and surprises the viewer throughout the lowland forests west of the Cascades. Dogwood ranges from southern British Columbia all the way to southern California. It attains its best growth (in size and abundance) in the Douglas fir forests of Puget Sound country. An isolated colony on the Selway–Lochsa forks of the Clearwater River drainage in west-central Idaho should give heart to those who would hope to grow it in colder areas of our region.

Distinguishing Features. Western flowering dogwood is easily the showiest of those species of the dogwood genus *Cornus* that have their true flowers aggregated into tight pincushion-like heads. The floral beauty comes from the large petal-like bracts that radiate from each pincushion flower cluster. The four to seven bracts are broadly ovate, each up to 3 inches long, and soft white or cream white, often changing to pale pink with age. Though most individual trees bloom in late spring (April to June), some plants flower profusely a second time, in mid-

Pacific flowering dogwood *(Cornus nuttallii)* in spring bloom to late summer when the plant is in full foliage. The spring flowering period comes on naked branches, before the leaves emerge, a feature which gives the bloom more spectacular background.

Trees are often multi-stemmed from the base, forming a cluster of trunks. Single- or multi-stemmed trees occasionally get to 50 feet tall, but the usual growth form is more shrub-like, not exceeding 20 feet in height. Foliage is distinctive; leaves and twigs are borne in pairs (opposite one another). Often the branching appears to be in whorls from the main trunk, with the side branching appearing forked. The leaves are usually clustered toward the tips of the branchlets. Leaves are much the shape of the colorful bracts—broadly ovate, 3 to 5 inches long, with arcuate veins (curving and parallel to the leaf margin). In fruit, although each of the tiny flowers of the bracteate cluster can be fertile, only a few of them produce the red fleshy berries.

Garden Uses. This dogwood is a native tree for all seasons: in fall, fine yellow to reddish foliage; in winter, superb tracery of the symmetrical branching pattern of naked twigs; and, of course, the glorious spring show in flower. Even in summer it has its ornamental value, both as a shade tree and for the occasional second episode of bloom. It seems to take well to partial shade in the garden and thrives in the not-too-dense companionship of coniferous evergreens. Well-established trees can do without summer watering; indeed, a well-watered tree seems to suffer. Either the single- or multi-stemmed trees make striking show specimens in the shrub border or open woodland glade. When planted in lawns or in shrub borders, an ample circle free of lawn must be provided as buffer against mechanical damage to the trunk from lawnmowers or other tools. Once wounded, dogwood is an easy prey to a killing fungus disease. A shaded trunk prevents sunburn damage to the bark on which microorganisms may feast.

A few cultivars of the dogwood are known. One has variegated foliage; others are recognized for their exceptionally large "flowers" (bracteate flower clusters or heads). The named cultivars include 'Colrigo Giant', 'Eddiei' (a variegated form, formerly 'Gold Spot'), and the hybrid with *Cornus florida,* called 'Eddie's White Wonder'.

Propagation. Seeds, planted soon after harvest in the fall, are the best means of propagation. The fleshy coat should be removed. Outdoor seedflats should be mulched with sawdust, conifer needles, or light leaf mold as protection against frost-heaving. Treated cuttings taken in early summer root fairly well, though not as abundantly as does the eastern flowering dogwood *(Cornus florida).* Air- or ground-layering of small branches should work well. Dogwood does not transplant too well, especially if the plants are over 2 or 3 feet high. Small saplings or seedlings from woodlot or garden can be grown in containers for eventual transplanting to a permanent site. A few nurseries stock this superb native tree. If none are available in the trade, a search in nearby woodlands or in a friend's garden will often yield the stray seedling, sown by passing birds. For eastside gardens with some shelter, it would be advisable to grow plants from seeds obtained in the Selway–Lochsa

River population; this is a small and isolated source in Idaho, so plants must not be dug there.

Though David Douglas discovered Pacific flowering dogwood around 1826, he did not recognize it as distinct from the eastern flowering dogwood *(Cornus florida)*. It was Thomas Nuttall ten years later who not only rediscovered our dogwood but recognized it to be a distinct species. The tree is first pictured in James Audubon's *Birds of North America;* on a sprig of the plant is perched the band-tailed pigeon, no coincidence to be sure. In the text to this classic work, Audubon provides the first description of dogwood and appends this note. "It is a superb species of dogwood, discovered by our learned friend, Thomas Nuttall, Esq., when on his march toward the shores of the Pacific Ocean . . . I have graced it with his name . . . *Cornus nuttallii.*"

Many years later, noted Harvard botanist Merritt L. Fernald solved the mystery of that apparently meaningless common name, dogwood. Fernald states:

> *Cornus,* the ancient name, from *cornu,* a horn, referred to the hardness of the wood, a European species having long been used for skewers by butchers and for daggers and other sharp implements, whence the colloquial names in some English provinces, skewerwood and *dagwood,* the latter coming from the Old English *dagge,* a dagger or sharp, pointed object. *Cornus* and *dagwood,* are, then, apparently closely related in meaning, and only by an erroneous etymology did dogwood become established as the English name of *Cornus.* [1942:27]

Maples (species of *Acer*). Maple Family (Aceraceae)

All three species of native maples have graced the urban scene as ornamental species. Big-leaf maple *(Acer macrophyllum)* is so common a native that it is ever-present in city landscapes, though most often without intention. The mountain maple *(A. glabrum)* only rarely appears in cultivation. But the third species, vine maple *(A. circinatum),* has, in recent years, captured the fancy of the landscape designer. It is a first-class plant and merits a detailed account here.

VINE MAPLE *(Acer circinatum). Distinguishing Features.* This is a large shrub or small tree with elegant form and texture. Most specimens have several trunks of bright reddish green bark, topped with foliage displayed in an exquisite, tiered pattern. Its palmate leaves are symmetrically seven- to nine-lobed, each lobe pointed and with a toothed margin. It flowers in April before leafing out, putting on a stunning show early. Each flower has wine-colored sepals and white petals. The showy upright clusters are enriched in color by the reddish bud scales sheathing the new leaves.

The habit of vine maples varies from upright small trees when grown in the open, to broadly spreading tall shrubs under the shade of forest trees. In moist valley bottoms and lower slopes of hemlock and cedar forests, vine maple is often the conspicuous understory shrub, forming

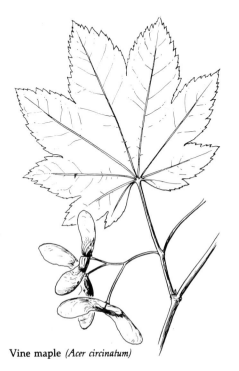

Vine maple *(Acer circinatum)*

impenetrable thickets as the drooping branches root and expand the tangled spread of the plant. It is most common in forests west of the Cascades from sea level to 2,500 feet, but is not infrequent in the forests on the east slope of the range. It is on the east side that its brilliant fall colors of yellows and reds are best developed.

Garden Uses The vine maple is best suited to woodland plantings, as it is tolerant by nature to the shade of conifers. Massed plantings under Douglas fir or other evergreens can achieve a spectacular display. It can also be grown singly in the open of a lawn or against a building, so long as it is not given too much exposure to the sun and can depend on a moist soil through the growing season. East of the Cascades, it can succeed in gardens with frequent watering, as much as a lawn would require.

Because it so closely resembles Japanese maple *(Acer palmatum),* vine maple has been grown in abundance in westside gardens and other urban settings. Much of the planting stock has come directly from the wild, usually dug on logged or young second-growth land. Mature specimens take rather well to transplanting from the wild, given special treatment from the initial digging to post-planting care. For the time being, this wholesale collecting from native sources has not seriously limited native stands, so plentiful is the species. But in time, gardeners and nurseries would do well to depend on propagating the plant from seed or layerings. Frequently, commercial plantings of clumps taken from the wild are doomed. They tend not to recover from the shock of transplanting if they are dug in flower or in leaf well into the spring growing season. Further loss may occur if they are placed in too severe exposure to light and wind. One authority (Bean 1970) comments: "It [the vine maple] is an admirable subject for a lawn in a small garden." We agree, but add that it needs partial shade or a moist root-run. A further recommendation is to plant it in groups or drifts—the effect is stunning.

Propagation. Vine maple can be grown from seeds or from well-rooted, layered branches. As with other maples, seeds should be sown soon after fall harvest. A seed bed of rich sandy loam fosters good germination. The best results from seeds are obtained by alternating with warm-cold stratification to break seed dormancy. The warm period takes 30 to 60 days at 68° to 86°F and the cold period 90 to 180 days at 38°F. However, we have had ample germination under outdoor conditions in the late fall and winter with only the natural day-night temperature regimes. Seedlings should be transplanted to containers or nursery rows soon after the first leaves mature.

DOUGLAS' MAPLE *(Acer glabrum)* (also called Rocky Mountain or Sierra maple). *Distinguishing Features.* This small tree has much the habit of vine maple, but tends to form multi-stemmed plants and does not spread by rooting of pendant branches. Its leaves are shallowly three- to five-lobed, each lobe double-toothed along the margin. *Acer glabrum*

Broad-leaved Deciduous

Rocky mountain maple *(Acer glabrum)*

is hardier than *A. circinatum,* as it is native in the mountains east of the Cascade crest and all the way to the Rocky Mountains. It should be considered a valuable substitute for vine maple in the colder areas of the Northwest. Though thought not quite as handsome as the vine maple, mountain maple does have fine fall color. This maple is also found infrequently on the western slopes of the Cascades, even growing side-by-side with vine maple. On the San Juan Islands, it can get up to 40 feet tall with trunks up to 2 feet in diameter. Forms with leaves divided into three leaflets show garden promise along with other three-leafleted small maples. Douglas' maple's autumnal colors range from orange and red to a soft "box-elder" yellow.

Propagation. Propagate by seeds, treated like vine maple; Douglas' maple has a higher germination capacity.

BIG-LEAF or COMMON MAPLE *(Acer macrophyllum).* In many other parts of the temperate world, big-leaf maple is considered "the noblest of maples," and is highly prized as an ornamental. Because it is so common—even invasive—in urban settings of the coastal Northwest, we tend to take it for granted or even resent its presence. It is a massive tree, of a size to dwarf the small garden. Where found in parks, open spaces, street parking strips, and in suburban and urban private residences, it is often preserved (or allowed to exist, like Douglas fir), an unplanned part of the urban landscape.

Distinguishing Features. No other tree has such a distinctive form. From its massive and squat main trunk arise several lateral branches soaring upward, each becoming huge vertical limbs. The whole dramatic form encompasses a spread of 50 feet or so and a stature up to 75 or 100 feet in height. Overwhelmingly majestic, it is a fine tree for intentional planting in *spacious* urban and suburban settings.

Broad-leaved Deciduous

Big-leaf maple is at home in the lower mountains and lowlands from southern California to southern British Columbia, mainly west of the Sierra–Cascade axis. It reaches its finest development in the coastal areas of the Pacific Northwest. It also grows in the moister canyons and hillsides on the east slope of the Cascades; good stands can be seen in the upper forested drainages of the Yakima and Wenatchee rivers. These eastslope populations should be tested for hardiness in the colder gardens of the east side. The tree attains its grandest expression in the temperate rain forests of the Olympic Mountains, where big-leaf maple serves as the massive, branching framework for the rich growth of moss, lichen, and ferns.

The leaves are often more than a foot in width, are deeply three- to five-lobed, with lobes entire (not toothed). Yellow is the predominant fall color of big-leaf maple foliage, with occasional salmon-tinted trees. The flowers are borne in large, vertical, chain-like clusters, creamy yellow, emerging in mid-spring before the leaves. Perhaps it is because of its great prodigality of seeds and seedlings that Northwesterners tend to regard it as dangerously invasive. Yet the mature outcome of that fertility is a tree of great beauty.

A word of caution for those who would attempt to garden beneath a huge specimen of big-leaf maple. Either from shade or by rapid moisture withdrawal in the summer, the soil beneath a mature tree can be inhospitable to growing even shade-tolerant ornamental shrubs or herbs. By judicious selection of other natives like salal, Oregon grape, sword fern, and others in the native understory, the big trees can have their own ground-level gardens.

Big-leaf maple *(Acer macrophyllum)*

Alder (species of *Alnus*). Birch Family (Betulaceae)

Why on earth include alder in an account of ornamental trees? Surely our lowland species, red alder *(Alnus rubra)*, seems much too common, aggressive—even weedy—to merit mention here. Red alder is more often dismissed as an invader of clear-cuts, burns, and waste places. But for use in the vital process of ecological restoration of blighted and barren wasteland in our urban midst, it is a tree to count on. Red alder can be used to reclaim bare ground of fills, dumps, dredge spoils, strip-mine spoil banks, and other ugly by-products of human activity. Alders fix nitrogen with the aid of microorganisms in root nodules and mycorhizae, and thus can serve as nutrient-giving pioneers in controlled land reclamation. Moreover, for any private or community beautification project involving what was once a woodland habitat, alder and conifers mix well in pattern as well as function, even though the association may not last. Alder may yield to the conifers eventually. Since the lowland red alder can become a tall (40 to 80 feet) tree, another less lofty alder can be tried if reduced height is important. The mountain, or Sitka, alder *(Alnus sinuata)* forms shrubby thickets or groves of small trees in high forested reaches of all our mountains, especially common in avalanche tracks. It is a beautiful small tree.

Propagation. Both alder species are propagated from freshly collected seeds. The light, flakey seeds are released from the female conelets in the fall.

Birch (species of *Betula*). Birch Family (Betulaceae)

Although three species are found in the Northwest, the two birches with tree habit (*Betula papyrifera* and *B. occidentalis*) are so similar that they can be treated as one. The paper birch *(B. papyrifera)* is commonest in northwestern Washington from Marysville north to the Canadian border and beyond; it is common in the lower Skagit River valley. Waterbirch *(B. occidentalis)* is frequent along streams east of the Cascades.

Distinguishing Features. Birch is rather easily distinguished from alder with which it commonly grows. The paper birch has a conspicuous white papery bark (in mature specimens) and smaller, softer-textured leaves. The native birches are well worth growing especially where a native woodland effect is desired. A low, shrubby birch *(Betula glandulosa)*, called the swamp birch, has potential for wet habitats.

Propagation. Birch propagates readily from seeds, treated like alder.

Deciduous Oaks (species of *Quercus*). Oak Family (Fagaceae)

Two deciduous oaks reach the Pacific Northwest. The California black oak *(Quercus kelloggii)* ranges into southern Oregon as far north as the McKenzie River, while the Oregon post oak or Garry oak *(Q. garryana)* can be found from the California border all the way to southern British Columbia.

Red alder *(Alnus rubra)*

Seeds of red alder

Broad-leaved Deciduous

Garry oak *(Quercus garryana)*

CALIFORNIA BLACK OAK *(Quercus kelloggii).* This oak resembles in foliage the more robust northern red oak *(Quercus rubra),* with its deeply cut leaves and sharp-pointed lobes. Trees are known to reach 50 to 75 feet in height in the wild. Mature specimens have a blackish brown and furrowed trunk, but upward in the limbs the bark is smooth and dark gray. Old trees with their irregular trunks and broad canopy are most handsome. Fine stands of California black oak can be seen in southwestern Oregon on the rather dry benches and slopes of mixed conifer-hardwood forests; it commonly coexists with yellow pine. Though it is drought resistant, it may not be hardy east of the Cascades. It is a prolific seeder, but with rather low viability. In cultivation, it is a slow-growing tree of smaller stature than the eastern red oaks like *Q. velutina* and *Q. rubra.* It should be a highly prized shade tree in the more arid sections of western Oregon and Washington, such as in the valley borders of the Rogue, Umpqua, and Willamette rivers, and in the gravelly prairie country of western Washington.

GARRY OAK or OREGON POST OAK *(Quercus garryana).* The Garry oak typifies the white oak group in the genus and resembles its European relative, English oak *(Q. robur).* Their features in common are the leaf with blunt tips and the several deeply cut, rounded lobes. Garry oak's white bark and elegant branching pattern, seen in the open parkland of the Willamette and Puget Sound country, lend an aspect of nobility to the landscape. From the Columbia River south, this oak is nearly continuous in the interior valleys and foothills west of the Cascades. Northward, it is discontinuous, usually occurring on the drier plains and prairies that frequently interrupt conifer forest of the western slopes. In Washington, it reappears eastward across the Cascades on the Yakima and other rivers tributary to the Columbia.

Around Puget Sound, Garry oak grows on the mainland around Olympia and Tacoma, on the islands of the Sound, and sparingly along the northeast edge of the Olympic Peninsula, near Sequim. It is plentiful in the San Juan Islands. British Columbians know Garry oak well, for it is a prominent tree member of the open, parklike landscapes of southern Vancouver Island. Its northern limit is around Nanaimo. Isolated stands may still be in existence along the lower reaches of the Fraser River.

At least two shrubby forms have been recognized. One is common in the Siskiyou Mountains of Oregon, called Brewer's oak *(Quercus breweri* or *Q. oerstediana)* or simply a variety of *Q. garryana* (var. *breweri).* The shrubby form that can be found on the more exposed headlands here and there in the San Juan Islands has not been named; it may be simply an ecological modification of the typical species, which is also found in the islands.

Garden Uses. Like so many of our noble native trees, Garry oak has been taken too much for granted. As urbanization continues to spread out into the oak-grass-Douglas fir prairies, specimens may be spared and become part of the cultivated landscape. But more often they succumb to the irreversible activities of housing, roads, and other development. Moreover, they are rarely planted on purpose, even to replace those lost to construction. Yet they should be planted, both to compensate for the loss and for their intrinsic ornamental value. Though perhaps not so attractive as California black oak, our native white oak has great appeal, especially as older specimens with intricate branching pattern. It is of slow growth and when young may tend to hold its dead leaves through winter. The best use is in the gardens on dryish porous gravelly soils where in time it can become a grand tree.

Propagation. Acorn crops are sporadic and may be riddled with insects, but good seeds germinate freely in moist soil enriched with leaf-mold. Young seedlings in the wild can be successfully transplanted.

Dr. John Tucker, oak specialist at the University of California (Davis), gives our Garry oak high marks as an ornamental: "Oregon oak is probably the most hardy of all Pacific Coast species, and the most widely adaptable for horticultural use in the Northwest. It is a splendid tree for spacious lawns, parks and avenues where climate and soils are to its liking."

Other Deciduous Trees

HAZEL *(Corylus cornuta).* Birch Family (Betulaceae). Though most often a tall, spreading shrub, our native hazel can become a small tree, much like open-grown vine maple. But there the likeness ends.

Distinguishing Features. Hazel produces long pendant male catkins in late winter, releasing its pollen before any other woody plant. It is this early emergence of elegant, pendant chains of tiny flowers long before leaf emergence that gives charm and ornamental value to the plant. Much less conspicuous are the targets of pollen release—the tiny female florets. They are barely more than reddish feathery pollen-catching plumes (stigmas). But from pairs of pollen-catching female flowerlets come the sizeable husks with their edible hazelnuts. The

Hazel *(Corylus cornuta),* early spring, male (pollen) tassels

Broad-leaved Deciduous

foliage resembles that of alder and birch, though it is softer to the touch (the underside of the leaves coated with a felty down). The leaves are oval in outline with pointed tip and double-toothed margin.

Hazel is a common member of forest communities on both sides of the Cascades. It, like alder and Douglas fir, seems to thrive in the disturbance of suburbia.

Propagation. If squirrels have not chanced to plant it, seedlings can be dug from the nearby woodlot or roadside for transplanting to the native garden. Hazel initiates the rites of spring hereabouts and will be a special omen for those who watch for signs of yearly rebirth in the garden.

BLACK COTTONWOOD *(Populus trichocarpa).* Willow Family (Salicaceae). To the fastidious gardener, the inclusion of our native black cottonwood as an ornamental will seem a bit extreme—a sure sign of regional chauvinism. By no means is the native cottonwood, *Populus trichocarpa,* a tree for the average-sized garden. What is more, it has a reputation as a common, invasive plant, massive in size, and has a runaway rate of growth. But for use in the reclamation of urban wasteland, black cottonwood shares high honors with red alder. It is especially valuable for periodically flooded lands or other wet habitats. This, the largest of North American cottonwoods, has an astounding rate of growth. Floodplain specimens at 7 years of age may reach 45 feet and at 27 years be 120 feet high with a girth of 120 inches. This phenomenal capacity for growth can be put to landscape advantage in situations demanding quick cover and fast growth—just the plant for restoring degraded moist habitats.

Distinguishing Features. Black cottonwood is easily recognized by its large triangular to broadly ovate leaves and straight trunks, greenish and smooth when young, but deeply furrowed and dark gray at maturity. In early spring, the pollen and seed tassels (catkins) festoon the leafless branches of all but the youngest tree, precocious like their relatives the willows; and, as in willows, the sexes are on separate trees. In late spring the air is snow-white with cottonwood fluff; seeds with their cottony down are shed in lavish quantities. The balsamic aroma emitted by the long black and sticky leaf buds adds to the singular character of the tree.

Found nearly everywhere in the West, it ranges from seashore to the Rocky Mountains, north to the Anchorage area of Alaska, and all the way south to southern California. Hardly continuous is this distribution, even in the Northwest. Cottonwood is mostly a plant of deep, moist soils of river bottoms and streamside.

For the harsher climates of eastern British Columbia and south to eastern California, there are other native cottonwoods that should be tried, especially in situations where the watertable is adequate. Hitchcock recognizes three such candidates as *Populus angustifolia, P. acuminata,* and *P. deltoidea.*

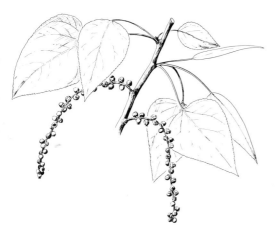

Black cottonwood *(Populus trichocarpa)*

Propagation. Cottonwoods can be propagated by seeds, cuttings, layering, or by transplanted seedlings from the wild. Seeds are shortlived unless stored under cold and dry conditions. In nature, the seeds can germinate on nearly raw mineral soil, as long as the soil is wet.

QUAKING ASPEN or WESTERN TREMBLING ASPEN *(Populus tremuloides).* Willow Family (Salicaceae). If black cottonwood merits mention only for its utilitarian value, then its nearest kin, quaking aspen, leaves no doubt as to its high ornamental value.

Distinguishing Features. Its quivering triangular leaves on long flattened stalks and a soft greenish white bark are the unmistakable recognition features of this small tree, so widespread in the West. Aspen is most common east of the Cascade crest, in wet openings of forest, moist seeps on brushy hillsides and in swales, and often in vast tracts in the mountains when conifer forest has succumbed to fire. In the Puget–Willamette trough, aspen can be encountered occasionally in wet areas bordering the oak parkland or gravelly prairies. Most often groves of aspen are clonal: each trunk may be part of a large, single individual. Aspen forms sucker shoots readily from its shallow roots.

Garden Uses. Aspen has become a most popular tree for garden, park, and wayside plantings. When grown in groups or drifts it can make a striking showpiece in the urban landscape. The fine foliage, brilliant gold in the fall, and elegant bark give it high rank as a native ornamental tree. In cultivation, aspen is usually a small tree, not over 25 to 30 feet high. But it may become intrusive in another direction. Because it sends up frequent suckers beyond the perimeter of the crown, it can wander; further, the moisture-seeking root systems can clog sewers or drainage systems.

Propagation. Easy to propagate from suckers or cuttings, though when available, seeds germinate readily and with a high percentage.

Quaking aspen *(Populus tremuloides)*

Broad-leaved Deciduous

Wild cherry (*Prunus emarginata* var. *mollis*)

Oregon ash *(Fraxinus latifolia)* in University of Washington Arboretum

BITTER CHERRY or NARROW-LEAVED CHERRY (*Prunus emarginata* var. *mollis*). Rose Family (Rosaceae). A rather common tree found in lowland westside wooded habitats, it seems to prefer open second-growth conifer forests. Old specimens may reach up to 50 feet high and have trunks a foot or more in diameter. The thin bark of large specimens is a shiny reddish brown with symmetrically horizontal stripes (lenticels). Leaves are broadly lance-shaped, 2 to 4 inches long. Flowers are small, whitish in flat-topped clusters. The small cherry-like fruits are inedible. Bitter cherry, in its stately tree form, comes naturally to a woodland setting, whether created by design or left by benign neglect. If natural plantings are not already present, then propagation is by seed sown in the fall; its germinative capacity, however, is rather low. The shrubby form of bitter cherry of the eastside forests and upper open slopes should be tried in the more demanding garden environments east of the Cascades.

OREGON ASH *(Fraxinus latifolia).* Ash or Olive Family (Oleaceae). This tree is most abundant in wet places in the lower reaches of the major river valleys west of the Cascades. It is especially common in the valleys of the Chehalis, Cowlitz, and lower Columbia rivers, often as pure stands, growing in flood waters during the winter. Trees reach up to

60 feet, with a narrow crown and straight trunks in thickets or with a broader crown in the open. The opposite leaves are compound, like mountain ash, up to a foot long, with 5 to 7 bright green, broadly tapered leaflets; their fall color is a good clear yellow. Flowers are inconspicuous, greenish, and in dense clusters; male and female are on separate trees. The fruits are winged, each resembling one-half of the two-winged maple fruit. Oregon ash should be a perfect native tree for revegetating wet, lowlying areas. Propagation is by seed, sown in the early fall. Stratification is essential for later sowings.

ELDERBERRY (*Sambucus cerulea* and *S. racemosa*). Honeysuckle Family (Caprifoliaceae). Our two native elderberries become tree-like in favorable conditions. Blue elderberry *(Sambucus cerulea)* is especially attractive when laden with masses of glossy, bluish gray fruit clusters. It is more common on the east side, especially along water courses, there attaining tree size; it extends from British Columbia to California and east to western Montana. Its fruits are edible, though not too palatable, raw or cooked. Red elderberry *(Sambucus racemosa)* is less often tree-like and is confined to the mountains and lowlands west of the Cascades. Though its large pyramidal clusters of red berries are most attractive, they are reputed to be toxic, at least when raw. Both elderberry species have large, oppositely arranged, compound leaves. They are vigorous colonizers, widely spread by birds, and make rapid growth as seedlings and saplings, though tending to become leggy. Severe pruning helps. Both in flower and especially in fruit they make attractive specimens in the wild garden. Those who would lure birds to their gardens would do well to grow either species. The blue elderberry is best for plantings on the east side. Propagation is by cleaned seeds sown in the fall or by cuttings.

CASCARA *(Rhamnus purshiana)*. Buckthorn Family (Rhamnaceae). "The plant is by no means unattractive, but is scarcely a valuable ornamental," so say Hitchcock and coauthors (1961, vol. 3). And I agree in both respects. Cascara is a small deciduous tree up to 30 feet tall, with 3-inch-long, broadly ovate leaves, embossed with bold veins. In the forest setting, its fine foliage is its real charm. But, alas, in the urban setting, the leaves rarely achieve their natural size and texture, nor their bright green hue. In the environment of cities, urban pollution and aphid attacks suppress the best expression of the handsome foliage. Cascara, then, is for the rural woodland garden or suburban park, either at home there by nature's chance or by gardener's intent. Propagation is by seeds, cleaned of their dark fleshy pulp and sown in the fall. An unnamed shrubby form, occurring in the eastside drainages of the Wenatchee and Teanaway rivers, shows real garden potential.

Cascara bark is harvested for making into a laxative. Bark-gatherers should cut down the trees after girdling (removing the bark) so that the tree may resprout, by coppicing.

Cascara *(Rhamnus purshiana)*

Hairy manzanita *(Arctostaphylos columbiana)*

Native Ornamental Shrubs

Shrubs in all their variety form the backbone plantings of most gardens. They give texture, form, and color in countless ways, serve as showpieces and as background for herbaceous plantings, define contour, path, and borders, and generally outline the garden setting. Northwest gardens use shrubs lavishly; most are woody plants from other lands. Yet, probably unrecognized by many gardeners, some of our common ornamental shrubs are natives of the Northwest. Oregon grape, red-flowering currant, ocean spray, and salal are outstanding examples of natives that have become a part of ornamental landscapes. But many more of our native shrubby species either have not been tried at all or are known only to a few connoisseurs of native plants. The potential for their garden use is unquestionably great; their introduction into our gardens needs only the efforts of zealous gardeners and enterprising nursery managers.

Shrubs will be treated here under three headings: coniferous needle-leaved shrubs, broad-leaved evergreen shrubs, and broad-leaved deciduous shrubs. The growth form of the shrub includes tall bushes, low shrubs, woody groundcovers, and woody climbers (vines).

Coniferous Evergreen Shrubs

The section on cone-bearing trees describes those native coniferous trees that have dwarf or shrubby cultivars (see pages 27–57). In addition, two native conifers are typically shrubs: (1) the common, or dwarf, juniper *(Juniperus communis)*, a fine needle-leaved evergreen shrub, grows as either a prostrate mat or low, spreading shrub. It is more fully described in the section on conifers; (2) the western yew *(Taxus brevifolia)*, though a small tree on the wet side of the mountains, takes on the shrub habit on the east slope of the Cascades. It is described on page 55.

80

Evergreen Broad-leaved Shrubs and Woody Ground Covers

Nearly fifty native species qualify as ornamentals in this category. Of that number, over half are members of the heather family (Ericaceae). This is hardly surprising to the field botanist who encounters the rich variety of the heather clan everywhere in our wetter forests. A sample of this ericaceous bounty would include salal, manzanitas, rhododendron, evergreen huckleberry, the mountain heathers, and that dwarf charmer, kalmiopsis. For openers, then, here are several members of the heather family.

SALAL *(Gaultheria shallon).* This robust evergreen shrub of heather affinity is nearly everywhere in forests and clearings of western Washington, Oregon, and lower British Columbia. So much a part of the natural landscape and yet so neglected (or even rejected) as an ornamental in former years, it is consoling to see salal now come into its own. For years suburbia has extirpated this lush shrub as though it were a weed. Now it is the "cinderella" plant of the developer and highway engineer.

Distinguishing Features. Typically, salal is a low to medium-sized evergreen shrub from 3 to 6 feet tall, but in the most favorable sites it may reach to over 10 feet. Usually it occurs in dense, continuous thickets under the forest canopy or at the forest border. Its dark lustrous green leaves are large (2 to 4 inches long by 1 to 3 inches wide), ovate and nearly glabrous, but finely toothed. The many intricately branched stems can root when reclining; underground stems commonly provide for rapid increase of a colony of salal. The flowers, abundant in late spring to early summer, are in showy clusters, sticky glandular and pinkish. Each flower is a dainty urn-shaped pendant goblet, white, tinged with pink, or even deep rose. The bland but pleasant fruits were prized by the coastal Indians and are used nowadays for preserves.

Salal *(Gaultheria shallon)*

Evergreens and Ground Covers

The fleshy, purplish "fruit" (actually, the epicalyx) encloses the ripened ovary with many tiny seeds, typical of many members of the heather family.

Garden Uses. Salal serves the garden best in habitats similar to its native setting: massed plantings in open park-like stands of evergreen trees. It can make a dense evergreen cover in a woodland garden, not too wet or too dry; yet it is versatile enough for open, sunny, south-facing banks. As long as it has good drainage and a dampish root-run, it will thrive in the open, although remain low in stature. It accommodates well to the small garden, used in a border or in a mass with overtopping rhododendrons or other larger shrubs. Once established, it spreads aggressively—so beware!

On banks, road cuts, freeway plantings, and other reclaimed ground, salal can make in time a continuous green ground cover. Since it develops an extensive and aggressive system of underground stems, the initial planting, at 3-foot center, will fill intervening space well.

Propagation. Now that salal belatedly has come into its own as a garden favorite, it is propagated intensively. And here is the bottleneck. To get vigorous gallon-can-size plants takes time, either from seeds or by vegetative propagation. The tiny seeds germinate well in moist peat-sand mix. Expect a wait of two to three years from seedling to 3- to 5-inch-high plants. From seedbed, seedlings are pricked out into loam-peat flats for a year's growing on, then moved to 4-inch pots or a holding bed. Vegetative propagation is almost as slow; plants dug in the wild must regenerate their underground stems, and it may take up to five years before the original "start" makes any new above-ground growth. Moreover, one should avoid digging even common salal in the wild; successful establishment is difficult and seems an ethically outdated practice these days. Perhaps the surest and fastest source of propagules will be from cuttings of new wood taken in late summer. Root cuttings have also worked well. More and more, salal is being sold in retail nurseries and being grown in quantity by wholesalers for open-space plantings— a winner among Northwest native shrubs. Its only major pest is strawberry-root weevil, an insect all too common and devastating to rhododendrons and other ericaceous shrubs. The newer sprays, like Orthene, seem to work well but are expensive.

Two close relatives of salal have garden merit. Both *Gaultheria ovatifolia* and *G. humifusa* are prostrate shrublets from the upper montane forests of the Pacific Northwest. They establish with difficulty in the garden, but should do well in a moist peaty site, with conifer shade. Both a curiosity and a fine garden plant is the cross between salal and *Pernettya mucronata*. It is given the hybrid name X *Gaulnettya* 'Wisley Pearl'. Since *Pernettya* is a South American plant, it is remarkable that the cross even occurred, and even more so that it is fertile. Brian Mulligan, director emeritus of the University of Washington Arboretum, worked out the nomenclature of this useful hybrid sometime after it was discovered in 1929 in the Royal Horticultural Society's gardens at Wisley,

England. In all respects a smaller version of salal, the hybrid makes a tidy evergreen shrub for the border. Later-generation progeny of the hybrid look too much like salal, so it is best to get plants from the small-leaved forms. Propagation is the same as with salal.

Salal attracts wildlife to the garden where birds and rodents make good use of the juicy fruits. Northwest Coast Indians have found the fruit useful, too, pressing the fruit into cakes, which were dried and kept for winter use. Dipped in fish oil, the salal cakes were considered a tasty condiment by the native coastal peoples. Modern-day salal gatherers turn the fruit into a sweet but strong-tasting preserve, or prefer a jam or jelly "cut" with other fruit—raspberries or strawberries.

Manzanitas and Kinnikinnik (species of *Arctostaphylos*)

Two distinct growth forms, shrub and ground cover, extend the gardener's choice in the manzanita clan. All are superb evergreens with glossy reddish brown bark, leathery leaves, exquisite, heather-like or *Pieris*-like flowers in clusters, and pea-sized fruits. They all like full sun and well-drained soils. Only *Arctostaphylos uva-ursi* (kinnikinnik), *A. nevadensis* (pinemat manzanita), and possibly *A. patula* are hardy in colder areas. Though propagation of manzanitas by seeds is difficult, cuttings dipped in hormone usually root well.

LOW SHRUB AND GROUNDCOVER MANZANITAS *(Arctostaphylos uva-ursi, A. nevadensis)*. The finest evergreen ground cover among our natives surely has to be kinnikinnik *(A. uva-ursi)* whose garden qualities have been fully exploited for many years. Long trailing branches, thickly clothed with small, dark green leaves adorn banks, highway plantings, rockeries, parking strips, and other open sunny places in urban plantings. The white or pink flowers add bright contrast to the foliage in spring.

Kinnikinnik *(Arctostaphylos uva-ursi)*

Kinnikinnik *(A. uva-ursi)*

Evergreens and Ground Covers

Pinemat manzanita *(Arctostaphylos nevadensis)*

Distinguishing Features. Kinnikinnik is found worldwide at higher north latitudes and is a frequent plant in the open woods, rocky glades, and prairies throughout our lowland environment west of the Cascades. On the montane east side, a close relative, pinemat manzanita *(Arctostaphylos nevadensis),* is not infrequent, especially in open yellow-pine and lodgepole-pine forests. The pinemat manzanita is distinguished from kinnikinnik by its pointed leaf tips; also, *A. nevadensis* tends to be less prostrate than *A. uva-ursi.* Kinnikinnik occasionally occurs at higher elevations in the Cascades and Olympics, and may also be found in the middle montane, forested zones of the east side. Though the leaf tip, rounded in *A. uva-ursi* and abruptly pointed (mucronate) in *A. nevadensis,* usually serves to separate the two, some eastside plants are difficult to name. A third low-growing manzanita, *Arctostaphylos X media,* may also coexist with kinnikinnik. It is a hybrid between *A. uva-ursi* and the tall, hairy manzanita *(A. columbiana).* The hybrid is a good garden plant, too (see below for details).

Garden and Open-Space Uses. Kinnikinnik does yeoman service as a ground cover on the more sterile and dry sites in the Northwest. It has become a favorite in highway plantings, eventually forming a dense mat on embankments. It thrives in full sun and low summer moisture, once established. Planted on the tops of rock walls, it will form a green drapery for the entire slope. Because it so easily roots at intervals along the prostrate stems, the long streamers anchor the soil as the prostrate stem grows. Kinnikinnik serves well as a replacement for lawn in parking strips and on steep, hard-to-mow, dry banks. Since it grows in so many different native habitats, forms for particular garden use can be chosen with ease. Slow-growing, small-leaved forms for the rock garden can be obtained from the high mountains, where kinnikinnik grows, often above timberline with common juniper, *Juniperus communis.* Or, if a salt-tolerant beach form is desired, cuttings from the coastal dune areas can be propagated. For eastside gardens, both kinnikinnik and pinemat manzanita from habitats ranging from the yellow-pine belt to timberline can be selected.

Propagation. Layering or rooted cuttings are the surest means of propagation. Heel cuttings, treated with hormone, strike best when taken in February, but late summer to late fall cuttings work rather well too. Well-rooted cuttings are ready for transplanting to potting soil in containers in two or three months. When collecting propagating material from the wild, the freely branched tips of the trailing shoots can be cut with shears and wrapped in moist toweling for the trip home. When naturally layered shoots are sought in the wild, we recommend their collection only in instances where the site is doomed by alteration. The rash collecting of rooted shoots in the field simply aids the erosion process that the plant cover served to prevent. Hardly anyone bothers with seeds, so easy is vegetative propagation. Seeds germinate only after treatment with sulphuric acid, a procedure requiring particular caution.

A note on the common name of the trailing manzanita: *Arctostaphylos uva-ursi* is known both as bearberry and kinnikinnik. The latter name has been commonly thought to have originated with Northwest Coast Indians; they used the plant for food and as smoking tobacco. But it now seems most likely that the name "kinnikinnik" came west with white trappers, voyageurs, and explorers, who got it from Indians of eastern North America. The name "bearberry" is a bit redundant, since both genus and species names mean bearberry. I am told that "kinnikinnik" is the longest palindromic word in our language; spelled either forward or backward it's still "kinnikinnik."

HAIRY MANZANITA *(Arctostaphylos columbiana).* This is the most wide-spread of the tall shrubby species of manzanitas in the Northwest. It ranges from coastal California into southern British Columbia. It is infrequent on the west slope of the Cascades in both Washington and Oregon.

Distinguishing Features. Mature plants can be up to 10 to 15 feet high with a broadly spreading, oval crown from a single trunk. Hairy, gray green leaves clothe the end of each twig, leaving the rest of the branching system naked. Thus is exposed the exquisite, reddish brown bark from ground level to well up into the canopy. Particularly fine stands can be found in dryish sunny openings in the forests of the Kitsap Peninsula and on the northeast corner of the Olympic Peninsula in Washington. The shrub often becomes more abundant following disturbance, especially removal of the forest. Witness the spectacular display of hairy manzanita in the large road cut just northwest of Port Discovery on Highway 101 to Port Angeles, Washington. And nearly everywhere that Christmas tree plantations of Douglas fir are encouraged, south and west of Bremerton in Kitsap and Mason counties, stands of *A. columbiana* can be found. Some of the largest specimens overhang the vertical gravel cliffs on the southeast edge of Hartstene Island in southern Puget Sound.

In Oregon, hairy manzanita occurs sporadically in drier habitats throughout the Coast Ranges and along the lower western slopes of

Flowers of hairy manzanita *(Arctostaphylos columbiana)*

Hairy manzanita, at Discovery Bay

Evergreens and Ground Covers

the Cascades. It is locally abundant on the lower western slopes of Mount Hood, where it coexists with kinnikinnik and pinemat manzanita. In British Columbia it is confined to the country just north of Vancouver and to the southern portion of Vancouver Island.

Garden Uses. Hairy manzanita makes a handsome display in sunny south- or west-facing exposures, doing especially well on sandy, well-drained soils. It will reach 6 to 8 feet high in the garden where it takes on a broadly rounded form. The exquisite pattern of forked branching, the glossy-smooth, dark brown bark, the charming clusters of white to pale pink *Pieris*-like flowers, and the clusters of showy fruits, all are features affording distinctive and pleasing character for a garden shrub. Unfortunately, it is probably not hardy east of the Cascades, nor is it easily available in local nurseries.

Propagation. Hormone-treated cuttings in sand-peat, and seedling plants carefully collected in the wild, are effective for propagation.

MEDIA MANZANITA *(Arctostaphylos X media).* The hybrid between the tall hairy manzanita and the trailing kinnikinnik seems an improbable outcome, but it does indeed occur nearly everywhere the two species coexist. It is especially abundant on the Kitsap Peninsula of Washington, near Rhododendron west of Mount Hood in Oregon and in the Cheakamus Valley north of Squamish, British Columbia. The most usual form of the hybrid is a slightly more shrubby form of kinnikinnik, with branches erect or spreading outward, rather than prostrate. Specimens may be up to 3 feet tall, but spreading in habit. One garden form, *Arctostaphylos X media* var. *grandiflora,* is a most attractive erect shrub, with small leaves and deep pink flowers. The more spreading forms of *A. X media* can be grown as ground covers much like *A. uva-ursi.*

Propagation. Its fruits appear to be sterile; however, any of the forms of this variable hybrid propagate readily from cuttings. It is well worth growing for low borders, on banks, and in rockeries. In the Mount Hood area of Oregon, *A. columbiana* hybridizes with *A. nevadensis.* Plants of this parentage should also have high garden value.

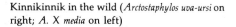

Kinnikinnik in the wild (*Arctostaphylos uva-ursi* on right; *A. X media* on left)

Four other manzanita species found in Oregon (Jackson, Josephine, and Curry counties) are of ornamental value: *Arctostaphylos canescens* (hairy manzanita), *A. viscida* (white-leaved manzanita), *A. parvifolia* (small-leaved manzanita), and *A. standfordiana* var. *hispidula* (rough manzanita). Eastside gardeners will want to try *A. patula* (green manzanita), a 3- to 6-foot-tall shrub with dark bark and bright green leaves. It grows on both sides of the Oregon Cascades from Mount Hood southward into California.

Other Evergreen Members of the Heather Family

BOG ROSEMARY *(Andromeda polifolia)*. An outstanding plant for the bog garden, bog rosemary is a low shrub with narrow, leathery leaves with inrolled margins. Its flowers are few in a cluster, pendant (like Irish or bell heather), and soft pink.

Unconfirmed reports assert its presence in Washington and Idaho; its occurrence in north-central British Columbia to Alaska is amply confirmed. Bog rosemary can be grown without re-creating bog conditions, so long as a surface layer, 2 to 4 inches thick, of sphagnum peat is provided in a wet sunny position. Propagation is by seeds or cuttings, although layering is easiest. Choice dwarf forms with longer flowers than the type are known as *Andromeda polifolia* var. *grandiflora compacta,* var. *congesta,* and var. *compacta alba.*

LABRADOR TEAS *(Ledum groenlandicum, L. glandulosum)*. These bog-loving plants thrive in the Pacific Northwest. The most common in the lowland bogs is *Ledum groenlandicum*. It is an evergreen shrub of 3 to 5 feet high, with long narrow leaves inrolled along the margins; a dense mat of rusty hairs covers the underside of the leaf. The foliage is highly aromatic when crushed and can indeed be brewed as a tea. Lest you plan a Labrador tea orgy, the precaution of one or two changes of boiling water should be noted. Hardy (1942) says: "It is said to have narcotic properties so that care should be used by the unaccustomed." All *Ledum* species have copious white flowers in tight clusters, appearing in summer.

Our other ledums are *L. glandulosum* and its variety *columbianum*. Both are more widespread in our area, but less common. The typical form, variety *glandulosum,* is locally frequent in moist seeps and swales on conifer-clad slopes of the Wenatchee Mountains. The coastal variety *columbianum* can be found trying to compete with the cultivated cranberry in bogs of southwestern Washington and adjacent Oregon. Beware! All parts of *L. glandulosum* and its variety are reputed to be poisonous if eaten.

Of the three ledums, I am partial to the Wenatchee Mountain form of *L. glandulosum*. It has a tidy compact habit, with small flat oval leaves and dense summer bloom. It merits a place in the garden, preferably in a moist peaty site, or in the artificially contrived bog garden.

Labrador tea *(Ledum groenlandicum)*

Evergreens and Ground Covers

BOG LAUREL *(Kalmia occidentalis).* Our two bog laurels are low shrublets, hardly in a class with their robust, tall relative *Kalmia latifolia* (mountain laurel) of the eastern United States. But as small evergreen bog plants, the bog laurels are delightful little gems. *Kalmia occidentalis* is a common associate of Labrador tea in lowland bogs, while *K. microphylla* is a tiny mat-forming shrublet in the wetter heather meadows of our subalpine. Both have small revolute leaves and unusually large, rose purple flowers. Given a cool, moist peaty soil, either variety should make an eye-catching spot in the garden. Propagation is by seeds, as with rhododendrons, or by late summer cuttings.

WESTERN LEUCOTHOE *(Leucothoe davisiae).* According to Bean (1970), the only native Northwest *Leucothoe* is one of the best in the genus for the garden. This bog-inhabiting shrub is a neat evergreen from 1 to 3 feet high, bearing leaves like a small salal and a glorious flower cluster raised well above the foliage. The little white goblets are pendant, appearing in mid-June. It grows in the northern Sierra Nevada of California and in the Siskiyou Mountains of southwestern Oregon. It is perfectly hardy in the Seattle garden and needs only a damp spot in a semi-shady portion of the garden. It propagates well from seeds or cuttings of half-ripened wood. It colonizes readily by salal-like underground stems.

KALMIOPSIS *(Kalmiopsis leachiana). Distinguishing Features.* This little shrublet has captivated garden devotees of the heather family. It is an evergreen not more than a foot high with a trim, compact habit. Its small evergreen leaves are oval and its flowers appear just above the compact mound of foliage. The flowers are a lovely rose pink, touched with purple. Though it could pass for a hybrid between *Kalmia polifolia* and a dwarf Kurume azalea, *Kalmiopsis leachiana* is an undisputed, distinctive species, the only one in the genus.

Garden Uses. Kalmiopsis likes open sunny sites with a peaty root run, like other small-leaved ericaceous shrubs. It does well in a relatively dry and partially shaded rock garden. Since its discovery by the Leaches in 1930 in the virtually inaccessible back country of the Siskiyous in southwestern Oregon, several additional localities, especially on the Umpqua River, have been reported, From these additional localities have come rather distinct variants, such as the 'LePiniec' form or the 'Umpqua River' form. Even with the slightly increased natural range, the plant is rare and local. The U.S. Forest Service has designated the major home range of the species as the Kalmiopsis Wilderness.

Propagation. The plants are rather easy to propagate, both from cuttings and from seeds. They can be treated as if they were dwarf Lapponicum rhododendrons.

PACIFIC RHODODENDRON *(Rhododendron macrophyllum).* The state flower of Washington hardly needs description. The large evergreen shrub with the big bold leaves and large trusses of pale purple flowers

Pacific rhododendron *(Rhododendron macrophyllum)*

is a familiar sight in many coastal and montane areas from northern California to southern British Columbia. Where they occur in conifer woods, the plants become small trees up to 25 feet high, often leggy, in a pleasing way. But in the open, the bushes are compact and dense with gray green foliage.

Since rhododendrons are so much a part of the garden scene in the Pacific Northwest, the addition of a not so spectacular native member of the Ponticum series may seem superfluous. Certainly *R. macrophyllum* cannot match kin of the Asiatic Fortunei series in beauty. But for the native garden or the naturalized woodland setting, the Pacific rhododendron is charmingly at home.

Propagation. Propagate from seeds, cuttings, or by layering. Digging plants in the wild should now be totally frowned upon. Many will remember in the 1950s seeing trucks parked along Seattle highways advertising their forlorn wares—rather sad-looking, spindly specimens of *R. macrophyllum* that had been collected in the wild and balled and burlapped for the carriage trade. No more, let us hope!

Rhododendron macrophyllum can be seen at its best on the Kitsap Peninsula of Washington where the local citizens still put on a Rhododendron Festival week at the height of the plant's spring display. Oregonians have easy access to the plant, too; the rhododendron thickets along the upper Sandy River east of Portland are outstanding. It is occasionally seen in the San Juan Islands and on Vancouver Island in British Columbia.

EVERGREEN HUCKLEBERRY *(Vaccinium ovatum).* This shrub is a charming surprise. Though huckleberries or blueberries are commonly deciduous, this one is a superb evergreen. The plant is quite common throughout the lowland Pacific Northwest, especially abundant on the Kitsap and Olympic peninsulas of Washington. In the forest it may get up to 15 feet high, with many erect branches from the base. But on cutover forest land and in the dwarfed forests of Christmas-tree farms, the full exposure to sun dwarfs it to 3- to 5-foot heights. The

Evergreens and Ground Covers

Ripe fruit of evergreen huckleberry *(Vaccinium ovatum)*

glossy, dark green leaves are small and ovate, with a serrate margin; they densely clothe the entire branch system. In sun the mature foliage often turns reddish purple and the new shoots are a bronzy red. It flowers profusely with small pinkish white bells in tight clusters. The buckshot-sized blackish purple fruits follow, much sought after by berry pickers.

Garden Uses. In the garden, vigorous plants can be used to great display in sun or shade. As a foil for a rhododendron planting, they are outstanding. Given any slightly acid soil site, it can be a good native substitute for the look-alike box *(Buxus sempervirens),* Japanese holly *(Ilex crenata),* or *Osmanthus delavayi.* The cut foliage is excellent for use in flower arrangements. Alas, this use has been commercially exploited. Wherever it is plentiful, it has been harvested by "brush-pickers" for the florist trade.

Propagation. Huckleberries can be propagated by hardwood cuttings or by seeds. As with other heath family plants, the seeds are tiny and, though germination is fairly good, the time between seedling and nursery-sized plant can be two to three years. We have found that cuttings of this huckleberry strike only sporadically. Until propagation techniques are improved, the garden public will have to make do with trial-and-error methods to get their own progeny of this choice plant. Unfortunately, it is not at all common in the nurseries. Plants dug in the field are seldom successful. What may appear to have been a small digging-size plant, will most likely be the new shoots of a much older plant reviving after logging or a fire.

PIPSISSEWA *(Chimaphila umbellata).* This lovely woodlander is mentioned only to forewarn the eager gardener. It prefers to stay in the wild, and attempts to cultivate it mostly fail. It is probable that the plants are partial root parasites. Should there be a way to keep host and parasite together, then the pipsissewas would add groundcover charm to the woodland setting. A smaller version is *Chimaphila menziesii.*

Other Native Heather-like Plants

Often near timberline in the Pacific Northwest, heather meadows dominate the green landscape. Yet our three "alpine heathers" are only heathers by familial relationship, while the true heather is the European *Calluna vulgaris* and the heaths are a group of Old World species of *Erica.* Our western look-alikes are in distinct genera of the heather family. Most like *Erica* in foliage are the two species of *Phyllodoce,* the purple *P. empetriformis* and the less common yellow *P. glanduliflora.* Both are low shrubs, from 6 to 18 inches high, with dense foliage of dark green, short-needle leaves. Often where the two species coexist in the alpine, they create an attractive hybrid, *P.* X *intermedia.*

The other look-alike, is *Cassiope mertensiana,* which resembles foliage of the Ling or Scottish heather *Calluna vulgaris.* The tiny scale leaves of *Cassiope* are closely overlapping on the branchlets, giving a squarish geometry to the twig. But the dainty white bells of *Cassiope,* borne in three-to five-flowered clusters are hardly like those of *Calluna.*

These three western alpine "heathers" require special care to keep them happy in a sea-level garden. They best endure the cool nook in the rockery or in a peaty, gritty raised bed in sun, but with a damp soil. Propagation is best by layerings and cuttings; by seeds, increase is slow.

Still two other heath-like plants earn the gardener's touch. *Loiseleuria procumbens,* the "dwarf azalea," is an ericad in many cool north temperate habitats. It barely gets into our area, in the North Cascades of Washington, but is a bit more common in British Columbia. This choice prostrate shrublet is widely known to rock gardeners, who give it a cool damp spot near the base of the rockery. From the tufted branchlets beset with tiny oblong leaves emerge dainty flower clusters; each flower, a rose to white bell perched upright in the cluster. It is easily propagated by cuttings or layering.

The other heath mimic is the crowberry, *Empetrum nigrum,* easily mistaken for a smallish *Phyllodoce.* Its leaves are a bit shorter and more densely inserted on the short, erect branchlets. Though its flowers are small and inconspicuous, the purplish black berries are a nice surprise. *Empetrum* is in its own small family, Empetraceae, and not in the heather family. In the Northwest, crowberry is both at timberline and along the coast. The montane form is best seen above Paradise on Mount Rainier or on Table Mountain in the Mount Baker area, while the coastal form is quite sporadic in Washington (e.g., Whidbey Island) and Oregon (Coos Bay area). It is easily propagated from cuttings and behaves as a low, dense green mound. It is more easily grown than its heather look-alikes, the phyllodoces.

Evergreens and Ground Covers

Twinflower *(Linnaea borealis)*

Shrubs and Ground Covers of Other Families

TWINFLOWER *(Linnaea borealis).* Honeysuckle Family (Caprifoliaceae). This utterly charming woodland creeper is best known for its dainty paired blooms hovering in profusion over a carpet of tiny evergreen leaves in the spring. Each of the pair of flowers is a small, pink, funnel-shaped bloom, the pair hanging upside down on their Y-shaped stalk. The ½-inch-long leaves are joined in pairs along the trailing stems. Mats of this superb carpeter can cover many square feet of forest floor and appear in many different forested communities throughout the Pacific Northwest.

Garden Uses. Of its ornamental value, Hitchcock says: "One of our most desirable native ground-covering shrubs, easily introduced from the wild and tending to spread rapidly but not aggressively" (4:455). Along with bunchberry *(Cornus canadensis), Linnaea borealis* makes the finest of ground covers for woodland or other partially shaded habitats. It is of sterling quality in or out of flower.

Propagation. Twinflower is fairly easy to propagate, especially from rooted pieces carefully detached from parent plants occurring in disturbed places in the wild. There seems to be no information on starting it from seeds.

CALIFORNIA WAX MYRTLE *(Myrica californica).* Sweet Gale Family (Myricaceae). No other woody plant is more typical of the dune landscape in the Northwest than the evergreen wax myrtle. All the way from Grays Harbor County, Washington, to northern California, stabilized dunes support a distinct flora, and this special habitat is the home

California wax myrtle *(Myrica californica)*

Pacific rhododendron
(Rhododendron macrophyllum)

Mountain heather *(Phyllodoce empetriformis)*

Mountain heather
(Phyllodoce glanduliflora)

Red-flowering currant *(Ribes sanguineum)*

Gooseberry *(Ribes lobbii)*

Hedgehog cactus *(Pediocactus simpsonii)*

Far left: Camas *(Camassia quamash)*

Left: Yellow bell *(Fritillaria pudica)*

Fawn lily *(Erythronium oregonum)*

Brodiaea *(Brodiaea ida-maia)*

Tiger lily *(Lilium columbianum)*

Iris *(Iris innominata)*

Blue-eyed grass *(Sisyrinchium douglasii)*

Bitterroot *(Lewisia rediviva)*

Tweedy's lewisia *(Lewisia tweedyi)*

Lewisia cotyledon

Stonecrop *(Sedum obtusatum)*

Catch-fly *(Silene hookeri)*

Partridgefoot *(Luetkea pectinata)*

Scarlet gilia *(Gilia aggregata)*

Alpine forget-me-not
(Eritrichium nanum elongatum)

Phlox adsurgens

Shooting star *(Dodecatheon conjugens)*

Douglasia *(Douglasia laevigata ciliolata)*

Cliff penstemon *(Penstemon rupicola)*

Penstemon *(Penstemon davidsonii)*

Synthyris *(Synthyris schizantha)*

Monkey-flower *(Mimulus lewisii)*

Scotch bluebell *(Campanula rotundifolia)*

Piper's harebell *(Campanula piperi)*

Showy townsendia *(Townsendia florifer)*

Balsamroot *(Balsamorhiza hookeri)*

of the wax myrtle. Fine stands can be seen on the Oyhut Peninsula around the tourist village of Ocean Shores in Washington, as well as on the famous dunes at Florence, Oregon.

Distinguishing Features. Pacific or California wax myrtle is a densely bushy shrub up to 15 feet tall, with long, narrow, dark green leaves, serrated on their margins. Its peculiar floral parts barely form a minimal flower; rather, they are little more than sessile bumps of tiny male or female sex organs scattered in clusters among the leaves of the upper branchlets. The waxy sessile fruits add a good purple hue to the branchlets in the fall.

Garden Uses. It is ideally suited for coastal plantings where tolerance to salt spray is necessary, and yet it thrives in inland plantings, sun or shade. A peaty, slightly acid soil favors its growth. It can be used to advantage as a screening hedge plant, interspersed with other broad-leaved evergreens, especially *Rhododendron,* or as a specimen shrub in border plantings. Wax myrtles or bayberries are famous for their fragrant foliage and candle-making wax, rendered from the fruits. Alas! The California wax myrtle has only faintly scented foliage and not much wax to give the candlemaker. Though less showy in the garden, the other bayberry in Washington, *Myrica gale,* has foliage of pleasant fragrance, hence its name, sweet gale. This deciduous shrub of coastal bogs has a unique use; its leaves have been used to flavor "home-brew." Yorkshiremen called the tasty beverage "gale beer."

Propagation. California wax myrtle can be increased by seeds, cuttings, or by layering. Seeds gathered in the fall require three months' stratification, and germination may take over one hundred days. For the more impatient, layering will be preferred.

Garden view of California wax myrtle

SAGEBRUSH *(Artemisia tridentata).* Aster Family (Compositae). Perhaps in time forgiveness will come to one who proposes that the common sagebrush be given a place in the garden. But in Britain it is already a favorite, its gray foliage making a pleasing contrast with the usual green of garden shrubs. And the strongly aromatic foliage adds another aesthetic dimension to the sun-baked garden.

Distinguishing Features. Artemisia tridentata gets up to 8 feet tall in its most luxuriant stands in eastern British Columbia, Washington, and Oregon. More usual are the 3- to 5-foot-high shrubs that seem to populate arid plains in all directions, the endless expanse of gray flannel only broken by human intervention. Man is making devastating inroads on sagebrush. Besides conventional agriculture and other developments, the newest gargantua, the circle-irrigation system, now makes a much more frightening assault on the land of the sagebrush.

The attractive gray green foliage consists of small, entire to tridentate leaves, copiously bunched along the upper stems. The gray caste to the foliage comes from the dense felt of hairs plastered on leaves and young stems. Older branches and the main trunk have a shaggy bark. Sagebrush flower heads are tiny, unglamorous things, but the total mass of plume-like clusters makes a pleasant effect.

Garden Uses. Though perfectly hardy in lowland gardens west of the Cascades, the wet side of the mountains may try the endurance of sagebrush with too much moisture. Dry, sunny sites, especially against a wall, can give the needed drought conditions. The inner court of the Forest Resources buildings on the University of Washington campus seems a propitious microhabitat for the thrifty specimen planted there.

Propagation. Half-ripened wood under glass gives some success as cuttings. But this is one plant that can be collected in moderation in the field. Young seedlings, taken after fall rains, establish well. No mention is made in the propagation literature about the use of seeds; when available they should germinate easily, like most members of the sunflower family.

COYOTE BRUSH *(Baccharis pilularis).* Aster Family (Compositae). Though mostly a plant of coastal central California, this evergreen shrub reaches Tillamook County along the Oregon coast. Like the olearias of New Zealand and Australia, this large shrub is a bush daisy, in the sunflower family. The best form for cultivation is the low mounded one, native to coastal central California. It merits trial as a utilitarian ground cover in sheltered coastal gardens in the Northwest. Its small wedgeshaped leaves are a pleasingly varnished bright green. The tall form, var. *consanguinea,* is too leggy a plant for us.

BUSH CHINQUAPIN, SIERRA CHINQUAPIN *(Chrysolepis sempervirens).* Oak Family (Fagaceae). *Distinguishing Features.* Like the golden chinquapin tree (p. 60), bush chinquapin is easily recognized by two distinctive features: the golden sheen to the lower leaf epidermis, and the spinose ''bur'' or fruit. For these attributes alone, it can claim a prominent place in sunny gardens. One specimen in my garden, propagated by Carl English some fifteen years ago, is now 10 feet high with a broad round-tipped form, densely leafy from tip to ground level. Any time of the year, in flower, fruit, or in-between, it is a magnificent, bold evergreen shrub.

The leaves are oblong, 1 to 3 inches long, gray green above and golden beneath, all densely set on stiff branches. The catkins are at the tips of terminal and side branches; their slender terminal portions bear the male flowers and the basal segment produces the female flowers, later to become the bristly, bur-like fruits. When in bloom in late summer, the bush is covered with cream-white spikey pollen flowers, which emit a strong but not unpleasant odor. The bright green burs mature in the fall of the second year, making a brown spiny cluster as big as a sea urchin, and drop to the ground through the winter.

Its name, Sierra chinquapin, delimits the shrub's major territory: mostly in the High Sierras from 8,000 to 12,000 feet. But the species ranges into southern California and north into the Siskiyou–Klamath country of northwestern California and southern Oregon. Throughout its range it usually forms dense thickets on dryish mountain ridges

Seed burs and male tassels of bush chinquapin *(Chrysolepis sempervirens)*

or it may occur in rocky clearings in open conifer forests. Mount Ashland in Jackson County, Oregon, is a good place to see it and look for seeds.

Garden Uses. In the garden, it likes sunny well-drained sites and can be a good companion to native species of *Ceanothus, Cupressus,* and *Arctostaphylos.* Since it is a large and bold shrub, it should be given ample room in a sunny well-drained spot. Though not sufficiently tested for hardiness, the single plant in our garden has endured the worst of Seattle winters without any signs of suffering. Plants for the garden should come from the northern end of the bush chinquapin's extensive natural range.

Propagation. Seeds are available in the wild during the fall harvest, although one must beat the squirrels and other harvesters. Seeds germinate readily when planted fresh in moist peat. Propagation by cuttings usually fails, even under mist and with hormone; layering is worth trying.

MOUNTAIN LOVER, OREGON BOX, MYRTLE BOXWOOD *(Pachistima myrsinites).*

Staff-tree Family (Celastraceae). This low evergreen native looks like two well-known garden plants, Japanese holly *(Ilex crenata)* and boxwood *(Buxus sempervirens).* Its low stature, prostrate to 3 feet high, and its opposite, toothed, darkly evergreen leaves match well these two exotics. In disposition, *Pachistima* can perform in the garden with equal vigor and versatility.

On closer look, Oregon box can claim its own distinctive features. Though the small, finely toothed evergreen leaves arrayed in pairs along ascending branches are not unique, the tiny red flower, borne in axillary clusters, is the telling feature. The flowers clearly relate *Pachistima,* not to *Buxus* or *Ilex,* but to *Euonymus,* in the family Celastraceae.

Oregon box is common throughout the West. It occurs in dense woods or open rocky places, with an altitudinal range from sea level (around Puget Sound) to nearly timberline. Though not uncommon west of the Cascades, it is at its best on the drier slopes east of the crest, in open woods, rocky glades, or on ridge tops. Besides growing in Oregon and Washington, it can be found south and east to New Mexico and north to Alberta. It is never better than in northern Idaho, where it is harvested for the floral cutgreens trade in quantities. Mountain lover, Oregon box, or just plain "pa-kissed-ma" *(Pachistima's* memory gimmick), it is a plant of many haunts.

Garden Uses. In the garden, *Pachistima* has just as many roles to play as the exotics it resembles. Border, woodland, rockery, low hedging for delineating paths, or in the foreground of a shrub bed, all suit this good-tempered plant. Partial to full sun in well-drained soils suits it best. Although it may get a bit taller and more leggy in the shade, it serves well as a medium-sized shrub around the trunks of conifers in the woodland garden. In the Innis Arden district of Seattle it thrives in the wild on a south slope under the open crowns of madrone.

Propagation. Oregon box is so easily increased by cuttings that seeds

Bush chinquapin *(Chrysolepis sempervirens)*

Oregon box *(Pachistima myrsinites)*

Evergreens and Ground Covers

may not have been tried. When judiciously done, naturally layered (and rooted) stems in the wild can be severed from the parent plant and safely introduced into the garden.

MOUNTAIN MAHOGANY *(Cercocarpus montanus, C. ledifolius)*. Rose Family (Rosaceae). Two species of this shrub occur in the Northwest. Both *Cercocarpus montanus* var. *glaber* and *C. ledifolius* have garden value. The unique feature of both is the startlingly beautiful plumed fruit perched solitary or in small clusters on the many dense and stiff branchlets of these tall evergreens.

Distinguishing Features. Cercocarpus montanus var. *glaber,* a tall shrub or small tree to 20 feet high, has small leaves not over an inch long, oblong in outline, dark green above, and silky beneath. Seen from beneath, the lateral veins are deeply embossed and the leaf margin is serrate above the middle. This more temperate species can be found in dry shrub thickets and chaparral in southern Oregon from the Umpqua Valley east to Lake County.

In late summer, a bush of mountain mahogany is a soft blur of silk, so profuse are the 4-inch-long, twisted and fuzzy tails of the bony achenes. These on a background of tiny alder-like leaves make a dazzling sight, especially when accentuated by morning's dew and backlight from the sun.

Though similar in fruit, *Cercocarpus ledifolius* has leaves more like Labrador tea (thus its species' name), utterly distinct from the foliage of *C. montanus.* An inhabitant of more arid regions in the West, *C. ledifolius* has long and narrow, dark green leaves, with entire but inrolled margins. Look for this tallish, sparse looking shrub on the rim-rock or talus slopes of the bunch-grass and yellow-pine country east of the Cascades.

Garden Uses. Both species of mountain mahogany like a dry well-drained site. Carl English has grown *C. ledifolius* with some success at the Locks Gardens in Seattle, and it should be hardy enough for most eastside gardens. Both species should grow well with *Ceanothus* and *Arctostaphylos* species in full sun.

Propagation. Outdoor germination of fresh seeds over winter works best. Stratification increases germination, but is not necessary. De-plumed seeds should be soaked in water for thirty minutes before sowing. Germination may take from seventy days to a year. Stored seeds retain viability up to five years. Heel cuttings of summer wood are worth trying.

SHRUBBY MONKEY FLOWER *(Mimulus aurantiacus)*. Snapdragon or Figwort Family (Scrophulariaceae). Though most monkey flower species are annual or perennial herbs, a very few are definitely woody. One shrubby *Mimulus* (= *Diplacus*), *M. aurantiacus,* gets as far north as Curry County in Oregon where it is a plant of the coastal bluff flora. It is a charming little shrub with showy snapdragon-like trumpet flowers scattered along the upper portions of the stiffly erect stems. Flower colors range from yellow to salmon. Its leaves are widely spaced in

Mountain mahogany *(Cercocarpus ledifolius)* in fruit

pairs, glossy and leather-textured above, but sticky beneath (as are the flowering stems). Sticky monkey flower is another good common name.

Garden Uses. The bush monkey flower should be grown in an open, warm, well-drained site, with some protection from cold. Some years in Puget Sound gardens it may die down to the ground, but if mulched with pine needles, it will survive a winter, to recover its shrubby stature and showy bloom the next season.

Propagation. It is easy to propagate from the dust-sized seeds. Expect copious germination in less than two weeks from sowing. Seedlings need early thinning to ensure vigorous plants.

SILK-TASSEL BUSH *(Garrya elliptica).* Silk-tassel Family (Garryaceae). *Distinguishing Features.* This is the best of a superb clan of evergreen shrubs, highly prized by discerning plantsmen. Silk-tassel bush lives up to its name in late winter when the pendant male catkins elongate and open. Then, the 6- to 12-inch-long floral chains erupt in cascades of cream-yellow stamens on a silvery gray background. In westside gardens the plants may become small trees up to 20 feet high, yet remain densely leafy and elegantly shrubby in form. The gray green leaves are in pairs, 2 to 4 inches long, oval to oblong, and have a conspicuous wavy margin. Such choice foliage, beset with tinsel-like bloom makes striking indoor floral arrangements.

The glory of silk-tassel finery is largely males. Female plants produce much shorter, less attractive catkins, but do yield the precious seeds and have the same fine foliage.

Garrya elliptica is restricted to coastal bluffs and hills in southwestern Oregon from Cape Perpetua south into California. Two other species live in our area: *G. fremontii* grows in woodlands and on brushy slopes in the Oregon Cascades and just barely gets into Washington (Wind Mountain and the Big Lava Beds of Skamania County); *G. buxifolia* is found in Josephine County, Oregon, usually on serpentine soils.

Garden Uses. Gardeners have found silk-tassel bush to do best in a moderately sunny position, with sharp drainage and a light warm soil. Add protection from the north winds and the male plants will respond with the largest catkins, up to 12 inches long. Carl English used *Garrya elliptica* liberally at the Seattle Locks Gardens, along the north fence and shrub borders. Grown against a wall or as a free-standing plant, it can be an eye-catching delight all year around.

Propagation. Since it is the male plants that are preferred, propagation must be by cuttings, unless one is willing to cull out female plants after several years when the plants first bloom. Cuttings taken in late summer strike best with bottom heat. Seeds, collected in the fall and cleaned of their purple pulp, require some form of pretreatment. Low temperature stratification in sand or peat for 30 to 120 days, followed by a 17-hour soak in 100 p.p.m. gibberellin is prescribed.

A selected form of a garden hybrid between *G. elliptica* and *G. fremontii* received an Award of Merit when shown in Britain. The clonal form

Silk-tassel bush *(Garrya elliptica)*

is called *Garrya* cv. 'Pat Ballard', in honor of a great lady and a champion of worthy horticultural causes. The cultivar, 'James Roof', has exceptionally long catkins. The other Northwest species, though of botanical interest, are thought by some to be less attractive than *G. elliptica*. The glossy, bright green foliage of *G. fremontii* has its own distinction, even if its tassles do not come up to the mark of *G. elliptica*.

Shrub tan oak (*Lithocarpus densiflorus* var. *echinoides*)

SHRUB TAN OAK, DWARF TANBARK *(Lithocarpus densiflorus* var. *echinoides).* Oak Family (Fagaceae). In all but the technical features of flower and fruit, the tanbarks are good oaks. And this one, the shrubby variety of the tree-sized tan oak (see p. 61) ranks high among the gardener's choice showpieces. The gray green foliage clothes a shrub of 3 to 5 feet in height. The oblong leaves are mostly 2 to 3 inches long, smaller than those of the tree form of the species. The finely stellate pubescence disappears with age to reveal bold lateral veins; the leaf margin is entire or obscurely toothed. Tan oak flowering catkins are stiffly erect at the tips of branches, distinguishing them from the drooping catkins of species of *Quercus*. Like the huckleberry oak, dwarf tanbark likes the sterile open brush-covered slopes of serpentine soils in southwestern Josephine County, Oregon. It ranges south into California on serpentine both in the Siskiyou–Klamath country and down the Sierra Nevada to Tuolumne County.

Find a moderately sunny, well-drained spot in the garden for this prized plant to thrive. It is perfectly hardy in the western sections of the Northwest.

Propagation. Propagation of these three evergreen shrub oaks is by acorns, planted fresh from the fall harvest. Discard acorns with holes; good seeds germinate well in about twenty to forty days from sowing in a light, oak-leaf mold soil or peat.

TREE LUPINE *(Lupinus arboreus).* Pea Family (Leguminosae). Though not a native in the Northwest, this Californian has become thoroughly naturalized in some northern coastal areas. It can be seen frequently on sand spits above the high-tide zone at Anacortes, on Whidbey Island, and elsewhere along the shores of Puget Sound.

Tree lupine attains its 6- to 9-foot height in three to four years, an amazingly rapid growth rate. The habit is really that of a largish rounded bush with one strong central trunk. The 1- to 2-inch digitately compound leaves are covered with a silky pubescence. The superb sulfur-yellow pea flowers appear on erect terminal stalks up to 10 inches long.

Garden Uses. Lupinus arboreus thrives in a sunny site on sandy soils. While it is perfectly suited to inland gardens, it should be particularly happy in seaside plantings, since it is apparently tolerant of salt water.

Propagation. It can be raised easily from seeds, sown fresh from harvest. Stored seeds of lupins have hard seed coats and require pretreatment for germination. Soaking in hot water, mechanical scarification, or cold stratification for 72 days at 35° F., all induce rapid germination.

RESINWEED, GUM PLANT *(Grindelia integrifolia* var. *macrophylla).* Aster Family (Compositae). Like the tree lupin, the grindelias are subshrub kin of largely herbaceous plants. This somewhat woody yellow daisy grows in maritime habitats around Puget Sound: from salt marsh to rocky shoreline. The 2- to 4-foot tall plants have smallish strap-shaped leaves and flowering stalks bearing many yellow daisy-like heads. Both the herbage and the flower heads are copiously gummy. A good plant for reclaiming seaside land. Grown from seeds or cuttings.

COFFEEBERRY *(Rhamnus californica).* Buckthorn Family (Rhamnaceae). This highly variable and distinctive evergreen shrub is primarily a Californian, with only var. *occidentalis* reaching Josephine County in southern Oregon. The attractive light green foliage makes up for the insignificant flowers. The shiny black pea-sized berries make a pretty contrast with the foliage. Leaves are alternate, 1 to 3 inches long, usually oblong to ovate. The shrubby buckthorns require sun.

Propagation. Germination is easy; cuttings are difficult. Seeds should be cleaned of pulp before sowing. Other varieties (vars. *crassifolius* and *tomentella*), though only reaching northern California, are worth trying in our more northern gardens. Both varieties have attractive, gray green foliage, often white and woolly beneath.

SHRUBBY PENSTEMON *(Penstemon fruticosus).* Figwort or Foxglove Family (Scrophulariaceae). Though much more will be said about the elegant penstemon clan as herbaceous perennials,* one species makes a low shrubby form—a woody evergreen. *Penstemon fruticosus* is widely distributed from the east slope of the Cascades east to the northern Rocky Mountains, and south from British Columbia to Oregon.

Distinguishing Features. Its low, compact bushy form and dark green, toothed leaves in pairs remind one of *Pachistima* (Oregon box). But in flower, its *Penstemon* glory is revealed. The exquisite tubular, rose-purple to lavender flowers are inserted horizontally on the 6-inch scapes. Insects, especially bumblebees are attracted to the showy flowers. As a consequence, when *P. fruticosus* grows with other penstemons of the *Dasanthera* section (especially *P. rupicola, P. barrettiae,* and *P. davidsonii*), hybrids are sure to occur. (See color section.)

Garden Uses. A sunny, dryish bank or rock garden suits this neat shrub well. Since all its attributes are four-star in quality—compact stature, good foliage, superb flower, exceptional hardiness, and easy propagation—this plant should be seen more widely in cultivation. It should be especially good for eastside gardens where colorful shrubs of a hardy constitution are rarely available. Plants grown in westside gardens seem to be shortlived; but propagation by cuttings is so easy that it can be perpetuated at will. Seeds germinate without treatment, but the yield of seedlings is low. Take precautions against damping-off of the young seedlings.

* The peerless Columbia Gorge endemic, *Penstemon barrettiae,* also has a somewhat shrubby habitat, though it will be treated as a herbaceous perennial (chap. 4).

Oregon Grapes (species of *Berberis**). Barberry Family (Berberidaceae)

Next to salal our two Oregon grapes are the most common evergreen shrubs in the westside lowlands. The berries, coated with a gorgeous blue gray sheen, are especially attractive in their heavy terminal clusters. Besides being favorite bird food, the berries are often harvested for making preserves. Oregon grape jelly is a Northwest delicacy.

The pinnate-leaved barberries of Oregon grapes seem a far cry from the simple leaved barberries, despite their sharing the genus *Berberis*. Many botanists and horticulturists prefer to put all the pinnate-leaved *Berberis* species in the genus *Mahonia*. That simple-leaved barberries and compound-leaved mahonias are close relatives is confirmed by the bizarre garden hybrid, X *Mahoberberis*.

Propagation. All the Oregon grapes are best grown from seeds. Cold stratification is advisable for good germination. Cuttings taken in fall root best. Field-collected transplants do poorly, and are slow to establish. Often *Berberis aquifolium* seedlings can be collected in the garden nearby the parent plants; seeds germinate well after their trip through a foraging bird.

TALL OREGON GRAPE *(Berberis aquifolium).* This grape has had a long history of garden value since it was first introduced to Britain in 1823. For a while it was a costly ornamental, single plants selling for as much as ten pounds each.

Distinguishing Features. Berberis (or *Mahonia*) *aquifolium* is a plant of open woods and clearings from British Columbia to California, mostly west of the Cascade range. It can get as high as 8 to 10 feet, though typically does not reach over 5 feet in gardens. Most often it produces several erect unbranched canes bearing glossy compound leaves. The 6- to

* Oregon grapes are known under two generic names, *Mahonia* and *Berberis*. Some botanists place all the compound-leaved barberries in *Mahonia,* others retain the Oregon grapes with the simple-leaved barberries, in *Berberis.*

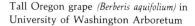

Tall Oregon grape *(Berberis aquifolium)* in University of Washington Arboretum

Evergreens and Ground Covers

Tall Oregon grape

12-inch pinnate leaves have from five to nine leaflets, each with spinose teeth along their margin. The showy bloom in early spring is confined to the tips of the canes. The large clusters of smallish golden yellow flowers set on the lustrous green foliage are a glorious sight.

Garden Uses. Tall Oregon grape is widely used in gardens: it serves well in formal hedges, border plantings, and as background for deciduous shrubs. When naturalized in open woodland, it is outstanding.

Tall Oregon grape in Elsa Frye's garden

Evergreens and Ground Covers

Fruit of Cascade Oregon grape *(Berberis nervosa)*

The bronzy copper color of the new growth in spring, like that of evergreen huckleberry, is a bonus attribute. Since it takes to all degrees of exposure to light, it will be at home in a variety of garden settings, ever adding lustrous, holly-like texture to its surroundings.

CASCADE OREGON GRAPE *(Berberis nervosa)*. The Cascade Oregon grape is a much smaller shrub than *Berberis aquifolium,* rarely over 2 feet tall. Its short stem bears a basal rosette of 12-inch-long compound leaves, each with 9 to 19 leaflets, dull green but boldly veined, and with spinose teeth on the leaf margin. The long flower stalks emerge erect from both the stem tip and the axils of the leaves, forming a showy spray of yellow bloom in spring. Though more common in our woods than *B. aquifolium, B. nervosa* is less frequently grown. While slow to establish, it can in time be a fine low evergreen for the border or woodland scene. It was introduced to horticulture in 1822, one year earlier than tall Oregon grape.

An even smaller version of Oregon grape comes from east of the Cascades. *Berberis repens,* creeping or low Oregon grape, is widespread in open conifer woods. It has found a place in gardens on both the wet and the dry side of the mountains. It can spread from underground stems, but is easily checked by occasional root pruning. *Berberis pumila* of southern Oregon is another low-growing Oregon grape, a gray-leaved version of *B. repens;* it is a fine garden plant for dry sunny banks.

Wild Lilac or Buckbrush (species of *Ceanothus*). Buckthorn Family (Rhamnaceae)

Evergreens and Ground Covers

Mountain balm, or wild lilac *(Ceanothus velutinus)*

The five evergreen *Ceanothus* species found in the Northwest all have garden worth. Three of the local evergreen species are tall shrubs. *Ceanothus velutinus,* variously called buckbrush, mountain balm, Indian tobacco, or sticky laurel, is a widespread species, growing mainly in the drier conifer belt of the slopes of the Cascades and Sierra Nevada east to the Rockies. Its large and shiny leaves, with a sticky varnish finish, make it easily recognizable, in sight and in smell. Prominently three-veined and minutely toothed, the sticky leaf surface emits a turpentine-like odor like no other native evergreen. In flower, the cream white flowers profusely cover the twiggy 3- to 8-feet-tall shrubs. A form, var. *laevigatus,* grows west of the Cascades especially in the Hood Canal area. It is taller (up to 20 feet) and has a more open, branching pattern. *Ceanothus velutinus* and its variety take well to open sunny sites in the garden; even the least amount of shade will cause it to get leggy. Variety *laevigatus* is more suited for westside gardens. Once established, it needs no summer watering, and, indeed, resents it.

Blueblossom, *Ceanothus thrysiflorus,* is the hardiest of the California wild lilacs. Its gorgeous plumes of deep lilac blue flowers, dotted with yellow stamens, clothe in spring a fine evergreen foliage on a 6- to 15-foot shrub. Its leaves are 1 to 1½ inches long, oval, toothed, with three prominent veins and a bright lustrous green. Blueblossom can be found along the coast in Oregon from Coos County southwards to central California. Many fine forms of this species are grown: var. *griseus,* has a low spreading habit, to 4 feet (it is a bit more tender than the type from Oregon). Other garden forms are selected progeny of hybrids. It crosses easily in the garden and in the wild with other wild lilac species. Blueblossom, in its many forms, adds an exquisite beauty to the sunny shrub border, open slope, or south-facing exposure of buildings. Indeed, it is the best all-around native *Ceanothus* for the

Mountain balm in flower

Evergreens and Ground Covers

Puget Sound garden. On the other hand, the coastal *C. thrysiflorus* and its variety *griseus* are not suitable for eastside gardens. As with most *Ceanothus* species, these dislike summer watering once established.

The other tallish species, *Ceanothus cuneatus* (the common buckbrush of Oregon) has small, gray green, opposite leaves, usually entire. Its dull white flowers might lessen its value as a garden plant. Yet for naturalizing on a dry slope in milder westside localities, the plant can fill a useful landscape niche.

Two closely related species of prostrate wild lilacs are both a delight and a challenge to the gardener. When successfully grown, they make lovely evergreen mats, bathed in bloom with lilac blue flowers in spring. But the trick is to get them established and then keep the plant thriving. The more widespread mahala mat or squaw carpet *(Ceanothus prostratus)* ranges from the south just into Washington in Klickitat County, while the even smaller leaved *C. pumilus* is restricted to serpentine soils in the Siskiyous of Oregon and California. Both species are less rampant than the Point Reyes creeper, *C. gloriosus.* They should do well in the sunniest rock garden.

Propagation. Some species of *Ceanothus* come well from seeds, following a hot water treatment. Bring water to a boil and then steep the seed for 10 to 15 minutes; germination occurs in from fifteen days to over three months. *Ceanothus velutinus* and *C. cuneatus* require three months' stratification after the hot water treatment. Start seeds in mid-winter; precautions against damping-off should be taken. Cuttings of most California species (especially the alternate-leaved ones) strike easily; cuttings should be tried of our own Northwest species. Layering may work best for the two prostrate species.

Evergreen Oaks (species of *Quercus*)

Shrubby evergreen oaks are in great demand currently, and as long as acorns set, we can be assured of a supply of them. Though it may be arbitrary to pick favorites among our three natives, *Quercus sadleriana* would rank high on anyone's list.

DEER OAK, SADLER'S OAK *(Quercus sadleriana).* Oak Family (Fagaceae). Sadler's oak is a 6- to 10-foot, spreading evergreen (or semi-evergreen), forming dense thickets in open coniferous forests and dry open slopes in the Klamath–Siskiyou Mountains from northeastern Curry County, Oregon, into northern California. Its lustrous, rich green leaves are unusually large for an evergreen oak: 2 to 4 inches long, broadly oval, toothed, and with dominant lateral veins. Mature specimens flower and fruit handsomely in cultivation. Partial sun at the edge of a conifer canopy or in a moderately sunny shrub border suits Sadler's oak best.

HUCKLEBERRY OAK *(Quercus vaccinifolia).* Oak Family (Fagaceae). Though sometimes considered a shrubby variety of Canyon oak *(Quercus*

Sadler's oak *(Quercus sadleriana)*

Evergreens and Ground Covers

Huckleberry oak *(Quercus vaccinifolia)*

chrysolepis), it seems best to recognize as a unique species this distinctive and handsome low, shrubby evergreen oak. While huckleberry oak is commonest in the granitic slopes of the high Yosemite country of California, it is locally plentiful in places in the Siskiyous as far north as southern Josephine County, Oregon. Here it likes dry, open brushy slopes, often growing on serpentine soils.

Huckleberry oak is a low and compact shrub up to 4 feet, with small mostly entire ovate to lanceolate leaves. It thrives on a south-facing slope. The drier portions of a rock garden make good habitats.

Mention should be made of another low-growing evergreen oak, even though its natural range is just south of the range of this book. The leather oak, *Quercus durata*, reaches northern California in Trinity County and so should be fairly hardy in our more northern gardens. We have found it perfectly hardy in Seattle and have admired its fine gray green, holly-like foliage for years. *Quercus durata* in the wild is nearly wholly confined to serpentine soils.

Leather oak *(Quercus durata)*

Shrubby Forms of Evergreen Tree Species

A few evergreen trees can be used as shrubs, given proper selection of forms and judicious manipulation. In most instances, the tree habit has to be artificially modified early in the life of the plant. Yet, in a very few instances, there are available in nature those individuals or even populations of evergreens that are hereditarily endowed with the shrubby habit. In the latter category, three or four exceptional examples come to mind: western yew, Oregon myrtle (or California bay laurel), golden chinquapin, and tan oak.

Though usually a small tree on the west side of the Cascades, there is an attractive shrubby form of western yew *(Taxus brevifolia)* that is

Evergreens and Ground Covers

common in the upper drainages of the Cle Elum and North Fork Teanaway rivers, Wenatchee Mountains, Washington. This shrubby yew with fine glaucous (gray green) foliage is most commonly found on serpentine soils, a demanding habitat that usually provokes the appearance of unusual plant life (see Kruckeberg 1969; Whittaker 1960; or Proctor and Woodell 1975, for accounts of the fascinating plant life on serpentine and other high magnesium soils).

A similar response to serpentine occurs in populations of bay laurel *(Umbellularia californica)* and in tan oak *(Lithocarpus densiflorus,* the variety *echinoides* in southwestern Oregon). The deciduous tree *Rhamnus purshiana* makes a shrubby form that grows on serpentine in the Wenatchee Mountains, Washington. All these can be propagated in the manner of their tree counterparts.

Other evergreen trees with a heredity for shrubbiness may occur as single, isolated genetic "freaks" (mutants); these are exceptional individuals in populations of the normal tree form of the species. Dwarfs in conifers like western hemlock, Douglas fir, western white pine, and western red cedar have made their way into cultivation. Most often they are detected in nurseries where out of thousands of seedlings from wild seeds, one or two dwarf mutants can be found. Occasionally such mutants may be found in the wild, surviving long enough to display their freakish dwarf character. *Tsuga heterophylla* 'Iron Springs', a fine dwarf western hemlock, is one such named mutant. Such forms must be propagated vegetatively (by cuttings, layering, or grafting).

A transient shrubbiness can be induced to last for some time with most any evergreen tree species if the proper manipulations are performed. Well-established but young saplings, 1 to 3 feet high, can be dwarfed by pinching back new growth, or by shearing and pruning. This is the procedure used by Christmas tree farm operators in producing symmetrical bushy trees for the holiday trade. The same techniques can be used for garden evergreens. Another approach is now within the gardener's reach. Though well tested on a variety of popular garden shrubs, chemical control of the growth form of native evergreen trees has hardly begun. The enterprising gardener will want to look into this intriguing technique, using the chemical maleic hydrazide (as appropriate dilutions of 30 percent MH-30[R] or Slo-Gro[R]).

Native Cacti (species of *Opuntia* and *Pediocactus*).

Cactus Family (Cactaceae)

Three native cacti are the only members of a vast desert clan that can be grown outdoors in the Northwest. Two species of prickly pear, *Opuntia fragilis* (with somewhat rounded joints) and *O. polyacantha* (with flat joints) occur in our area, mostly east of the Cascades. *Opuntia fragilis* also finds a native home in drier habitats around the Puget Sound Basin, as at Sequim and in the San Juan Islands. The hedge-hog cactus

Hedge-hog cactus *(Pediocactus simpsonii)*

(Pediocactus simpsonii), with a globose, miniature growth, ranges from eastern Washington to Colorado (see color section).

Growing these hardy cacti is something of a challenge. For westside gardeners, the sunniest place, protected from winter damp, is needed. Moreover, these native cacti are hard to come by, especially since collecting plants in the wild is now to be thoroughly discouraged. Fortunately the two opuntias can be propagated from their joints or pads. The hedge-hog cactus is now becoming rare to extinct in many of its localities, both due to the inroads of agriculture and to the indiscriminate and wholesale collecting of these gems. They must not be collected. These plants should be secured from nurseries that have propagated the species under cultivation.

Deciduous Shrubs

Nearly every kind of habitat from coastal bluff to the alpine summit has its share of shrubs that lose their leaves. They are particularly common in the understory of our coniferous forests. Huckleberry, serviceberry, snowberry, salmonberry, ocean spray, currant, and gooseberry plants form a dominant thread of the living fabric beneath the forest tree canopy. A number of these deciduous shrubby natives are choice subjects for the garden. Two lists will be developed here: the first singles out the ten or so best deciduous shrubs, and the second deals with other shrubs of redeeming (though perhaps not outstanding) value. Since subjective choice enters here, it will repay the user of this manual to study both lists. Plants in the second list, while not always best for a choice site in the garden can be charming in a woodland setting, or can do yeoman service to aid wildlife and soil conservation in other places under cultivation or ecological restoration.

Ten Choice Deciduous Shrubs

1. SERVICEBERRY, SASKATOON BERRY *(Amelanchier alnifolia)*. Rose Family (Rosaceae). There is scarcely a habitat in the Pacific Northwest that does not support stands of serviceberry (often pronounced sarvisberry). At low elevations on both sides of the Cascades, specimens are mostly 4 to 6 or even 10 feet tall, often with a broad, multi-branched habit. With superior foliage, flower, and fruit, our native serviceberry merits wider use in the garden. English gardeners learned about it a long time ago.

Distinguishing Features. Its leaves are broadly oval, up to 2 inches long, with margins toothed on the free end of the leaf and the leaf base often cordate (heart-shaped) and free of marginal teeth. The foliage in fall turns to glorious reds or yellows, bright splashes of color among the evergreens in hills and mountains. The flowers are in compact clusters, up to 2 inches across and of the purest white. The five free petals are broadly strap-shaped, widely spreading at full flowering,

Serviceberry *(Amelanchier alnifolia)*

Deciduous

Serviceberry *(Amelanchier alnifolia)* in spring flower, cultivated in University of British Columbia Botanical Garden

but enveloped in a pearly white bud at first. The exquisite flowers are in a class of two well-known garden shrubs, pearlbush *(Exochorda)* and mock-orange *(Philadelphus).* By late summer, clusters of pea-size, purplish black fruits (really small "apples" or pomes) are nestled in the colorful foliage. Brian Mulligan, former director of the University of Washington Arboretum, has called attention to the variety *cusickii* with its larger flowers; it grows on the east side of the Cascades. Serviceberry likes partial to full sun and will do well in open woodland, shrub border to sunny bank.

Propagation. Propagation by seeds requires cold stratification for three to six months (33° to 44° F.). Seeds should be free of pulp. Treated cuttings under mist can also be tried. So common a plant gives seedlings frequently in places of disturbance, and careful collecting of plants from such transient spots may be condoned.

Many have eaten serviceberry fruits in a variety of ways—cooked, raw, or dried. Doug Benoliel in *Northwest Foraging,* extolls their quality: "Use the fruit raw, cooked or dried. Their flavor makes for fine pies or jams. A handful of fresh fruit can liven up a bag of granola. The fruit can be dried and used as a substitute for raisins or currants" (p. 67). Roy Davidson, skilled Northwest plantsman, tells of yet another use: "Certainly [serviceberry] was one of the constituents of the American Indian food caches—pounded fruit and meat together giving today's 'mince meat.' "

2. DEER BRUSH *(Ceanothus integerrimus).* Buckthorn Family (Rhamnaceae). On down to the Columbia River from Mount Adams, many of the back roads of Skamania and Klickitat counties are lined with this delightful shrub. The time to see it is late spring, April and May, when the roadsides are a dazzling mixture of deep blue lilac to nearly

Deer brush *(Ceanothus integerrimus)*

white where deer brush grows. The wide variation in color of this species of wild lilac gives the landscape rich splashes of color. And the mixture in the native habitat is wholly charming. But, unless the gardener is able to grow a thicket of deer brush, he may have to be content with only one of the many color forms. The recovery of a deep lilac individual from seeds or wild-collected seedlings is a longshot chance. Fortunately, wild lilacs take rather easily from cuttings.

Distinguishing Features. Deer brush is a tall (6 to 15 foot high), openly branched shrub with pale green leaves, rather more sparsely clothing the plant than with other species of *Ceanothus.* The alternate leaves are broadly oval, 1 to 2 inches long, with entire margins and soft pubescence on both surfaces. The tiny flowers are in large open clusters, projecting from the ends of the branches, *en masse* forming a lovely froth of lilac to white bloom.

This is a shrub of open woods, usually in a conifer-hardwood setting of Douglas fir or yellow pine and Garry oak. Though southern Washington is its northern limit, it occurs south through Oregon (mostly west of the Cascades) into California and east to New Mexico and lower California. The northern localities produce perfectly hardy plants for Northwest gardens.

Propagation. The shrub can be propagated by seeds (hot water treatment needed), by collected seedlings, or by cuttings. Only the latter method assures a desired color form.

Oregonians will want to look for good forms of this shrub in Hood River County, on the northeast slope of Mount Hood, or in southwestern Oregon, as in the Medford–Ashland area. As to garden culture, let it have partial to full sun in light, well-drained soil and it will thrive. Since it is best grown in massed plantings, the open woodland setting or the large wild garden should be preferred sites.

Deciduous

Oceanspray *(Holodiscus discolor)*

3. CREEK DOGWOOD, RED OSIER DOGWOOD *(Cornus stolonifera),* Dogwood Family (Cornaceae). This is an ideal native shrub for moist places: boggy areas or along the shores of streams and ponds, or simply in wetter parts of the conventional garden. The rewards for its presence come from all its phases—foliage, flower, and fruit.

Distinguishing Features. The red osier dogwood is a many-stemmed tall shrub, up to 15 feet and often widely spreading from root sprouts. Its 3- to 5-inch-long, paired leaves have an untoothed margin and show bold, curving veins. In fall, the foliage colors a deep red. Twigs of this highly variable species are often red, whence the name, red osier. Unlike the Pacific flowering dogwood *(Cornus nuttallii),* the creek dogwood has no showy bracts surrounding the clusters of tiny white flowers. But when clothed with the flat-topped clusters of white flowers, the effect in bloom is pleasing. Bunches of white or bluish berries are copiously produced by fall. The white-berried forms display their fruits grandly against the red foliage.

Cornus stolonifera is common at low elevations in moist habitats throughout western North America. In some places it can form dense thickets along streams. Though several species names appear in earlier literature (e.g., *C. pubescens, C. glabrata, C. occidentalis*), Hitchcock et al. (1959) consider these all part of one highly variable species. Most of the variation is in rather minute features of foliage and fruit. Hitchcock recognizes two varieties; the one called var. *occidentalis* is the Northwest's common red osier dogwood.

Creek dogwood occupies a valued niche in the woodland garden or in open-space plantings. Its tolerance of water gives it special merit for wet spots in the urban garden. *Cornus stolonifera* is one of our most valuable native shrubs for habitat reclamation, wildlife cover, and other environmental plantings.

Propagation. Propagation by seeds requires cold stratification after removal of the pulp. From thirty to sixty days at 35° to 41° F. will yield high germination of seeds sown in ordinary loam, and 2- or 3-inch branch tips, taken in late summer, root readily. Since wild plants sucker freely from underground stems, collected sprouts can be easily established.

Several cultivars are in the trade, among which cv. 'Flaviramea' (yellow twigs) and cv. 'Kelseyi' (dwarf, up to 2 feet) are noteworthy.

4. OCEANSPRAY, CREAMBUSH, MEADOWSWEET *(Holodiscus discolor).* Rose Family (Rosaceae). Though widespread in the Northwest from the Pacific Coast to Montana, oceanspray is most at home in the lowland westside country.

Distinguishing Features. Everywhere in dryish open woods of Douglas fir and madrone, this tall many-stemmed shrub is covered with a creamy foam of flower in mid-summer. The foliage has pleasing texture and form. Its leaves are up to 1½ inches long, broadly oval or triangular in outline, but deeply lobed, the symmetrical lobes coarsely and doubly toothed. The tiny cream white flowers are borne in large clusters, often pendant under their own weight. In full flower, the shrub can be entirely clothed with bloom, awash with a sea of creamy white. This member of the rose family produces its seeds in tiny dry capsules like its close relative *Spiraea.* The clusters of fruit may persist until next season, giving the plant a rather spent, bedraggled look.

Oceanspray lends charm to the sunny woodland setting and is a colorful reclaimer of open or disturbed land. Witness its everpresence in logged-over areas, recent second growth, and roadbanks throughout the coastal sectors of the Pacific Northwest.

Propagation. The plant is easiest to propagate from seedlings, often abundantly available in the wild. The tiny seeds require cold stratification at 41° F. for as much as eighteen weeks. Semi-hardwood cuttings or suckers have been tried with success.

For eastside gardens, hardier sources of this plant are available in nearby forests. Also, arid eastside gardens should prove hospitable to a related species, *Holodiscus dumosus* (desert oceanspray), that grows in the lava, pumice, and volcanic ash soils of south-central Oregon. It is an attractive shrub, smaller in stature and foliage than *H. discolor.*

5. MOCK-ORANGE, SYRINGA *(Philadelphus lewisii).* Hydrangea Family (Hydrangeaceae). Introduced into Britain by David Douglas in 1825, our native mock-orange has long been a highly prized ornamental in Europe. Bean says of it: "It is one of the most elegant and floriferous of all the taller species." So fine a plant, then, should be known more to gardeners in its native land.

Distinguishing Features. Though highly variable in stature and leaf size, there are a few dependable traits. First, it is the only species of *Philadelphus* in the Northwest, so its generic traits are easily applied. It is a medium-to-large, many-stemmed, and branched deciduous shrub. The paired leaves are broadly ovate, sparingly but coarsely toothed (or entire); the leaf surface tends to be slightly sand-papery to the touch. The flowers, in elongate clusters, are snow-white, large and fragrant. A hillside covered with mock-orange in full bloom in late June is an unforgettable sight.

Mock-orange is common on both the west and east sides of the Cascades, ranging inland to central Montana. On the west side it tends to be rather infrequent in open glades of dryish Douglas fir forest, especially near the coast. The shrubs are taller, more openly branched in such places. Where it occurs in basalt rimrock and talus east of the Cascades the bushes are more floriferous. Mock-orange is glorious along the rocky walls of the Yakima Canyon.

Garden Uses. Western mock-orange can be used in shrub borders, as isolated specimens on lawns, or to decorate sunny parts of the garden. It grows vigorously and flowers faithfully. To assure continued flowering from year to year, prune out the old branches that have borne flowers, leaving the long vigorous shoots of the current year for next season's flowers. Eastside gardens should welcome this dependable, hardy native of great beauty.

Mock-orange *(Philadelphus lewisii),* southern Washington

Deciduous

Propagation. Easy to propagate from cuttings of not too brittle young wood, taken in mid-July. Seeds should be stratified for good germination—eight weeks in coarse sand at 41° F—and then planted in a coarse sand medium at 75° F. The seeds are so plentiful, however, that sowing large quantities of them directly, without stratification, will yield enough seedlings for all but commercial uses.

6. SHRUBBY CINQUEFOIL *(Potentilla fruticosa).* Rose Family (Rosaceae). On every north temperate continent, often in the alpine, the traveler is likely to encounter this mound of golden yellow bloom. In our area, shrubby cinquefoil thrives in open, sunny places in the mountain hemlock zone to above timberline. At lower elevations it is more partial to wet meadows and swampy shrubfields. The best areas—and the best plant forms—are at timberline: Mount Rainier, Wenatchee Mountains, the Olympics, and elsewhere in the mountainous Northwest.

Distinguishing Features. It is a low- to medium-sized shrub (6 inches to 3 feet tall) with distinctive short pinnate to trifoliate leaves. The divisions (pinnae) are finger-like, narrowly elongate, usually less than an inch long. The large, golden yellow flowers resemble those of a yellow buttercup; the compact shrub of the alpine form in full flower is a golden glory.

Garden Uses. In recent years, garden varieties* of *Potentilla fruticosa* and its Asiatic kin have become increasingly popular as low border shrubs in full sun. Commercial and public plantings of it are common and the home garden sees more and more of these cultivars. Little has been done to select from our own native types superior forms for the garden. They should be sought in the high country of the North

* The many cultivars, with white, fawn, orange, or red flowers, are all derived from Eurasian plants.

Shrubby cinquefoil *(Potentilla fruticosa)*

Cascades. Low, compact types with large flowers are found in the Harts Pass area of Washington.

Propagation. Propagation is usually with soft-wood cuttings taken in early summer at low elevations, late summer in the subalpine. Hard-wood cuttings will strike, but the plants are slow to develop. Seeds, though produced sparingly in the wild, can be germinated without stratification, if sown fresh.

7. RED-FLOWERING CURRANT, BLOOD CURRANT, WINTER CURRANT *(Ribes sanguineum).* Gooseberry Family (Grossulariaceae). Of thirty or so currant and gooseberry species in the Northwest, no other has had such a long preeminence as a garden plant. Discovered in 1793 by Archibald Menzies in Puget Sound and introduced to horticulture by David Douglas in 1826, the red-flowering currant has been a European favorite ever since. It is just possible that our own Northwest garden plants had to come all the way back home from England to make their place in cultivation here.

Distinguishing Features. The red-flowering currant is an 8- to 10-foot-tall shrub with many upright stems from the base. On older twigs its leaves are in clusters on short, lateral spur branches. The pubescent (soft-hairy) leaves are round in outline, but usually three-lobed, the lobes rounded and slightly toothed. The pendant flower clusters are closely set with gorgeous red to pink (or even white) flowers. Color range is highly variable, from deep hues to paler pinks; the calyx is usually darker than the petals. The fruits are black, covered with a conspicuous glaucous bloom. There is some difference of opinion on their edibility. Hitchcock says they are unpalatable, while Erna Gunther claims that the Clallam Indians ate them. Books on edible plants do not mention this currant. Though not poisonous, its fruits are probably not worth gathering for food. Two other currants, *Ribes aureum* (yellow currant) and *R. cereum* (squaw currant) are recommended edibles.

Garden Uses. At its best in early spring with the glamorous bloom emerging before the leaves, this shrub can be worked into the garden in a variety of places. It is tolerant of sun or shade, although may get a bit leggy in a woodland setting. Several cultivars are in the trade, emphasizing double white or deep crimson flowers. These are mostly of English garden origin, following the original introduction of Douglas. Although *Ribes sanguineum* is most commonly a plant of lowland westside forest and glades, it does reach the east slope of the Cascades in Oregon and Washington. Plants of this colder origin should be tried for eastside garden color.

Propagation. The easiest source of plants from the wild is seedlings from self-sown plants, often abounding in places around Puget Sound and other coastal areas where disturbance has created a suitable seed bed for bird-disseminated seed. For quantity propagation, seeds are the surest method. Cleaned fresh seeds require three months' cold stratification at 32° to 36° F. Hardwood cuttings taken in fall can be used, and the currant can easily be layered as well.

Red flowering currant *(Ribes sanguineum)*

Deciduous

Other Species. Several other native currants and gooseberries are of ornamental value. *Ribes aureum,* the golden currant, produces precocious golden yellow flowers on tall wand-like stems. It is found along streams and washes on the east side. *Ribes lobbii,* a montane forest species of the east side has exquisite, pendant flowers (red calyx and white petals, like a small fuchsia). The observant collector will find other species worth trying in the garden, such as *R. viscossisimum* (sticky currant), *R. lacustre* (swamp currant), *R. menziesii* (prickly or Menzies' gooseberry), and *R. cereum* (squaw currant). Since some species can serve as the alternate host to the white-pine blister rust (a severe pathogen of five-needled pines), introduction of *Ribes* species to the garden should be made with disease-free stock.

8. WESTERN AZALEA *(Rhododendron occidentale).* Heather Family (Ericaceae). Nearly every garden that grows hybrid azaleas has plants with this fine western native in their "blood." *Rhododendron occidentale* continues to be a source of superior azalea crosses. Witness the famous Knaphill and Koster hybrids, all with *occidentale* parentage. But our native azalea can be grown to perfection without benefit from other species.

In the wild, western azalea likes moist thickets and stream banks. It is especially common in coastal Curry County, Oregon, though it is known inland in the Umpqua Valley and south into California. It is happy on serpentine soils in the Siskiyous, as long as its feet are in moisture.

Distinguishing Features. Plants in the garden can form many-stemmed bushes up to 10 feet high, with slender, upright twiggy branching. The leaves are thin, narrowly oval to lance shaped, usually wider at the tip than at the base. The flower clusters are tightly compact, often densely glandular. Flower color varies from pale rose to white, blotched with yellow. Rhododendron specialists in Oregon have been diligent in their search for exceptional forms: good color, large flowers, and superior growth form. The dependable flowering in June and July makes it one of our finest summer-blooming natives.

Garden Uses. Western azalea is perfectly at home in the moister, acid places of the garden. It can take full sun, but is particularly charming in open woodland with evergreen rhododendrons as companions. The native azalea is best used in massed plantings, interspersed with evergreens. Propagation is from suckers, cuttings, and seeds, treated like other azalea species.

9. SITKA MOUNTAIN ASH *(Sorbus sitchensis).* Rose Family (Rosaceae). While similar to the common European mountain ash *(Sorbus aucuparia),* this native shrub has its own virtues. It is a shrub, not a tree; and its fruits are large, orange red, not small and dull crimson. Sitka mountain ash *is* different and can adapt well to the garden.

Most often it is found wild in upper montane to subalpine areas where it forms thickets on avalanche slopes or grows in association with subalpine fir and mountain hemlock.

Sitka mountain ash *(Sorbus sitchensis)*

Distinguishing Features. The bushes are 3 to 10 feet tall, usually with many erect to spreading stems from a common base. Its alternate leaves are compound, with from seven to nine leaflets, each toothed above the middle. Flowers are small and white, in dense flat-topped clusters with a bit of an unpleasant (or unusual) odor. Its glory is in fall, when the yellow to bronzy red foliage sets off the huge clusters of big reddish orange fruits.

Garden Uses. It can be grown at lower elevations, but tends not to be as floriferous, and hence has less of the choice fruit. It takes well to the sunny, moist shrub border and can be worked in with rhododendrons and azaleas to good effect. The native *Sorbus scopulina* merits garden use, too.

Propagation. Usually propagated by seeds; cold stratification at 32° F. for two to four months is recommended. Unstratified seeds freshly sown outdoors in fall or winter for cold conditioning also yield seedlings. Mountain ash is difficult to start from cuttings.

10. RED HUCKLEBERRY, RED WHORTLEBERRY *(Vaccinium parvifolium).* Heather Family (Ericaceae). Of all the deciduous bushes, this is the most well known to Northwesterners living on the west side of the mountains. It is everywhere in the lowland westside forests, from southern British Columbia to Oregon, and thence to the Bay Area of central California. It likes open to dense conifer forest, dryish to moist sites, and is habitually found thriving perched on logs or stumps. The dispersal of seeds by birds assures that unique habitat.

Distinguishing Features. The bushes are 3 to 12 feet tall, with many tiny angular twigs from a many-branched stem. The small, oval leaves are entire, emerging before the flowers in spring. Its flowers are small, greenish to flesh-colored, borne inconspicuously as single or few-flowered axillary clusters. Its fruits are an attractive salmon-egg red and quite edible.

Garden Uses. Red huckleberry enjoys the hospitality of the rhododendron bed or woodland garden best. Partial shade and the forest-floor

Mountain ash *(Sorbus scopulina)*

Red huckleberry *(Vaccinium parvifolium)*

humus or rotten logs foster its growth. Where it grows nearby as a native wildling, the gardener never deliberately has to plant it, since seedlings are sure to appear beneath the garden conifers. These can be moved easily in late winter to a desired spot.

Propagation. For those who have no handy wild source of plants, collected seeds or layerings can start the huckleberry. Seeds of huckleberries require no special treatment. They are small, however, and the seedlings must be handled through two or three transplantings (like rhododendrons) before they can be put out in the garden.

Other Deciduous Shrubs

Personal prejudice biases the choice of the ten best native shrubs of deciduous habit. For other eyes, and for special situations, other deciduous shrubs native to the Pacific Northwest call for honorable mention. Brief accounts of these worthy garden natives appear below.

BOG BIRCH, SCRUB BIRCH *(Betula glandulosa).* Birch Family (Betulaceae). A 6- to 8-foot miniature of birch in foliage and flower and fruit, bog birch occurs infrequently in swamps and bogs from British Columbia to California. It is a fine choice for wet places in the wild garden, and is best propagated from seeds.

DESERT SWEET *(Chamaebatiaria millefolium).* Rose Family (Rosaceae). Shrub, 3 to 5 feet tall, with finely divided leaves (like yarrow), pungently aromatic. Cream-white flowers in terminal clusters, reminiscent of mock-orange, though smaller. It is native to rocky slopes of semi-desert areas in eastern Oregon, south and east to Utah and Arizona. Despite its desert-like home, it takes rather well to open, sunny places in Northwest gardens, especially in sandy soils. It can be increased from seeds, probably with stratification, as well as from hormone-treated cuttings. Plants in my own garden, from seeds collected by Carl English, are 4 feet tall and have bloomed repeatedly, so it seems to be perfectly hardy in Seattle. Given its eastside habitats, it should do well in the colder and drier parts of the Pacific Northwest.

COPPER BUSH *(Cladothamnus pyroliflorus).* Heather Family (Ericaceae). A distinctive shrub of the heather family, 2 to 5 feet high, with salmon- or copper-colored flowers resembling those of herbaceous wintergreens, *(Pyrola)* or pipsissewa *(Chimaphila):* flat open flowers with separate petals and a recurved style. Leaves are narrowly oblong, up to 2 inches long. Copper bush is uncommon in montane forests of the Cascades and Olympics of Washington and extends south to Clatsop County, Oregon. Though slow to establish, it can be a neat shrub for peaty, damp sites in the garden.

RABBITBRUSH *(Chrysothamnus nauseosus, C. viscidiflorus).* Aster Family (Compositae). Sagebrush country shrubs with golden yellow flower heads in early autumn, this member of the compositae family is wide-spread in the more arid West. *Chrysothamnus nauseosus,* the common rab-bitbrush, comes in many variants; the montane ones are of better, more compact stature. The sticky rabbitbrush, *C. viscidiflorus,* with sticky linear, partially evergreen leaves, has much the same range as the white woolly-leaved species, *C. nauseosus.* Useful for naturalizing in open, waste places on the east side. Propagate from seeds or collected seed-lings.

Deciduous

ROCK CLEMATIS *(Clematis columbiana).* Buttercup Family (Ranuncula-ceae). A fine trailing shrub of rocky places in the mountains east of the Cascades, from British Columbia to northern Oregon. Look for a scrambling vine with opposite, compound leaves and large, four-parted blue flowers on long stalks. Rock clematis merits naturalizing in sunny garden sites or in the rock garden. Sow freshly collected ripe seeds (plumes of seeds in billowy clusters) or take *internode* cuttings.

MORMON TEA *(Ephedra viridis, E. nevadensis).* Ephedra Family (Ephedra-ceae). These are curious leafless shrubs of low stature; their upper branches resemble small horsetail *(Equisetum)* shoots. Two species, *Ephedra viridis* and *E. nevadensis,* are native of dry desert-like areas of southeastern Oregon and on southward. The ephedras are intriguing links between conifers and flowering plants, and are of some ornamental value, espe-cially in dry areas east of the Cascades. On the west side of the moun-tains, they need full sun and good drainage. They are grown from seeds.

Rock clematis *(Clematis columbiana)*

WESTERN SPINDLEBUSH, WESTERN WAHOO, BURNING BUSH *(Euonymus occidentalis).* Spindlebush Family (Celastraceae). Many species of spindlebush are in cultivation. Hitchcock describes it as a tall (8 to 15 feet), straggly shrub, an understory species in woods. In the garden, he says, it is "of little horticultural importance." Why include such an unprepossessing plant? Perhaps it is unremarkable for its large ovate leaves in pairs, with finely toothed margins and axillary, small, greenish red flowers. Its fall yellows and reds and its reddish purple fruits, however, are redeeming qualities. It is of infrequent occurrence in south-central Washington (Lewis and Clark counties) and is fairly abundant in woods on the south side of the Columbia River, east of Portland. The more venturesome of gardeners should try it. It comes easily from cuttings.

SPINY HOPSAGE *(Atriplex spinosa = Grayia spinosa)* and WINTER FAT *(Eurotia lanata).* Goosefoot Family (Chenopodiaceae). These two low shrubs grow in more alkaline areas of the sagebrush country east of the Cascades. Both have gray green foliage and curious fruits (flat and winged in hopsage; densely hairy in winter fat). They are suitable for revegetation purposes in alkaline areas in the cold, dry, steppe-desert country. *Eurotia* has been cultivated in Britain.

Deciduous

Fool's huckleberry *(Menziesia ferruginea)*

Devil's club spines and opening leaf bud

RUSTY LEAF, MOCK-AZALEA, FOOL'S HUCKLEBERRY *(Menziesia ferruginea).* Heather Family (Ericaceae). Despite its deceptive similarity to some azaleas and to taller huckleberries, rusty leaf has its own character. It is a tall (6 to 10 feet), twiggy shrub, with leaves clustered at the tips of the twigs. Its open reddish yellow, urn-shaped flowers resemble those of huckleberry; but the fruits mature to a dry capsule, not a fleshy berry. It is common in the Pacific Northwest, from southern Alaska to northern California and east to the Rockies. It prefers cool, moist habitats in forests, from coastal regions to well up in the mountains.

Though it is no rival in flower to its showier Japanese relatives, *Menziesia ferruginea* has its own charm, especially with its good fall foliage. It finds a welcome home in the woodland garden, or interspersed with rhododendrons and azaleas beneath partial shade. Small plants make good bonsai or planter subjects. Peaty soils suit it best.

It propagates rather easily from seeds or cuttings; like other ericads, the seeds are small and the seedlings require two or three moves before setting out.

The genus name, *Menziesia,* commemorates Archibald Menzies, who first collected it on Puget Sound in 1792. Though the Menzies' plant was *M. ferruginea,* all other species in the genus carry his name to remind us of that early exploration. There are two species of *Menziesia* in the eastern United States *(M. pilosa* and *M. glabella)* and four species in eastern Asia.

SWEET GALE *(Myrica gale).* Sweet Gale Family (Myricaceae) Despite their close botanical affinity, the deciduous sweet gale and the evergreen California wax myrtle (see p. 92) differ markedly in habitat and appearance. Sweet gale's home is the coastal bog, where it may replace Labrador tea as the dominant shrub. It is a low bushy shrub with long narrow leaves. Its flowers are insignificant, but show off well in their many-clustered terminal spikes; male flowers are on one plant and females on another. Propagated from seeds or by layering, it is grown in moist spots in the garden, as much for its sweet-scented foliage as for its interesting form.

DEVIL'S CLUB *(Oplopanax horridum).* Ginseng Family (Araliaceae). Though notorious for its formidable covering of irritating spines, devil's club must be given high praise as a garden ornamental. Look, but do not touch, and you will see a tall, wand-like stem, naked (except for spines) up to the tip where the huge palmate leaves surround the flower and fruit clusters. In the wild, devil's club forms extensive clumps in wetter habitats in low elevation coniferous forests. Here is where it gets its nasty reputation for impaling trespassers with its stout spines.

Though rare in cultivation, it has proved highly decorative in a variety of settings: naturalized in a wet woodland or wild garden, intermixed in the shrub border with evergreens, as a single showpiece speci-

Devil's club *(Oplopanax horridum)*

men against a shaded wall, or grown in a large planter box under shade. Propagation is slow, either from seed or cuttings or by layering. Small plants from the wild should be tried, giving due regard to when and where they are dug.

INDIAN PLUM, OSO BERRY *(Osmaronia—or Oemleria—cerasiformis)*. Rose Family (Rosaceae). No other westside shrub better celebrates the spring rebirth of our lowland landscapes. By early March the tips of its leafless branches begin to burst with green and white flower clusters, becoming pendant as they mature. Indian plum performs its spring rites every-where in the brushy, second growth forest land. It is especially eye-catching in groves of alder and maple, where its early flowers light up the leafless woods. Indian plum grows to 15 or 20 feet tall, with open, arched branching and, often, sucker growth from the base. Its summer foliage is undistinguished, much like Scouler's willow—except for the unique odor. Crushed leaves of Indian plum smell like cucum-bers or watermelon rind. The flowers in short terminal clusters are either male or female, on separate bushes. The "plums" in fall are olive-sized purple berries, somewhat bittersweet in taste. They are a favorite of birds and other wildlife.

Indian plum grows in moist to somewhat dry places in westside forests and open woodland, from British Columbia to California.

Though it is not intended as an ornamental for a choice place in the formal garden, it has great value in urban and suburban landscapes. For the wild or woodland garden, for native plantings in parks and open spaces, and for land reclamation, Indian plum is a superior shrub. It is easy to grow from seeds, and seedlings are often abundant in the wild. Bean remarks that "it is easily propagated by taking off small pieces from old plants," by which he means that it takes well from twig cuttings.

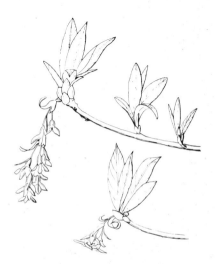

Indian plum *(Osmaronia cerasiformis)*

Deciduous

Indian plum in early spring

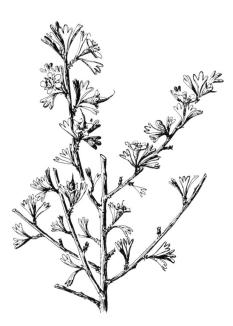

Bitterbrush *(Purshia tridentata)*

Bean also extolls its worth as a garden plant: "The oso berry is useful for its early, almond-scented blossoms, which are usually fully open by the third week in March [in Britain], being produced from the leafless shoots of the previous year."

NINEBARK *(Physocarpus capitatus).* Rose Family (Rosaceae). Look for this tallish shrub in open woods, along water-courses and in moist hedge-rows throughout the westside country at low elevations. Though its leaves look like those of a mallow, currant, or even small-leaved maple, ninebark's affinity is with spiraea and oceanspray in the rose family. Its smallish white flowers are borne in dense pompoms, reminiscent of the snowball bush *(Viburnum opulus).* On the east side, a hardier species, *Physocarpus malvaceus,* inhabits drier places in yellow-pine and Douglas fir country. Ninebark shrubbery fits well in the wild garden, open woodland, or shrub-grass meadow. It is easy to start from cuttings, but slow from fall-sown seeds. The subtle rose brown fall color is attractive *en masse.*

BITTERBRUSH, ANTELOPE BRUSH *(Purshia tridentata).* Rose Family (Rosaceae). Easily mistaken for sagebrush, bitterbrush fits much the same ecological niche. Sagebrush and bunchgrass plains, open yellow-pine forests and even high in the drier eastside mountains, all are home to this widespread, rugged plant. The twiggy shrubs, either nearly prostrate or up to 8 and 10 feet high, bear small three-pronged (trident) leaves that resemble sagebrush foliage. But in flower and fruit, the resemblance ceases. *Purshia's* neat and dainty yellow star-flowers dot

Ninebark *(Physocarpus capitatus)*

the bush in spring; by fall the flowers have made their fuzzy short-tailed nutlets (achenes).

Bitterbrush can be the salvation of many an eastside revegetation project: roadsides, urban open spaces, dam sites, and all other such places of disturbance on the dry side of the mountains. Already, selection of superior layering forms is providing a choice native for roadside beautification where stressful environments prevail. And for big game browsing, there is no better shrub: bitterbrush and game management east of the Cascades go well together. Westside gardeners should contrive a dry, sunny place for *Purshia* to grow; it is worth the effort. It grows best from seeds with winter stratification, but layering also works. Cuttings need to be tried.

BREWER'S OAK *(Quercus garryana* var. *breweri).* Oak Family (Fagaceae). This shrubby version of Oregon post-oak or Garry oak lives in dryish places in the Klamath–Siskiyou mountain country of southwestern Oregon and adjacent California. Brewer's oak is a "must" for connoisseurs of the oaks; it will remind the collector of another deciduous shrub oak of the intermountain region, Gambel's oak *(Quercus gambellii).* Both are shrubs up to 10 feet high, with small, round-lobed leaves. Start Brewer's oak from acorns and in a few years a miniature Garry oak can adorn the garden.

SHRUB CASCARA *(Rhamnus purshiana* var. *"arbuscula").* Buckthorn Family (Rhamnaceae). Several years ago we came across a 4-foot-high, spreading cascara on serpentine slopes in the Wenatchee Mountains. Though its leaves are only slightly smaller than the tree cascara of the west side, the shrub habit is distinct and persistent. Grown from seed, the plants retain the bush habit. The spreading cascara has done well as a shrub in open, drier places in my garden. It comes best from

Deciduous

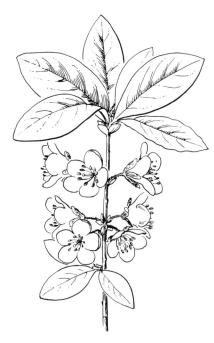

Cascade azalea *(Rhododendron albiflorum)*

stratified seeds, and we have had no success yet with cuttings. As yet it has no official name.

CASCADE AZALEA *(Rhododendron albiflorum)*. Heather Family (Ericaceae). Nature tantalizes us with this beautiful shrub. Lovely cream bells and glossy, bright green foliage mark it as a great beauty in the upper montane forest of mountain hemlock and subalpine fir. Yet successful establishment of *Rhododendron albiflorum* seems next to impossible. The one recorded success in Scotland was compounded of luck, sunny position, and rather poor stoney soil. It should be tried with persistence and with the canny foresight to get the right exposure and moisture for a garden trial. Why it is so difficult is a mystery. After all, so many of our easy rhododendrons come from much higher altitudes in the Himalayas. Seeds or cuttings should be tried, in the manner of azalea propagation, and with a bit of witchcraft.

SUMAC *(Rhus glabra)*. Sumac Family (Anacardiaceae). The handsome sumacs of North America have long been favorites in the garden for their striking growth form, superb, deep red fall color, and showy fruit clusters. Our *Rhus glabra*, closely related to the eastern *R. typhina*, ranges throughout the West in sagebrush, bunchgrass, and lava rimrock country, from British Columbia to the Southwest. The tall (3 to 12 feet) shrubs have a distinctive forked (dichotomous) branching pattern and large, pinnately compound leaves; the many terminal flower clusters develop into attractive conical masses of reddish fruits.

Though best grown in *wild* gardens east of the Cascades, it should do well in drier sites on the west side, especially in the Willamette and Rogue River valleys of Oregon. Note my underscoring of the *wild* garden for this shrub. Handsome though it is, sumac "spreads by greatly elongate shallow roots and tends to form large thickets"; with this cautionary remark by Hitchcock, the gardener will be aware of sumac's rampant nature.

Rhus glabra cultivar 'Laciniata' is a highly regarded garden form with handsome deeply cut leaflets. According to Bean (1970), "Its greatest beauty is obtained by cutting it hard back every spring, and thinning down the young shoots to one or two, thus obtaining broad feathery leaves 3 ft. long, very striking in their autumn colour."

Propagation. It is easiest to propagate from generous pieces of the horizontal roots, or from cuttings. Seed requires mechanical or chemical scarification; a hot water treatment may be sufficient. Outdoor stratification in the fall is recommended. Germination for *R. glabra* has been aided by constant temperature conditions (68° F.) for 20 to 60 days.

Two other species of the genus *Rhus* are well known as poison oak *(R. diversiloba)* and poison ivy *(R. radicans)*. They are easily recognized by their compound leaves of three leaflets. Only gardeners either too innocent or with diabolical intent would plant them. The Squawbush *(R. trilobata)*, though also having the trifoliolate (but smaller) leaves, is harmless and a good low shrub for dry, sunny spots.

BUFFALO BERRY *(Shepherdia canadensis* and *S. argentea).* Oleaster Family (Eleagnaceae). These close relatives of the widely planted exotic, Russian olive *(Eleagnus angustifolia)* have their own garden merit. The russet-leaved buffalo berry *(Shepherdia canadensis),* though widespread east of the Cascades, is also at home in the drier open woods and headlands of the San Juan Islands. It is a "natural" for drier open places in westside gardens and especially for revegetating the summer place in the islands.

The silver-leaved buffalo berry grows in the Rocky Mountain country. *Shepherdia argentea* does not grow wild in our region, but is so close in southeastern Oregon that it should be included. It is a rugged shrub for the colder and drier parts of the Northwest.

Both species of buffalo berry are low- to medium-sized shrubs with opposite leaves and separate sexes. Their most telltale feature is the tiny flat scales that cover all parts of the plant: stem, leaf, flower, and fruit. This "flocked" or plastered sheen on the plant surfaces is a hallmark of the whole oleaster family. These two buffalo berries, with their cast-iron hardiness are perfect for cold, dry gardens east of the Cascades.

Propagation. The plant is propagated best from cuttings. Seeds need both scarification (to soften the hard seed coat) and stratification (to break dormancy). Interplant both sexes to get berries.

WESTERN WILD GRAPE *(Vitis californica).* Grape Family (Vitaceae). Oregonians living in the Umpqua and Rogue River valleys know this climbing vine. It frequents stream banks and wet deciduous woods of valley bottoms in southwestern Oregon, and on south into California. This aggressively rampant vine is best left to the woodland or for naturalizing in open spaces where it can attain its exuberant growth best. The wild grape of Oregon has large, three- to five-lobed leaves and glaucous, purple fruit. It is said to grow easily from seeds; grapes also come quickly from cuttings.

YERBA DE SELVA, WHIPPLE VINE *(Whipplea modesta).* Hydrangea Family (Hydrangeaceae). This dainty charmer grows in open woods and sheltered rocky places near the coast from the Olympic Peninsula to California. It is a low, almost herbaceous trailing shrublet, with decided possibilities as a ground cover. It and mock-orange are our native members of the hydrangea family (Hydrangeaceae). Whipple vine has opposite, semi-deciduous leaves on short lateral upright branches, each branchlet usually tipped with a delicate puff of tiny white flowers. Since it roots freely as it travels along the ground, rooted pieces can serve to bring it into the garden, even in dense shade.

A look-alike in trailing habit and opposite leaves is the half-woody yerba buena *(Satureja douglasii).* It likes dryish open woods west of the Cascades. It can be used in place of *Whipplea* or *Linnaea* where a ground-cover tolerant of drier situations is wanted. And yerba buena foliage is both exquisitely aromatic and medicinal.

Yerba buena *(Satureja douglasii)*

Twinberries, Honeysuckles (species of *Lonicera*). Honeysuckle Family (Caprifoliaceae)

Members of the honeysuckle clan come in two forms—shrubs or climbing vines. Both types are represented in the Pacific Northwest. The twinberry *(Lonicera involucrata)* is the largest of the shrubby honeysuckles: 10 feet tall, with large opposite leaves; pale yellow flowers in pairs at the ends of twigs; and purplish black fruits, two-by-two in saucerlike bracts. Easily grown in moist, open sites, it occurs wild on both sides of the mountains, from sea level to well up in the mountains.

Three other shrubby species, *Lonicera utahensis, L. caerulea,* and *L. conjugialis* are smaller in all attributes than *L. involucrata.* They should naturalize well in eastside gardens.

The best of the native climbing honeysuckle is the orange, or trumpet, honeysuckle, *L. ciliosa.* It is widespread in open woods on both sides of the Cascades. It can run free on the ground or clamber up into trees with ease. The large, orange, trumpet-shaped flowers are clustered just above a large round "leaf" (two opposite leaves wholly fused). Of it, the British authority Bean (1970) says: "Although rare in gardens, it is a fine species, which should be more widely cultivated." It won an Award of Merit at a British garden show in 1919.

Two other climbing honeysuckles are suitable for the wild garden: *Lonicera hispidula* (California or hairy honeysuckle) and *L. interrupta* (chaparral honeysuckle). Both are west of the Cascades: *L. hispidula,* with yellow flowers, extends from Washington to California in open woods, while *L. interrupta* is in dry thickets of southern Oregon and California (as on Table Mountain, near Medford, Oregon).

Species of *Lonicera* come easily from cuttings: hardwood cuttings outdoors or young summer shoots placed over bottom heat. Germination of seeds is slow unless given stratification treatment. All species should be more widely used either as ornamentals or for wildlife plantings.

Honeysuckle *(Lonicera ciliosa)*

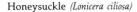

Wood's rose *(Rosa woodsii)*

Wild Roses (species of *Rosa*). Rose Family (Rosaceae)

Though the rose has a traditional and honored place in the garden,
it is only the roses of ancient domestication that are commonly grown.
Yet, all around us, nearly everywhere throughout the Pacific Northwest,
are delightful native species to try. Here is a trio of species as starters
to bring the wild native roses into the garden:

Nootka rose *(Rosa nutkana).* Dryish to moist habitats both west and
east of the Cascades; large, solitary flowers; big purplish pear-shaped
hips.

Wood's rose *(R. woodsii).* Widespread east of the Cascades; small flowers in showy clusters; hips round or pear-shaped.

Bald-hip rose, or little wild rose *(R. gymnocarpa).* Hips brilliant red;
flowers small in attractive clusters. The common name tells something
of its character: naked hips, meaning that the sepals do not remain
on the mature hips. This rose is common west of the Cascades, but
is also found in western Idaho and western Montana.

Seeds removed from dried rose-hips germinate slowly; outside stratification over a winter helps; and small offsets from the parent root
transplant easily.

Berried Shrubs of the *Rubus* Clan. Rose Family (Rosaceae)

The two tall *Rubus* species, thimbleberry *(R. parviflorus)* and salmonberry
(R. spectabilis) are easy and often spontaneous in the wild garden. The
big white flowers followed by the soft, bland-sweet fruits of thimbleberry are known to all Northwesterners.

Early spring is the best time for the transient glory of salmonberry.
The big reddish purple flowers appear before the foliage as bright
and gaudy specks in the yet dormant underbrush in the forest. In

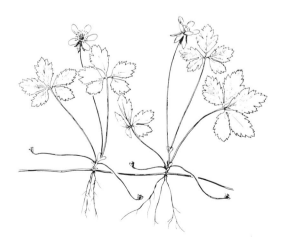

Strawberry bramble *(Rubus pedatus)*

Deciduous

Scouler's willow *(Salix scouleriana)*

Willow *(Salix nivalis)*

late summer the bright red salmonberries rarely go begging along a well-traveled trail. The garden use of both these brambles is best limited to naturalizing in wilder and wetter sections of a suburban garden.

Two other *Rubus* berries fit a very different garden niche. Since both are trailing woodlanders, they make fine groundcover carpeters in shaded situations. Both the strawberry bramble *(R. pedatus)* with five distinct leaflets, and the dwarf bramble *(R. lasiococcus)* are "excellent trailing ornamentals," so says Hitchcock, and I agree. Both are easily planted from rooted runners. The dainty white flowers at ground level rarely seem to set fruit—too close to slugs and rodents, perhaps. Since the two brambles occur on both sides of the Cascades, the eastside gardener should look for hardy strains.

Willows (species of *Salix*). Willow Family (Salicaceae)

Like brambles, there is a willow for nearly every occasion and place. Among the taller (5 to 15 feet high) types, Scouler's willow *(Salix scouleriana)* and Hooker's willow *(S. hookeriana)* naturalize well in the wild garden. Hooker's willow is well suited to seaside plantings, for its home is on the coastal dune, just back of the sea. Inlanders on the east side of the Cascades should try the several narrow-leaved willows like *S. exigua* and *S. fluviatilis.* They are perfectly hardy, but do require moist places.

A very different willow way of life enriches the garden from the alpine. Tiny ground-hugging shrublets of *Salix arctica, S. nivalis,* or *S. cascadensis* amaze the backpacker above timberline with their show of dainty foliage and bold, erect flower tassels (catkins). And for the rock gardener at sea level, the dwarf willows are both a challenge and a delight. Like their taller kin, they can be started from cuttings or seeds. But the trick is to get them to persist. A gritty, moist soil with good drainage and an open, sunny setting give the best chance of success. These dwarf willows should be tried in container plantings, too.

Native Spireas (species of *Spiraea*). Rose Family (Rosaceae)

Spireas from other lands have been garden favorites for many years. Yet we have a trio of native species that measure up well with the garden exotics. Each of our natives occupies a characteristic natural habitat. The most common and widespread northwesterner is *Spiraea douglasii.* It is at home in moist, but open, sunny places; bogs, swamps, borders of streams, and lakes are usual habitats. Some lowland bogs are dominated by the species, and are often called hardhack bogs. Hardhack spirea is a tall, many-stemmed shrub (6 to 12 feet high) with 1 or 2 inch long oval leaves. Each stem in summer can be extravagantly tipped with the purplish pink plume of tiny flowers. It is a fine, though aggressive, plant for wet places in the wild garden and for naturalizing in watery wastes of suburbia.

A far different habitat is required by the shiny-leaved spirea *(S.*

betulifolia var. *lucida).* It is common in open conifer woods mainly east of the Cascades. The plants are rarely over 3 feet tall, with leaves like hardhack spirea but of a brighter green. The oval leaf margin is toothed above the middle, resembling the leaves of serviceberry. The tiny cream-white flowers of this dryland spirea are gathered into large flat-topped clusters. It is a good understory plant for the dryish woodland garden. Eastside gardeners should give it a try, too.

Where bog and dry land meet, one can often find the hybrid between *Spiraea douglasii* and *S. betulifolia.* It is intermediate in features of stature and flower. Its soft pale-pink flowers form a pyramidal or obconic cluster of *S. douglasii* with the flat-topped inflorescence of *S. betulifolia.* The hybrid name, *Spiraea* X *pyramidata,* acknowledges this in-between character of the inflorescence. Pyramid spirea is an easy and attractive garden plant, tolerating sun or shade and dry to rather moist sites.

The third species of spirea is a glory of the high country. *Spiraea densiflora,* called by Hitchcock "subalpine spirea," thrives in open sunny but wet places in the meadows of the West's higher mountains. It has the general habit of *S. betulifolia,* both in low stature and in its flat-topped flower clusters. But the flowers are a shocking dark pink to purple. A large patch of subalpine spirea is a dazzling sight. It has been cultivated successfully, especially as a rock garden plant in a fairly moist spot.

Propagation. Spireas grow easily from seeds or cuttings. Since all our natives grow from creeping underground stems, offshoots of these can be readily established in the garden.

Snowberries (species of *Symphoricarpos*). Honeysuckle Family (Caprifoliaceae)

A common sight in winter is a low deciduous shrub covered with snowwhite balls. The leafless phase of snowberry is certainly the most conspicuous, as the fruits can last throughout that inhospitable season. There are four species of snowberry in the Northwest, adding snowberry charm and richness to a wide array of habitats from the seashore to the Rockies. Species of *Symphoricarpos* are much alike: many-branched, low twiggy shrubs with small opposite leaves, smallish flowers in honeysuckle-like pairs, and distinctive white fruits. The search for wild garden introductions of snowberry need not take the gardener far afield. Forest, shrub thicket, and open slopes from sea level to the mid-montane on either side of the Cascades support snowberries of one species or another. And beside its value as an ornamental, snowberry is yet another woodland garden plant that attracts wildlife, both for food and shelter.

Propagation. Snowberries start easily from suckers or offshoots; cuttings should also be tried. Seeds sown in the fall require warm stratification (80° F. for 90 to 120 days). Spring sowings need an additional cold stratification (41° F. for 4 to 6 months).

Hardhack *(Spiraea douglasii)*

Deciduous

Spiraea X pyramidata, a hybrid spirea in eastern Washington

Snowberry (*Symphoricarpos mollis* var. *hesperius*)

Deciduous huckleberries (species of *Vaccinium*). Heather Family (Ericaceae)

Besides the red huckleberry, described on page 115, there are several other native species of *Vaccinium* worthy of cultivation. In the mountainous westside country, two tall species (*V. alaskense* and *V. membranaceum)* are common in the conifer forest understory; and in the subalpine meadows, that dwarf delight, *Vaccinium deliciosum* grows. The grouseberry *(V. scoparium),* a low twiggy plant of dry coniferous forests on the east side, has yet to be successfully introduced into gardens. Its angular stems and low twiggy habit in winter remind one of a particularly attractive species of broom.

And for the bog garden there are the two cranberries: the native *(V. oxycoccus)* and the escaped cultivated cranberry *(V. macrocarpon).* Vacciniums are propagated by seeds, cuttings, and rooted suckers or offshoots.

High-bush Cranberries, Viburnums (species of *Viburnum*). Honeysuckle Family (Caprifoliaceae)

For a continent so rich in viburnums, it seems the Pacific Northwest was short-changed, with only three native here. While ours are not of outstanding quality, they are worthy of cultivation. One is of course the widespread commonly grown New and Old World species *Viburnum opulus* (snowball, high-bush cranberry, wild guelder rose). It reached our area as a native in northern Idaho and the Columbia River Gorge. *Viburnum edule* (moosewood viburnum, high-bush cranberry, or squashberry) is infrequent in moist woods and swamps on both sides of the Cascades. The third species, oval-leaved or Oregon viburnum *(V. ellipticum),* is found occasionally in thickets and open woods west of the Cascades. Any of them will take to the woodland garden with ease. Because of their attractive red fruits, dense clusters of white flowers, and pleasing foliage, any of these viburnums merit garden trial. They are best propagated from cuttings as germination of seeds can be difficult.

Chapter 4

Native
Ornamental
Herbaceous
Perennials

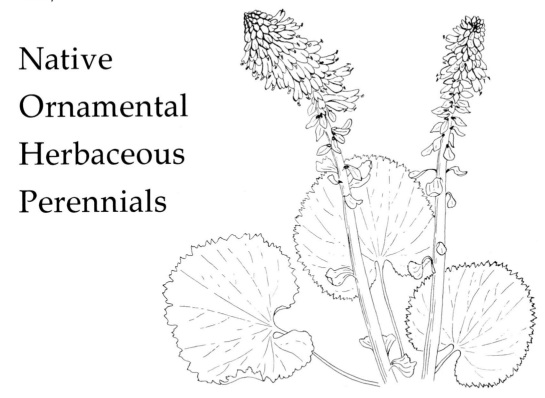

Mountain kittentails *(Synthyris missurica)*

Most wild places in the Pacific Northwest bear witness to a near universal design in nature—plants in groupings or communities. The design
of most plant communities uses the three dominant life-forms of plants:
trees, shrubs, and herbs. Whether it be dense or open forest, or the
park-like savannas of the oak prairies, or the tree-studded meadows
of the subalpine, nature nearly always displays a *stratified* pattern of
vegetation. The trees tend to form the dominating framework of the
grouping, with shrubs adding an eye-level tapestry under the tree layer.
And beneath the canopy of trees and shrubs, the observer at ground
level meets the rich texture and variety of herbaceous plants. It is no
wonder that cultivated gardens develop the same stratified composition
of trees, shrubs, and herbs. By intuition or perhaps by ancient birth-
right, a garden fashioned by humans is often patterned after nature.
Formal garden or woodland setting for wildlings—whatever the landscape objective—the gardening tradition assures that woody plants define the setting, and that the herbaceous plants shall embellish the
scene.

Far from being "frosting on the cake" in nature, herbaceous plants
are part of the well-being of the wild landscape: they hold the soil,
they add nutrients, they host insects and fungal pathogens, they serve
up food to wildlife. Though we may tend to use herbaceous perennials
as the final decoration in the garden, they should be used not as after-
thoughts, but as integral parts of the garden setting.

129

What are herbaceous perennials? Take away all trees and shrubs—woody plants of any sort—and the herbs are left. Then take away annuals—herbs that live but one year—and the herbaceous perennial is left. Often simply called perennials, they live year after year, annually sending forth new shoots from a bulb, taproot, or rhizome. And every fall, their above-ground growth of the year sinks back to the ground, compost for the next season. The term "herbaceous" means the stems and leaves are not woody or leathery but are of a more delicate and fleshy texture. The term "perennial" means existing for two or more years. Familiar garden examples are daffodils, primulas, violets, and columbines.

Herbaceous perennials can be catalogued in many ways. Our system will be the most familiar garden-oriented categories. First come the ferns, then the bulbs, orchids, and grass-like plants. This leaves a large miscellany comprised of mostly "dicots," the botanist's term for a vast clan of flowering plants like larkspur, columbine, anemone, strawberry, and cow parsnip, to pick a few herbaceous dicots at random. To deal with this unwieldly group, three size categories will be used: tall herbs (3 to 10 feet), herbs of medium stature (1 to 3 feet), and low herbs (1 foot and under). The account of each species (or genus) includes botanical and common names, form (habit) of plant, key recognition features, natural habitat, garden uses, and methods of propagation.

Use of Herbaceous Perennials from the Wild

Native perennials come in so many sizes, shapes, textures, and colors that their use can only be judged on the merits and qualities of a particular species. By meshing our view of the wild landscape with the aesthetics of gardening, however, a general function for the herbaceous perennial becomes apparent. In the garden, as in nature, perennials give the textural cohesion that holds the scene together. In a word, they embellish the basic garden defined by the trees and shrubs. And, the great variety of herbaceous perennials can enrich in-between garden spaces with unlimited possibilities.

Though each kind of perennial should be judged on its particular merits, there are some universals that dictate their use. Unlike trees or shrubs that often stand as single specimens when well placed, the perennial looks best when planted in multiples. There is nothing more distracting to the eye than trying to focus on a bed or rockery daubed with one of a kind, however placed, at random or in soldierly rows. Far more pleasing is the effect when generous drifts of a single species are used. Massed plantings are natural plantings, more so with herbaceous plants than with any other. Even three of a kind is better than the forlorn loner.

Propagation of Native Perennials

In general, herbaceous perennials are easier to propagate than woody plants. There are fewer setbacks with seed dormancy, hard seed coats, and other problems that often plague the propagator of woody plants. Scarification, stratification, and other pre-treatment of seeds are less often required. Two kinds of native perennials—ferns and orchids— do require special handling if grown from spores (ferns) or from seeds (orchids). Raising ferns from spores takes special techniques, but these are now within reach of the ambitious amateur. They are described in a recent article by Mareen Kruckeberg in *Pacific Search* (June 1976), in the *Fern Grower's Manual* by Hoshizaki, and in other gardening literature, listed in the bibliography. Briefly, fern spores can be sown on the surface of moist sterilized soil in glass-covered dishes under eighteen hours of artificial light per day. The first plantlets are tiny heart-shaped flecks of sex-cell-bearing green tissue (called gametophytes) that must reproduce sexually in the dish to become young fern plants. Then two to three months can elapse before the young fern plants (sporophytes) are ready to be separated. After six months to a year, they will be big enough to pot or set out . . . a long process, but rewarding.

For propagation of native orchids, the techniques are more demanding and less certain of results. While tropical orchids can be propagated from seeds on artificial media in flasks, the cool temperate species seem much less cooperative. Successes, using the standard orchid-grower's procedures, are meager with seeds of our native ground orchids. Vegetative propagation of these orchids is as yet the only solution. Since digging of native orchids is forbidden in some states and to be deplored in any case, must we give up the possibility of having them in the garden? For the commoner species, collecting in the wild can be done, if the procedures indicated earlier are followed. With the rarer lady's slipper orchids, it is better to leave them alone. Only when an area where they grow is in imminent danger of disturbance should the orchids be "rescued."

Native Ferns (Family Polypodiaceae)

Though we tend to think of ferns as moisture-loving woodlanders, they may grow in a variety of habitats. Some are rock ferns with considerable drought tolerance, like *Aspidotis densa, Cheilanthes gracillima,* and *Woodsia oregana.* Other species prefer cool and moist rock crevices or talus. Woodland ferns in the Pacific Northwest are both common and easily recognized as shade-tolerant, forest-dwelling species (sword fern, oak fern, deer fern, for example). Since our ferns have such diverse habitat preferences, it is best that they be dealt with one at a time.

Propagation of ferns by spores has already been discussed above. It is a rewarding enterprise, once the simple techniques are mastered and early successes are achieved. Propagation by division of clumps or of rhizome is easier and a much quicker way to get mature plants. Digging ferns in the wild, either for whole plants or to make divisions of clumps, must be done sparingly and with good judgment. It should

Ferns

Maidenhair fern *(Adiantum pedatum)*

Dwarf maidenhair *(Adiantum pedatum* var. *subpumilum)*

be possible to subdivide wild plants by carefully severing a piece of the underground stem and firming the remainder back into its spot. Wholesale collecting of ferns, even when common, absolutely must be discouraged. And taking whole plants of the rarer types like the aspleniums, some species of *Polystichum,* and the rare *Woodwardia fimbriata* can be condoned only when their habitat is threatened.

MAIDENHAIR FERN *(Adiantum pedatum).* Found in moist places (seeps, waterfalls, edges of streams) from sea level to mid-montane in wooded areas throughout the Pacific Northwest. It is a deciduous fern, 1 to 2 feet tall with five to seven fingerlike branchlets each bearing many wedge-shaped, toothed leaflets (pinnae); spore-bearing areas are on the margins of the pinnae. Maidenhair fern is a delicate, lovely plant for the garden, doing best at the edge of ponds, streams, or in boggy areas. It takes partial shade and a heavy-textured soil, and is a deciduous species.

The question of a proper varietal name for the fine dwarf of our native maidenhair fern has finally been settled. Fern expert, Dr. Warren H. Wagner, Jr., gives the name of var. *subpumilum* to this popular garden plant. It has gone under various names—Aleutian Island Form, Japanese Form, var. *minor,* 'Dyce's Dwarf', and forma *imbricans.* This dwarf variety is native of coastal rock cliffs of northwestern Vancouver Island.

Another form with imbricate pinnae, intermediate in size between var. *subpumilum* and the typical maidenhair fern, often occurs on serpentine soils in the Pacific Northwest. It is not known as yet if this should be called var. *aleuticum.*

SPLEENWORT *(Asplenium trichomanes).* Spleenwort grows in rock crevices and moist talus slopes in the lower to mid-montane forest belt and is infrequent throughout our area. It is a low, tufted fern (6 to 10 inches tall), with several delicate fronds (leaves) per clump. The fronds bear many small, toothed leaflets; the leaf "stem" (rachis) is black. In the garden, it does well in cool shaded places in the rockery, or an artificial crevice sets it off well. It is one of our best rock garden ferns, and a superb container plant.

ROCK BRAKE, POD-FERN, INDIAN'S DREAM *(Aspidotis densa).* This rock fern can be found in dry stony ground in many places in the Pacific Northwest, though rarely common. A favorite haunt is on serpentine soils from British Columbia to northern California. It is a densely tufted, low fern (4 to 6 inches high), with fronds broadly triangular in outline. Each frond is dissected into many linear leaflets (pinnules). On the wet side of the mountains this fern needs the protection of a rock overhang. When the crown is protected from winter sogginess and a cool root-run is provided, this evergreen fern excels as a rock garden subject. In Washington, it is best seen in the Wenatchee Mountains; in Oregon, look for it on serpentines southwest of Grants Pass (as at Rough and Ready State Park). In Hitchcock et al. (1969), the new name *Aspidotis densa* had not yet been decreed; it is listed there as *Cryptogramma densa,* just one of its many botanical synonyms. The origin and meaning of one of its common names, Indian's dream, is wholly obscure. But by whatever name, it is a charming plant, which should do well in the drier gardens of the east side, if given winter protection.

Spleenwort *(Asplenium trichomanes)*

Indian's dream *(Aspidotis densa)*

Ferns

Deer fern *(Blechnum spicant)*

LADY-FERN *(Athyrium filix-femina)*. This nearly cosmopolitan fern abounds in moist woods, wet meadows, and streambanks from sea level to well up in the mountains. In the most favored sites, lady-fern fronds may be 6 feet tall, spreading fan-shaped from a tuft of clustered leaf bases. Each frond in outline is tapered at tip and base, and the leaf is twice divided (doubly pinnate) with the ultimate leaflets coarsely toothed. This is a fine fern for the wetter parts of the wild garden. Its bright, yellow green herbage is at its best in mid-summer. Alas, it dies back completely in the winter, leaving a soggy mess at its crown, best composted soon after dying. Moreover, it is aggressive, coming easily from wild-sown spores. It can be used in the more un-tamed reaches of a garden, but with caution.

The high mountain lady-fern, alpine lady-fern *(Athyrium distentifolium)*, is rarely cultivated, but does merit more of a trial. It is a tidier, smaller version of its rank lowland sister.

DEER FERN *(Blechnum spicant)*. There is no more distinctive a woodland fern than the exquisite deer fern: a tall (1 to 3 feet) plant with several spreading leaves from a basal tuft. The fronds are of two types: a series of outer sterile fronds with broader, simple pinnae; these sur-round one or a few fertile (spore-bearing) fronds, equal in length to the vegetative fronds, but the simple pinnae much narrower and darker in color. Deer fern grows nearly everywhere in our moist conifer forests from sea level to mid-montane elevations. Of it, Hitchcock says: "[Deer fern is] a truly choice fern usable in many places in the garden, but so common as to have little appeal to most gardeners." Let not its commonness stand in the way of introducing it into the garden. Though it can be grown from spore, prudently collected young plants move handily. Sporelings are often found on banks of logging roads and other disturbed places in the woods, where they can be safely dug.

LACE FERN *(Cheilanthes gracillima)*. Our commoner species of *Cheilanthes* is one of a sizeable clan of temperate and sub-tropical dryland ferns. All are of a small stature. The native lace fern, widespread in the Pacific Northwest, is a rock crevice plant of mid-altitudes in all our mountains. The small, gray green fronds in a cushion-like rosette, have wiry "stems" (rachises) and deeply dissected pinnules. The effect is of a beautifully textured lacework. It deserves a choice, fairly dry spot in the rock garden. Propagation by spore is to be encouraged, since collection of wild-grown plants cannot be justified. Rarely does this slow-growing gem leave its inaccessible rock-crevice for a disturbed and more accessible habitat. Plants dug from a safe home in a crevice never come out with sufficient roots, in which case, the life of the transplanted victim is hardly assured. Collect only with restraint in areas destined to be destroyed.

Two other species, *Cheilanthes feei* and *C. lanosa*, are rare in the Pacific Northwest. They should be sought from sources where they are most common, or from dealers in spore-propagated ferns.

Lace fern *(Cheilanthes gracillima)* in rock garden

PARSLEY FERN *(Cryptogramma crispa)*. Perhaps our most common rock fern, parsley fern is a tufted, low plant, 6 to 9 inches tall, with both sterile and more stiffly erect fertile fronds. It grows on rocky talus under rather moist to dryish conditions. We fully support Hitchcock's recommendation of it as a garden plant: "Parsley fern is an ideal small fern for the garden, where it thrives in the rockery, under logs, or even on moist shaded banks. It is a lighter, somewhat more yellowish-green than most ferns and is arresting in its natural beauty" (1:69). Where plentiful, it might be collected with restraint, preferably in areas of previous disturbance. It can be grown from spore, as well.

Parsley fern *(Cryptogramma crispa)*

Ferns

BLADDER FERN *(Cystopteris fragilis)*. This is a delightful, deciduous rock fern, of easy culture in the garden. It likes moist to moderately dry sites in rock crevices in all our mountains. Its short, 4- to 12-inch-long fronds are deeply cut (two or three pinnate), giving it a delicate, lacy look. Readily grown from spores.

SHIELD FERN *(Dryopteris austriaca = D. expansa)*. Of the several shield ferns in the Northwest, *Dryopteris austriaca* is the most common. The fronds of this rather large (1 to 3 foot high) deciduous woodland fern has a broadly triangular outline. Each frond is a delicate lacework of finely dissected pinnae. The common shield fern is at home in our lowland forests; it takes to westside gardens well, thriving in partial shade. The other Northwest species listed in Hitchcock should be sought also as garden subjects. They all do well from spores; prudently dug small plants establish well.

OAK FERN *(Gymnocarpium dryopteris)*. This exquisite woodlander is smaller than most ferns of the forest, though it forms rampant patches beneath the forest canopy from lowlands to mid-montane habitats. The small (6 to 10 inch tall) delicate fronds, triangular in outline, are divided in threes; each member of the triad has deeply cut or compound pinnae. The underground stem spreads beneath the forest floor to create extensive colonies of this superb fern. It is this spreading habit that makes oak fern so amenable to transplanting into the garden. Small pieces dug in the wild can be easily established in shady garden spots.

CLIFF BRAKES *(Pellaea* species). Any of these rock-crevice ferns are miniature show pieces in a fern fancier's collection. All are small, wiry,

Oak fern *(Gymnocarpium dryopteris)*

Oak fern with rhododendron, in University of Washington Arboretum

tufted ferns with leathery fronds bearing simple to lobed, bluish green pinnae. Since they are arid land or high mountain plants they are best grown in dryish places in gritty soils. As all are rare in the Pacific Northwest, they should be obtained from plantsmen who raise them from spore. Three of our natives are representative of the group: *Pellaea breweri, P. bridgesii* and *P. glabella.*

GOLDBACK FERN *(Pityrogramma triangularis).* Choice but difficult, this fern tasks the patience of those who garden on the wet side of the mountains. Either find a dry spot under a rock overhang or keep it in a dryish alpine coolhouse over winter, if it is to survive. Gardeners in southwestern Oregon will fare better with this charming, yet challenging plant. It is a small evergreen rock fern with a triangular leaf and boldly dissected pinnae. The frond is dark green above and golden beneath (due to yellow powdery scales). It is infrequent in western Washington and Vancouver Island, becoming more common southward in Oregon and California.

LICORICE FERNS or POLYPODIES (*Polypodium* species). The three common species of polypody tend to have distinct habitats. First is the evergreen *Polypodium scouleri* that hugs the coastline from southern British Columbia south into California. Its bold, simple pinnate frond has a tough leathery texture. It seems to thrive on the salt spray just back of the sea. As Hitchcock says, it is both the most attractive and the most difficult to cultivate of our native polypodies.

Next is *Polypodium glycyrrhiza,* licorice fern, so faithful to the moss-covered bark of big-leaf maples, and on logs and stumps on the west side. Since it does occur on wet mossy banks and rocks, it can be

Licorice fern *(Polypodium glycyrrhiza)* growing from trunk of big-leaf maple

Licorice fern *(Polypodium hesperium)* in rock crevice

grown in similar garden settings. The simple pinnae of its fronds are pointed at the tip. Though it is the largest of the three native polypodies, the fronds are only 10 to 12 inches long, best displayed in their downward arching habit from the limb of a maple.

The third polypody, *P. hesperium,* takes a bit drier sites, mostly on rocks on both sides of the mountains. It has simple pinnae, rounded at the tip. A neat, low growing plant of fine form for the rock garden.

All these polypodies have the same general attributes: smallish fronds that are divided just once into right-angled pinnae with undivided and uncut margins. On fertile fronds, the underneath side of the pinnae are boldly and regularly dotted with yellowish oval clusters (sori) of spore cases, each devoid of a covering, or "indusium." The boldly dotted undersides of polypody leaves are the tell-tale sign of the genus.

Propagation. All three propagate rather well from spores; the short-creeping rhizome can be divided to make offshoots for the garden. The two deciduous species, *Polypodium glycyrrhiza* and *P. hesperium,* are easiest to grow.

SWORD FERNS and HOLLY FERNS *(Polystichum* species). Every one of our eight species of evergreen holly ferns gets high marks as a garden plant. First, attempt the large woodland types: the majestic sword fern *(Polystichum munitum),* with 3- to 5-feet-tall fronds, will be familiar to every westside gardener and woodland naturalist. It grows everywhere in the lowland conifer forests; especially luxuriant is its growth in hemlock-cedar forests. The massive clumps can produce up to a hundred of the long arching fronds, each with an artful symmetry of simple, toothed pinnae or leaflets. When not already growing

Sword fern *(Polystichum munitum)*

naturally in the suburban subdivision, the gardener can easily introduce sword fern, as it transplants well. It gives a look of lushness to the woodland garden and the rhododendron shrub bed. It looks best planted in groups or drifts. The so-called "sun" form (var. *imbricans*) of *Polystichum munitum* is now raised to the rank of species. It is a smaller, more compact version of its close kin, the sword fern. Some "sun" forms are simply stunted *P. munitum,* when growing on a road bank or logged area. But *P. imbricans* as a distinct species inherits its compact form. It prefers full sun and is especially happy in a rock wall or similar sunny spot.

The other woodlander, Anderson's sword fern *(Polystichum andersonii),* is rare in the Northwest, and for most gardeners this lovely fern will have to be sought at specialty, rare plant nurseries. Unlike our other holly ferns, it is doubly pinnate, each large leaflet once more divided. The ultimate pinnules have a serrate margin. Its most distinctive feature is the invariable occurrence of a bulblet on the upper surface of the frond near the tip, which can grow into a new plant when the old frond touches the ground. Single clumps may produce ten or fifteen fronds, each up to 3 feet tall. It is evergreen, as are all our holly and sword ferns. *Polystichum andersonii* and the common sword fern form a natural hybrid nicely intermediate in characters of the frond. It is a superb—but very rare—garden subject, as yet unnamed.

Next are the holly and sword ferns of smaller stature, all choice plants for the rock garden. The mountain holly fern, *Polystichum lonchitis,* is found on the three north temperate continents. In western North America it grows mostly at high elevations in shaded natural rockeries. It looks like a miniature sword fern, except that its toothed pinnae

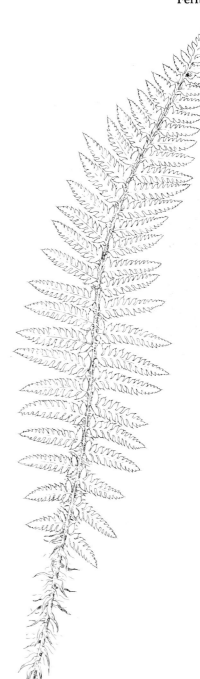

Anderson's Sword fern *(Polystichum andersonii)*

Elmera racemosa with Kruckeberg's sword fern *(Polystichum kruckebergii),* Olympic National Park

Ferns

Shasta fern *(Polystichum lemmonii)*, Wenatchee Mountains, Washington

are more all of one size. Lucky gardeners seem to get it to perform well, though it is not as easy to grow as our lowland ferns. A good place to see quantities of it is along the Perry Creek trail, in Snohomish County, Washington. This, the finest fernery in the state, is the home of many of our choice native ferns. The area is protected as a preserve by the U.S. Forest Service.

A close look-alike to holly fern is *P. kruckebergii,* found at widely scattered localities from British Columbia to Oregon and Idaho. Fern specialists believe that it is a stabilized (self-perpetuating) hybrid between *P. lonchitis* and *P. lemmonii.*

The rock sword fern, *Polystichum scopulinum,* has nearly bipinnate fronds, 12 to 18 inches long, with pinnae somewhat overlapping (imbricate) like shingles on a roof. It too is widespread in the Northwest, but never common. It grows in rocky places mostly at high elevations. Washingtonians see it frequently in the Wenatchee Mountains east of the Cascade Range.

The Shasta or serpentine fern, *Polystichum lemmonii* (or *Polystichum mohrioides* var. *lemmonii*) is absolutely faithful to ultrabasic rocks (serpentine and others high in magnesium). Every high montane serpentine area from northern California to the Canadian border is likely to support this charming dwarf sword fern. It can form great drifts bordering massive boulders and become tenacious tufts in rock crevices. Its 4- to 8-inch-long fronds are bipinnate and the neatly scalloped pinnules form a tightly overlapping pattern. It seems a smaller, more imbricate edition of *P. scopulinum.*

The four rock garden polystichums described here are special challenges to the gardener. Since they should not be collected in the wild, it is necessary to get plants grown from spores. A few rare plant nurseries carry them. The next challenge is to keep them alive and vigorous. Gritty soil with a cool, moist root run and reduced winter sogginess should give some assurance of success.

BEECH FERNS *(Thelypteris* species). Two of these ferns, *Thelypteris neva-*
densis and *T. limbosperma,* are close to *Dryopteris* and *Athyrium* in appearance
and woodland preference. The common beech fern, *T. phegopteris* is perhaps the best of the three natives and resembles oak fern, though a
bit larger and darker green. It is recognized by the downward-pointing
lowermost pair of pinnae.

WOODSIA *(Woodsia oregana, W. scopulina).* Both are densely tufted, low
rock ferns of deciduous habit. Despite their delicate, lacy bipinnate
fronds they grow in harsh dry environments mostly east of the Cascades. The short fronds (6 to 8 inches) have a finely scalloped tracery
and a lush look in late spring. But by late summer, they dry out to
tufts of fern "hay." This parched stage may lessen their garden value,
but when trimmed back after they dry, they are unobtrusive until
next season when they again emerge to grace a dryish spot in a rockery
or next to a log. *Woodsia oregana* has little or no hairs on the frond,
while *W. scopulina* is glandular hairy, at least on the underside of the
blade.

CHAIN FERN *(Woodwardia fimbriata).* This is a Hitchcock favorite among
our larger native ferns. Of it he says, "This is surely our choicest
large fern, its leathery leaves usually persisting in excellent condition
until the new fronds have uncoiled. It prefers moisture and some shade,
but will do well in full sunlight with only infrequent summer watering.
If grown in wet areas it often produces sporeling plants rather freely"
(1:98).

Chain fern forms large clumps with evergreen bipinnate fronds up
to 4 (even 6) feet long. From a distance, it can look like lady fern.
But a closer look reveals the leathery texture of the coarsely bipinnate
frond. The clusters of spore cases are distinctive: elongate patches next

Chain fern *(Woodwardia fimbriata)*

to the midrib of the pinnule. Though much more common in southern Oregon and California, chain fern can be found sporadically north of the Umpqua River of Oregon. In two or three known localities around Puget Sound, it grows on shaded vertical banks in dripping water, usually just above the salt water. It is best obtained from nurseries where it is frequently offered. It does well from spores.

Fern Allies (Ground Pine, *Lycopodium;* Little Club Moss, *Selaginella;* and Horse-tail, *Equisetum*)

GROUND PINE or CLUB MOSS *(Lycopodium clavatum, L. selago).* Family Lycopodiaceae. These large moss-like plants are often conspicuous ground covers in the woods from sea level to the subalpine. Though most decorative in their natural settings, they are difficult to grow well. Perhaps we should accept Hitchcock who says: "All the species are attractive ground covers, but rarely can successfully be transplanted into the garden, so should be left strictly alone in the wild." *Lycopodium clavatum* might be tried as cuttings or rooted segments in the propagating bed in a rich forest duff. It has been reported to do best when grown with living salal *(Gaultheria shallon). Lycopodium selago* can be grown from its tiny vegetative propagules (gemmae = scattered bulbils amongst the upper leaves).

Always select wild material intended for propagation with concern for preserving the wild population. Good conservation practice is essential with these uncommon and tempting plants.

The little club mosses (species of *Selaginella*) are easier than *Lycopodium* to bring into the garden. They are low cushion-forming herbs with needle- or scale-leaves; some grow on rocks *(Selaginella wallacei* and *S. densa)* while others grow on logs or tree trunks *(S. douglasii* and *S. oregana). Selaginella oregana* is the most conspicuous "moss" of the Olympic rain forests.

HORSETAILS and SCOURING RUSHES *(Equisetum hyemale, E. scirpoides).* Family Equisetaceae. Rest assured, we will not recommend the more pestiferous horsetails as garden plants. But certain of the evergreen scouring rushes have gained acceptance in the garden. *Equisetum hyemale,* the common scouring rush, is handsome against a layer of cobble rock or a cedar log, or as a container plant. *Equisetum scirpoides* is a dainty ground cover for wet places; it is a nothern species that barely gets into the Northwest, having been found only in the Okanagan Highlands of British Columbia and northeastern Washington.

Native Ground Orchids (Family Orchidaceae)

Native orchids of the Pacific Northwest are a far cry from the gaudy plants of the tropics. Some are downright insignificant and hardly claim the gardener's attention. Others are charming woodlanders and do tempt the plantsman to try them. But at this stage of our ignorance on ways to propagate them from seed, we had best heed Hitchcock:

> [Native orchids] should be left strictly alone in their native habitat in the hope that they will somehow be preserved for others to see and enjoy. Most of the showy species, but especially *Calypso* and species of *Cypripedium,* are becoming rare if not already obliterated in most areas. The person who cannot resist the temptation to move native orchids into his garden will surely regret his covetousness if he has a conscience, because they do not do well in cultivation, and will persist but a few seasons at best. [1:825]

Fortunately, botanists are working on the tricky business of seed propagation. When they come up with a proven recipe we will be prepared at least with a list of desirable species to grow *from seeds:* calypso or fairy slipper *(Calypso bulbosa)*, lady slipper (species of *Cypripedium,* especially *C. montanum* and *C. californicum*), helleborine *(Epipactis gigantea),* rattlesnake plantain *(Goodyera oblongifolia),* and rein-orchids (species of *Habenaria,* especially *H. dilatata* and *H. orbiculata*). For now though, orchid viewing—not collecting—in the woods must suffice, despite temptation.

Lilies and Irises (Families Liliaceae and Iridaceae), *and Their Kin*

These are all plants with parallel-veined leaves and flower parts in threes or multiples—the "monocots" of the botanist. Besides lilies and irises, the two monocot families include trilliums, wild onions, blue-eyed grasses, false Solomon's seal, bead lily, false hellebore, and several other Northwest delights. All are perennial, arising from a bulb, corm, tuber, or rhizome. For the garden, they fit nicely into two or three groups: plants for the woodland, the border, and the rock garden. First the woodlanders and border plants of the lily-iris families (*Liliaceae* and *Iridaceae*):

NATIVE LILIES (*Lilium* species). Five of the six native lilies* prefer woodland or moist open habitats. The most common, *Lilium columbianum* (tiger lily), ranges from near sea level to mid-montane on both sides of the Cascades. Its smallish flowers (for a lily) are orange and spotted red and hang bell-like in open clusters from 2- to 4-feet-tall leafy stems. The other species are less common. Lilac (or redwood) lily *(L. rubescens)* grows in woods from southwestern Oregon southward and has pink flowers. Western lily *(L. occidentale)* is found in sphagnum bogs of Curry County, Oregon; it has flowers tinged crimson and orange. The alpine lily, or small tiger lily *(L. parvum),* extends into Josephine and Jackson counties, Oregon, from California. Its flowers are orange to dark red, erect, and bell-shaped. Wiggins lily *(L. wigginsii)* extends

* See p. 154 for *Lilium bolanderi,* a dryland lily.

Tiger lily *(Lilium columbianum)*

from coastal Curry County east to Jackson County in Oregon and into the Siskiyou Mountains of California. The flowers are clear yellow and spotted purple. The leopard lily (*L. pardalinum*) ranges from southern Klamath County in wet places west to the Coast and south into California; flowers are orange, spotted maroon. A taller species, *L. washingtonianum*, gets north as far as the south slopes of Mount Adams in Washington and has large trumpet-shaped, fragrant flowers, nearly white with reddish dots. Other species in the Klamath–Siskiyou country and the North Coast counties of California deserve the gardener's attention. They are *L. vollmeri, L. kellyanum, L. maritimum,* and *L. kelloggii.*

Such a treasure of wild lily species and yet so few of them are grown in gardens! In days before an awareness of the need to preserve rare plants had surfaced, amateurs and nurserymen dug the bulbs, but no longer can that be condoned.

Propagation. Lilies can be grown from seeds, or garden-grown bulbs can be divided, or their bulb scales can be used for propagation, rather than digging bulbs in the wild. From seeds, it is a long wait, perhaps three to five years, but the grower has the satisfaction of knowing that the parent plant was left to perpetuate its kind in the wild. A standard garden cyclopedia can be consulted for details on propagation.

BEAD LILIES (*Clintonia uniflora, C. andrewsiana*). The two native bead lilies are so different that each must have its own praise. Queen's cup or bead lily (*Clintonia uniflora*) is an abundant and familiar ground lily of the lowland country and on up to mid-montane conifer forests, where it often carpets the forest floor. Two broad, tongue-shaped basal leaves form the rosette backdrop for a simple flower stalk (3 to 8 inches tall) bearing one large, pure white flower. The angelic bloom is replaced by an equally exquisite single berry-like fruit of amethystine hue.

The other native, red clintonia (*C. andrewsiana*), has four or five basal leaves and a taller inflorescence (12 to 18 inches high) with many deep rose purple flowers in a cluster. Its fruits are a steely blue. It is a glorious plant in flower and in fruit. Red clintonia is at home in the deep shade of coastal redwood forests, coming as far north as southwestern Curry County in Oregon (the coincident limit of the coast redwood).

Propagation. Both bead lilies are not too difficult to propagate. The quickest method is by root divisions taken in spring. Clintonias have fibrous rootstocks, not bulbs. As with most lily relatives, seed propagation is a slow process; though germination is quick, the maturation to flowering goes at a snail's pace. By the way, slugs are fond of clintonias. Whatever the obstacles, the bead lilies are well worth the patience and care needed to bring them to flower.

FAIRY BELL (*Disporum smithii*). This is one of three woodland genera (*Disporum, Streptopus,* and *Smilacina*) that have much the same growth form and habitat preferences. So similar are they, that botanists and

Queen's cup *(Clintonia uniflora)*

amateurs alike must pause for a discriminating look to tell them apart. All three genera produce several stem leaves that often clasp the branched stem; the leaves are prominently parallel-veined. Each differs mainly by position and number of flowers. Fairy bells produce either single flowers or from three to five in a cluster. The delicate bell-shaped flowers are flesh-colored and demurely pendant from the leaf axils (joints) at the ends of the leafy stem. The fruits of *Disporum* are salmon-red. Of the three Northwest natives, *Disporum smithii* has the largest flowers. Propagation is from root-cuttings or from seeds.

Lilies, Irises, and Kin

FALSE SOLOMON'S SEAL *(Smilacina racemosa, S. stellata).* Like the fairy bell, species of false Solomon's seal have ample leafy stems, but the latter are unbranched. *Smilacina* flowers come in profusion, small and white, clustered at the tips of the stems. The large false Solomon's seal *(Smilacina racemosa)* can get up to 3 feet tall, with one to several stems from its branched rhizome and a large number of cream-colored flowers in ample, branched inflorescences. It is a bold plant for wetter woodland or even partially open sites. *Smilacina stellata* is a smaller, more dainty plant, not over 10 inches high. Its unbranched, leafy stems bear terminal, few-flowered clusters of star-shaped white blossoms.

Both smilacinas can be grown from rhizome pieces with ease. Their best growth is achieved in open woodland, the tall *S. racemosa* as accent and the short *S. stellata* as a carpeter.

TWISTED-STALKS *(Streptopus* species). The leafy, often zig-zag stems of twisted-stalk are nearly indistinguishable from those of fairy bells *(Disporum).* But look for the key difference: *Streptopus* bears its axillary flowers one at a time at the base of each leaf. Characteristically the flower stalk (pedicel) is jointed, giving it an angled or twisted look. *Streptopus amplexifolius* is our largest species of native twisted-stalk, getting up to 2 feet tall, with an elegant symmetry of branching stem. The low-growing species *(S. roseus* and *S. streptopoides)* are tidy woodlanders suitable for groundcover effects. All are propagated by pieces of rhizome and from seeds.

Twisted stalk *(Streptopus amplexifolius)*

False Solomon's seal *(Smilacina racemosa)*

Lilies, Irises, and Kin

Fawn lily *(Erythronium oreganum)*

Glacier lily *(Erythronium montanum)*

FAWN LILIES, AVALANCHE LILIES, DOG'S TOOTH VIOLETS (*Erythronium* species). Like the true lilies (species of *Lilium*), the erythroniums come from deep-seated bulbs. And, like their lily relatives, the erythroniums are outstanding beauties. Though most of us know best by sight the great drifts of fawn lilies in our high mountain meadows, (*Erythronium montanum* and *E. grandiflorum*), it is the species of the lowland woods that take best to garden culture. These lowland erythroniums all have mottled basal leaves and tallish flower scapes bearing few to several large, open lily-like flowers. *Erythronium revolutum* and *E. oreganum* are the best of the clan and take well to moist, shaded parts of the garden. When these two self-sow themselves, they will increase to form delightful drifts of their lily-like splendor. The spectacular avalanche lilies of the high country will have to be left in their native haunts; they just do not acclimate well to the garden.

Propagation. The growable species, such as *E. revolutum* and *E. oreganum*, can be propagated by seeds; bulb-snatching in the wild is to be frowned upon. From seeds to bloom takes from three to six years; if impatient one can get bulbs from specialty nurseries. Sown in flats or pots in the fall, seeds usually germinate well. The containers should then be "plunged" in the soil of a shady place, patiently held there for four or five seasons until the bulbs get large enough to support a flowering. Erythroniums prefer a well-drained soil rich in leaf mold; the bulbs reach deeper and deeper into the ground as they get older.

The adventuresome gardener will want to try still other lowland species from seed: *Erythronium citrinum, E. hendersonii, E. howellii,* and lowland forms of *E. grandiflorum*. These less common forms occur in southwestern Oregon and in California.

There is scarcely a more bewitching sight in a woodland garden than the prim ranks of fawn lilies adrift in generous numbers—nodding bells, mottled leaves, and superb color make for a breath-taking picture.

SLINK LILY, SLINK POD, FETID ADDER'S TONGUE *(Scoliopus hallii).* Such unbecoming names for this neat woodland lily seem hardly fetching lures to tempt the gardener. Though the flowers of *Scoliopus* do have a carrion-like odor (no doubt to attract their fly pollinators), our visual sense is utterly charmed by this dainty plant.

Species of *Scoliopus,* wholly restricted to woods in northern California and southern Oregon, are a blend of lily family features.

Distinguishing Features. The overall form and fibrous root system reminds one of the bead lily *(Clintonia uniflora),* while the broad basal leaves are purplish-mottled like some of our erythroniums. *Scoliopus* flowers combine some features of both *Erythronium* and *Fritillaria.* One to four leafless stalks each bear a single smallish flower with mottled and veined outer sepals, and the inner wiry petals overarch the center of the flower. After flowering, a most curious seed release mechanism is set in motion. The stalk bearing the capsule is erect when the flower is present; then the stalk begins bending to the ground. At maturity the capsule simply disintegrates by decay on the ground, releasing the seeds. Hence the name, *Scoliopus*—"crooked foot"—referring to the bent stalk. I first saw it to admire in the Hitchcock garden. Hitchcock himself extolls the adder's-tongue lily and gives even higher praise to the larger Californian species, *S. bigelovii.*

Propagation. Scoliopus is propagated by seed or by divisions of the short-rhizomatous root-stalk. Slugs adore the lovely foliage.

FALSE LILY-OF-THE-VALLEY *(Maianthemum dilatatum).* Some hesitancy should temper the introduction of this aggressive carpeter to the garden. Only when invasiveness is desired should *Maianthemum* be given a foothold. But in the right spot—a deserted wild corner in a woodsy setting, a shady bank, or a neglected stretch of ground—this glossy green ground cover is unexcelled.

Distinguishing Features. An erect stalk, 2 to 4 inches high, bears two broad heart-shaped leaves and a terminal spiky cluster of tiny white flowers. Since each stalk comes from an underground system of vigorous horizontal stems, a single plant can, in time, produce hundreds of above-ground triads—two leaves and one flower cluster. False lily-of-the-valley, so-called because it resembles *Convallaria majalis,* the "true" lily-of-the-valley, grows everywhere in moist woods and along streams from sea level to mid altitudes in the mountains. It can be found in favorable sites east to northern Idaho and central British Columbia.

The gardener will surely want to use it, but cautiously. And remember *where* you have planted it, for it will seem to have disappeared without a trace over winter. On its garden uses, Hitchcock shall have the last word: "An attractive addition to the wild garden that seems happiest when invading areas where it is not wanted."

False lily-of-the-valley *(Maianthemum dilatatum)*

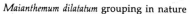

Maianthemum dilatatum grouping in nature

TRILLIUMS or WAKE ROBINS (*Trillium* species). The rites of spring are gloriously celebrated when trilliums come into bloom. Then the forest floor, where winter moisture has gathered, will be dotted with the unmistakable little flags of trillium: single stalks bearing three large leaves forming a three-cornered collar around a large single flower. The commonest trillium of the Northwest, *T. ovatum,* has sessile leaves and a large white flower that perches above the trio of ample leaves. It is also the most widespread of our four native species, thriving in moist woods from the sea coast to interior British Columbia and western Montana. Bizarre variants of *T. ovatum* continue to crop up. Plants with double flowers (with extra "petals" or tepals) as well as variant color forms occur in nature.

Propagation. Only when trilliums really need rescuing should they be transplanted. Indeed, trillium culture demands a generous pinch of the conservation ethic. Take from the wild only when the colony is doomed; better yet, propagate them from collected seed or by careful division, leaving a portion of the plant in place. We are reinforced in this admonition by sage words from Hitchcock:

Lilies, Irises, and Kin

Western wake-robin *(Trillium ovatum)*

The trilliums are rather easily grown, and *T. ovatum* in particular is an excellent addition to the native garden in the partial shade of such shrubs as rhododendrons, but it is a shame to dig them, especially since they grow readily from seeds. It has been said that the gathering of the flowering stem results in death of the plant, which is scarcely true, but it does rob the rhizome of stored food needed for the growth of the succeeding year's flowering stem, often resulting in failure to flower. If the admonition was invented to discourage picking of the flowers, the statement should be that the picker, not the picked, will die, but justice rarely is so obvious. [1:807]

A more diminutive trillium, *Trillium rivale,* is not at all common in southern Oregon (stream banks from southern Josephine and Curry counties to California). It is a charming little wake-robin with white flowers tinged rose carmine, often nodding in full flower.

The giant trillium *(T. chloropetalum)* lives in moist woods wholly west of the Cascades. Its three large, mottled leaves surround a single sessile flower with stiffly erect flower parts. Color varies from red through greenish yellow to white. An arresting sight it makes in the open woods.

The round-leaved trillium *(T. petiolatum)* from east of the Cascades is more of a curiosity than a trillium of charm. Its three large leaves are on long stalks (petioles), at the base of which nestles a rather gloomy maroon flower.

FALSE HELLEBORES, CORN LILIES (*Veratrum* species). Nature was generous with her pattern for lily-making when creating veratrums. Lilies they are in family resemblance, but the similarity stops there. False hellebores are surely the most distinctive of all the lily family in our region. All are stiffly erect, up to six feet or more, with great clasping, strongly ribbed leaves all the way to the crowning glory at the top. There, in place of tassels of corn pollen, are the hundreds of smallish flowers, green or white in loose clusters. A mountain meadow with a soldierly array of these great corn lilies is an unforgettable sight. Two species with white and somewhat congested flowers are rather common at low to mid elevations: *V. californicum* ranges from western Washington to California and east to Montana, while *V. insolitum* just gets into southwestern Oregon from the south. The pride of the open tree-studded meadows of the mountain hemlock–subalpine fir zone is *V. viride.* Its soft green flowers hang in graceful, pendant chains from the tall stalk. When successfully brought into the garden, false hellebores will live on for ages, increasing the stout underground rhizome (both poisonous and medicinal) to a massive storage and regenerative organ. Corn lilies like a heavy-textured moist soil and need full sun. But success with these proud giants of the lily family is still uncertain. According to the Royal Horticultural Society *Dictionary of Gardening,* they are easy to grow from seeds and from divisions of the root-stock. Our native westerners seem more intractible than other false hellebores, but certainly they are worth the try.

BEAR GRASS, INDIAN BASKET GRASS *(Xerophyllum tenax).* When great clumps of "grass" leaves come to harbor in their midst a tall, bold wand of white flowers, our sensibilities are jolted. No grass at all is this lily with the grass-like leaves. Bear grass is fastidious of habitat, preferring open, dryish woods; yet it ranges across 3,000 feet of elevation from near sea level to subalpine forests on Mount Rainier. Eastward, it extends to British Columbia and Montana, and south, to northern California. Though it likes best the meadowy openings in conifer forest, it is shy of flowering here. But let fire sweep through a stand and the next year every grassy clump bears its 1- to-3-foot-tall mace of white flowers. After flowering, the leafy tuft supporting the flower stalk dies, but young offset clumps will have already formed to replace the old. The offsets can be used for propagation; seeds are a much slower source of new plants. Well-drained, partially open slopes in the garden suit bear grass best.

SKUNK CABBAGE *(Lysichitum americanum).* Calla lily Family (Araceae). Though boggy areas in the garden may seem vexing problem spots, they can be turned into places of living beauty. The great lady of English gardening, Gertrude Jekyll, once told a friend burdened with boggy ground: "Go down on your knees and thank God for the bog." And, of course, no native is more suited to the garden bog than our amazing skunk cabbage. A pity it is that such a repugnant name is fixed to this grandly handsome perennial. Its beauty first comes in "flower"—that bizarre fabrication of brilliant yellow "wrapper" around a club of male and female flowerlets. Following its March flowering to October's seasonal demise, a great leafiness dominates. The skunk "cabbage" leaf is neither particularly offensive in odor, nor is it fit for the kitchen. But such magnificent leafiness cannot be overlooked.

Lilies, Irises, and Kin

Bear grass *(Xerophyllum tenax)*

Skunk cabbage *(Lysichitum americanum)*

Tapertip onion *(Allium acuminatum)*

A set of 2- to 3-foot-long "paddles" form the summer rosette around the spent flower stalk, now well into seed-making on the elongate axis (spadix). The large underground stem can be divided to make transplants; seeds should be tried as well, as they are reputed to germinate easily.

Lily and Iris Kin for Rock Gardens and Border Plantings

Several genera in the lily family make their home in open meadows, rocky slopes, or on shifting talus. All have deep-seated bulbs and simple, usually basal, strap-shaped leaves. All but camas *(Camassia)* like sharp drainage, and most are happiest in open, sunny habitats. Collection of bulbs has been the usual mode of bringing plants into cultivation. For rarer kinds, this thoughtless harvesting must cease. Though it takes more time, plants come easily from seeds. We will take up the rock garden types genus by genus in alphabetical order.

WILD ONIONS (*Allium* species). The more than thirty species of wild onions in the Pacific Northwest hang together botanically around two or three features held in common: (1) all have an onion—or garlic-like—odor from the thin strap-shaped or grass-like leaves; (2) all have bulbs, usually with the same odor; (3) flowers are held in clusters called umbels, much like the inflorescences of carrot, parsley, and their kin. But once getting to know the general *Allium* habit, the task of putting a name to a particular kind of wild onion becomes exasperating.

Distinguishing Features. Species of *Allium* are distinguished by technical features of flower, foliage, and, not least, by bulb. A true test of perseverance and keen observation—with a bit of luck thrown in—is to be able to distinguish the reticulations of the bulb scales (the tiny cross-hatched pattern of cells), which are the "fingerprint" unique to a species.

Garden Uses. Northwest alliums are either wet meadows plants or dry habitat species. The former group should be cultivated in moist but sunny borders. The best of this group are: *A. cernuum* (nodding onion, common along the coastal bluffs), *A. douglasii* (common in winter-wet soils of the Columbia Plateau), *A. madidum* (swamp onion of the wet meadows along our eastern borders), and *A. validum* (Pacific onion, a tasty onion of swampy mountain meadows). Most of these have tallish scapes, surpassing the leaves. Their flowers are lavender or white.

The wild onions from dryish habitats are best suited for more arid sites in a rockery. Many produce long strap-shaped leaves that may sprawl and twist over the ground, several times longer than the short flowering stalks. Of the many dryland onions to choose from, here is a tempting sample: *Allium acuminatum* (tapertip onion, widespread on dry hills and flats mainly east of the Cascades, but also in drier places around Puget Sound; flowers pink to rose-purple); *A. crenulatum* (scalloped onion, on exposed ridges and summits in the mountains); *A. robinsonii* (on benches and flats along the Columbia River; flowers white to pale pink with pink stripes); *A. falcifolium* (sickle-leaf onion, on serpentine outcrops in southwestern Oregon; flowers deep rose purple); and *A. macrum* (rock onion, nowhere common but widespread on sterile stony soils east of the Cascades).

Propagation. Wild onions set seeds plentifully and are easy to germinate, using a gritty mixture (sand and loam). After germination it is best to plunge the deep seed pans on a safe site. The bulbs can then be thinned two or three years later. Avoid digging bulbs in the wild, unless the collecting site is obviously disturbed or doomed.

BRODIAEAS, BLUE DICKS (*Brodiaea* species). Though much like wild onions, brodiaeas do not have the onion- or garlic-like odor in any of their parts. Usually *Brodiaea* flowers are larger than those of *Allium* and tend to be few per umbel. Most of our Northwest brodiaeas choose habitats where their tall and wiry flowering scapes can be supported by other tall herbs, especially grasses, or by the branches of shrubs. For this reason, the taller species in the garden will flop about when planted free of surrounding plants. Given some fellow plant to lean on, however, the showy flowers make a pleasing sight emerging from the foliage of a dry shrub border or braced against other plants in a perennial bed. (See color section.)

Hitchcock lists 7 species, and Peck 16, the greater number for Oregon is a symptom of brodiaea's affinity for California where there are 29 species. Several Pacific Northwest brodiaeas occur on the west side of the Cascades, mostly in grassy, dryish prairies and on open headlands near the coast. The best of these are *Brodiaea coronaria* (flowers violet purple), *B. elegans* (flowers violet purple), and *B. hendersonii* (flowers yellowish, tinged purple). Of the southern Oregon brodiaeas, *B. ida-maia*, the fire-cracker brodiaea, is the most remarkable. Its tight clusters of tubular flowers, fire-engine red, are on the ends of long leafless scapes that poke through the protective twiggery of chaparral shrubs.

Propagation. Brodiaeas, like onions, should be started from seeds or as nursery-grown bulbs.

MARIPOSA or SEGO LILIES (*Calochortus* species). *Distinguishing Features.* The flowers of mariposa lilies are some of nature's most exotic productions. From a deep-seated bulb issues forth a flower scape with two or three broadly strap-shaped leaves, all supporting the crowning achievement: from one to three large flowers, each with three broadly wedged-shaped petals. The outer half of the petals may be white, pink, or yellow, but the basal inner portion is a riot of intricate design— the highly ornamented glands.

The gland is a broad, arc-shaped zone of contrasting color, tessellated glands, and a texture of hairs. Look inside the cup of a mariposa lily and see a microcosm of design and color. And often within the gland, an animated scene: a small army of insects (usually tiny beetles) that suggests the purpose of the rococco design.

Garden Uses. Such rare beauty has tempted many a gardener. Bushels

Lilies, Irises, and Kin

Mariposa lily *(Calochortus uniflorus)*

of bulbs, dug with great expectations in the wild, have been transplanted to the rockery or perennial bed. But not a single species of mariposa lily has succeeded in cultivation. Hitchcock raises only guarded expectations: "Collected bulbs may survive for a few years in a raised bed or on a dry bank in full sun if kept completely dry from midsummer to late fall. Most species, however, propagate freely only from seeds, and it takes from three to five years of exacting care to produce a flowering bulb in this way." If we turn to British plantsmen whose past successes with demanding plants ever amaze us, we get not much more solace. Reginald Farrar, the patron saint of English rock gardening, offers little hope of success with them: "The race is vast and lovely, and apparently in nature fitted for every unpleasant diversity of soil, whether in bog-land [hardly that extreme], heavy and hard, or in the lightest of hot sands. None the less the utmost they will do in England (except in the gardens of the specially favoured) is to arise just once from their elaborate beds, wave at the world their painted waxen heads and delicate fringes, then go on to join the Onocyclus Irids in a better land."

Undoubtedly the most difficult ones are the taller mariposa lilies that thrive only in their naturally parched sagebrush "desert" country. They are best left there, or tried by the gardener who lives in similar demanding country. The garden carved out of Palouse prairie, scabland, or basalt rimrock east of the Cascades might just succeed with these intractable taller species by growing them from seeds.*

A bit more amenable to cultivation are the more dwarf species of the open woods and meadowlands from the Cascades and Siskiyou mountains westward. These are called star tulips or cat's ears (their hairy petals suggesting the whiskery fur of a cat's ear). The star tulip section of *Calochortus* includes *C. tolmiei* (and *C. purdyi*), *C. apiculatus, C. uniflorus,* and *C. eurycarpus,* all native of the Pacific Northwest. Culture of these from seed is much to be encouraged. Fresh seeds should be sown in the autumn of harvest in a mix of leaf mold, loam, and sand. Seed pans (clay pots of wide and rather shallow dimensions) should be plunged in the cold frame, covered to keep out excessive damp. Seedlings should be left to the end of the second year in the seed pans; then in the dormant period of the second year, the young bulbs can be removed and planted outdoors. Deep trough or pan culture may be the safest approach, or a dryish, protected spot in the rockery just may keep them alive.

One may properly ask, "Why bother with a race of such demanding prima donnas?" To be sure, most gardeners will not be tempted, after learning of the risk and painstaking care needed for their culture. But a few intrepid souls will want to try them—to those, we offer the best of luck. And great will be the reward in eventually flowering any one of these gems.

* Dr. Marion Ownbey, noted Washington botanist, had remarkable success in growing sego lilies, on an unwatered slope of heavy Palouse clay-loam.

CAMAS, INDIAN HYACINTHS (*Camassia* species). Scarcely any other perennial is so closely tied to the culture of native western Americans as the camas. It was one of the mainstay foods of the Plains Indians and a supplemental vegetable for coastal Indians. The commoner species, *Camassia quamash* is widespread on both sides of the Cascades, especially gregarious in areas of winter wet (meadows, swales, depressions in prairies, and on moist slopes).

Distinguishing Features. Camassia quamash has several daffodil-like leaves, surrounding a tall (1 or 2 foot) scape of lovely blue violet, wheel-shaped flowers. *Camassia leichtlinii,* the great camas, is a more robust species, best known in its yellow phase. It frequents grassy meadows and open slopes in the Umpqua Valley of Oregon. A purplish blue form of this same species ranges north from western Oregon to southern British Columbia. Another stout species, *Camassia cusickii,* occurs in the Blue and Wallowa mountains of northeastern Oregon, and has a bulb two or three times the size of the bulb in other species.

Garden Uses. Camas bulbs do well in the sunny perennial border or bulb garden or grown wild. Though they like their feet wet in winter and early spring, they need to dry out after flowering, much like most other native bulbs. They are far less fastidious than the species of *Calochortus* or *Lilium* and do best in heavy soils. Plants come easily from seeds and will flower in four years.

FRITILLARIES, CHECKER LILIES, CHOCOLATE LILIES, RATTLE-PODS (*Fritillaria* species). Bulb fanciers the world over worship at the feet of this captivating clan of lily-like plants. Species of Old World fritillaries have been grown in gardens for years, much as have species of tulips. Though only a small part of *Fritillaria* diversity is represented in the western United States, some of the best are here, mainly in California. In the Pacific Northwest province, we can count eight or nine species, several of superior garden quality.

Distinguishing Features. From a deep-seated bulb emerges one (rarely more than one) tallish stalk bearing both leaves and terminal flowers. In several species, the stem leaves are symmetrically whorled (three or more per node). The flowers are usually nodding and bell-shaped, largely maroon in a checkered pattern. One native, *Fritillaria pudica,* is clear yellow.

Garden Uses. The westside fritillaries are more amenable to garden culture, taking rather well to the sunny border or rock garden. *Fritillaria lanceolata* is the most common of these, a plant of prairies, oak woodlands, and grassy headlands on both sides of the Cascades in Washington and into northern Idaho; in Oregon it stays on the west side only. Though increasingly more abundant from British Columbia to Alaska, *F. camschatcensis* is known only from two localities in western Washington. The prize species, *Fritillaria pudica,* is not for westside gardens. This charming little yellow "tulip" is wholly an eastsider, at home in sagebrush and yellow-pine country. Gardeners in the cold dry side of the mountains will want to try this dainty bearer of yellow bells. Gardeners

Camas *(Camassia quamash)*

in southwestern Oregon have it nearby, growing wild in the Rogue River Valley. By studying its native haunts in the spring, the gardener can plan a strategy for its successful growth.

Other species of southern Oregon are largely found on sterile, stony ground or grassy openings in the woods, where they get baked in the summer. Watch for the following: *Fritillaria recurva, F. glauca,* and *F. atropurpurea* (also its ally *F. adamantina*).

Propagation. The collecting of bulbs can no longer be countenanced as fritillaries are fast disappearing from their native habitats. As with other bulbous plants, the patient approach with seeds is to be encouraged. Treat them in the same way as described for *Lilium* and *Erythronium.* Seed pans may show no seedlings for up to six months. On emerging, the seedlings send their tiny bulblets rapidly down to the bottom of the pot. Hold young plants until the dormant (fall) period of the second year before replanting. Fritillaries are best suited for dryish bulb beds or the rock garden.

BOLANDER'S LILY *(Lilium bolanderi).* This lily was omitted from the woodland listing for two reasons. First, it is such a remarkable and unique lily, with its amazing purplish red flowers, more funnel-form than the open bell-shaped corollas of most other lilies. And then it is not a woodland species at all. Native to southern Oregon and northern California, *Lilium bolanderi* grows in open stony ground, often on serpentine, poking up through manzanita, buckbrush, or other shrub species of brushy hillsides. A most unlikely habitat for a lily! Nowhere common, it is now succumbing to the ravages of rapacious bulb-snatching. It must no longer be dug. Nursery-grown bulbs from seed, or do-it-yourself seed sowings are the only ethical ways to bring this prized lily into the garden.

DEATH CAMAS *(Zigadenus elegans, Z. venenosus).* There is a shy grace about these smaller, cream-colored versions of camas. The smallish flowers are borne in dense spiked clusters on single stalks, tethered at their base by daffodil-like basal leaves. Heed the common name well: death camas is poisonous to humans and livestock. The plants can be grown in sunny places in the rock garden where moisture does not gather. They are best planted in drifts for a showier effect.

Zigadenus elegans has the showiest flowers of the four or five species in our area. It prefers cool, moist openings in upper montane coniferous forests, while the other species are found on prairies, sagebrush plains, and rocky slopes. *Zigadenus venenosus* is the commonest species and is found on both sides of the Cascades; cream-yellow flower spikes dot the grassy openings in the San Juan Islands and the coastal prairies of the west side. Propagation is by seeds, although dividing larger plants or digging bulbs can be tolerated, where permissible.

IRISES, GRASS IRISES *(Iris* species). "The native irises are well known and highly prized rock garden to bog plants" (Hitchcock 1:817). Our

Death camas *(Zigadenus elegans)*

Northwest corner of the large world of *Iris* is blessed with some outstanding attractions. Indeed it is the West Coast that seems to have a monopoly on one whole section of the genus *Iris*, an alliance of about fifteen species called the "grass iris" (section Californicae).

Distinguishing Features. For the most part our native iris is a low-growing, tufted perennial, with narrow grass-like blades and showy flowers on thin, wand-like stems, usually not over 18 inches tall. The seven species of grass iris in the Northwest are restricted to west of the Cascades where they grow in a variety of habitats at low elevations. They may occur in open, dryish woods of yellow pine, oak, and Douglas fir. All are well worth cultivating and some garden forms are highly prized cultivars here and abroad. First, a sketch of several of the *Iris* species:

I. bracteata (Siskiyou iris). Flowers yellow, streaked with maroon, tube short. In shade of yellow-pine woods, from southern Josephine County, Oregon, to Del Norte County, California.

I. douglasiana. Leaves broader (¾-inch wide), flowers from cream to reddish purple. In woods and meadows near the coast from Coos County, Oregon, to southern California.

I. innominata (golden iris). Flowers deep golden yellow to clear yellow; also in purple. On sunny to partly shaded slopes in open mixed evergreen forest, from Josephine and Curry counties to northern Del Norte County.

I. tenax. Flowers lavender to dark purple (var. *gormanii* with pale yellow flowers); tube short and stout. In open sunny places (pastures, meadows, oak forest, and logged lands) from southwestern Washington through the Willamette, Umpqua, and Rogue River valleys, and inter-

Lilies, Irises, and Kin

Oregon iris *(Iris tenax)*

Iris innominata

mittent to northern California (var. *klamathensis*). The most common and certainly the most beautiful grass iris in the Northwest. At its northern limit in Washington, locally common around Napavine and Winlock in Lewis County.

I. tenuis. Flowers whitish with variable markings (purple venation, yellow or purplish blotching). A rare and local iris, known only from Clackamas County, Oregon, yet easy in dampish open woodland soils. This iris is now allied with *I. cristata* of the Evansia section; it is entirely deciduous.

Three other grass irises merit a place on the gardener's palette: *Iris chrysophylla* (cream yellow to nearly white), *I. tenuissima* (pale cream with darker veining), *I. purdyi* (cream yellow with lavender-tinged sepals), all grow wild in the border counties of southern Oregon and northwestern California.

From these basic species can be compounded an exotic array of floral types, all through hybridization and selection. Nature has taken a bold hand in the mixing of grass iris "blood." Nearly every bi-species combination has occurred in the wild and even some hybrid populations are the result of at least three species pooling their heredities.

The stimulus to interspecies crossing has been disturbance. Logging, farming, and roadbuilding have blurred the boundaries between habitats of the different species. And though this hybridity has confused the botanist, it has rewarded the gardener with new beauty. Iris specialists can count many named cultivars that have come from both natural crossing and the hand of the hybridizer.

Garden Uses. It is easy to duplicate the rather undemanding conditions needed for grass irises. Partial shade to full sun in well-drained loamy sand should make them happy. Although favored in the rock garden, they can be used in other garden niches: along borders, in drifts in grassy areas, and in the sunny edges of the woodland. Specialty plantsmen around the Northwest can supply a wide variety of the better-known types. And the persistent collector can enrich his garden with plants from the wild. Careful collections of small off-shoots taken in the fall and heeled-in in the propagation frame will give quick rewards. Seed harvesting in the fall, especially in known hybrid colonies, can yield a surprise catch of recombined progenies. Not all seedlings will be worth saving by the iris fancier, but the fun comes in picking out good variants.

Propagation. Seeds germinate with ease, and may give flower the second season.

Other Species. The species mentioned thus far are happiest when grown west of the Cascades. Perhaps with a winter protection of pine needles or other dry mulch, they can be kept in sheltered nooks of gardens in the more austere eastside country. But a "consolation-prize" species grows naturally east of the Cascades. *Iris missouriensis* (western iris) ranges widely in the arid sagebrush and yellow-pine country from British Columbia to California and east to the Dakotas. In such dry country it has claimed a niche that satisfies its demand for moisture, at least through flowering. Moist seeps, vernal pools, stream banks, lake borders, and all such wet sites are havens for this tall (1 to 2 feet) iris with pale to deep blue flowers, infrequently snowy white. Good color forms of this extensively rhizomatous species can be easily removed to the garden; small pieces of rhizome transplant safely. East-siders will want to watch for the best colors in the Palouse and scabland country of eastern Washington and adjacent Idaho. Botanists puzzle over the sporadic occurrence of *I. missouriensis* in the Puget Sound area (Whidbey Island and in San Juan County). How did these maritime outlier populations get this far west? It is known that 5,000 to 8,000 years ago the climate of western Washington was warmer and drier. A number of other species with requirements for more continental climates existed west of the Cascades then, some of them persisting to the present. Perhaps the isolated colonies of western iris in the islands are vestiges of that former period of warm dry climate. These westernmost colonies are fast disappearing as the island habitats succumb to development. They need protection—and where protected, must not be collected.

BLUE-EYED GRASSES, SISYRINCHIUMS (*Sisyrinchium* species). Neither grasses nor all blue-eyed, yet the common name "blue-eyed grass" persists to embrace a clan of dainty native relatives of the iris, nearly all desirable for the garden.

Distinguishing Features. Like irises, the grasslike leaves of *Sisyrinchium* are flattened parallel to the flowering stem; also like irises, the flower stalks of blue-eyed grasses bear one to several leafy bracts, the uppermost one arising just beneath the cluster of two to five smallish, regular flowers. Flowers of *Sisyrinchium,* unlike the more flamboyant ones of the iris, are rather dainty and are wholly symmetrical in floral structure. Their six "petals" (called tepals) are all alike and tipped with from one to three points. While the flowers of most species are blue to reddish purple, one has yellow flowers *(S. californicum).* All but *S. douglasii* find a moist situation to their liking. The best of our native blue-eyed grasses for the garden are:

Sisyrinchium bellum. Flowers dark blue with yellow eye. In coastal meadows, valley grasslands, oak woodlands, then east to sagebrush country in eastern Oregon; always near water. Willamette Valley south to California.

S. hitchcockii. Essentially a larger flowered edition of *S. bellum;* a beautiful plant, coexisting with *S. bellum* from Willamette Valley to Humboldt County, northern California.

S. douglasii. Flowers deep reddish purple to magenta (or rare forms of pink and even white flowers). Inhabits springtime-wet places in sagebrush, juniper–yellow-pine woodland, grassland, and oak savannahs; mostly east of the Cascades in Oregon and Washington. Colonies known from the drier rain-shadow country of the Olympic Peninsula on the San Juan and Gulf islands; likewise, in the drier interior valleys of southwestern Oregon (the Rogue–Umpqua–Klamath rivers country).

Blue-eyed grass *(Sisyrinchium bellum)*

An exquisite plant, so much at home in places of moisture in the early spring.

Propagation. Culture of sisyrinchiums is easy: offshoots of the short rhizome or tufted leaf rosette transplant well, and, once established, they seed themselves readily. All are suited for moister parts of a rock garden. Seed germination is dependably low (10 to 20 percent).

Other Herbaceous Perennials

Everywhere in the Pacific Northwest, wild landscapes are adorned with perennials that are neither grasses, lilies and their kin, orchids, nor irises. Botanists recognize these "others" as dicots: *dicotyledonous* plants with net-veined leaves and flower parts, not in threes or multiples of threes. Lupines, violets, potentillas, mustards, phloxes, penstemons, and daisies are some familiar examples of dicots. Many are of considerable ornamental value. So diverse in size, habitat, and other features is the great herbaceous dicot assemblage, that we must deal with them in more convenient groupings. Stature is a handy distinction and usually correlates well with habitat: (1) tall herbaceous plants, 3 to 10 feet high, are open, wet meadow or moist woodland species; (2) herbs of medium stature (1 to 3 feet) are woodland or open habitat species; (3) plants of low stature (1 foot or less) are usually good rock garden subjects, though a number may prefer garden sites similar to their forest floor habitats.

Tall Herbs (3 to 10 feet)

MONKSHOOD *(Aconitum columbianum).* Buttercup Family (Ranunculaceae). Spectacular in bloom and with foliage of elegantly dissected hairy leaves, monkshood urges its beauty upon us all over the mountainous Northwest. Its many brilliant purple, large, hooded flowers are displayed on tall, spike-like inflorescences. Aconite grows in moist glades in conifer forests and at the edge of water. It is common at mid-montane to subalpine elevations east of the Cascade crest to the Rockies. For the garden, give it a place in boggy areas, at water's edge or in other moist places. Partial to full sun, with its feet wet, suits it best. Collected seedlings or seeds sown soon after fall harvest are the best methods of propagation.

WESTERN ARALIA, SPIKENARD *(Aralia californica).* Ginseng Family (Araliaceae). This relative of devil's club may remind one more of goat's beard or cow parsnip. Generous-sized palmately divided leaves surmount a tall (1 to 2 meter) stalk of many tiny whitish flowers and dark purple fruits in globose clusters. Its succulence and great size, for an herbaceous perennial, suggest its affinity for moist, shady habitats. Western aralia is found near streams and seeps all through

California on up to southern Oregon. It has been a most effective and decorative plant for similar wettish habitats in Northwest gardens. Aralias come easily from seeds collected in late summer.

GOAT'S BEARD *(Aruncus sylvester).* Rose Family (Rosaceae). A graceful woodlander with ferny foliage and huge billowy plumes of tiny white flowers. Several erect stems with large compound leaves is its usual habit. The male plants are preferred as they bear showier flower clusters and do not seed themselves. Goat's beard is at home in moist woods and along streams, mostly west of the Cascades in Washington and Oregon, but it wanders east to British Columbia to the Selkirk Mountains. A lovely native for dampish openings in woods or near pools and streamside in larger gardens. Easy to grow from seeds and collected seedlings, its propagules may need to be culled after blooming to get the more desired male plants.

THISTLE *(Cirsium edule, C. foliosum).* Aster Family (Compositae). While some are rank, invasive, and pernicious, a few Northwest species of *Cirsium* are lovely with their graceful, nodding heads and exquisite foliage. A worthy entry for the moist garden is *Cirsium edule* (horse thistle, Indian thistle) with bold purple heads (aggregates of tiny flowers), a short-lived perennial from the Cascades, which ranges eastward to central British Columbia in Canada.

Several other species are native east of the Cascades in yellow-pine to bunch-grass prairies; they should be tried in eastside gardens. The stemless form of *C. foliosum* from east of the Cascades makes an exquisite pincushion rosette for the rock garden, but do avoid the weedy introductions like *C. arvense* (Canada thistle) and *C. vulgare.* Can be grown from seeds sown in spring or from collected seedlings. Some species may be monocarpic—dying after flowering, a demise that may wait until three or four years from seed.

CORYDALIS *(Corydalis* species). Bleeding-heart Family (Fumariaceae). Three of these graceful kin to bleeding heart *(Dicentra)* are tall, succulent perennials native to our area. All have stout stems and finely divided, gray green smooth leaves and bear large, open panicles of flowers, from white to rose lavender. Each prefers moist ground in conifer woods and can flower in reduced sunlight. The best of them, *Corydalis aquagelidae,* is much too rare for us to reveal its limited natural habitat in northern Oregon. It is to be hoped that plantsmen will learn to propagate it for the garden trade. *Corydalis aqua-gelidae* (coldwater corydalis) has the best foliage, finely dissected, and flowers of a deeper lavender hue; *C. scouleri* is rather frequent in deep moist forests west of the Cascades at low elevations from southern British Columbia to northern Oregon; *C. cusickii* (fitweed corydalis) is a hardier plant of moist woods in the Blue Mountains. Its flowers are white or purple-tinged. Propagation is by seeds.

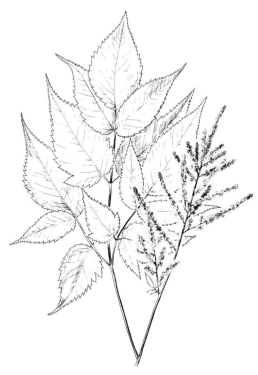

Goat's beard *(Aruncus sylvester)*

FIREWEED *(Epilobium angustifolium).* Evening Primrose Family (Onagraceae). For a fleeting two-week period in summer, the bold, rose violet to magenta pink color of fireweed in full bloom atones for all its robust, weedy character. Fields of fireweed in late summer come ablaze with glorious color all over the Northwest, and are especially common in recent burns and in other disturbed areas in the forest. And it can enliven even a drab vacant space in the city. But from one flowering season to the next there is not much to recommend the plant, though the young shoots have a lush attractiveness in spring. It is best that it be exiled to the wilder, self-perpetuating parts of the garden. Fastidious gardeners will want to cut it back to the ground just before it goes to seed. Pieces of underground stem transplant easily. Lest it be thought that we are recommending a rank wayside weed as a garden plant, one has only to recall seeing lush stands of fireweed everywhere in the more moist open meadows of the high country. Perhaps these montane native forms of lower stature (2 to 3 feet tall) should be sought for garden use.

Durand, in *Taming the Wildlings,* says of fireweed: "Not difficult to establish, and both useful and attractive in rather dry situations, provided it is placed where its color will not clash with that of other flowers." As a parting recommendation, do not forget that fireweed is a source of an excellent honey. A lovely non-invasive white form is in limited cultivation.

TALL or RUSH BUCKWHEAT *(Eriogonum elatum).* Buckwheat Family (Polygonaceae). The tallest of our wild buckwheat has, in bloom, the look of Queen Anne's lace or baby's breath, a fleecy cloud of tiny white puffs on a diffusely branched flower stalk. Fine rosy color forms occur in Snake River Canyon country. The large basal leaves are triangular to lance-shaped in outline. Tall buckwheat ranges down along the east flank of the Cascades from northern Washington to northern California. It grows best in open dry plains and hillsides with sagebrush, juniper, and yellow pine. Like most other buckwheats, *Eriogonum elatum* cannot abide the wet side of the mountains; but give it hot and dry wild-garden conditions and its robust nature and dainty flowering will generously charm. It is excellent as dry bouquet material, and grows from seeds or collected seedlings.

DEER'S TONGUE, GIANT FRASERA *(Frasera speciosa).* Gentian Family (Gentianaceae). These giant "gentians" are fairly common in open woods and wet meadows east of the Cascades. Their stately spires of greenish yellow, fringed flowers rise from a rosette of lush green, "deer's tongue"-shaped leaves. These tall, symmetric herbs are something less than perennials: the rosette may live for two to several years before it "bolts" to produce the elongate flower stalk. The whole plant then dies—another example of the monocarpic (one-fruiting) condition. It comes from seed with difficulty, but young plants can be established in moist wooded areas in the colder eastside gardens. It seems to do especially well in wet grassy meadows; it is the glory of summer-moist meadows in Jackson Hole, Wyoming. English rock garden sage Reginald Farrar is too hard on it: *"Frasera speciosa* lies in so calling itself [*speciosa* = showy]. For in reality it is an ugly thing, rather like a *Swertia* with greeny-white flowers. It comes from North America, loves shade, hates lime, and grows a yard high." Although it is certainly not a plant for the rock garden, its lovely candelabra-like grace is well suited for other settings.

COW PARSNIP *(Heracleum lanatum).* Parsley Family (Umbelliferae). Every feature of this wild spectacular is on the massive side: stout stems, huge compound leaves, and a great display of white to cream flowers in flat-topped umbels. Cow parsnip is widely distributed in the Northwest from sea level to montane, typically in moist sites (bogs, seeps, streamsides, or damp open meadows); in fact this single species represents the genus throughout North America. If your garden has been favored with a bog or other wet habitat, cow parsnip can add a bold splash of green and white to the scene. Its size demands ample space. It may not be very long-lived, however, and some botanists even list it as a biennial. It is grown from seeds, planted soon after harvest, or from carefully collected seedlings.

GLOBE MALLOW *(Iliamna rivularis, I. longisepala).* Mallow Family (Malvaceae). Globe mallow, a close relative of hollyhock and hibiscus, is a stout perennial of stiffly erect stems, several to a clump. Its largish leaves, though alternate, resemble those of many a maple. The lovely pinkish lavender to rose purple flowers are borne in erect terminal racemes. This attractive, robust perennial lives east of the Cascades, happiest in moister situations of the sagebrush and yellow-pine zones. *Iliamna rivularis* is the most widespread of the two globe mallows, ranging from British Columbia to Oregon and east to Colorado. It is rather common in the Methow Valley of Washington and makes a spectacular show around the Jackson Hole country of Wyoming. Globe mallows will be happiest in eastside gardens with full sun, but in not too dry a situation. Seed germination is low; seedlings are occasionally collectable. The two species differ only in minor details.

YELLOW-PINE COLTSFOOT *(Luina nardosmia).* Aster Family (Compositae). Conjure up a warm spring day in an open yellow-pine forest. Then, along with the delicious pineapple smell from the pines, expect to encounter the tall yellow daisy that we have named yellow-pine coltsfoot, standing in close ranks on the forest floor. In massed display or singly, this robust perennial has special charm. First are the elegantly cut basal leaves, nearly as big and as alike in shape as our commoner coltsfoot, *Petasites frigida.* From the cluster of basal leaves will grow a flower stalk that rapidly reaches 3 or more feet. From well above its leafy stem extends a beautiful, stalked cluster of large, orange yellow heads, each bearing only disc florets (like the central florets of a sun-

Tall Herbs

Sabin's lupine *(Lupinus sabinii)*

flower head). Given a rich forest soil in yellow-pine country on the east side, this bold native will give perennial delight to the native gardener. Best grown from seeds, but one must compete with beetles for viable seeds.

BIG-LEAF LUPINE *(Lupinus polyphyllus).* Pea Family (Leguminosae). It was from wild Northwest stocks of this species, in combination with our introduced tree lupine, *Lupinus arboreus,* that the famous 'Russel Lupines' were developed. But *L. polyphyllus* has garden virtues of its own. The tall, more succulent varieties are plants of moist, open meadows and coastal valleys at low elevations west of the Cascades. These taller forms are mostly glabrous (without hairs, except in var. *pallidipes*) and have stout, hollow (fistulose) stems and large, digitately divided leaves. The tall spikes bear large showy "lupine" flowers, blue to violet in hue. It is excellent for naturalizing in open, moist meadowy areas, or in the wildflower border. Seeds germinate well when steeped for twelve hours in water brought just to a boil. Some eastside lupines of tall stature, e.g., *L. leucophyllus* and *L. laxiflorus,* merit trial in drier garden sites; they are happiest east of winter wet. Roy Davidson of Bellevue and the Palouse, who has a keen eye for choice plants, feels that the Blue Mountain endemic, *L. sabinii,* must not be overlooked: "It is notable for low golden spikes from gray-leaved bushes—a David Douglas plant."

EVENING PRIMROSE *(Oenothera biennis, O. hookeri).* Evening Primrose Family (Onagraceae). The golden yellow, tall evening primroses, though rank in stature, are showy in flower. They seem perfectly happy in the most untended garden habitats, just so they get ample sun. These evening primroses (not at all related to "real" primroses) may act either as biennials or short-lived perennials. Both are natives widespread east of the Cascades. The introduced species, *O. erythrosepala,* with pale yellow flowers frequents disturbed areas near the coast from Washington to California, and may be used in the wild garden.

BLACK-EYED SUSAN *(Rudbeckia hirta).* Aster Family (Compositae). The charm of these rather coarse meadow perennials is in the unusual flower "heads." Each head consists of a central "pincushion" of reddish brown flowerlets (disk florets), which can be broadly or steeply (narrowly) conical. In *Rudbeckia hirta* the disk florets are surrounded by gay orange-colored, strap-shaped ray florets, not unlike some wild sunflowers.

Rudbeckia hirta has presumably been introduced to the Northwest from the central United States; it frequents disturbed places and open meadows. Our common native black-eyed Susan, *R. occidentalis,* lives near streams and in the woods mostly east of the Cascades. It has an elongate conical pincushion of disk florets, but no rays. These rudbeckias are for the wild garden or for other untamed places in suburbia—not choice, but deserving of a corner in our human environment. The related coneflower, *Ratibida columnaris,* has heads with yellow or purple rays and an elongate cylindrical spike of disk florets. It may be an escape in our area. Propagate from seeds or collected seedlings.

FIGWORTS *(Scrophularia californica, S. lanceolata)*. Snapdragon Family (Scrophulariaceae). These curious relatives of penstemon, snapdragon, and monkey flower are widespread in North America and Eurasia. They are lushly rank, tall herbs with square stems and openly branched systems of herbage and flowers. It is their flowers that claim the gardener's eye: small maroon goblets fringed with cleft petal tips. Produced in great profusion, the massed effect of the stubby flowerlets can be most attractive. *Scrophularia californica* ranges from British Columbia to Southern California in moist coastal habitats. A species of mountain meadows, *S. lanceolata,* occurs east of the Cascades. Moist sunny places in the wild garden will make either of these figworts happy. They can be cut to the ground before going to seed. Propagate by seeds or collected seedlings.

ARROWLEAF GROUNDSEL *(Senecio triangularis)*. Aster Family (Compositae). For those who like tall yellow daisies, *Senecio triangularis* will please. It grows in moist areas in woods up to nearly timberline (there, in moist meadows and along streams), and is a familiar, bright signpost to the hiker seeking water in our mountains. Several leafy stems clothed with narrowly triangular leaves, each stem leading up to a simple cluster of pure yellow flower heads. From seeds or collected plants the progeny are suited to a moist spot in the wild garden, with partial to full sun. Other tall senecios, especially for eastside gardens: *S. serra* (wet places), S. *integerrimus* (winter wet/summer dry), and *S. crassicaulis* (moist habitats).

GOLDENRODS *(Solidago* species). Aster Family (Compositae). To some, goldenrods are pesky, aggressive weeds, inflicting hayfever on the susceptible. But to others, notably English gardeners like Gertrude Jeckyl, these plumes of late summer gold are part of the harmony of an old-fashioned flower bed. Our larger ones do so often appear along water ditches, railroad tracks, and other waste places as to evoke disdain or rejection by the gardener. But look closer and marvel at the elegant symmetry of a flowering stalk of goldenrod. Hundreds of tiny flower heads on slender arching branchlets make a golden glow on into autumn. All the taller ones, like *S. canadensis, S. graminifolia,* and *S. occidentalis,* can be easily grown from pieces of the extensive rhizome system. Goldenrod also comes readily from seeds.

Medium-sized Herbs (1 to 3 feet)

VANILLA LEAF, SWEET-AFTER-DEATH *(Achlys triphylla)*. Barberry Family (Berberidaceae). No other perennial seems so much a part of the shaded understory in our lowland woods as vanilla leaf. On both sides of the Cascades from British Columbia to northern California,

Medium-sized Herbs

Vanilla leaf *(Achlys triphylla)*

the forest floor is sure to be carpeted with this herbaceous marvel of the barberry family. From a widely spreading underground stem, there emerges at close intervals a tuft of long-stalked leaves, cleft in threes, like a huge cloverleaf. From the same tuft arises the stiff slender flower-stalk bearing many tiny flowerlets in a spike, devoid of petals. It is the stamens and the dark purplish capsular fruit that display vanilla leaf fecundity. A peerless carpeter, a foot high, for the woodland garden. This, with lilies in a planting of rhododendrons can make an enchanting sight. Propagated from seed or collected rhizomes. The common names refer to the sweet smell of the dried herbage.

TRAILBLAZER, PATHFINDER, STICK-TIGHT *(Adenocaulon bicolor)*. Aster Family (Compositae). A stroll through a patch of this trailside herb will surely be remembered. The green foliage when overturned by the hiker shows its white felty underside to mark the trail; and, in fruit, the long sticky seeds attach to clothes and fur, remembrances of footfalls long past. *Adenocaulon* is a woodlander, but seems to prefer slight disturbance, such as alongside a trail or in a clearing. Trailblazer has large triangular leaves, green on the upperside and white beneath. Its tall flower stalk bears many scattered and small "heads," revealing its kinship with the aster family. It is an easy, cheery plant for the wilder parts of the open woodland garden, and grows readily from seeds or as seedlings transplanted from nature.

BANEBERRY *(Actaea rubra).* Buttercup Family (Ranunculaceae). This beauty packs danger in its exquisite, red fruits. How can one grow a plant in the garden with so blatant a capacity for poisoning the innocent? Up to six berries can cause severe symptoms of acute stomach cramps, vomiting, delirium, and circulatory failure. Yet, with the caution borne of knowledge, baneberry need not be excluded from the wild garden. The plant has from one to three large leaves just above the ground, each leaf divided by threes into broad ultimate segments with a serrate margin. The flowering stem, reaching beyond the leaves, produces a tight racemose cluster of smallish white flowers at its tip. The full glory of the plant comes in late summer when the fully elongated flower stalk bears the large red (or white) fruits. White-fruited plants can occur sporadically through the range of our common red-fruited baneberry. The plant thrives in moist woods and along water courses at moderate elevations from coast to coast. It comes easily from seeds. It makes a pleasing woodlander when interspersed with swordfern or shield fern. For the curious, its poisonous principle, a glycoside or essential oil, is most concentrated in roots and berries.

PEARLY EVERLASTING *(Anaphalis margaritacea).* Aster Family (Compositae). For dried bouquets or for persistent flowering in the garden, this is the best of our native "everlasting" plants. Each individual has many leafy stems up to 2 feet tall. The leaves are narrow and usually white woolly when young, though the leaf's upper surface greens with age. Beyond the leafy summit of the stem, unfurls a compact cluster of small dry "heads," aggregates of tiny yellowish flowerlets. Each head is shrouded with papery white bracts, with the tiny yellow flowerlets in the center. The papery bracts give the everlasting feature. Pearly everlasting grows nearly everywhere in open sunny sites from lowlands to the subalpine. It ranges right across North America and on into eastern Asia. So variable in character it is that one should seek the better forms for the garden. The compact variants from the high country are to be preferred over the rather coarse ones from lowland roadsides. It is easy to grow from pieces of the rhizome; seeds from female plants germinate without difficulty.

Pearly everlasting *(Anaphalis margaritacea)*

COLUMBINES *(Aquilegia* species). Buttercup Family (Ranunculaceae). The columbines of North America are the most elegant of a greatly admired group of perennials. Our most common Northwest species is the red *Aquilegia formosa,* living in open, rocky places, streamsides and mountain meadows, from British Columbia to California. Its nodding red flowers with short spurs (the five downward projecting nectar tubes) catch the eye of both man and beast—hummingbirds thrive on columbine nectar. A more alpine species with pale yellow flowers and longer spurs is *A. flavescens,* occurring in the northern Cascades to the Wenatchee Range of Washington, and then reappearing in the Wallowa Mountains of Oregon. Both species are superb garden plants

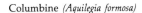

Columbine *(Aquilegia formosa)*

Medium-sized Herbs

Columbine in nature, Wenatchee Mountains, Washington

and thrive in sunny, moist sites. Columbines come well from seed. And when two or more species are mixed in the garden, a rich array of hybrid progeny can result.

Two other columbines, while just beyond the boundaries of our region, demand recognition as beautiful acquisitions for our gardens. The tall flamboyant blue *A. coerulea*, state flower of Colorado, reaches northward into the Rocky Mountains of western Montana and central Idaho. *Aquilegia jonesii*, the tantalizing, tiny rock columbine, is a limestone scree and crevice plant in Wyoming and Montana. Even from seeds it is a trying plant to keep, but it may persist with fastidious pan culture in the alpine cool house.

ARNICAS (*Arnica* species). Aster Family (Compositae). Though without a common name, arnicas abound all over the montane Northwest. These yellow "daisies" with opposite leaves take to the garden with ease. The better ones are *Arnica cordifolia*, *A. amplexicaulis*, and *A. chamissonis*. They look best in a sunny wild garden, intermixed with other perennials, much as in their wild habitats. They can be propagated from rhizomes or seeds. Besides the commoner arnicas, the Siskiyou *A. cernua* is an especially nice little woodlander. Most species of *Arnica* live in conifer woods: dryish habitats suit *A. cordifolia* and *A. cernua*, and moister places suit most of the others.

WORMWOODS (*Artemisia* species). Aster Family (Compositae). Besides the shrubby sagebrush, *Artemisia tridentata*, there are many herbaceous perennials of tall to low stature in the genus. Several of our natives have good gray foliage and decorative tassels of small "heads" with flowerlets. Those high plains or montane species with dissected leaves, like *A. frigida*, *A. norvegica*, and *A. trifurcata*, are tidy little plants for the rock garden. *Artemisia frigida* makes contorted natural "mingtrees" in the Snake River basalt. Propagation is from seeds or from pieces of the root crown.

ASTERS, DAISIES (*Aster* species). Aster Family (Compositae). Traditional cultivated asters like the Michaelmas daisy have been at home in the old-fashioned border garden for years. Some of our native asters can fill that same niche: *Aster foliaceus*, *A. ledophyllus*, *A. radulinus*, and doubtless other tall leafy species. Asters occur in nearly all habitats from seashore to sagebrush. The better ones for perennial border use are those of the open high meadows. Easy to start from seeds or pieces of the root crown.

BALSAMROOTS, DESERT SUNFLOWERS (*Balsamorhiza* species). Aster Family (Compositae). The rites of spring in sagebrush country are truly celebrated when fields of yellow appear. Spring's golden display in ponderosa pine and eastside plains is often dominated by the common balsamroot, *Balsamorhiza sagittata*. Bold triangular leaves of a stiff sandpapery texture, and several tallish (1 or 2 feet) scapes of big yellow sunflowers are perched on a thick taproot. The whole plant takes poorly to transplanting, thus seeds should be used. Other tall species of merit include *B. careyana, B. deltoidea,* and *B. macrophylla.* The westside gardener is usually defeated by the damp climate when attempting these desert sunflowers. But balsamroots are happily easy to establish in gardens on the dry east side. They will thrive in rocky pastures, winter wet but summer dry. No doubt westsiders with the right situation (dry gravelly soils with sharp drainage) could succeed with balsamroots, too. Indeed, though they are most common east of the mountains, some do grow wild on the west side in the drier Tacoma prairies, Whidbey Island, Sequim, and then in southwestern Oregon.

BOYKINIA *(Boykinia elata, B. major).* Saxifrage Family (Saxifragaceae). These tall relatives of the saxifrages do nicely in moist shady places in the wild garden. The two Northwest species are the smaller (12 to 18 inches) *Boykinia elata,* with small rounded and lobed leaves, and the stout *B. major* (up to 2½ feet), with coarsely toothed rounded leaves. Both have elongate, dense clusters of white flowers. Propagate from seeds.

BRICKELLIA *(Brickellia grandiflora).* Aster Family (Compositae). This is a tallish (1 to 2 feet) composite with broadly triangular leaves and copiously leafy, open clusters of cream-colored heads (all disc florets). It likes open rocky places east of the Cascade crest. A nice perennial for eastsiders with rocky open ground or for the wild garden. Propagate from seeds.

CLEMATIS, VASE FLOWER, SUGARBOWLS, LEATHER FLOWER, LION'S BEARD *(Clematis hirsutissima).* Buttercup Family (Ranunculaceae). Most *Clematis* species are woody vines. But of those that are herbaceous perennials, *C. hirsutissima* is an outstanding example. From tufts of large deeply dissected leaves emerge leafy 2-foot-high flower stalks, each bearing a single exquisite flower: a brownish purple nodding bell with recurved tips and a woolly exterior. In fruit, clusters of tiny feathery plumed achenes adorn the now erect peduncle. This lovely native graces meadows, sagebrush plains, and yellow-pine woodland in the cold, dry country on the east side. Gardeners on the wet side of the mountains will envy eastsiders who can grow this excellent plant. It comes well from *fresh* seeds, planted in the fall.

CALIFORNIA PITCHER-PLANT, COBRA PLANT *(Darlingtonia californica).* Pitcher-plant Family (Sarraceniaceae). One of the most curious and intriguing plants of our flora is this lone western member of the pitcher-plant family. Its leaves are marvellously converted into long insect-trapping tubes: the hooded tips of each leaf look like an alert cobra's head, with moustache. The 2-foot-tall flower stalk bears one large terminal flower, greenish yellow and nodding at maturity. *Darlingtonia* is rather widespread in coastal southwestern Oregon from Florence

Medium-sized Herbs

Boykinia *(Boykinia elata)*

Medium-sized Herbs

California pitcher plant *(Darlingtonia californica)*

Larkspur *(Delphinium glareosum)*

south to the Siskiyous and then on into northern California. It is faithful to bogs and moist seeps, the latter often on serpentine soils. Leland Stanford Stamper, a character in Ken Kesey's *Sometimes a Great Notion*, gives a delightful account of an encounter with this weird bog-lover.

So bizarre a plant is inevitably collected for trial in the garden. In fact, commercial extraction of *Darlingtonia* for sale as a curio plant has gone beyond propriety and good conservation practice. Bogs have been stripped of this slow-growing curiosity. Yet it cannot be made to persist at all well in cultivation. Wholesale collecting must be discouraged. Only when a *Darlingtonia* bog is destined to be destroyed, should one attempt to save the plants by digging transplants for the garden. Then, and only then, transplants may work, especially if the recipe in the Royal Horticultural Society Dictionary is followed: "*Darlingtonia* is hardy and will grow in a damp shady position in a compost of peat and chopped sphagnum with plenty of sharp sand and small pieces of limestone, or better still, charcoal, provided it is kept well supplied with water. . . . The plants are best potted when least active, usually in early July and repotting is needed every second year. The pots should be stood in saucers so that the soil never becomes dry, and the spaces between the pots filled with sphagnum." Preferred increase is by seeds, which are sown on a flat bed of moist sphagnum under glass. Bog conditions can be created outdoors by placing a plastic wading pool just below ground level. Darlingtonias have been known to succeed in such a contrived bog, growing in a wet, heavy-textured soil.

DELPHINIUMS or LARKSPURS (*Delphinium* species). Buttercup Family (Ranunculaceae). The delphiniums and larkspurs of old-fashioned gardens are robust things in their summer glory and are known to most gardeners. It is when we venture into species *Delphinium* from North America and Eurasia that a treasure of garden beauty is revealed.

All our delphiniums have dissected basal and stem leaves; the flower stalk bears few to many flowers in colors from red, purple, or lavender, to yellow. Each flower has a single spur projecting beneath the open petals. The spur is a nectar tube made of the upper pair of sepals and petals. The fruits are erect capsules with many small dark seeds. Note that the word "larkspur" is usually applied to the annual Old World species of *Delphinium;* all ours are perennials and thus take the common name, delphinium.

About twenty species of *Delphinium* are native to the Pacific Northwest, some of which (*D. multiplex, D. xantholeucum,* and *D. viridescens*) are very rare and local; they must not be collected. The taller species like *D. trolliifolium, D. burkei,* and *D. glaucum* grow in moist sites. The familiar dryland types are exemplified by *D. nuttallianum,* a widespread species of sagebrush plains and eastside mountain slopes and valleys. A choice low-growing species of mountain talus and scree is *D. glareosum,* found in the Olympics and in the Cascades from northern Washington to central Oregon.

The fibrous or tuber-like roots grow deep in the soil and seem most fragilely connected with the above-ground portions. Indeed, they seem to defy safe extraction for transplanting. Fresh seeds sown in fall for outdoor stratification should be tried.

BLEEDING HEARTS (*Dicentra* species). Fumitory Family (Fumariaceae). Three dicentras, all fine garden plants are native to the Pacific Northwest. Each has some slight variant form of the predictable *Dicentra* foliage—fleshy-textured, deeply cut, and smooth glaucous leaves, coupled with pendant, jewel-like flowers (deeply saccate or spurred petals). The most commonly grown bleeding heart, *D. formosa,* is a charming plant for moist shady places; it ranges from southern British Columbia to California, mostly on the west side of the Cascades. Besides the common form with pink to purple flowers, a good albino is often seen in gardens. The variety *oregona,* with intensely blue glaucous foliage and pale yellow flowers, is frequent on serpentine in southwestern Oregon and adjacent California. It and the typical *D. formosa* are easy to grow from seeds or collected plants.

Dicentra cucullaria, the Dutchman's breeches, although commoner in eastern and central North America, appears in the West as isolated populations in the Columbia River Gorge area and Saddle Mountain, east to Idaho. Its flowers are white to pink, tipped with yellow. A charming little alpine is *D. uniflora,* the steers head. Its pink flower is a miniature horned head of a steer. It is rather infrequent in the mountains all through the West and much the most difficult to grow.

FLEABANES, ERIGERONS (*Erigeron* species). Aster Family (Compositae). Ours are members of a vast genus of aster-like daisies, some of

Bleeding heart *(Dicentra formosa)*

Medium-sized Herbs

which are showy plants of middling stature—and of doubtful virtue as the bane of fleas. The best is surely the common *Erigeron peregrinus* of subalpine meadows. Its leafy scapes bear several heads, the largest of the genus, of deep lavender rays and yellow centers. It is rather easy to grow from seed or collected segments of the short rhizome. Given full sun in rich, somewhat damp soil, it should do well in both west- and eastside gardens. The low-growing erigerons are treated in the next section with low herbaceous perennials.

WILD GERANIUMS, CRANE'S BILL (*Geranium* species). Geranium Family (Geraniaceae). Wild geraniums are familiar plants of meadows and open forest, mainly east of the Cascades. The two common species have many coarsely dissected leaves in large clumps and 1- to 2-feet-tall leafy flower stalks with saucer-shaped flowers up to 1 inch across. *Geranium richardsonii* with white to pale pink flowers prefers moist, shady habitats, while *G. viscossisimum* thrives in the full sun of grassy meadows.

These are plants for the wild garden and should be tried on either side of the mountains. A better plant for westside gardens is the rather showy *G. oreganum*, growing west of the Cascades from southern Washington to northern California. All of the geraniums can be established from seeds.

WILD FORGET-ME-NOTS (*Hackelia* species). Borage or Forget-me-not Family (Boraginaceae). Forget-me-not flowers on tall wand-like stems are close relatives of *Myosotis*, the true 'Vergissmein Niss.' The chief distinction is the fruit, which in *Hackelia* is armed with intricate bristles, a gem to behold with the hand lens. The dozen or so species in the Northwest are all from east of the Cascade Crest. The montane species, *H. jessicae* and *H. floribunda*, grow in rocky open thickets, meadows, and swales, while most other species grow in drier sites—ponderosa pine forests, cliffs and talus slopes, and sagebrush-bunchgrass plains. All arise from a rosette of narrow leaves (on a deepseated taproot), and flower in open panicles of small mostly blue flowers with a yellow eye. With the rarest, *H. venusta*, *H. davisii*, and *H. arida*, enjoy looking but don't collect!

The common species of *Hackelia* are best grown in the more arid gardens, where winter moisture can be minimized. The eastside or Rogue–Umpqua gardeners should try these showy forget-me-nots, best from seeds or young collected plants.

ALUM ROOTS (*Heuchera* species). Saxifrage Family (Saxifragaceae). Though most heucheras are of a smaller stature and best suited to the rock garden, *H. micrantha* is a distinctive, large species, best for open forest glade or sunny wild garden. Its large basal rosettes have many long-stalked leaves of rounded and scalloped outline. The several tall (1 to 2 feet) flowering stems have many small white flowers in a diffuse, open display. *Heuchera micrantha* (and the closely allied *H. glabra*)

Alum root *(Heuchera micrantha)*

prefers moist rocky banks and swales all through the Northwest, from coastal to interior habitats. Propagate by seed or from cuttings (lateral rosettes) or collected plants—when common.

Medium-sized Herbs

WILD SWEET PEAS (*Lathyrus* species). Pea Family (Leguminosae). Several different sweet peas are native to the more montane or arid Pacific Northwest. The smaller ones are tufted, erect to sprawling, perennials, with several stems from a deep taproot. The pinnately compound leaves usually have climbing tendrils in place of the terminal leaflet. The pea flowers are in racemes and are usually bluish lavender to white. Wild sweet peas need a deep root-run in heavy-textured soil; since they succumb to winter wet, the eastside gardener will do better with most species. *Lathyrus rigidus* (white), *L. nevadensis* (variable from blue to purplish red), and *L. polyphyllus* (purplish red) are good subjects for the sunny wild garden. Propagation is best from seeds.

A few introduced species are attractive, but best used in neglected or disturbed sites as they can be rampant in growth. Of these naturalized foreigners look for *L. latifolius* (a coarse rhizomatous perennial with showy flowers) and *L. sylvestris* with red flowers. For coastal gardens, especially in sand dune areas, the native dune peas are showy, yet durable as they pin down the shifting landscape: *L. japonicus*, reddish purple to light blue, and *L. littoralis*, white, pink, or purple.

Wild sweet pea *(Lathyrus rigidus)*

WILD BLUE FLAX (*Linum perenne* var. *lewisii*). Flax Family (Linaceae). This showy perennial is widespread in prairie, open woodland, and rocky places east of the Cascades. One thinks of it as a natural companion of sagebrush, yellow pine, and bunch grass. The several, clustered, 1- to 2-foot-tall stems bear many grayish linear leaves. Each stalk produces only one or two flowers at a time, but a new batch comes on each day during the flowering season.

Wild blue flax is a charming, dependable plant for the sunny border and rockery. Low-growing races from high elevations make the best rock garden subjects. Easily grown from seeds.

STONESEED, GROMWELL, PUCCOON (*Lithospermum* species). Borage Family (Boraginaceae). Rather coarse, many-stemmed perennials of arid areas, our native lithospermums are best for naturalizing in the sunny wild garden. Each of the many leafy stems is coated with stiff hairs and is topped by clusters of yellow tubular flowers. Each flower matures four large, shiny white, and hard nutlets. *Lithospermum incisum* has showy bright yellow flowers early in the season; its later flowers are smaller but more fecund. *Lithospermum incisum* barely reaches our area in western Montana and southern British Columbia. The commoner species of the arid east side, *L. ruderale*, has smaller pale yellow flowers. This is the puccoon of Native Americans for whom its roots served as a source of a red dye. The seeds, hard though they are, germinate fairly well.

Stoneseed *(Lithospermum ruderale)*

Medium-sized Herbs

Silverback luina *(Luina hypoleuca)*

SILVERBACK LUINA *(Luina hypoleuca)*. Aster Family (Compositae). This distinctive composite has bicolor leaves, woolly white below (thus, "hypoleuca") and green above. The several leafy stems, up to 1½ feet tall, terminate in a tight cluster of cream yellow heads, with only disc florets. Though widespread throughout the Northwest, it is nowhere very common. Look for it in rock crevices and on talus slopes, from the Cascades west to the Olympics and Coast Ranges into California. It should be happy in the rock garden where it can have a cool, deep root-run and a warm, sunny soil surface. Grown from seeds or pieces of the branched woody base.

BOG BUCKBEAN *(Menyanthes trifoliata)*. Buckbean Family (Menyanthaceae). A curious plant of fresh-water lakes and bogs where it often grows in great drifts partly submerged. From a horizontal rhizome, emerge three to five large, three-parted (clover-like) leaves for each 1-foot-high flowering stalk. The several small whitish flowers are in an erect raceme. Each flower, like so many gentian relatives, has small, erect scales that cover the surface of the petal.

A near relative, *Nephrophyllidium crista-galli*, likes similar habitats, but is only common north of our range from British Columbia to Alaska. Deer cabbage has been found in a few isolated localities on the Olympic Peninsula. Its largish rounded leaves, reminiscent of some robust saxifrages are simple, not trilobed. *Nephrophyllidium* flowers have jagged crests, instead of scales on the petals. Both this plant and *Menyanthes* are suitable for the edge of ponds or in boggy places in the garden, though *Nephrophyllidium* is more attractive. Both are easily grown from pieces of rhizome.

BLUEBELLS (*Mertensia* species). Forget-me-not or Borage Family (Boraginaceae). A lovely race of perennials are the bluebells, of forget-me-not kinship. Almost all of our natives have clusters of elegant blue flowers, tubular and pendant. There are two rather distinct species groups in *Mertensia*, based on size range. Those less than a foot high, like *M. longiflora* and *M. oblongifolia*, are eastside plants of sagebrush plains and yellow-pine foothills. The taller ones, up to 3 feet—*M. bella*, *M. paniculata*, and *M. platyphylla*—are plants of moist thickets and streambanks in the Cascades and Coast Ranges. Of these, *M. paniculata* is the common bluebell of lush mountain meadows, so familiar a plant and habitat to hikers in the high country. The plants have four to many leafy stems from a thick root crown. The leaves are usually smooth and blue gray, ovate to long, and lance-shaped; the stems are leafy right up to the drooping clusters of the most lovely skyblue flowers.

The more dwarf species are eminently suitable for the rock garden. They are partial to full sun and need a deep root-run. The taller species are happiest in sunny but moist places in the wild garden. Mertensias are grown from seeds, although divisions of the woody root crown take root with fair success.

Monkey flower *(Mimulus guttatus)*

MONKEY FLOWERS (*Mimulus* species). Snapdragon or Figwort Family (Scrophulariaceae). Three tallish *Mimulus* species, all quite distinct from one another, are outstanding members of a genus whose flowers are said to wear the face of our simian brethren. *Mimulus cardinalis,* with great crimson, bugle-shaped flowers, grows in moist shady places in lowland southwestern Oregon and southward the full length of California and into the southwest. The broadly ovate and sticky leaves are opposite and clasping; each leafy flowering stem bears a succession of red "monkey flowers." A species with similar foliage and flower shape is the rose purple flowered *M. lewisii,* the glory of wet places in all our mountain meadows and high streamside places.

The common monkey flower, *M. guttatus,* has rounded, smooth leaves, usually coarsely dentate, and large yellow trumpets, often with spots on the petal lips. Although a coarsely succulent plant, its showy yellow flowers are redeeming. *Mimulus guttatus* is all over the West in wet ground: water ditches, swamps, stream banks, and wet cliffs.

All these tall monkey flowers put on a show in wet, sunny places in the wild garden. The tiny seeds germinate with ease.

WOODLAND PENSTEMON, WOODLAND BEARD-TONGUE *(Nothochelone nemorosa).* Snapdragon or Figwort Family (Scrophulariaceae). Formerly in the genus *Penstemon,* the distinctive attributes of this plant have warranted its attachment to *Nothochelone.* It is a robust perennial with several stems from a woody root crown and has broadly ovate, opposite leaves, coarsely toothed. The open inflorescence bears several large and fat tubular flowers of a rose purple hue. The woodland beard-tongue grows in the Cascades, Coast Ranges, and Olympic Mountains from rather low elevations to the upper montane. It is frequent in

Medium-sized Herbs

partially sunny glades in the woods, on lightly wooded talus slopes, cliffs, and rock ledges. It is a good, even-tempered penstemon for the wild garden and propagates well from seeds.

SWEET CICELY (*Osmorhiza* species). Parsley Family (Umbelliferae). Ferny foliage and attractive fruits make these wild parsleys desirable for the wild garden. Plants 1 to 3 feet tall have erect stems clothed with large leaves finely dissected into a beautiful lacework of green. The tall umbels bear tiny white flowers that each become the 1-inch-long, needle-like fruits. Cut stalks with ripe seeds make good dried bouquet material. Each of the many elongate fruits finally split lengthwise to be held dangling by wiry threads. Our two common species are *Osmorhiza chilensis* (woodlands at low elevations) with barbed fruits, and *O. occidentalis* (mountain meadows and thickets) with smooth fruits. Sweet cicely is not easy to start from seeds, and seedlings collected in nature may have to suffice.

WESTERN PEONY *(Paeonia brownii)*. Peony Family (Paeoniaceae). West-side gardeners may have to visit gardens on the arid east side to witness successful cultivation of this charming but difficult peony. Though not as glamorous as many Old World cultivated species, western peony has exceptional garden potential. Exquisite foliage—a steely blue gray leaf cut into many narrow segments—and a single large flower perched on a leafy stalk up to 2 feet tall. Its flower nearly defies description: the outer greenish sepals, faintly purple-tinged, surround five petals that Hitchcock valiantly describes as "brownish-reddish-purple." The petals form a shallow saucer around many yellow stamens. The mature fruits form a cluster of three to five erect capsules (follicles) that release large blackish purple seeds.

Paeonia brownii ranges throughout much of the arid Far West; look for it in open yellow-pine woods or sagebrush slopes, especially in deep lava-derived soils. Its natural habitat is the key to its garden needs: a dormant winter under snow, a spring of transient wet to give it bloom and fruit, and a hot summer to bake it into dormancy again. Eastside gardeners should try it from seed; though slow to flower from seeds, it is a surer way to bring it into the rock garden. Quoting Farrer, "It delights the west with the fragrance of its red blossoms and the leaves also are tipped with the same rich tone of scarlet." One can only surmise that it would not fare well in damp Britain.

Western peony *(Paeonia brownii)*

SHIELDLEAF, UMBRELLA PLANT, INDIAN RHUBARB *(Peltiphyllum peltatum)*. Saxifrage Family (Saxifragaceae). Of all our native water plants this marvel of nature deserves the highest praise of its regal beauty. Stately leaves, great plumes of flowers and ease of cultivation in springy bogs and stream sides—it has all any wet spot in the garden could deserve. Each big leaf is nearly round, with a toothed margin and centrally attached to an erect leaf stalk (petiole) up to a yard or so long, a form that easily evokes the common names for the plant. The stout fleshy flower stalks, leafless their full length, support a galaxy of white to deep pink flowers. Size is so variable in *Peltiphyllum* that it can be accommodated in either the tall or the medium-size categories.

Oregonians can discover this magnificent plant along many west Cascade streams from Benton County south to the California border and beyond. It has proved to be quite hardy further north: in Seattle, a fine planting made by Carl English at the Locks continues to fascinate visitors year after year. Pieces of rhizome establish readily, but the wait from seeds to flowering takes patience.

PENSTEMONS, BEARD-TONGUES (*Penstemon* species). Snapdragon or Figwort Family (Scrophulariaceae). Of the fifty or so species of penstemons in the Pacific Northwest, nearly all have garden value—and some few are superb. In the medium-size range, there is a multitude of treasured—and untried—species for the garden. These taller ones, though not suited to the rock garden are choice additions to the wild garden or border planting and for naturalizing in open ground. Since most of the taller ones are native east of the Cascades, gardeners who live with the cold-hot-cold and winter wet–summer dry terrain can have a great show of penstemon variety. Some of the best in the medium-size range of the *Penstemon* species are:

P. acuminatus. Large glaucous leaves and bright blue flowers
P. cyaneus. Bright blue flowers
P. laetus. Flowers deep blue-violet
P. lyallii. Flowers lavender
P. richardsonii. Sharply toothed leaves and flowers bright lavender
P. speciosus. Large smooth leaves and bright blue flowers
P. venustus. Serrate leaves and flowers bright lavender to purple violet

Though the above seven are best suited for eastside conditions, *P. serrulatus* of the western Cascade slopes takes well to the mild, damp winters of the wet side of the mountains.

This list just scratches the surface of suitable penstemons of medium stature. The woody-based *P. fruticosus* is dealt with in the shrub section. And gems of lower stature are placed in the next section with other rock garden species.

So vast and fascinating is penstemon lore for the garden that enthusiasts have formed the American Penstemon Society to learn more about these fascinating western plants. The members exchange ideas, seeds, and plants and make trips to penstemon country.

But what is a penstemon? Most are herbaceous perennials with leathery to fleshy, thick to thin, opposite leaves, usually from basal rosettes on branched root crowns. Leaves of the basal rosette are larger than the stem leaves and tightly clustered at the base of the stalk. Flowers are in congested to open arrays and range in size from ½ to 2 inches long. They project as horizontal trumpets from the floral stem. The five stamens (thus the name "penstemon") are really a 4-and-1 cluster: four fertile (pollen-bearing) stamens and one sterile (often bearded)

Penstemon *(Penstemon lyallii)*

Medium-sized Herbs

stamen. The showy tubular flowers with their horizontal display are visited by a great variety of insects and even by hummingbirds.

Culture is easy. Cuttings or pieces of the root crown and attached rosettes of leaves root well. Seeds germinate without difficulty, though seedlings are easy prey to damping-off. Some specialty nurseries carry a number of our native penstemons. But growing your own, especially ones not available, can be rewarding. In a gardener's world of many temptations, penstemons claim much deserved attention.

If they can be faulted at all, it is their shortlived disposition. As Farrer says, "Penstemons usually having but a lush constitution, prefer a crowded hour of glory rather than a long existence of mere usefulness."

COLTSFOOT (*Petasites* species). Aster Family (Compositae). "The great coltsfoots are only fitted for the remotest parts of the wildest bog or wilderness. . ." (Farrer 1930)—true, indeed, for some coltsfoots like the exotic *Petasites japonica* and our giant natives, *P. frigidus* and *P. sagittatus.* For sheer rampant growth, these are "bracken ferns" of the sunflower family. But wilder wet places in suburbia do need lush and bold plant cover, so why not the elephantine footprints of coltsfoot? Our westside native, *P. frigidus* var. *palmatus* covers wide swaths of wet banks and moist sunny openings in the lowlands everywhere. It has large lobed leaves, rounded in outline, 1 to 2 feet tall, from a fast-growing underground, repent stem. Before leaves emerge in spring, the first sign of coltsfoot is the nearly naked 1- to 2-foot-tall flowering scape, beset with whitish heads.

In wet places of northeastern Washington and adjacent northern Idaho and western Montana, *P. sagittatus* with large triangular leaves invites introduction into the bog garden. Arrowleaf coltsfoot is commoner to the Northeast, in Canada, and north to Alaska. One subalpine variety, *P. frigidus* var. *nivalis,* is scaled down to a modest size for wet places in smaller gardens.

A rare hybrid is found in the Swauk Creek drainages of Kittitas County, Washington. It is thought to be an ancient cross between *P. frigidus* and *P. sagittatus* when they coexisted in earlier interglacial times. The true coltsfoots of *Petasites* are close relatives of the yellow-pine coltsfoot, *Luina nardosmia* (p. 161). All are easy to start from pieces of rhizome. Seeds, found only on female plants, should be tried. All coltsfoots disappear from above ground over winter, but come back exuberantly in the spring.

PRIMROSES (*Primula* species). Primrose Family (Primulaceae). Of this vast north temperate clan, we count only three natives for the Pacific Northwest. Despite Hitchcock's terse warning: "Our species not satisfactory ornamental plants," *Primula parryi* should be grown along with its more tractable Asiatic relatives like *P. nivalis* and *P. japonica. Primula parryi* is a lush beauty of wet seeps and dripping rock from central Idaho all the way to Arizona in the intermountain and into the Rockies.

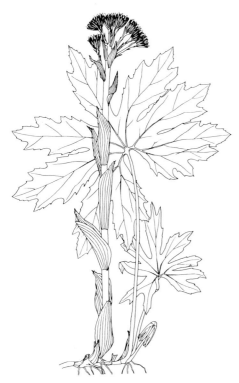

Coltsfoot *(Petasites frigidus var. palmatus)*

From robust rosettes of large coarse leaves emerge scapes of brilliant purple primula flowers, each with a yellow eye and tube. Getting it to grow well is the problem. Even when given a moist situation to match the natural habitat, good performance is not assured. Gardeners of the colder interior who have the happy combination of a wet place that congeals in the winter should have the best chance for success with this superlative primrose, which can be started from seeds.

The other two native species, *P. cusickiana* and *P. incana*, are rather insignificant little primulas easily surpassed by Eurasian types in garden value.

CHECKER-MALLOWS, SIDALCEAS (*Sidalcea* species). Mallow Family (Malvaceae). Farrer (1930) praises our western checker-mallows as suitable garden subjects: "These tall mallowy wands belong more rightly to the herbaceous border . . . all bushy handsome things of a yard or more in height, with lavish show of silky pink or white Mallows throughout the late summer." The Northwest is the heartland of these graceful border mallows. All have basal rosettes with long-stalked, scalloped leaves, rounded in outline; the leaves of the flowering stem are deeply dissected. The copiously flowered tips of the stem bear miniature (1 inch) hollyhock blooms. Several have been grown for years in gardens: *Sidalcea oregana* from sagebrush and grass meadows on the east side, with pink flowers; *S. hendersonii* on mud flats along the coast from British Columbia to California; and the many forms of *S. malvaeflora* from west-central Oregon to California. Easy to grow from seeds or pieces of the multiple crown.

CATCH-FLIES, CAMPIONS (*Silene* species). Pink Family (Caryophyllaceae). Though highest praise must be reserved for the low-growing silenes, some of the taller ones are good wild border plants. The *Silene* clan, represented by nearly 500 species on all north temperate continents, are herbs with opposite leaves and swollen nodes. *Silene* flowers have united sepals and separate petals, variously fringed or appendaged. Some taller native species for the border include *S. douglasii* (in dryish montane meadows and rocky places, with white flowers and non-sticky herbage), and those with sticky, "catch-fly" herbage, like *S. oregana* (pale pink flowers; on eastside ponderosa pine and sagebrush slopes), *S. parryi* (Cascades and Olympics in dampish subalpine meadows; white to pink flowers), and *S. scouleri* (meadowy bluffs along the coast; flowers pink to purple.) All grow rather easily from seeds.

WESTERN SOPHORA (*Sophora leachiana*). Pea Family (Leguminosae). This rare Oregon legume might be taken for a tallish *Astragalus* (locoweed). But a closer look at the flower discloses the distinctive feature of free (not united) stamens. The copious herbage of long, pinnately-compound leaves surrounds an erect spike-like cluster of yellowish pea flowers, followed by long thin pea pods. This unusual herbaceous kin of the woody sophoras is restricted to the canyon of the Rogue

Campion (*Silene scouleri* var. *scouleri*)

River around Galice. As it is a rarity, only seeds should be collected for propagation—and sparingly.

It makes an attractive, compact low and bushy perennial of silky foliage and pale yellow blooms. Perhaps its limited cultivation in gardens can help keep it from becoming extinct.

SWERTIA *(Swertia perennis)*. Gentian Family (Gentianaceae). A curious relative of the gentians, but looking for all the world like a silene, except for the telltale flowers with their gentian-like scales on the petals. The 1- to 2-foot-tall stems arise from rosettes of oval-pointed leaves; stem leaves are opposite. The erect somewhat congested flower clusters are composed of small pointed stars of a bluish purple to mottled purple-on-white pattern.

Certain species of similar foliage and flower are placed in the neighboring genus *Frasera* (along with the tall, succulent deer's tongue, *F. speciosa*, p. 160). The fraseras of lower stature are tufted perennials. *Frasera albicaulis* and *F. montana* are montane plants of drier habitats. *Swertia perennis* differs in having more congested flower clusters. Depending upon their preferred native haunts, the *Frasera–Swertia* group of species are suited for moist to dryish sunny sites in the wild garden, more adapted to the eastside garden. Grown from seeds or collected seedlings.

FRINGECUP *(Tellima grandiflora)*. Saxifrage Family (Saxifragaceae). This bold edition of a saxifrage is a welcome woodlander everywhere in lowland Northwest habitats. Since it frequents roadcuts and other disturbed places, it foretells a somewhat aggressive nature. It has round, coarsely toothed basal and stem leaves and one to several flower stalks up to 2 feet tall. Above the last stem leaf comes a procession of charming flowers, each a fringed jewel of pale cream color. It likes dampish open ground and is easy to naturalize.

MEADOW RUES (*Thalictrum* species). Buttercup Family (Ranunculaceae). Meadow rues accentuate the delicate element in plant texture. Even though they are sturdy perennials, meadow rue foliage and flower evoke a fragile ambience. The tufts of basal leaves are compounded of delicate leaflets remindful of maidenhair fern. The tips of the leafy flower stalks display further fragile grace, especially so in male plants which bear many small flowers with numerous maroon red stamens. Female flowers have hardly more than conspicuously red, seed-bearing pistils. Meadow rues delight in open woodland or semi-shaded border plantings. They go well with arnicas, sidalceas, and meadow asters. The turgid achenes (swollen single-seeded fruits) germinate well if planted soon after harvest. Pieces of rhizome transplant easily.

GOLDEN PEA, BUCKBEAN *(Thermopsis montana)*. Pea Family (Leguminosae). Easily mistaken for tall yellow lupines, this woodland pea has three-parted leaves with conspicuous petiolar stipules, while lupines

Youth-on-age *(Tolmiea menziesii)*

have digitately compound leaves and seldom have yellow flowers. (Stamen filaments are not united in *Thermopsis,* but are connate as a cylindrical collar in lupine flowers.)

Thermopsis montana is a montane meadow and open conifer woods legume, coastal to well inland (east of the Cascades) throughout our region. Hitchcock gives it deserved praise: *"Thermopsis montana* is easily grown and well deserving of a place in the wild garden, having excellent foliage and showy, attractive flowers. Although transplantable with difficulty, the plant is best propagated from seeds" (3:351).

YOUTH-ON-AGE, PIGGYBACK PLANT, THOUSAND MOTHERS
(Tolmiea menziesii). Saxifrage Family (Saxifragaceae). Those of us who know our Northwest woodland flora may smile at the houseplant craze that numbers this wildling among the favorites for indoors. Far from being a tender tropical, like coleus and begonia, youth-on-age is a saxifrage that grows wild in moist woods and streamsides in our coastal country from southern Alaska to central California. Its notoriety comes from the amazing capacity to produce plantlets at the juncture of petiole and the rotund, toothed leaf-blade. The several wand-like flower stalks produce modest flowers of an unusual chocolate color with bright yellow anthers. Its broad sepals contrast with the filamentous petals. It is the easiest of plants to naturalize in woodland gardens, either from seeds, leaf propagules, or from pieces of rootstalk. To further convince indoor gardeners of its native origins in the Northwest, both its botanical names commemorate prominent Northwest botanical explorers: John Tolmie, physician at Fort Vancouver, and Archibald Menzies, of the Vancouver Expedition.

FALSE BUGBANE *(Trautvetteria caroliniensis).* Buttercup Family (Ranunculaceae). Ignore the infelicitous name and behold the plant! A pretty woodlander should not be afflicted with such a repugnant common

Medium-sized Herbs

name. Though its affinity is with the buttercup family, it looks more like a small goat's beard *(Aruncus),* with large triangular, deeply lobed, and toothed basal leaves, and small cauline leaves to decorate a white foam of tiny petalless flowers. *Trautvetteria* grows in moist woods all across the continent and then reappears in Japan. The woodland garden will be a perfect home for it. Roy Davidson reports that it has been successful in a watered shade garden in the Palouse. It is grown from rhizome pieces or seeds.

SITKA VALERIAN, MOUNTAIN HELIOTROPE *(Valeriana sitchensis).* Valerian Family (Valerianaceae). This stately herb is a faithful landmark of our high mountain meadows. Conspicuous to dominant in lush, open parkland, Sitka valerian is a familiar trailside companion for the hiker. The rather coarse compound leaves may look like those of a potato plant and may have a somewhat unpleasant odor, but the best is above all that herbage. A graceful yet sturdy, 2- to 3-foot-tall flowering stalk bears many symmetrical clusters of small white tubular flowers of most redeeming odor. And in fruit, each flower is transformed into a tiny plumed parachute, perched for the flight of valerians yet to come. Worthy of a place in the moist and sunny wild garden, it can be grown from seeds or pieces of rhizome.

INSIDE-OUT FLOWERS, VANCOUVERIAS (*Vancouveria* species). Barberry Family (Berberidaceae). These remarkable herbaceous relatives of Oregon grape and barberry are perfect upright ground cover or carpeter plants in semi-shade. The three species are all restricted to the Northwest and have a common set of features: stems horizontal and underground (rhizomes); large erect basal leaves geometrically compound in two sets of triplets; and, above the exquisite basal leaves extends a flower stalk up to 12 inches tall, bearing an open paniculate array of yellow or white, inside-out flowers. "Inside-out" because the petals and sepals are reflexed (abruptly drawn back along the flower stalk, exposing the stamens and pistil). The lovely foliage of hexagonal segments and the dainty flowers have made this a garden favorite here and overseas. The genus is confined to our Northwest coastal region, from the Tacoma prairies in Washington to northern California. Its closest relative is *Epimedium,* a Eurasian genus of fine, tall woodland ground covers. The three species of *Vancouveria* are distinguished as follows:

V. hexandra. Large white flowers and dull green deciduous leaves; the most widespread of the three species, from western Washington to coastal northern California. A fine vigorous grower, best suited to ramp in shady open spaces between shrubs like rhododendrons, *Pachistima,* and salal.

V. chrysantha. Evergreen with dark glossy green leaves and dainty yellow inside-out flowers; occurs from southwestern Oregon and adjacent California. The best of the three by connoisseur standards.

V. planipetala. Evergreen with white flowers, smaller than those of

Inside-out flower *(Vancouveria hexandra)*

V. hexandra; occurs from southwestern Oregon to central California.

All vancouverias can be propagated from pieces of rhizome. Seeds must be sown soon after harvest.

MULE'S EARS (*Wyethia* species). Aster Family (Compositae). A rather coarse race of desert sunflowers that can be naturalized in neglected places where winter wet becomes baked clay in the summer. A bit more leafy than the balsam roots, the wyethias have nearly identical sunflower-like heads of yellow. Of the three Northwest species, *Wyethia helianthoides* from the eastern Cascades and mountains surrounding the Snake River basin, is the handsomest with white to cream ray florets. Propagate wyethias from seeds or segments of the rhizome.

Plants of Low Stature (less than 1 foot)

Plants of low stature have great appeal in the garden. Their native habitats rather closely define the kind of garden use for which they are best suited. A number of low-growing herbs are forest dwellers, happiest on the forest floor. In the garden, these will require shade, soils rich in humus, and moisture most of the time. Another group of the low herbs come from the talus, scree, and cliff habitats of the mountains, all the way to timberline and beyond. Suitable garden habitats for alpines include the rock garden, the alpine cool house, outdoor containers (troughs, wooden trays), and rock walls. A third natural habitat of low herbs is the arid country east of the Cascades, especially sagebrush plains, basalt rimrock, scablands, and coulees. These latter are perhaps the most fastidious herbs, requiring sharp drainage, dry soil surface, a hot dry summer, cold winters, and a brief wet spring. Plants of such rigorous habitats will take either painstaking manipulation of the garden habitat or the good fortune of growing in gardens in the right climates.

Our native flora has many plants of low stature that have made their way into gardens all over the world. Those low-growing species suitable for the rock garden have provided the greatest measure of gardening pleasure. Every book on rock gardening has paid high homage to the Northwest for its rich contribution to this genre of gardening.

In now taking up plants of low stature (1 foot or less), it will be necessary to qualify the attributes of each species, since each will have its own requirements of habitat.

ANEMONES, WINDFLOWERS, PASQUE FLOWERS (*Anemone* species). Buttercup Family (Ranunculaceae). Three rather distinct types of anemones decorate Northwest country. First, species of mountain pasque flower, or pulsatilla, are widely known in the Old World but are represented in the West by only *Anemone nuttallii* and *A. occidentalis.* Pasque flowers have deeply dissected leaves, large single flowers, and clusters of plumed fruits. *Anemone occidentalis* is the famous pasque flower of the high meadows in the Cascades, especially common on Mount

Western pasqueflower *(Anemone occidentalis)*

Small Herbs

Anemone *(Anemone drummondii)*

Rainier. The next group embraces the wind flowers of the mountains and high plain. They also have dissected leaves but the seeds are in cottony knobs tipping the flower scape. Typical of this group are *A. cylindrica, A. drummondii,* and *A. multifida.* Both the pasque flower and the wind flowers are rock garden subjects, showy in flower and picturesque in fruit. The third group comprises the woodland anemones. Three species of the Pacific Northwest typify these more delicate, shade-loving plants: *A. oregana, A piperi,* and *A. lyallii.* All are grown from seeds, sown soon after fall harvest.

EVERLASTINGS, PUSSY-TOES (*Antennaria* species). Aster Family (Compositae). Like pearly everlasting *(Anaphalis),* the antennarias have small "heads" of flowerlets, each head with a papery, everlasting quality. Many are alpines that form extensive ground-hugging mats of woolly white leaves and short erect tassels of everlasting heads. The better ones for the rock garden include *Antennaria alpina, A. microphylla,* and *A. parvifolia.* An everlasting for partial shade is the neat little woodlander, *A. racemosa,* with bicolor leaves (green above and woolly white below).

The most distinctive antennaria is the shrublet, *A. suffrutescens,* which makes a most attractive living bonsai subject. It is native to serpentine in southwestern Oregon and adjacent northwestern California. A number of carpeting antennarias are species of dryish meadows or sagebrush–bunchgrass plains. They should be most useful for edging the more arid wild garden or border, especially on the east side.

SANDWORTS (*Arenaria* species). Pink Family (Caryophyllaceae). The perennial arenarias tend to be mat- or cushion-forming plants with tiny needle-like leaves, much like our native phlox. Arenarias, however, are kin to the very different pink or carnation family; their other close relatives are chickweeds and catchflies. The common attributes are opposite needle leaves, swollen nodes, flowers in distinctive clusters called cymes, and floral parts in fives. The better cushion types in *Arenaria* are either high mountain or sagebrush plains species. *Arenaria obtusiloba* is an alpine, often on serpentine in the Wenatchee Mountains, whose long decumbent branches festoon barren talus slopes. More of the clump or cushion form are *A. capillaris, A. congesta,* and *A. franklinii.* All are easy plants for the rock garden: white flowers on short wiry stems and rosettes of short, pointed needle leaves. They start easily from seeds, or rooted offsets from the parent clump.

WILD GINGERS (*Asarum* species). Birthwort Family (Aristolochiaceae). Our native gingers must be ranked among the finest of woodland carpeters, as every one of their attributes proclaims high garden quality: lovely deep green leaves, large and heart-shaped and deliciously scented besides; then, the intriguing brownish purple, thimble-like flowers that nestle like little-tailed shrews hidden in the leafy rosette. Ginger spreads its loveliness by a robust system of spreading rhizomes. The most common species, *Asarum caudatum,* is a Cascades to Coast plant from British Columbia to California. Less frequently is it found east of the Cascades in northern Idaho and western Montana, but ever faithful to a comfortable habitat in moist shaded woods.

A particularly striking species of southwestern Oregon is *Asarum marmoratum (A. hartwegii),* its mottled leaves of an attractive delicately marbled pattern—green and gray. Unfortunately, this species is avidly sought by slugs. Both species are propagated from rhizome pieces or from seeds. Both are easily grown in moist shady garden nooks, banks, edges of rhododendron beds, and woodland glens.

LOCOWEEDS, RATTLE PODS, MILK VETCHES (*Astragalus* species). Pea Family (Leguminosae). Out of this vast and intricate swarm of legumes, the rock gardener can find a number of tempting items. Though many locoweeds are lank perennials, the persistent seeker of gems will discover prostrate types, cushion forms and low-growing ones with richly textured foliage and intriguing pods. Locoweeds all have pinnate leaves, pea flowers, and distinctive pods, often inflated, twisted, or curved. A sampler of desirable species includes *Astragalus kentrophyta* (prostrate, needle leaves, blue flowers), *A. agrestis, A. newberryi, A purshii,* and *A. whitneyi.*

A closely related genus, *Oxytropis,* is mostly high montane to alpine; they have a low tufted or caespitose habit, perfectly suited to rock gardens. *Oxytropis campestris* and *O. sericea* are typical of this group of stemless locoweeds. All must be grown from seeds.

KITTENTAILS *(Besseya* species). Figwort Family (Scrophulariaceae). All seven species of *Besseya* are restricted to North America, and six are wholly western. They are intriguing both for their unique features and their in-between status as relatives of both *Veronica* and *Synthyris* in the same family (Scrophulariaceae). *Besseya rubra,* frequent in open yellow-pine woods and dryish meadows east of the Cascades, has large, round to heart-shaped basal leaves and a spiky stalk of quite exceptional flowers. Unlike all other members of the family, flowers of *B. rubra* have only the rudiments of a corolla (petals). The colorful spike of flowers is a consequence of the hundreds of long stamens—two per flower—each tipped with a bright yellow ball of pollen. After blooming, the stalk further elongates and the capsules, like the fruits of the shepherd's purse, ripen. Plants come easily from seeds and do well in the rock garden. So close is *Besseya's* link to the woodland *Synthyris* (p. 214) that a natural hybrid is known: *B. rubra* X *Synthyris missurica,* which is sporadic in the Clearwater River drainage of central Idaho.

MARSH MARIGOLDS (*Caltha* species). Buttercup Family (Ranunculaceae). Marsh buttercups would be a better name for these swamp-

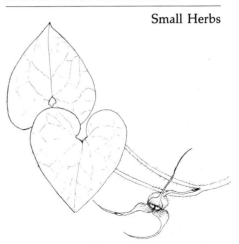

Small Herbs

Wild ginger *(Asarum caudatum)*

Small Herbs

Bog marigold *(Caltha asarifolia)*

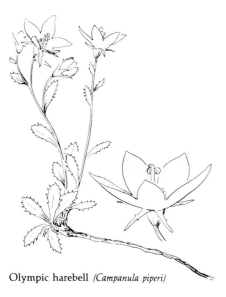

Olympic harebell *(Campanula piperi)*

loving members of the buttercup family. Perfectly charming plants for the bog garden, they have attractive foliage—succulent-fleshy, round basal leaves—and one to several leafless flowering scapes, each with a single or pair of yellow or white buttercups perched on top. They are most evident in montane meadows, often standing in the running water of snow melt, a true glory of our high country. *Caltha biflora* is the most common species. Fresh seeds sown on a wet peaty medium is the preferred mode of propagation, since digging them out of their mucky home is messy and destructive. Other species are *Caltha asarifolia* of coastal bogs from Alaska to Oregon and *C. leptosepala* of the Rockies, but reaching west into the Wallowa Mountains of northeastern Oregon.

HAREBELLS, BELLFLOWER (*Campanula* species). Harebell Family (Campanulaceae). Campanulas have had a proud place in gardening for centuries. And since the nineteenth century, the low-growing ones have come to be at home in many a rock garden. Though most are Eurasian introductions, the New World Northwest has given the gardener some lovely types. All have alternate leaves, which when bruised yield milky juice. The bell-shaped flowers can be deep thimbles, like the cosmopolitan *Campanula rotundifolia* and the Alaskan harebell *C. lasiocarpa,* or the blooms can take the form of flaring shallow bells with protruding clappers (styles), like *C. prenanthoides* and *C. scouleri.*

   Much the most common is *Campanula rotundifolia,* the Scotch bellflower or lady's thimble. Its pendant bluebells adorn open fields, rock outcrops, and roadsides from sea level to timberline. Two lowland species, *C. prenanthoides* and *C. scouleri,* have shallow bells of lavender hue and prominently exserted stamens and style. Both are in open woods and sunny banks on the west side.

The prize of the genus in the Northwest, Piper's harebell *(Campanula piperi,* see color section), should be attempted only by the most skilled and passionate rock gardeners. It grows in high, inaccessible crevices of the Olympic Mountains. Lincoln Foster, in his useful book *Rock Gardening,* reserves *C. piperi* for the connoisseur, both for its rarity and its demanding cultural conditions: gritty soil with a cool, moist root-run at the height of the growing season and a continued cold, dry root and crown environment for the winter. Most localities of *C. piperi* are within the National Park boundary, which precludes any collecting. But colonies just outside the park can be sources of seeds, which germinate well in cold, protected seed pans of gritty soil. Other alpine species worthy of the rock garden or alpine cool house are *C. lasiocarpa* (toothed leaves), *C. parryi* (glabrous, entire leaves), and *C. scabrella* (faintly hairy, entire leaves).

BITTER CRESSES, TOOTHWORTS (*Cardamine* species). Mustard Family (Cruciferae). Only two species of this otherwise weedy genus are of garden value. They are the toothworts, formerly placed in the genus *Dentaria.* Both *Cardamine integrifolia* and *C. pulcherrima* are pretty little woodlanders, with divided to lobed basal leaves and clusters of pink to purplish red "mustard" flowers. They prefer moist shady places and are easily grown from seed or pieces of the short fleshy rhizome. They occur wild in moist lowland woods from Puget Sound to California, strictly westsiders.

INDIAN PAINTBRUSHES (*Castilleja* species). Figwort Family (Scrophulariaceae). Few gardeners have learned the secret of growing these colorful native perennials. Of great beauty with their paintbrush spikes of red, purple, or yellow flowers, they all are partial parasites on other herbs. Those who have succeeded in growing them have been just plain lucky. Seeds broadcast among other herbs of the rock garden or low perennial border must germinate in the proximity of roots of other plants, which they then parasitize. The association of *Castilleja* with other herbs seems not to injure the host plants. The paintbrushes can carry on some foodmaking of their own and thus not wholly deplete the host plant.

The foliage of castillejas consists of alternate, entire to lobed leaves. Along the floral stalk leaves are modified as toothed bracts, richly colored and often overshadowing the adjacent flowers. Each flower is a hooded, saccate tube with the upper lip overshooting the lower in length. There are so many choice species that it would be futile to single out certain ones to try, using the seed broadcast method. Note, however, that paintbrushes can have rather different habitats. Some are sagebrush and high meadowy plains species, others are subalpine meadow plants, and not a few grow in open forests. Collect seeds of any of these types for sowing in compatible garden sites—and wish for luck.

Small Herbs

Alpine spring-beauty *(Claytonia megarhiza* var. *nivalis)*

FALSE YARROWS, CHAENACTIS (*Chaenactis* species). Aster Family (Compositae). These are biennials or short-lived perennials of the aster family, with finely divided leaves, the segments of which are usually covered with a white wool. The flower heads may be single or in loosely branched clusters. Each head is a pincushion of dainty flesh-to-cream-colored disc florets. The better *Chaenactis* species are rock garden plants, suitable for the scree. *Chaenactis ramosa* and *C. thompsonii* are found in the Wenatchee Mountains, often on serpentines, while *C. alpina* and *C. douglasii* var. *montana* are Rocky Mountain plants. The biennial *C. douglasii* is suitable for dry sunny border plantings. Any of these distinctive herbs should be happiest in eastside gardens.

CHIONOPHILA *(Chionophila tweedyi).* Figwort Family (Scrophulariaceae). A dainty alpine relative of penstemons with pale lavender leaves. It barely touches our borders in the high Seven Devils Mountains above the Snake River Canyon. It should be given a dampish open spot in gritty soil of the rock garden.

SPRING-BEAUTIES (*Claytonia* species). Purslane Family (Portulacaceae). The two very different claytonias of the Northwest are both lovely plants for the rock garden. *Claytonia lanceolata* has from one to a few basal strap-shaped fleshy leaves from a deepseated underground corm. The short flower stalk bears a pair of cauline leaves and short racemes of pale pink (rarely yellow) flowers. The spring-beauties emerge in great profusion on spring-wet open slopes from sagebrush foothills all the way to the alpine. Grown from seeds; corms may be collected with due concern for habitat preservation.

The other species, *Claytonia megarhiza,* is a succulent beauty of the alpine, its thick taproot growing in talus and rock crevices east of the Cascade crest. The variety *nivalis* of this species is rather common in the Mount Stuart region of Washington. The many basal leaves are fleshy and spoon-shaped; the short racemes bear gorgeous deep rose red flowers in profusion. When successfully introduced into the rockery this *Claytonia* can vie with the best of rock plants for crevice-hugging beauty. Though like their close relatives, the lewisias, in habit, *Claytonia megarhiza* is never as easy to grow as *Lewisia cotyledon* or *L. columbiana.* For westside rock gardens, it should be given shelter beneath a rock overhang. Best grown from seeds stratified outdoors over winter.

ALPINE COLLOMIA *(Collomia debilis).* Phlox Family (Polemoniaceae). This is a rock gardener's delight—and challenge: to simulate the cameo beauty of those dainty but tenacious tufts that festoon the unstable talus of pumice and rock screes throughout the high mountains of the Pacific Northwest. The tight clusters of small, entire to deeply dissected leaves, usually with a grayish cast, arise from several slender, partially buried stems that emerge from a deeply buried root crown. At the ends of the short leafy shoots, tubular flowers of a soft salmon pink are borne. Plants from collected seeds take a gritty soil in the rock garden—a place where surface grit is dry and the deeper soil needed for the long root-run is kept moist. Westside gardens might succeed with this charming talus species by providing winter shelter with an overhanging rock. Pan culture in the alpine house may be the surest way to success for this little gem.

GOLD THREADS (*Coptis* species) Buttercup Family (Ranunculaceae). Any of our several species of gold thread is admirably suited for use as a ground cover in the shadier parts of the garden. Each has a cluster of deeply dissected to divided evergreen leaves, often darkly shining. Though the flowers are inconspicuous, the spokelike clusters of fruits are attractive. Of the four species native to our damp woods, *Coptis laciniata* and *C. asplenifolia* are most often seen west of the Cascades. The yellowish rhizomes propagate rather easily.

WHITE FORGET-ME-NOTS, CRYPTANTHAS (*Cryptantha* species). Borage Family (Boraginaceae). Only a few of the perennial species of *Cryptantha* can claim a place in the drier rock garden. They have basal rosettes of bristly, lance-shaped leaves and leafy, flowering stems bearing tight clusters of pure white forget-me-not flowers, they too in a bristly setting. Each flower produces four tiny pockmarked nutlets, and these—rather than collected plants—should be used for propagation. The species of drier sagebrush country, such as *C. leucophaea* and *C. propria,* will be happiest in eastside gardens. The more montane species, *C. nubigena* (Wallowa Mountains) and *C. thompsonii* (Wenatchee Mountains), are for the more meticulous rock gardener, who can pamper them in an alpine cool house or cool dry spot outdoors.

DWARF DOGWOOD, BUNCHBERRY, DWARF CORNEL *(Cornus canadensis).* Dogwood Family (Cornaceae). Pure delight comes from any encounter with this carpeting woodlander. A 6-inch-high circle of broad leaves supports a single dogwood "bloom," a singular pattern often repeated in great swaths on the forest floor. Just like the tree dogwood, the white "flower" is in reality a set of four white bracts surrounding

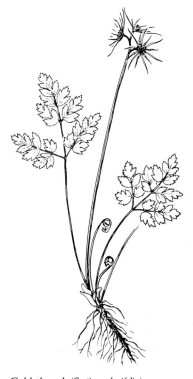

Gold thread *(Coptis asplenifolia)*

Bunchberry *(Cornus canadensis)*

Small Herbs

Shooting star *(Dodecatheon dentatum)*

a tight pincushion of tiny flowerlets. These mature as an exquisite bunch of red berries in fall. Farrer raves about our North American species as much superior in showiness to the European *C. suecica.* Though called a subshrub by Hitchcock, hardly any hint of woodiness is apparent in these lush low, carpeting herbs. Perhaps some success can be had from transplanted clumps, but well-grown seedlings established in pots may be set out with greater chance of establishment. The dwarf dogwood should be given preeminent placing in shaded portions of the garden, under azaleas or vine maple. They like an acid, gritty soil, somewhat damp for most of the year.

SHOOTING STARS (*Dodecatheon* species). Primrose Family (Primulaceae). "The race supplements the Poverty of Primula in America," so says Farrer. Indeed, the Far West may lack native primulas in any great diversity, but the "poverty of primula" is richly compensated for by the presence of a related group of the primrose family, the dodecatheons or shooting stars. Species of this striking primulad occur in many different habitats, from sagebrush country to high meadows and in coastal prairies. All have flat or tufted rosettes of basal leaves and a primly erect, umbellate flower cluster bearing the most amazing flowers. Like the inside-out flowers of *Vancouveria* (no relation), the colorful petals are abruptly reflexed back over the short floral tube and flower stalk (pedicel). Each looks like a jet-propelled missile with its "nose-cone" the showy yellow stamens and pistil. The reflexed petals are mostly purple, though there are white to rose pink forms. Two species of wet habitats are easy for compatible garden sites: *Dodecatheon jeffreyi* grows in wet meadows in the upper montane all over the Pacific Northwest. It comes in a great range of color, but reddish purple colonies seem to predominate. The more delicate *D. dentatum,* of stream banks, seeps, and edges of waterfalls east of the Cascade crest, has creamy white corollas.

Other species prefer only spring moisture and a dry summer habitat. *Dodecatheon conjugens* of seeps in sagebrush to open forested habitats occurs east of the Cascades from British Columbia to California, and can carpet spring-wet swales early in the year (see color section). On coastal prairies of the Puget Sound basin and Willamette Valley, spring-wet places host *D. hendersonii* and *D. pauciflorum.*

So there is a shooting star for almost every garden spot: heavenly places in woodlands, rockery, and border, as long as the moisture is compatible with the plant's temperament. Seeds seem the surest way to bring these delights into the garden. It is sad to see 'divots' left in springy places where collectors have dug the shooting star, because the chance of successful transplantings is slight.

DOUGLASIAS (*Douglasia* species). Primrose Family (Primulaceae). A happy union of exquisite plant and intrepid explorer is this association of the fine primulad with the name of David Douglas. Probably Douglas collected the first specimens in the Canadian Rockies in the 1820s.

All North American species are rock talus and cliff dwellers at middle to high elevations, though *Douglasia nivalis* may also occur in sagebrush country. All are nearly prostrate, cushion- or mat-forming plants, with small evergreen leaves and proud little candelabras of reddish purple "primrose" flowers.

The two species in our area are easily distinguished. *Douglasia laevigata,* found mainly west of the Cascade crest from Snohomish County south to Mount Hood, has dark green, toothed leaves. The mats of dense foliage can have extensive spread. It is especially showy in the high Hurricane Ridge sector of Olympic National Park. Its flowers are deep pinkish rose, fading to lavender. *Douglasia nivalis* forms smaller cushiony mats with its decidedly gray foliage (caused by minute stellate hairs). The variety *dentata* of *D. nivalis* is especially common on serpentine in the Wenatchee Mountains. Typical *D. nivalis* (without dentate leaves) ranges from northeastern Washington well into the Canadian Rockies.

Douglasias are incredibly beautiful subjects for the rock garden, alpine cool house, or trough garden. They need some winter protection from excessive moisture. It may be possible to root small cuttings taken from the mats in nature, but seeds are a bit more reliable.

Douglasia *(Douglasia nivalis* var. *nivalis)*

DRABAS, WHITLOW GRASS (*Draba* species). Mustard Family (Cruciferae). The better of these little crucifers (mustards) are far from drab. The rock-inhabiting cushion types are acclaimed by rock gardeners the world over. It has been mostly the Eurasian species that have captured the eye of the rock gardener. Yet many western drabas merit careful trial. Beware, the genus has some weedy species of no interest to the gardener, so concentrate on the tiny rock polster species of the high country.

Dwarf drabas of the alpine have deep taproots with one to many short, above-ground stems. Leaves are tiny, narrow to paddle-shaped, often in dense clusters. The leaves are usually grayish due to a covering of star-shaped or branched hairs. The short erect flower stalks bear yellow or white flowers in dense showy clusters. The small seed capsules are oval to elliptic and when seeds are released a thin, see-through partition remains. A selection of the rock garden drabas native in the Northwest includes *Draba aureola* (yellow flowers; on volcanic peaks from Mount Rainier to Mount Lassen), *D. densifolia* (yellow flowers; at mid altitudes in the Cascades and Blue–Wallowa mountains), *D. douglasii* (white flowers; rocky places in sagebrush country), *D. incerta* (yellow flowers, fading to white; in the Canadian Rockies south to the Olympics and North Cascades), *D. lemmonii* (yellow flowers; on high peaks of Wallowa Mountains), *D. lonchocarpa* (white flowers; alpine areas of western mountains from Alaska to northeast Oregon), *D. oligosperma* (flowers yellow to off-white; Rocky Mountains west to central Cascades and Wallowa Mountains), *D. paysonii* (flowers yellow; British Columbia to California and Rocky Mountains in the subalpine to alpine), and *D. ventosa* var. *ruaxes* (flowers yellow; rare in our area: Glacier Peak in Washington and Mount Waddington in British Columbia).

Though only a few of our native drabas have been tried in the rock garden, they are likely to respond to similar culture conditions as their Old World relatives: gritty soil with cool root-run and with some winter protection (snow, pine needles, or a rock overhang) mostly against root rot. Propagate from seeds.

SUNDEWS (*Drosera* species). Sundew Family (Droseraceae). These diminutive dwellers in sphagnum bogs are famous as insectivorous plants. Small insects trapped by the sticky leaves are digested by the plant's secretions to become a part of sundew nutrition. Nearly all sphagnum bogs from sea level to mid-montane regions have one or both species of our area. *Drosera anglica* has narrowly oblong leaves and the more common species, *D. rotundifolia,* has roundish leaves. They can be raised as curiosities—and for their fragile beauty—from seeds sown in damp sphagnum. The maturing plants must continue on the moist sphagnum habitat to endure. It is their glistening leaves with the glandular hairs, not the rather insignificant flowers, that attract attention.

MOUNTAIN AVENS (*Dryas* species). Rose Family (Rosaceae). Many arctic and alpine habitats at high latitudes nurture these ground-hugging marvels. Two widespread species just penetrate our Northwest high country. *Dryas drummondii* with yellow flowers grows on alpine summits of northeastern Washington and in the Wallowa Mountains of northeastern Oregon. The white or cream-colored *D. octopetala* appears on high ridges and peaks in the North Cascades of Washington and again in the Wallowas. Mountain avens forms extensive mats on rocky surfaces. The many-branched woody and prostrate stems take root as they inch along on gravelly soils. The small evergreen leaves are oblong with a scalloped margin and leathery texture. Each of the numerous 3- to 4-inch-high flower stalks bears a large rose-petaled yellow or white flower. And there is more splendor to come when in fruit: twisted tufts of feathery plumes atop the maturing seeds. Though *Dryas octopetala* is widely grown in rock gardens, our native forms seem not to take well to cultivation; *D. drummondii* is more tractable. And yet Farrer reminds us that *drummondii,* so pregnant with expectation in bud, fails to fulfill with fully opened flowers. Perhaps the answer is to grow the hybrid *D.* X *suendermannii* (available from rock garden nurseries), and thereby have the best of both worlds: cream buds and fully opened white flowers.

Rooted cuttings after establishing in pots can be set out on an artificial rock scree. Seeds are slow and not too sure. *Dryas,* so much at home in the high country, has been brought down the mountain to behave well year after year in many a lowland garden. Its evergreen foliage reacts favorably to the reflected heat of paving whereas many other plants "burn out."

ELMERA *(Elmera racemosa).* Saxifrage Family (Saxifragaceae). This neat little alum root (related to *Heuchera*) forms great sheets on subalpine

Mountain avens *(Dryas octopetala)* in University of British Columbia alpine garden

Elmera *(Elmera racemosa)* in garden trough

talus and rock cliffs in the Olympics, the Cascades, and the mountains of northwestern Oregon. The lovely cream-colored flowers on short stalks are raised 4 to 6 inches above a capacious rosette of round, scalloped leaves of a richly embossed surface. Each leafy rosette is linked to another to form patches up to a yard across. Though some success might come from rooting individual rosettes, plants from the tiny seeds are a more dependable way to propagate *Elmera,* which does well in rockeries or in troughs if given some winter protection against damp.

ALPINE WILLOW-HERBS (*Epilobium* species). Evening Primrose Family (Onagraceae). Only a few of the low-growing fireweeds merit garden culture. All the rest are either too coarse or have insignificant flowers—weeds, in short. But the very few worthy of the garden are superb. First on the connoisseur's list would be *Epilobium obcordatum* (in the Steens Mountains of Oregon, south to California) and its close kin, *E. rigidum* (in the Siskiyou region of Oregon and northern California). Both have lovely glaucous foliage from prostrate stems and large rose-colored flowers on short stalks. Both species occur on dry talus in their respective mountain habitats. A willow-herb from the wetter subalpine is the low, rambling *E. latifolium,* with lance-shaped, glaucous leaves and large, rose purple flowers. It is fairly common in moist places high in the North Cascades to British Columbia and beyond.

A yellow-flowered willow-herb, a color unique to the genus, is *Epilobium luteum.* It grows to 1½ feet high in moist meadowy places and along streams in the Cascades, the Olympics, and on north to Alaska.

Most willow-herbs when in seed are a bit messy. The long narrow pods emit cottony tufts, each bearing a tiny seed. But they do come easily from seeds so prodigally produced.

Alpine willow herb *(Epilobium obcordatum)*

Small Herbs

Subalpine daisy *(Erigeron peregrinus)*

Cut-leaved daisy *(Erigeron compositus)*, Wenatchee Mountains, Washington

Desert fleabane *(Erigeron poliospermus)* near Vantage, Washington

FLEABANES (*Erigeron* species). Aster Family (Compositae). The many low-growing fleabanes invite testing in the garden. In nature, those of low stature are gorgeous little daisies often smothered with yellow or lavender "heads." As in other genera, such as *Astragalus, Aster,* and *Lupinus,* species of low stature may occur in vastly different habitats: rocky alpine, desert-like rimrock or dry coulees, and scattered amongst the big shrubs of the sagebrush plains. Of the fifty or so species in the Pacific Northwest, nearly half are of low stature and suitable for some sunny spot in gardens, preferably in the rock garden setting. Rather than name all those that could be tried, we offer here some of the best and pre-tested species. First would be that golden glory of the alpine, *Erigeron aureus.* It has narrowly ovate rosette leaves and one to several flower stalks, each bearing a single large head of golden yellow ray and disc florets from May until freezing weather. The golden fleabane ranges from southern British Columbia to the Washington Cascades and is especially common in the Wenatchee Mountains. Another common fleabane of even more compact stature is *E. compositus.* It has small, finely dissected leaves, reminiscent of sagebrush or bitterbrush foliage, that form a dense cushion. The many short flowering stems bear single "heads" of showy ray florets (white, pink, or blue) and yellow disc florets. It can be found in sandy open habitats in the mid-montane, all the way to the alpine in rocky places. It is everywhere at high altitudes in the Northwest—in the right habitat.

A charming fleabane of sagebrush plains and dry foothills is *Erigeron linearis.* It has numerous linear (very narrow) longish leaves in dense rosettes with many yellow heads, each on its own peduncle.

These three fleabanes just open the door to the group's potential for the rock garden. They invite garden trial on both the "wet" and "dry" side of the mountains. Some of the more common ones might be collected as seedlings in the wild, but they do grow easily from seeds.

WILD BUCKWHEATS (*Eriogonum* species). Buckwheat Family (Polygonaceae). Gardeners on the wet side of the mountains may despair of ever being successful with these temperamental plants. Yet *Eriogonum* is so captivating a genus that we continue to try them. The low-growing ones are especially tempting: mats or cushions of deserty, lovely foliage and perky balls of tiny flowers, some white, reddish, others pink or yellow. It is the lucky owner of a dry, well-drained garden situation that can experiment with the many buckwheat possibilities. They are all nearly dryland eastsiders, from the alpine down into the sagebrush, basalt rimrock, and coulee habitats. Plants from seeds, well-established in pots, can be placed in sunny well-drained sites in the rockery with the prospect of living at least a few years. Even here on the west side we have had middling success with *Eriogonum umbellatum* (prostrate, with yellow flowers) and subalpine forms of *E. compositum* (yellow or white flowers). A fine plant of volcanic pumice and serpentine scree is *E. pyrolaefolium* with its bright wintergreen-like leaves and its little pompoms of pale pink flowerlets. The fine cushion-forming variant of *E. ovalifolium* is best grown on the east side; the more alpine forms of this wide-ranging plant are preferred. A plant of great beauty in the sagebrush and scabland country is *E. thymoides,* but of exacting cultural requirements. This is the little "ming" plant or dried bonsai that has been so ruthlessly exploited by commercial collectors. Well-grown plants from seed should be tried in eastside rock gardens. *Eriogonum thymoides* with its tiny thyme-like leaves and its usually yellow flowers is an outstanding wildling.

Here is a further sampling of the many other buckwheat possibilities: *Eriogonum flavum* (sulphur-yellow flowers), *E. douglasii* (flowers lemon to pinkish), and *E. sphaerocephalum* (flowers yellow or white). I have singled out only those low perennials with flowers in dense globose clusters, but some enthusiasts will want to try some of the low profile buckwheats with open, lacy-textured inflorescences. Turn to Hitchcock for a feast of possibilities.

GOLDEN YARROW, OREGON SUNSHINE *(Eriophyllum lanatum).* Aster Family (Compositae). Like its namesake, the common yarrow *(Achillea),* this single widespread species comes in many forms, from dense, low cushion plants to rather tall floppy mops. Since the several variants reflect habitat by their inherited fidelity to size, it is well worth collecting seeds of the low-growing montane forms. Golden yarrows have small divided rosette leaves, usually dense, white, woolly, and leafy flowering stems with single yellow heads. The forms from serpentine in the Wenatchee Mountains are especially pretty little plants. Easy to grow from seeds. The larger lowland golden yarrows need not be completely ignored. They make fine splashes of mid-summer gold in sunny wild gardens and neglected places in suburbia.

ALPINE FORGET-ME-NOT *(Eritrichium nanum).* Borage Family (Boraginaceae). If ever there was a Holy Grail sought by the rock gardener, it must be *Eritrichium.* From the Alps of Europe, all across Asia, into Alaska, and on down to northwestern North America and the Rocky Mountains, this exquisite, woolly, cushion plant with the heavenly blue flowers and yellow eye bedazzles all who behold it (see color section). But for many it is a love affair blighted with failure when tried in cultivation. A few gardeners can grow it and even fewer bring it to flowering, but whenever seeds come available it must be tried. The American rock garden authority Lincoln Foster gives a tempting, but exacting recipe for its culture:

> Success is most likely if the seeds are sown thinly in a large pot with a stone chip mulch. Thin the seedlings to stand about an inch apart. Water the pot only by plunging. Plenty of light and air but no baking sun are requisite, and, above all, protection from the heavy beating of thunderstorm rain. Soil should be a gritty leaf mold, though in nature they may be found growing in a stony, red-gumbo clay. With luck they will flower the third year from seeds on tuffets about two inches across. Spare seedlings may

Wild buckwheat *(Eriogonum umbellatum)*

Wild buckwheat *(Eriogonum compositum)*

Small Herbs

be potted singly or set in the scree on the north side of a rock when the single rosette has begun to make new rosettes. [1968:277]

In our area, *Eritrichium nanum* is rare, occurring in a few high alpine stations in the North Cascades and in the Wallowa Mountains. It is more common in the Rocky Mountains, as is its relative, *E. howardii.*

WALL FLOWERS *(Erysimum* species). Mustard Family (Cruciferae). The more alpine of these yellow mustards are well worth garden culture. In the class of fine alpines is *Erysimum arenicola,* of high rocky places in the Cascades and Olympics. Scapes of showy lemon-yellow "crucifer" flowers, 4 to 8 inches high, reach upward from a rosette of narrow leaves of a somewhat sandpapery texture. The pods (siliques) are long, straight, and nearly erect. The more alpine forms of *E. arenicola* should be successful in the rock garden.

Other taller wall flowers, typified by *Erysimum asperum,* are best suited to the drier wild garden. They are of good color (yellow, orange, or reddish), with showy flowers, but rather coarse in foliage and in fruit. *Erysimum asperum* is abundant from sagebrush plains to open conifer forests on the east side. All are easy to start from seeds.

WILD STRAWBERRIES (*Fragaria* species). Rose Family (Rosaceae). All our native strawberries are easy of cultivation and have well-deserved reputations as dependable groundcover plants. The wild strawberries have basal, trifoliate leaves (clover-like) on long leaf stalks, creeping, horizontal runners from each rosette, lovely white, five-petaled flowers, and edible fruits (small strawberries). The maritime *Fragaria chiloensis* thrives on sand dunes and beaches. It makes a fine sand-binding ground cover in coastal gardens, but is equally useful inland. It is one parent of the cultivated strawberries.

Fragaria vesca comes in two varieties in our area. Variety *bracteata* is a taller form (up to 8 inches) and is well suited as a ground cover in open woodland places. Variety *crinita* is a smaller plant of open rocky places west of the Cascades. It is a good, low carpeter, with soft tawny green leaves.

Forms of *Fragaria virginiana* always have gray green (glaucous) leaves, an easy distinction from the other two species. Ordinarily they are low-growing plants (2 to 5 inches), freely spreading by runners. The two varieties of *F. virginiana* are specially common in open woods and dryish meadows east of the Cascades. Any of these most accommodating ground covers can be grown from the offset plants produced by the many runners.

BEDSTRAWS (*Galium* species). Madder Family (Rubiaceae). Although the most choice rock garden galiums are Eurasian, our western *Galium multiflorum* surely should be given honorable mention. It makes a thrifty shrublet with its many short stems in dense tufts from a woody rhizome. The short slender stems are square (four-angled), and bear four

Wild strawberry *(Fragaria vesca)*

small linear leaves per node. The upper portion of each stem produces a branched flower cluster, which in fruit bears many tiny bristly burs, the whole effect a smoky halo. This galium grows on dryish montane slopes east of the Cascades, and is most plentiful in the Wenatchee Mountains of central Washington. Grown from seeds or pieces of rhizome, it is fine for the sunny rock garden scree.

GENTIANS (*Gentiana* species). Gentian Family (Gentianaceae). In a clan of superlative garden plants, our Northwest gentians are not of the first rank. Even our best native, the lovely blue, high meadow *Gentiana calycosa* is often disappointing in the garden, unless the conditions approaching a wet and cold mountain meadow can be met. *Gentiana affinis* of eastside boggy places and *G. detonsa* of coastal bogs should be tried in the bog garden. All have deep blue, funnel-shaped flowers, often fringed or notched, and have stems with opposite leaves. Grown from seeds or from rooted pieces of stem.

GILIAS (*Gilia* species). Phlox Family (Polemoniaceae). The two perennial gilias of the Northwest perform best in arid gardens on the east side. The scarlet gilia *(G. aggregata)* decorates its 1- to 2-foot-high leafy stem with red trumpets—a glorious sight on a midsummer's rocky slope. Its rosette and stem leaves are finely divided into linear segments. Never long-lived, *G. aggregata* will usually die after flowering. It is widespread east of the Cascades from British Columbia to California, occurring in sagebrush and rocky openings in yellow-pine forests. *Gilia congesta* has dense heads of short tubular white flowers; its short flowering stalks emerge from sparse rosettes of woolly divided leaves. *Gilia congesta* is confined to the Wallowas and southeastern Oregon in the Pacific Northwest. For other gilia-like plants, see *Leptodactylon* and *Linanthastrum*. Grown from seeds.

HAPLOPAPPUS (*Haplopappus* species). Aster Family (Compositae). The lower growing of these near-woody yellow asters include *Haplopappus acaulis, H. lyallii,* and *H. uniflorus,* each of good temperament for the rock garden. Although mostly to the east of our area in Idaho and Montana, *H. acaulis* appears in the Steens and Wallowa mountains of eastern Oregon on high ridges; *H. lyallii* stays around timberline from British Columbia to Oregon; and *H. uniflorus* var. *howellii,* with narrow grass-like leaves and stems with single yellow heads, is at high altitudes in the Steens and Warner mountains of southeastern Oregon. Grown from seeds or rooted offsets.

HESPEROCHIRONS (*Hesperochiron* species). Waterleaf Family (Hydrophyllaceae). Dainty cousins of *Hydrophyllum* and *Phacelia,* these ground-hugging plants can grow in great profusion in spring-wet swales, meadows, and open slopes east of the Cascades. Individual plants are like tiny lewisias, with a few prostrate strap-shaped leaves and short flowering stems, each with a single saucer-shaped white flower tinged with

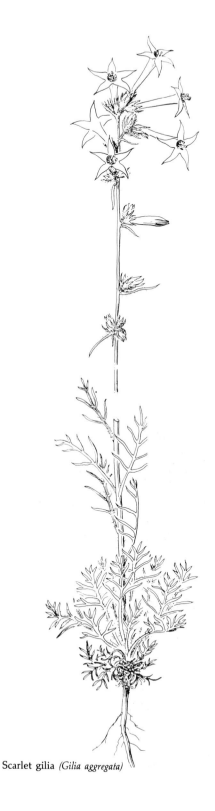

Scarlet gilia *(Gilia aggregata)*

Small Herbs

purple. After a few weeks of spring glory, they disappear from view, living on underground from deep slender taproots. Foster recommends growing them from seeds or spring offshoots. They show off best in clumps, or drifts, in a cool moist place in the rockery—but in full sun. The Northwest has both species: *H. californicus* and its miniature replica *H. pumilus*.

ALUM ROOTS (*Heuchera* species). Saxifrage Family (Saxifragaceae). Besides the taller ones described earlier, there are low-growing alum roots suited to the rock garden or low border area. All have one to several basal rosettes from a thick taproot. The leaves are round with a scalloped margin, often with a glandular surface. The flowers are borne in usually dense clusters. *Heuchera cylindrica* is found in almost all mountainous areas of the West, but east of the Cascades. The better garden forms of lower stature come from the high country. *Heuchera cylindrica* has cream-yellow flowers in dense spikes. It can easily be mistaken for *Elmera racemosa,* though the latter has more widely spaced flowers. A more diminutive plant is *H. grossulariifolia* with smaller flowers on slender scapes. It is found in the Columbia River Gorge and the Wallowa Mountains, as well as the mountains to the east of our region. The heucheras grow easily from seeds or division and are not too fussy as to habitat in the garden.

HORKELIAS (*Horkelia* species). Rose Family (Rosaceae). Though only technically distinct from potentillas, these little westerners of the rose family seem to stay put in *Horkelia.* Unlike *Potentilla,* they have white flowers and only ten stamens. Our two species have short, pinnate leaves, each leaflet neatly incised or toothed. *Horkelia congesta* grows in open dryish woods from the Willamette Valley to the Rogue River country in Oregon; *H. fusca* can be found in dampish meadows to open woods east of the Cascades, from central Washington to the Sierras. Both take well to the rock garden, low border, or wild garden, and are easy to start from seeds or division.

HULSEAS (*Hulsea* species). Aster Family (Compositae). These are exquisite alpine daisies with yellow heads, large for the low-tufted plants. The brilliant yellow rays seem to glow with a luminescence—like buttercup gold of a celestial quality. Our two Northwest species have rosettes of narrow leaves, quite sticky (glandular) and coarsely cut along their margins. *Hulsea algida* is the taller of the two (up to 8 inches), and its floral stalks are leafy. It is an alpine of granitic talus and rock crevices in the Wallowa Mountains. *Hulsea nana,* smaller and with leafless (scapose) flowering stems, prefers the hot rocky summits of volcanic peaks, pumice flats, and cinder cones, from Mount Rainier (Washington) to Mount Lassen (California). They are both suited to the rockery and are grown from seeds.

Dwarf hulsea *(Hulsea nana)* in lava rock garden, Mt. Adams

WATERLEAFS (*Hydrophyllum* species). Waterleaf Family (Hydrophyllaceae). Singularly unsuited is the common name for these relatives of phacelias, the fiddlenecks (see p. 207). Hydrophyllums are woodland to open slope plants from near sea level to nearly alpine. All have rather coarsely divided basal leaves and short flowering stems, leafy or scapose. The flowers are in dense balls (capitate clusters), made plumose by the hairy calyces and protruding stamens. The woodlanders—*Hydrophyllum fendleri, H. occidentalis* and *H. tenuipes*—are a bit rank and aggressive and best confined to the wild garden. The preferred rock garden species is *H. capitatum:* ground-hugging rosettes of purplish cut leaves and low dense balls of lavender to deep purplish blue flowers. The better forms are from open upper montane slopes. This waterleaf makes its home east of the Cascades, from southern British Columbia to central California, and is grown from seeds.

Ivesia *(Ivesia gordonii)*

IVESIAS (*Ivesia* species). Rose Family (Rosaceae). Of the three genera that rally round the cinquefoil *(Potentilla)* theme, *Ivesia* is the most diminutive in foliage. Its glandular rosette leaves are pinnately compounded into the tiniest of fingerlike divisions. As the flowers on the scapose stems have rather insignificant pale yellow flowers in globose clusters, the rock gardener is attracted to the pretty foliage. The three species are much alike in habit and garden requirements: dry sunny spots in the rock garden, with a good rock to cover the taproot. *Ivesia tweedyi* is mostly restricted to serpentine rock in the Wenatchee Mountains; *I. gordonii* is widespread in subalpine to alpine reaches of mountains east of the Cascade crest; *I. baileyi* comes from the desert summits of the Steens Mountains in southeastern Oregon. Eastside rock gardens will be the happier places for these ferny cinquefoils, which are grown from seeds or by division of root crowns.

KELSEYA *(Kelseya uniflora)*. Rose Family (Rosaceae). Such an impossible wonder of the vegetable world from central Idaho! Better to enjoy its rock-hugging beauty in the wilds of central Idaho than try to bring it into culture. A few have succeeded with this tiny polster-forming member of the rose family, but only with painstaking attention to its limestone needs. Young plants from seeds may be inserted into soil-filled holes drilled into limestone rock and kept in an alpine coolhouse. Foliage of *Kelseya* consists of tiny leaves in tough-textured, thick crusts, a startling sight on high limestone cliffs in the mountains of central Idaho. The mats of tiny, hard leaves in overlapping shingle pattern, are covered in early summer with small, rose pink flowers.

SHRUBBY PHLOX, PRICKLY PHLOX, GRANITE GILIA *(Leptodactylon pungens)*. Phlox Family (Polemoniaceae). This desert shrub combines the foliage of heather with the flowers of a phlox. It grows in scabland basalt rimrock and sagebrush country in the Pacific Northwest, but is widespread elsewhere in the West in similar arid habitats. The shrub is intricately branched, the stems bearing sweet-smelling foliage of needle-like ''leaves'' (actually the points are part of the compound leaf with linear divisions). The large single phlox flowers, one per stem, vary in color from white, tinged rose, to salmon, and are usually nocturnal. Prickly phlox takes well to the arid garden, grown against rocks, and comes from seeds or rooted cuttings.

LEATHERLEAF SAXIFRAGE, FALSE SAXIFRAGE *(Leptarrhena pyrolaefolia)*. Saxifrage Family (Saxifragaceae). Both common names tell much about the qualities and affinity of this small evergreen mountain herb. It has leathery oblong leaves, with a toothed margin. The foliage is in dense rosettes from a system of spreading rootstocks. Its small greenish white flowers are congested at the tip of slender erect stalks. In leaf and flower it does look like its close kin, saxifrage. False saxifrage grows along streams and snow-melt slopes in the upper montane from the Cascades and Olympics, south to the Sisters in Oregon. The reddish follicles at fruiting stage add a late summer beauty to the large patches of *Leptarrhena*. It does well in cultivation when it is placed in a sunny wet spot. Grown from seeds or from rooted pieces of rootstock.

BITTERROOTS, LEWISIAS (*Lewisia* species). Purslane Family (Portulacaceae). A rock garden in the West is rarely without one of the glamorous and showy succulents of the genus *Lewisia*. Wholly western in native origin, the lewisias have diversified into fifteen or so species, of varied habitat and form. All are tidy little plants with succulent foliage and showy flowers. The family resemblance (purslane family) to *Claytonia*, especially to *C. megarhiza* is at once apparent. But so diverse are the kinds of lewisias that only the most general of attributes suffice. Though all are of rock garden quality, their particular requirements vary from species to species.

Lewisia rediviva. This is the bitterroot of western Indian lore, dug for the nutritious roots. In late spring the rimrock, scabland, and rocky slopes of the arid West come alive for a brief spell to dazzle the eye with floral beauty. The prize of all such dry, rocky places is surely this tiny plant, with its fleshy long cylindrical leaves beset with oversized flowers of deep to pale rose pink. By summer all above-ground sign of the plant is gone, leaving the thick branched taproot to hold over until next spring's wet spell. Even westside gardeners have succeeded with bitterroot in either container or rock garden; sharp drainage, winter protection and a spell of summer baking-out dormancy, matched with a bit of luck, can hold them for a time. They are even known to seed themselves in suitable dry places in the rockery. Eastsiders, of course, can enjoy bitterroot without such exacting care.

Lewisia cotyledon. Siskiyou Mountains country and the North Coast ranges of California host this much-acclaimed wonder. Though there are a number of named variants, botanist Janet Hohn sees them all as rallying around the *L. cotyledon* theme: basal rosettes with large, strap-shaped, fleshy leaves and erect inflorescences, each bearing several to many quarter-sized flowers from white to rose pink to salmon, variously candy-striped or in plain colors. The Oregon forms are var. *purdyi*,

Bitterroot *(Lewisia rediviva)*, eastern Washington

with short entire rosette leaves and pink-striped petals, found in the Kalmiopsis Wilderness Area. The typical variety (var. *cotyledon*) has large entire leaves and white to yellow petals, with pink median stripes. It is found in the high country of Josephine and Jackson counties. Three other variants are in northwest California: *howellii, heckneri,* and *fimbriata.* A distinct but closely related species, *L. leana,* has cylindrical, linear leaves and somewhat smaller flowers. When it grows with *L. cotyledon* in the wild, a hybrid of charming intermediate character is invariably produced.

All the *Lewisia cotyledon* forms are dependable rock plants, even on the west side—and lovely rock plants to boot. They come well from seeds; divisions of the root crown can be established, though collecting lewisias in the wild any more can hardly be condoned. Several rock garden and rare plant nurseries now carry most of the wild forms as well as some of the good garden hybrids (e.g., 'Insriach'—Jack Drake hybrids). Despite their fleshy nature they prefer some shade and a cool damp root-run; rock garden or low border is called for.

Lewisia columbiana is a montane plant of dry rocky slopes and cliffs from the yellow-pine zone to timberline. It is widespread from southern British Columbia, the Olympics, the east slope of the Cascades, and on into northern Oregon. The many variants all have basal succulent leaves, usually much longer than broad, a deep-seated taproot, and an open inflorescence of smallish lavender to magenta rose flowers. The two smaller varieties, var. *rupicola* (Mount Rainier, the Olympics, and Oregon Coast Ranges) and var. *wallowensis* (in mountains above the Grand Canyon of the Snake River), both have short, narrow leaves. Though not as showy as the aforementioned lewisias, *L. columbiana,* especially when grown in drifts, makes a charming sight in the rock garden. They are easy-to-please rock plants for most sunny gardens.

Lewisia cotyledon in mat of *Penstemon davidsonii*

Lewisia columbiana in natural rock garden

Small Herbs

Lewisia tweedyi, the crowning glory of the kingdom of lewisias, is both the rarest and the most difficult to grow of those discussed. Attend to these superlatives first, before mention of caveats: large strap-shaped, succulent leaves (up to 8 inches long and broadly spatula-shaped) in often lavishly large multiple rosettes. Then emerging from the leaves are 6- to 8-inch-long inflorescences, each bearing from one to three silver dollar-sized flowers of the most exquisite apricot to salmon hues. Large plants in nature may bear more than one hundred flowers at a time over a long blooming period in late spring. The caveats are two: first, the plant is not widespread, and though it may be locally common, its total range is both limited and discontinuous. Its center of distribution is northern Kittitas County to Chelan County in Washington, with more remote populations in the Methow River drainage of Okanogan County, Washington. The northernmost population is reported from Manning Park in British Columbia. The second caveat is that it must not be collected, both because of losses to wild populations and because dug plants do not take well to transplanting. Plants from seeds or from nurseries then must pass the test of garden conditions. As with most dry land perennials with a fleshy rootcrown, rotting of the crown at ground level is the greatest danger. Charles Thurman, Spokane plantsman who has had fabulous successes with *L. tweedyi,* recommends growing them nearly horizontal between rocks near the top of a dry rock wall, with enough rock overhang to prevent stagnating moisture. Sharp drainage and a fine rock mulch around the crown also works. (Note that this lewisia need not have full sun.) They are often found in dry conifer duff under yellow pine or Douglas fir, or if in rock, they need a deep cool root-run and only partial sun.

The lewisias are some of our best rock garden plants, with fine succulent foliage and lovely in flower (see color section). The two easiest for the garden are *Lewisia columbiana* and *L. cotyledon.* For the more patient and ingenious gardener who can cope with cultural mysteries, *L. rediviva* and *L. tweedyi* give full value for the efforts when successful. All are best grown from seeds or as nursery-grown plants.

Lewisia tweedyi

WILD BLUE FLAX *(Linum perenne* var. *lewisii)* Flax Family (Linaceae). East of the Cascades, this durable perennial graces both hills and valleys of yellow-pine and sagebrush country, as well as the higher dry peaks of the east side. Depending on the source of seeds, the many erect stems from the woody rootstock may be anywhere from 6 inches to 2 feet tall. Leaves that freely clothe the stems are gray green and narrow. Atop each stem, the glorious, large blue flowers begin, one after another, daily for a long summer's blooming. Easily grown from seeds.

ALASKA SPIREA, PARTRIDGE FOOT *(Luetkea pectinata).* Rose Family (Rosaceae). If some alpines seem a bit too challenging for garden culture, here is one that seems every bit as happy at sea level as in its home in the subalpine. Moreover it is a superior, low ground cover for sunny moist places in the garden. Alaska spirea is indeed related to *Spiraea*, but is so distinctive a member of the rose family as to merit its own genus. The one species, *Leutkea pectinata*, has many low rosettes from creeping rhizomes and stolons, each rosette with finely dissected leaves. Short, 6-inch-high flower stalks bear a few smaller dissected leaves and a terminal plume of small, cream yellow flowers. A carpet of this luxuriant grower in the higher subalpine meadowlands and screes of the Northwest, or in the sunny rock garden down at sea level, creates an enchanting scene. Native to subalpine and alpine areas from Alaska to northern California, *L. pectinata* comes well from seeds and is easy to multiply from detached rosettes with rhizome. Though it may take full sun in the rockery, the site must not be dry; at the base of the rock garden where drainage may collect is preferred. *Luetkea* is used in the high country to restore areas suffering from human impact. It is a tough, aggressive, yet beautiful performer, a ground cover of first quality.

WOODLAND STARS, PRAIRIE STARS (*Lithophragma* species). Saxifrage Family (Saxifragaceae). These kin to the saxifrages are tougher than they look. Despite the slender above-ground parts, they come from underground bulblets, persistent long after the tops fade away in summer. The small digitately compound leaves form in rosettes and are also scattered along the flowering stem. When present, the pinkish flowers are graceful little stars. But many times all but the terminal flowers are replaced by small purplish bulblets. The lithophragmas appear in early spring, often in great patches in rocky places and open meadows, flowering and seeding while the soil is still moist. The common species on both sides of the Cascades is *L. parviflora.* Can be grown from seeds, bulblets, or young plants.

LUPINES (*Lupinus* species). Pea Family (Leguminosae). The one low-growing lupine, highly prized by rock gardeners is the ground-hugging alpine, *Lupinus lepidus* var. *lobbii.* One-inch-high tufts of tiny silvery, silky lupine leaves form mats a foot or more across. The blue lupine flowers decorate a neat little stalk less than 4 inches high. This dwarf

Lupine *(Lupinus lepidus* var. *lobbii)*

lupine is found on ridges and high slopes to the uppermost tundra habitats from southern British Columbia to southern California. It seems to favor gritty, sandy soils in dryish openings and pumice slopes of the subalpines to alpine zones. Best results with fresh seeds is to steep them in hot water for an hour, then sow immediately in seed pans with good drainage and a light gritty soil, topped with fine rock mulch. The plants are rather short-lived in the rock garden, especially on the wet side of the mountains.

ALPINE MONKEY FLOWER *(Mimulus tilingii).* Figwort Family (Scrophulariaceae). Besides the charming little annual monkey flowers of the sagebrush country, the only low-growing perennial is *Mimulus tilingii.* Either in shy little clumps or in great drifts, this high montane plant captures the eye with its large yellow snapdragon trumpets on dainty stalks not over 8 inches high. It prefers the wettest of seeps and snowmelt basins near timberline and often wanders into cold running water. If the gardener can approximate such conditions, then *M. tilingii* will be a great performer, and yet retain a more delicate grace than its coarser relative, *M. guttatus.* Besides growing from seeds, *M. tilingii* can be increased from pieces of its extensive fleshy rhizome system.

MITREWORTS, BISHOP'S CAPS (*Mitella* species). Saxifrage Family (Saxifragaceae). For those who garden with trowel, camera, *and* hand lens, the mitreworts offer hidden but exquisite beauty. While the foliage is pleasantly saxifrage in character (round basal leaves with scalloped margins), the flowers are miniatures of geometric beauty. The leafless scapes from 6 inches to 2 feet tall bear white or greenish blooms whose design is best revealed close up, aided with a lens. Each flower is a double star: the outer sepals form a simple five-pointed star; the petals accent the star pattern as five radiating branched filaments of the most exquisite design—feathery filigrees or dainty tridents. Each flower when so viewed has the intricate design and symmetry of a snowflake.

Bishop's caps are easy garden plants for the woodland or shady border, best obtained from seeds. Each of the eight species of the Northwest grows in wooded areas, some west, others east of the Cascades. A sampling of *Mitella* elegance can be had with the following:

M. caulescens. Flowers greenish; on the coastal to mid-montane west side

M. breweri. Flowers greenish; on the upper montane in Cascades and Olympics

M. stauropetala. Flowers white; in moist woods of Blue, Wallowa, and Ochoco mountains

M. trifida. White, three-pronged petals; on both sides of the Cascades in Washington, and in eastern Oregon to Grant County

The other four species deserve honorable mention: *M. diversifolia, M. nuda, M. ovalis,* and *M. pentandra.*

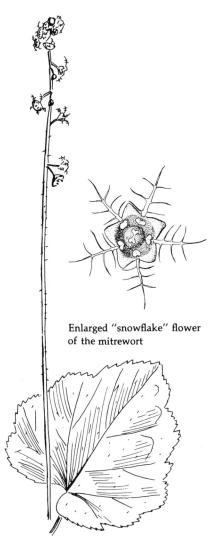

Enlarged "snowflake" flower of the mitrewort

Mitrewort *(Mitella pentandra)*

WESTERN BALM, MOUNTAIN MONARDELLA *(Monardella odoratissima)*. Mint Family (Labiatae). Sight and smell blend in heavenly form with this rock-loving member of the mint family (Labiatae). The blue gray foliage, giving off an unforgettably sweeter-than-peppermint odor, comes in attractive, low moundy heaps. Each of the many leafy stems (bearing opposite leaves) is tipped with a head-like cluster of lavender mint flowers. *Monardella* is a mountain plant of moderate to high elevations east of the Cascade crest from Washington well into California and ranges east to the Rockies. It is best to search out the more compact editions of this widely variable plant, then grow the better forms from seeds in dry, sunny places in the rockery.

DESERT EVENING PRIMROSE *(Oenothera caespitosa)*. Evening Primrose Family (Onagraceae). We are blessed with one low-growing perennial evening primrose of superior garden quality. *Oenothera caespitosa* gives a succession of white flowers that perch just above the 4-inch-long rosette leaves. The leafy tufts come alive with flowers in the late afternoon to enliven talus slopes and road banks in drier places east of the Cascades. The four-petaled flowers change to pink in their brief evening's life. But each new day in late spring and early summer brings a squad of new flowers. The toothed, narrow leaves sit on a woody rootstock that gets bigger with each passing year. This deep taproot needs a well-drained and coarse-textured soil. Plants grown from seeds will be happiest in the gardens of the more arid east side.

OXALIS, WOOD SORRELS *(Oxalis* species). Oxalis Family (Oxalidaceae). Two natives of this vast, world-wide genus are fine woodland garden plants. Our forest-carpeting wood sorrels form rosettes of attractive clover-like, three-parted leaves. Flowers are borne on short erect stalks above the leafy rosette. Both species expand their territory by underground stems (rhizomes). Hitchcock recommends the yellow-flowered *Oxalis suksdorfii* over *O. oregana,* and for good reason. The former is much less rampant. But if an aggressive carpeter is desired in the untamed woodland setting, the *en masse* spectacle of the pink-flowered *O. oregana* is worth the space given up to it. Both species, from our coastal forests, are easily propagated from rhizome pieces.

MOUNTAIN SORREL *(Oxyria digyna)*. Buckwheat Family (Polygonaceae). This little alpine buckwheat grows in scree and rock crevices in all north temperate continents. Whether in the Cascade Mountains of Washington, in Alaska, or in the European Alps, its distinct character is faithfully portrayed. Rather fleshy basal leaves (pleasingly sour), round or kidney-shaped, cluster about a short erect stalk, bearing little "knotweed" flowers. It is in fruit that mountain sorrel becomes a decorative garden plant. Each small flower turns into a round, single-seeded, dry fruit with a broad-winged margin. The flower stalk, with many pendant winged fruits, often turning purple with age, lends alpine grace to a rock garden crevice or scree. Best grown from seeds.

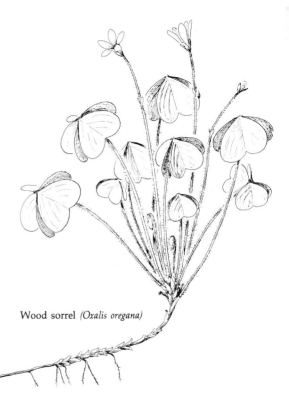

Wood sorrel *(Oxalis oregana)*

Small Herbs

Grass-of-Parnassus *(Parnassia fimbriata)*

MILK-VETCHES (*Oxytropis* species). See *Astragalus*, p. 183.

GRASS-OF-PARNASSUS (*Parnassia* species). Saxifrage Family (Saxifragaceae). If the gardener can simulate a high mountain streamside or wet meadowy spot, he must try species of *Parnassia*. Like marsh marigold, alpine coltsfoot, and the two wet-meadow monkey flowers *(Mimulus lewisii* and *M. tilingii),* these exquisite little saxifrages must have their bottoms wet at all times. Why the word grass should appear in the common name can only be attributed to poetic license. Parnassias are good dicots, though resting somewhat uneasily in the saxifrage family. Their basal leaves are round, often heart-shaped, making pleasing rosettes. The near-naked flowering stems bear large single white flowers, rather reminiscent of those of marsh marigold, at a distance. But in fine detail, *Parnassia* flowers have gone on a rococo binge like mariposa lilies and gentians. In *Parnassia* flowers the finely wrought filigree is a creation of sterile stamens (staminodes). Besides the five fertile stamens, each sterile stamen is converted into a series of tiny fingers, often tipped with miniscule globes. More filigree is found on the basal edges of the petals, with a fine comb-like margin. It is believed that the sterile stamens are false nectaries, lures for insect visitors.

The showiest of our two or three species is *Parnassia fimbriata.* It is widespread throughout the West in mountain springy places, in bogs, and along margins of streams. The plants come easily from fresh seeds sown in the fall.

LOUSEWORTS, ELEPHANT'S HEADS, BIRD'S BEAKS (*Pedicularis* species). Figwort Family (Scrophulariaceae). Just as tempting—and as intractable—as the Indian paintbrushes *(Castilleja),* are the enchanting louseworts of the high mountain forests and open subalpine meadows. Like *Castilleja,* all species of *Pedicularis* are assumed to be partial parasites on other seed plants. And herein lies the gardener's dilemma. Can other plants in the rock garden or bog bed serve as hosts to a lousewort? Some have succeeded, especially with broadcast seeds, in a suitable place already supporting plant life. If the alliance with a host plant takes, the reward is the sumptuous ferny foliage and the brilliant and bizarre flowers so familiar in our high country. The erect flower stalks bear closely set flowers of the most amazing design: the floral tube (corolla) is tapered and twisted in ways distinct for each species. The corolla of *Pedicularis groenlandica* has become a miniature elephant's trunk, while that of *P. ornithorhynchya* is in the shape of a bird's beak. These curious floral contrivances all appear to be adaptations for insect pollination, especially by bumblebees.

Besides the two species just mentioned, the gardener should try *Pedicularis contorta, P. bracteosa,* and *P. racemosa.* When collecting seed, one should take note of both the habitat (dry to wet meadow, forest border, etc.) and the neighboring plants likely to be hosts. The craftier gardener may thus simulate the conditions of successful growth of these mountain wonders.

PENSTEMONS, BEARD-TONGUES (*Penstemon* species). Figwort Family (Scrophulariaceae). By now it may seem that there is a penstemon for nearly every garden spot. First we offered the shrubby ones (p. 99), all eminently suited to the rock garden. Then in the section on medium-sized herbs (p. 175), we found a generous helping of species for sun, shade, and dry to dampish situations in the wild garden. And now, still more penstemons, this time those of low stature—all of four-star rock garden quality. Penstemon lovers will want to go beyond the six species recommended here. But why not start with the best?

Two bountiful mat-formers with evergreen leaves are *Penstemon davidsonii* (green leaves and purple flowers) and *P. rupicola* (gray glaucous leaves and reddish purple flowers). Both are common in the Cascades as mid- to high-montane plants whose stems hug the surface of cliffs and rock outcrops. *Penstemon davidsonii* is the more widespread, thriving in the subalpine from British Columbia and Vancouver Island to California, and in the Olympics and along the full length of the Cascades, on into the northern Sierras. A dazzling rock-crevice plant, *P. rupicola*, is found in the Cascades of Washington and northern Oregon.

Two somewhat woody species, closely allied to the above and to *Penstemon fruticosus* are most local in occurrence. Indeed, *P. barrettiae* should be considered one of those rare plants whose existence is threatened by habitat change. It is known only from a few places along the Columbia Gorge and tributary rivers, especially the Klickitat River. Barrett's penstemon has 1- to 2-foot stems from a many-branched rootcrown. Hovering over its large blue gray leaves are stiffly erect stalks of large rose purple to lilac flowers. It should never be collected in the wild. Luckily it is often available as seeds or as nursery-grown plants.

Penstemon cardwellii with large, bright green, toothed leaves seems to prefer volcanic and lava soils of the high central Cascades, from Mount

Penstemon *(Penstemon davidsonii)*

Saint Helens to southern Oregon. It tends to be a many-branched shrublet with 6- to 10-inch-long racemes of rose purple flowers.

One other semi-woody penstemon, *P. newberryi* var. *berryi* has foliage like *P. cardwellii* but on more reclining stems. Its flowers are reddish purple. Look for it in the Salmon–Trinity country of northern California and in the Siskiyous of southwestern Oregon.

These five species are members of a closeknit group, the Dasanthera penstemons: mostly all somewhat woody-stemmed and all with large tubular flowers standing horizontal along the 4- to 8-inch-long stalks. Since two or three species of the group may occur in the same place, natural hybrids usually result. Many are as fine as their parents. Both species and hybrids are easily propagated by stem cuttings; see *P. fruticosus* (p. 99) for seed culture.

Of a very different alliance in the genus is *Penstemon tolmiei* (or *P. procerus* var. *tolmiei*). It is wholly herbaceous and forms good-sized patches composed of dainty rosettes of short narrow leaves. From each rosette emerges a short flower stalk tipped with a dense cluster of brilliant blue purple flowers, each small and tubular. The whole effect of a mat of *P. tolmiei* in flower is striking. This penstemon occurs along our highest ridges near timberline in the Cascades, Olympics, and mountains of southern British Columbia. It propagates easily from rosette cuttings and from seeds, though it is a bit more capricious than the Dasanthera penstemons.

Of all our showy western plants, the penstemons in their glorious variety offer the greatest herb treasure to Northwest gardens. With fifty or so species to choose from, the gardener can find some penstemon delight for almost every spot: woodland, border, or rock garden.

DWARF SPIREAS, PETROPHYTUM (*Petrophytum* species). Rose Family (Rosaceae). What an apt name—"rock-plant"—for this rock-hugging

Olympic Mountain rockmat *(Petrophytum hendersonii)* in garden trough

wonder. All three species of this mat-forming relative of *Spiraea* live in the Pacific Northwest, always on cliffs or in rock crevices. The tiny, closely packed leaves form dense cushions 1 inch high and up to 2 to 3 feet across. The prostrate mat spreads from a woody rootstock to "pour" over the nearby rock surfaces. The tiny white flowers are congested in a short spiky stalk. The most widespread species, *Petrophytum caespitosum,* is mostly at home in the Rockies and the intervening desert mountains south and east of our area, but has been found in the Cascades of southern Oregon. *Petrophytum hendersonii* is restricted to the Olympics of Washington, at moderate to high elevations; and *P. cinerascens,* the most local species, hugs the vertical walls of cliffs above the Columbia River north of Wenatchee. The three species are separated on the most trivial of differences, but the gardener would do well to try the more common species, either from small cuttings or from seeds. Dwarf spireas, especially *P. caespitosum* are available at some rare plant and rock garden nurseries. They take rather well to the rock garden, especially where limestone chips are added to the coarse-textured, gritty soil. Planted next to a rock or in a rock crevice, they may slowly take on their natural cushion habit.

FIDDLENECKS, PHACELIAS (*Phacelia* species). Waterleaf Family (Hydrophyllaceae). The prodigious clan of fiddlenecks, though liberally stocked with annuals and perennials of dry habitats, has devoted some ingenuity to making alpine rock plants. The best bear lovely blue spikes of flowers in dense fiddleneck clusters, topping a closely set ferny foliage. *Phacelia lyallii* is a Rocky Mountain plant; *P. sericea* is frequent in rocky places at timberline in the Cascades and Olympics from British Columbia to northern California. Both have dense rosettes of basal leaves, deeply divided and beset with short gray hairs. The flower clusters, 3 to 8 inches long, are crowded with lavender to bluish purple flowers.

The lavender or pale purple forms of *Phacelia hastata* are often of low stature and dense habit. The gray green leaves may be entire and lance-shaped or have paired basal lobes.

These low-growing perennial phacelias are suited to the rock garden, especially where winter moisture can be controlled. An open gritty soil to permit quick drainage plus rock protection can avoid rotting of the root crown. Best propagated from seeds.

PHLOX, WILD SWEET WILLIAMS (*Phlox* species). Phlox Family (Polemoniaceae). Great expectations meet the challenge of temperamental behavior for any who are tempted by our lovely phloxes. Nearly all are of great beauty and compel trial in the garden. If their rootcrowns can be freed of soggy winter conditions, they may be grown west of the Cascades. More certain success will come to the gardener on the east side.

There are two distinct groups of native phlox, based on growth form. The erect types, with rather leafy stems, bear two to several

Small Herbs

Spreading phlox *(Phlox diffusa)* in University of British Columbia alpine garden

Phlox hoodii, eastern Washington

large phlox flowers on each flower stalk. Three are sagebrush, scabland, or yellow-pine species, local to widespread east of the Cascades: *Phlox colubrina* (Snake River canyon or eastern Oregon), *P. longifolia,* and *P. speciosa.* When grown well in eastside gardens they are handsome, showy things, especially if their somewhat weak stems can clamber into a low shrub. The one erect form from the west side, *P. adsurgens,* is in open conifer woods from Linn County, Oregon, to northwestern California. It offers the best opportunity for the westside gardener.

The cushion-forming phloxes, like *Phlox diffusa,* have tiny needle-like leaves and are fond of scree and other rocky open places from sagebrush to timberline. Though there are many of these ground-hugging phloxes in the West, *P. hendersonii* (from central Washington to Mount Hood) and *P. hoodii* (in sagebrush country of eastern Washington and Oregon) are the only other northwesterners with the cushion-forming phlox form.

Either erect or prostrate, phloxes are superb rock plants, if only their fastidious needs can be met: good drainage in full sun and moist spring conditions followed by a drying-off period until the winter. They are propagated by rooting small rosette or stem offshoots from a parent plant. Pieces of rhizome from plants of *P. adsurgens* can be tried. Seeds, though often scanty, offer the surest method of increase. Damping-off molds are to be guarded against in propagating phlox.

DAGGER-POD *(Phoenicaulis cheiranthoides).* Mustard Family (Cruciferae). A remarkable little crucifer for the fairly dry rock garden. Its several dense rosettes from a branched rootcrown have long narrow grayish leaves. The flower stems, up to 10 inches high, bear a few short stem leaves and a cluster of fragrant, brilliant reddish purple or pink mustard flowers on stiffly horizontal pedicels. The fruits are long and pointed, earning the name "dagger-pod." It is a plant of sagebrush and yellow-pine country and comes easily from seeds. This is the same plant as *Parrya menziesii,* praised by Farrer.

BLADDER-PODS *(Physaria* species). Mustard Family (Cruciferae). Here is still another rock garden crucifer, with inflated pods and yellow flowers. The physarias are all deep taprooted plants with fine silvery foliage in ground-hugging tufts. The leaves may be spoon-shaped or broad and dissected. The flowering stems are arched to erect, with many pale yellow flowers in early summer. The fruiting stems with the small inflated pods are decorative curiosities. *Physaria geyeri* and *P. alpestris* represent this western clan in rocky places east of the Cascades.

JACOB'S LADDERS, SKY PILOTS *(Polemonium* species). Phlox Family (Polemoniaceae). Like their kin the phloxes, polemoniums come in two growth forms, both of great garden value. The woodlanders like *Polemonium carneum* and *P. pulcherrimum* are 6 inches to over a foot tall, with many long pinnately compound leaves and flowering stems with loose clusters of rose pink, blue, or lavender flowers.

Mostly above timberline another race of Jacob's ladder greets the seeker of alpine plants. Tiny rock-hugging tufts of densely compound leaves and short flower stalks are capped with showy clusters of exquisite blue flowers. *Polemonium elegans* is at home in the highest volcanic Cascades of Washington, north into British Columbia. A very similar sky pilot, *P. viscosum,* grows in rocky alpine places in northeastern Washington and the Wallowa Mountains of Oregon; it also ranges the length of the Rockies from Alberta to New Mexico.

The woodland species will thrive in partial to full sun in a deep, well-drained soil of floral border plantings or in moister places of the rock garden. The more alpine sky pilots must have a gritty soil, a rock crevice, and a cool root-run. Grown from seeds or by dividing garden-grown plants.

CINQUEFOILS (*Potentilla* species). Rose Family (Rosaceae). Most of the native potentillas for the garden have been described in the early section on medium-sized herbs. Other species are of low stature or have low-growing alpine races, suitable for the rock garden. Some ground-hugging types are *Potentilla brevifolia* (high mountains of eastern Oregon), *P. breweri* (high Cascades), and *P. ovina* (eastern Oregon).

WINTERGREENS, PYROLAS (*Pyrola* species). Heath Family (Ericaceae). These handsome evergreen woodlanders are in a class with our native terrestrial orchids: several display charming flowers and foliage, but are reluctant to become established in the garden. The bond between the pyrolas and the orchids is the root environment where both have some degree of dependence upon the roots of other plants and upon the fungi of the forest floor. Perhaps we should be content with Hitchcock's wisdom on the matter of their cultivation: "Attractive in the wild where they should be left, since they cannot be cultivated successfully."

But persistent gardeners have had some success with the wintergreens, which are indeed hard to resist. Most have delightful glossy evergreen foliage in tidy compact basal rosettes; some (*Pyrola picta* and *P. dentata*) have a mottled pattern on the roundish leaves. *Pyrola asarifolia* is the most spectacular of the wintergreens: large round basal leaves, dark green to shiny, and from one to several erect flower clusters up to 1 foot tall with rose pink to reddish purple flowers.

The rock garden expert H. Lincoln Foster gives an exacting recipe for their culture: "The best means of establishment is to dig carefully the smallest, most compact clump to be found, shake off the soil, and plant in a pot containing ⅔ sharp sand and ⅓ acid peat. If not permitted to dry out thoroughly, and also not kept too moist, new feeding-roots will be encouraged to form. This will take up to six months. The plant will appear healthy and alive for long periods even without roots, but should not be set in a permanent site in duffy woods soil until new roots are assured" (1968). About seed propagation, he says: "The dustlike seed is reluctant to germinate, but with patience

Jacob's ladder *(Polemonium carneum)*

Small Herbs

will produce plants if sown on sphagnum moss." For those with neither the patience nor the capabilities to provide such tender-loving-care, it would be best to enjoy the pyrolas in nature's garden.

SILVERY RAILLARDELLA (*Raillardella argentea*). Aster Family (Compositae). This is a mat-forming alpine daisy of exquisite beauty: small, nearly linear leaves all silvery with fine wool and solitary yellow heads (rayless) on short (1 to 2 inches) spikes. The mats can become 1 or 2 yards in diameter in the wild, consisting of many small rosettes of the lovely silvery foliage. Though more common at and above timberline in the Sierra Nevada of California, it does extend well into Oregon. Look for it in the volcanic Cascades from Mount Thielsen and Crater Lake to the Three Sisters, as well as in the Siskiyous.

The plant has rarely been grown by rock gardeners. It should not be too difficult from rooted pieces of the branched rootstock and associated rosette leaves; seeds should be tried, too. *Raillardella* should be an outstanding carpeter for the alpine garden scree. It will need gritty soil in full sun with a cool root-run.

SAGEBRUSH BUTTERCUP *(Ranunculus andersonii)*. Buttercup Family (Ranunculaceae). This remarkable buttercup—unlike any others in the West—has red flowers. Its finely dissected foliage forms a compact rosette to set off a short erect and leafless stalk bearing a single showy red buttercup. The plant inhabits screes and other rocky places in sagebrush and yellow-pine country from eastern Oregon to central Idaho, south to eastern California, and Nevada. It should be tried in a shaded but well-drained spot in the rock gardens east of the mountains or in the warmer parts of southwestern Oregon. Some botanists prefer to keep it in its own genus, *Beckwithia,* so distinct is it from any other buttercup. Best propagated from seeds, freshly sown in fall.

SAGES (*Salvia* species). Sage Family (Labiatae). Two perennial sages are in our area. Both are fine plants in the wild and should be given a trial in suitable garden situations. Grayball sage *(Salvia dorrii)* grows in dry scabland and sagebrush territory. Yet, remember that it is no relative of *Artemisia,* the genus of sagebrush species. Plants of grayball sage are many-branched shrubs—up to 2 or 3 feet tall—with numerous silvery gray leaves. The long, erect spike-like clusters of blue violet flowers are glamorous exclamation points above the silvery foliage. This has to be a plant for dry gardens, baked in summer and frigid, but dry, in winter. It comes either from seeds or soft-wood cuttings.

The other species, creeping sage *(Salvia sonomensis),* just gets into our region in Siskiyou County, California. It is a prostrate shrublet, often reaching a diameter of 5 to 8 feet. Its narrow grayish leaves have a distinctive, deeply embossed veininess. Its short flower stalks bear numerous blue violet mint flowers. It should be a fine dryland carpeter in gardens of the lower Willamette, Umpqua, and Rogue rivers. Californians are just learning about its drought-loving habits and its ornamen-

Sage (*Salvia dorrii* var. *carnosa*)

tal virtues, especially from the pen of Marjorie Schmidt, author of *Growing California Native Plants*. She recommends starting creeping sage from tip cuttings taken any time of the year. Seeds require three months' stratification. Like all sages, both these natives have aromatic foliage.

SAXIFRAGES (*Saxifraga* species). Saxifrage Family (Saxifragaceae). Though we have used the term saxifrage for many members of the family that look, at least in leaf, like true saxifrages, we can now be charmed by the real thing. Old World saxifrages from woodland or rocky alpine habitat have long been a traditional part of the rock garden mania. Every rock garden manual devotes pages to the mossy, the encrusted, and the engleria saxifrages—the three main divisions of this vast army of plants. Native saxifrages of the Northwest, though a bit less glamorous than some of the gems in the European alps, do claim a place in the garden.

One common saxifrage way of life is the wet opening or streamside in forested high country. Plants of this habitat usually have silver dollar-size leaves with margins variously dentate or scalloped and with 1 foot tall inflorescences of small white flowers. Typifying the preference for the bog garden or for the edges of a pond or stream are *Saxifraga arguta, S. marshallii,* and *S. mertensii.* Some of these will replace some of their flowers with ready-to-grow bulblets—a kind of vegetable vivipary.

For the rock garden, there are several native alpines, notably *Saxifraga bronchialis* and *S. oppositifolia.* Hitchcock remarks that our Northwest race of the latter species is more vexing to establish in the garden than its Eurasian counterparts. *Saxifraga oppositifolia* has tiny oval leaves, oppositely disposed on short stems, the whole plant a neat mossy cushion. Each stemlet may bear a single, large (for the size of the plant), purple flower.

Saxifraga bronchialis is a more robust rock plant of the high country: many short stems with dark green needle-leaves and 6-inch-high stalks with many small flowers in open clusters. Each flower is white with purplish dots on the petals. Other alpines of dainty elegance are *S. caespitosa* and *S. tolmiei.* All but *S. oppositifolia* are common up high in our mountains.

As rock garden subjects, these alpine saxifrages need a dampish sunny place in the rockery, a top dressing of rock mulch and gritty soil with peat added. They are best grown from seeds.

STONECROPS, HENS-AND-CHICKENS (*Sedum* species). Stonecrop Family (Crassulaceae). Succulents for cool temperate climates seem almost a contradiction in terms. Yet the succulent habit need not always be associated with hot, dry climates. Succulents of the genus *Sedum* occur in the Northwest from sea level to the alpine and inland to the sagebrush country. To be sure, sedums avoid wet or shady places, so they won't be found in forest or bog. But in a rocky place or sunny outcrop-glade in the woods, expect to find a *Sedum.*

Saxifrage *(Saxifraga arguta)*

Small Herbs

Broad-leaf sedum *(Sedum spathulifolium)*

All sedums have small fleshy leaves either narrow or broad, and usually, star-shaped flowers. The broad-leaved species are fine rock garden plants. *Sedum spathulifolium* forms large patches on rocks and banks in low-lying coastal areas from the San Juan Islands and British Columbia to California. It makes numerous tight rosettes of small spatulate leaves. The short flowering stems bear leafy clusters of yellow flowers. *Sedum obtusatum* and the related species, *S. oregonense* and *S. laxum,* have larger and thicker, fleshy leaves and flowers from off-white and cream to yellow. The group is centered in the North Coast ranges of California and the Siskiyou Mountains, with extensions north in the Cascades and south in the Sierras. The obtusatums are fine plants with thick grayish foliage.

The best of the narrow-leaved sedums are *S. divergens* (Cascades from British Columbia to Oregon), *S. stenopetalum* (mostly east of the Cascade crest in yellow-pine forest and sagebrush to the subalpine), and *S. lanceolatum* (general and widespread from sea level to timberline; var. *rupicolum* in the Wenatchee Mountains is particularly choice).

Sedums are the easiest of plants for the rock garden. The smallest piece of leafy stem or rosette will root without any help. Some kinds tend to be invasive, and the broad-leaved group is the easiest to contain in a small space.

GROUNDSELS (*Senecio* species). Aster Family (Compositae). Only a few of these yellow daisies meet the criteria of low stature and garden acceptance. The best is certainly *Senecio neowebsteri,* a plant of moist talus in the high northeast sector of the Olympic Mountains. It has large solitary heads and woolly, often purple leaves from a creeping rootstock. *Senecio flettii,* also from the Olympics, and *S. porteri,* of the Wallowas, can also be recommended for the rock garden. Propagation can be achieved by seeds.

SIBBALDIA *(Sibbaldia procumbens).* Rose Family (Rosaceae). A tiny potentilla, *Sibbaldia* has only its compact grey green foliage to merit its inclusion here. The leaves are digitately compound like many other cinquefoils; but unlike potentilla, its tiny greenish yellow flowers have only five stamens. Sibbaldias are cosmopolitan at high elevations in the Old and New World, and can make a worthy ground cover for "in-between" places in the rockery. Can be propagated from seeds.

CAMPIONS, CATCH-FLIES, SILENES (*Silene* species). Pink Family (Caryophyllaceae). The Pacific Northwest boasts of two of the finest catch-flies in all the genus. *Silene hookeri* is an Oregonian of rare distinction. Large fringed flowers of shades of pink to salmon on short tufts of gray green foliage, all coming from a deepseated taproot of delicate branching underground stems. This lovely rock garden subject is at home in rocky openings and woodland glades in the oak and conifer woods from Yamhill County, Oregon, south into northern California. The fringed character of the flower comes from the deeply cut linear

Wild pink *(Silene hookeri)*

lobing of each of the five petals. Several forms, given names like *S. ingrahamii* and *S. pulverulenta*, are hardly more than distinct forms of this highly variable plant. Any of the variant forms is desirable for the rock garden.

A plant of rather similar form to *Silene hookeri* is *S. californica* with brilliant crimson flowers not as finely lobed as in *S. hookeri*. Its tufts of opposite leaves come directly from a stout taproot. *Silene californica* just enters Oregon in Josephine County; it is commoner in California.

Both *Silene hookeri* and *S. californica* are a bit fastidious for wetter westside gardens, especially north of Eugene, Oregon; they do need protection against winter wet. These, like all other silenes, are grown from seed. Seedlings are easy to come by, but keeping them happy until of flowering age in the rock garden is a matter of luck and location.

A few other native silenes of low stature can be grown in the garden. Recommended for trial are *S. campanulata* and *S. lemmonii*, both species of open dryish woods in southwestern Oregon and California.

Our last catch-fly is like no other in the garden or in nature. *Silene acaulis*, the moss campion, is a plant of worldwide rock garden fame. It is one of those few everpresent alpines that one finds in both the Old World and in North America. It makes the finest mossy cushions of dense, almost spiny, glossy leaves. Like *Petrophytum*, the dense, prostrate green mats seem to "flow" over rock. Even without flowers, one cannot fail to be charmed by the plant. But when the pink catch-fly flowers dot the mat in profusion, delight is multiplied. Farrer, on the other hand, quibbles about the quality of the flowers of moss campion: ". . . crude little chalk-pink stars . . . its color is never clean, however brilliant." Such a good-natured alpine should not be so dismissed. Most who grow it will be satisfied that this trouble-free alpine provides ever-increasing delight as the mossy mat increases. In the garden, some forms of moss campion tend to be a bit shy in flowering. Good color forms with dependable flowering can be propagated from stem cuttings. Plants come easily from seeds, and should be transplanted to the rockery when the rosettes get 1 to 2 inches across—neat little buns that grow and grow in rock crevices with full sun. *Silene acaulis* is a plant of the alpine in western North America; suitable alpine fell-fields and tundra occasionally occur in Oregon and Washington, more continuously so on north to Alaska.

SMELOWSKIAS (*Smelowskia* species). Mustard Family (Cruciferae). A better common name should adorn this charming little alpine crucifer. Since one or two species have the habit of some drabas, *Thlaspi* or *Alyssum*, they could be called "alpine penny-cress" or "alpine candytuft." Smelowskias form small rosettes of densely tufted compound leaves, so finely hairy as to appear gray. They produce short, spiky racemes of white candytuft flowers, followed by small pods. One or the other species, *Smelowskia ovalis* or *S. calycina*, will be encountered in the subalpine to alpine from British Columbia to California. They can be started from seeds and grown in the rock garden.

Small Herbs

Moss campion *(Silene acaulis)*, in University of British Columbia alpine garden

Small Herbs

Pussypaws (*Spraguea umbellata* var. *caudicifera*)

Snow-queen (*Synthyris reniformis*)

GOLDENRODS (*Solidago* species). Aster Family (Compositae). Our one alpine goldenrod, *Solidago spathulata* var. *nana,* will stay dwarfed in the rock garden. It will form spreading cushions of many tight rosettes of short spatulate leaves and brief stems of fine goldenrod flower heads. Forms from any high montane localities are easy from seeds or single rosette cuttings.

PUSSYPAWS *(Spraguea umbellata).* Purslane Family (Portulacaceae). These curious ground-hugging mats turn up at high elevations all over the West. Though relatives of claytonias and lewisias, they do not have fleshy leaves; rather the dense foliage is more like that of an alpine buckwheat *(Eriogonum):* short tapered leaves thickly crowding the ground above the deep taproot. The curious papery pink flowerlets in dense heads are at the ends of short nearly prostrate stems—altogether a most delightful rock garden subject. Hitchcock distinguishes between a "strong perennial" form, var. *caudicifera,* a plant of subalpine screes and rocky flats, and a nearly annual plant of lower elevations, var. *umbellata.* The perennial form is more to be desired.

As a garden plant, Hitchcock says of it: "This is a very interesting and attractive little plant that cannot endure irrigation but which would probably take well to the rock garden east of the Cascades." So, yet another of those choice alpines that take special care on the wet side of the mountains can be trouble-free in drier gardens. Propagation is from fresh seeds.

SUKSDORFIA *(Suksdorfia violacea)* and SULLIVANTIA *(Sullivantia oregana).* Saxifrage Family (Saxifragaceae). These are two saxifrage kin of moist habitats in the Cascades and the Columbia Gorge region. Both resemble *Boykinia, Tiarella,* and the leafier species of *Saxifraga.* Consult Hitchcock for their distinguishing features. Grown from seeds, both are suitable for moist sunny places.

SYNTHYRIS, KITTENTAILS (*Synthyris* species). Figwort Family (Scrophulariaceae). Wholly western North American, this small genus is the botanical home for some elegant garden plants. Like *Besseya* (p. 183), species of *Synthyris* are deep fibrous-rooted perennials with leaves in a single large basal rosette and flowers in compact scapes. *Besseya* and *Synthyris* are so closely related as members of the Veronica section of the figwort family that they occasionally hybridize in the wild.

There are two distinct growth forms in *Synthyris.* First come the lowland to mid-montane species with large, oval, merely toothed leaves. *Synthyris reniformis* grows in open woods and brushy clearings from northern California all the way through Oregon and to the oak woodlands and "prairies" around Tacoma and Olympia in Washington. It has small round leaves of scalloped margin and many weakly upright flowering stems, each with from three to seven lovely pale blue "veronica" flowers. It likes a duff-enriched forest soil but not too much shade. A bolder version is the elegant *S. missurica,* a plant of yellow-pine and mixed-conifer woods east of the Cascades. The large round leaves, also toothed, form a lush rosette from which emerge several stiffly erect succulent stems (4 to 8 inches tall), with deep blue flowers. Marion Ownbey located pale pink to nearly albino forms of *S. missurica* in eastern Washington. A form in the Columbia Gorge, often recognized as var. *stellata,* has more sharply toothed leaves and paler flowers.

A third species of the round-leaved pattern is *Synthyris schizantha* (see color section). This is a rare plant with only three known localities: two in western Washington and one in northwestern Oregon. Unlike the two evergreen species just described, *S. schizantha* completely disappears over winter, unless the dry flower stalks remain. It has large round leaves with doubly toothed margins and 1 foot tall flower stalks, bearing small blue flowers each with deeply dissected petals. The admonition against collecting whole plants must be strongly invoked where *Synthyris* is concerned. Not only are some rare and local, they are also the target of thoughtless plant-diggers. *Synthyris* does come well from seeds harvested in early fall from the heart-shaped capsules. The three large-leaved species are best grown in partial shade at the edges of a shrub border or in a woodland opening. They are dependable performers that delight the eye in early spring.

Other western synthyrises inhabit the very different subalpine to alpine country. Moreover, they tend to be smaller and have finely dissected leaves. Though most are plants of the intermountain country of Idaho and Utah, the Northwest is adorned by one of these alpine gems, *S. pinnatifida* var. *lanuginosa,* native to the high northeast sector of the Olympic Mountains. Its finely dissected leaves are white with a woolly pubescence and from the low tuft of foliage comes a short spike of blue flowers. This woolly little alpine is not the easiest plant for the rock gardens. But as a pan or container plant in the alpine cool house, it can share honors with many other alpines. It should be grown from seeds.

TALINUMS (*Talinum* species). Purslane Family (Portulacaceae). Miniature rarities of the *Lewisia* alliance, these rock plants have short spine-tipped, fleshy leaves, and flowers like *Lewisia columbiana* or *L. leana. Talinum spinescens* (red flowers) thrives in sagebrush country on the basalt outcrops of rimrock and scabland; it is restricted to central Washington. *Talinum okanoganense* (pink to white flowers) is a more prostrate version, confined to rocky places in the mountains of Okanogan County, Washington and adjacent southern British Columbia. These two charming deserty succulents will be happiest in eastside rock gardens. Both can be grown from seeds.

Okanogan fameflower *(Talinum okanoganense)*

ALPINE PENNYCRESS *(Thlaspi fendleri).* Mustard Family (Cruciferae). Only the most compact of these mountain crucifers should be admitted to the rock garden. They may have dense rosettes of glossy, dark green leaves, small and oval in outline, with short stalks of white crucifer flowers in dense spicate racemes. Though everywhere in our mountains, the better forms are likely to be from high exposed sites around timberline. Their curious heart-shaped to triangular pods, reminiscent of shepherd's purse, are an added attraction. They can be grown from seeds.

FOAM FLOWER *(Tiarella trifoliata).* Saxifrage Family (Saxifragaceae). This smallish woodland saxifrage combines neat foliage of maple-like leaves in a basal rosette with attractive clusters of dainty white flowers. Some forms have deeply cut leaves like some Japanese maples; others are trifoliate or merely lobed. In the wild shaded garden, massed plantings are a delight, and flowering can last through the summer. The species and its variant foliage forms are widespread in the forests of the Pacific Northwest. It is easily propagated by leafy offsets that are produced by its short rhizome.

TOWNSENDIAS (*Townsendia* species). Aster Family (Compositae). These are the cream of the showier alpine, low-growing daisies. Flower heads are large like *Erigeron peregrinus,* but perched low on dwarfed tuffets of narrow leaves. The flower heads have pink, blue, or lavender rays and yellow disc florets. Most townsendias are Rocky Mountain and Great Basin plants. Three species are found in the Northwest: *Townsendia florifer* is a dwarf daisy in sagebrush country of central Washington (see color section), while *T. montanum* and *T. parryi* get into our region in the Wallowa Mountains of eastern Oregon.

Though most are short-lived perennials, they may self-seed easily and are ideal for dry sunny places in the rockery.

STAR FLOWERS (*Trientalis* species). Primrose Family (Primulaceae). These dainty woodland "star-bearers" grow everywhere in Northwest conifer forests, often carpeting the forest floor. Because they have both creeping rootstalks (thin underground stolons) as well as small tubers, individual plants can both persist and spread in a woodland garden. Though placed in the primrose family, star flowers resemble more than

Star flower *(Trientalis latifolia)*

the dwarf species of *Trillium* in leaf: four or five ovate leaves in a circle (whorl), 2 to 4 inches above the ground, and topped by one to several wiry stems each bearing white to pinkish starlike flowers. This is an utterly carefree plant that once introduced will easily naturalize in shadier garden sites. The smaller species, *Trientalis arctica,* has white flowers; *T. latifolia* of larger size, has white to pink flowers. Both are easy to grow from the little tubers.

BIG-HEAD CLOVER *(Trifolium macrocephalum).* Pea Family (Leguminosae). This ground-hugging clover ranges over much of the dry forest, sagebrush, and scabland country in the Northwest. Unlike most clovers, it has an unusually large and beautiful head of pink to rose flowers. It should be a superb addition to dryland rock gardens east of the Cascades, and is best grown from seeds. Other species of native clover should be tested for garden use; there is a good native *Trifolium* for nearly every garden setting, from coastal dune, westside woodland, or wet place, to dryland garden. The rare Chelan County *Trifolium thompsonii,* sadly, must be omitted from the garden palette. It is both too difficult and probably too rare for garden testing.

GLOBE FLOWER *(Trollius laxus).* Buttercup Family (Ranunculaceae). Like marsh marigolds (*Caltha* species), the globe flower likes wet places in the mountains. Our species, *Trollius laxus,* is in all our higher mountains, emerging in flower and early leaf at the edge of melting snow. In foliage and flower, the globe flower resembles a showy buttercup. Its basal leaves are coarsely dissected; the several stems bear single large white flowers. A cool wet place, not too shady, should suit it best. Seeds should be sown soon after fall harvest.

SPEEDWELLS (*Veronica* species). Figwort Family (Scrophulariaceae). Only two Northwest species of this large worldwide clan are suitable for the garden. Both are common plants of the subalpine meadows throughout the Pacific Northwest: each has tufts of dainty, 6- to 8-inch stems with opposite leaves, topped by clusters of lavender to blue violet flowers, smallish but showy *en masse.* The stems spread by rhizomes to form dense or open patches beneath the taller herbs of the meadow. *Veronica cusickii* is devoid of hairs in the herbage and can stand conditions from moist to somewhat on the dry side, *V. wormskjoldii* has finely hairy herbage and prefers wetter sites in the subalpine. The seeds, borne in neat "shepherd's purse" capsules, germinate well, but the plant is not always easy to establish at low elevations.

VIOLETS (*Viola* species). Violet Family (Violaceae). If garden pansies seem a bit gross for refined tastes, then surely our rich wild violet treasure can produce the right substitute with restrained beauty. There must be a violet species for almost every major habitat in the Northwest, from sea level to the subalpine. Some are dryland plants, others woodlanders, and still others are confined to bogs and wet meadows. First

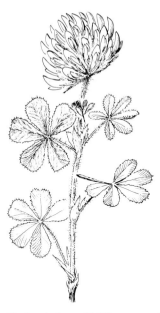

Big-head clover *(Trifolium macrocephalum)*

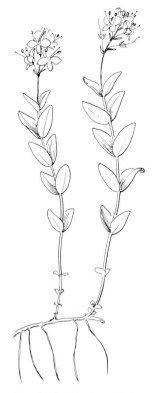

Speedwell *(Veronica cusickii)*

Small Herbs

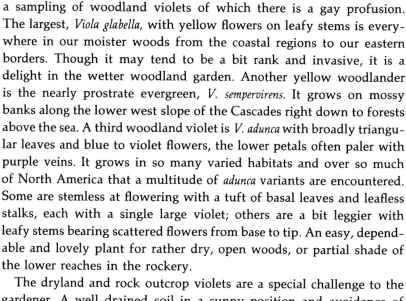

Violet *(Viola glabella)*

Violet *(Viola adunca* var. *adunca)*

a sampling of woodland violets of which there is a gay profusion. The largest, *Viola glabella*, with yellow flowers on leafy stems is everywhere in our moister woods from the coastal regions to our eastern borders. Though it may tend to be a bit rank and invasive, it is a delight in the wetter woodland garden. Another yellow woodlander is the nearly prostrate evergreen, *V. sempervirens.* It grows on mossy banks along the lower west slope of the Cascades right down to forests above the sea. A third woodland violet is *V. adunca* with broadly triangular leaves and blue to violet flowers, the lower petals often paler with purple veins. It grows in so many varied habitats and over so much of North America that a multitude of *adunca* variants are encountered. Some are stemless at flowering with a tuft of basal leaves and leafless stalks, each with a single large violet; others are a bit leggier with leafy stems bearing scattered flowers from base to tip. An easy, dependable and lovely plant for rather dry, open woods, or partial shade of the lower reaches in the rockery.

The dryland and rock outcrop violets are a special challenge to the gardener. A well-drained soil in a sunny position and avoidance of winter wet are called for. *Viola nuttallii* lavishes most of its variety on the east side of the mountains, in sagebrush, yellow pine, and other yet higher but fairly dry places. One form (var. *praemorsa*) grows in drier valleys and the gravelly "prairies" west of the Cascades. All forms of *V. nuttallii* have broadly lance-shaped basal leaves and short leafless flowering stems with single bicolor flowers (the two upper petals, yellow but backed with brown; the three lower, yellow and streaked brownish purple). *Viola purpurea* is widespread east of the Cascades from sagebrush lowlands to the subalpine; its leaves are coarsely toothed and often purplish beneath, or purple veined. Three sagebrush violets with finely dissected leaves entice trial in eastside rock gardens. Of the three—*V. beckwithii*, *V. sheltonii*, and *V. trinervata*—the last-named "is a 'must' for gardeners, east of the Cascades," according to Hitchcock, and with my full support. The dryland species from seeds do need hot dry summers after their spring flush of glory.

Some wet-meadow violets tame well in damp places in the garden. *Viola canadensis*, *V. mackloskyi*, and *V. palustris* are of this stamp.

The most challenging violet comes from the alpine. In the high Olympics, especially in the drier northeast sector, a lovely little violet, *V. flettii*, glorifies rock crevices and talus slopes of that exacting terrain. This local Olympic Mountain species may be raised in pans in the alpine cool house, with attention to drainage and a gritty textured soil. Because of its local distribution and the difficulties of garden culture, it must not be collected. Experts can try it from seeds, harvested outside the national park.

Violets come well from seeds; continued growth of seedlings is determined by the proper post-natal care, though only a skilled "plant pediatrician" can see the more difficult ones through to flowering. It may be noted that some violets have two flushes of bloom. The first is with showy flowers, freely out-crossed by insect pollinators. Later in the season, smaller flowers that never open, yield seeds by self-pollination, an uncommon seed-producing trick called cleistogamy by the botanist.

CALIFORNIA FUCHSIA *(Zauschneria latifolia)*. Evening Primrose Family (Onagraceae). This is the only member of a western clan of fuchsia-flowered willow-herbs that reaches our area. Its brilliant scarlet trumpets are borne on lax, clustered stems; its narrow felty-glandular leaves are about an inch long, often in opposite array on the stems. It can be found in southwestern Oregon, mainly in the drainage of the lower Rogue River.

Though *Zauschneria* belongs to the same family (Onagraceae or evening primrose family) as the true fuchsias of the tropics, it is a closer kin to the willow-herbs in the genus *Epilobium.*

Our northern race may be only a variety of the more wide-ranging *Zauschneria californica,* ranging from lower California to Curry County, Oregon. California fuchsias are easily grown from seeds and thrive in a sunny place in the rock garden or border. Give it plenty of root-run, as it can travel aggressively underground to pop up well away from the original planting.

Violet *(Viola flettii)*

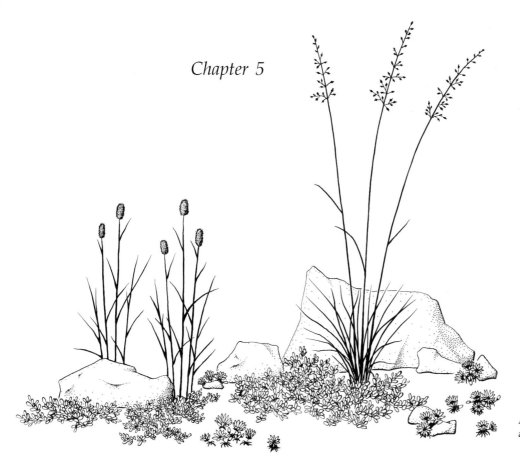

Alpine timothy (*Phleum alpinum*)
and green fescue (*Festuca viridula*)

Chapter 5

Grasses and Grasslike Plants

In nearly every vegetation type—seashore and dunes, woodland to alpine tundra—native grasses and their lookalike (monocot) kin appear as significant and faithful members of the plant community. Hence, in the gardener's desire to recreate a natural native plant setting, grasses and grasslike plants should claim pride of place. What is more, they have an appealing beauty as eye-catching elements in the garden decor.

For decades, grasses were a rare ingredient on the gardener's palette for homes or public places. But nowadays grasses and their kin—mostly exotics from other lands but some native to the Pacific Northwest—are commonly grown and are available commercially. There are a number of books devoted to the clan, often including some of our best natives (see Selected Bibliography).

What is meant by grasses *and* grasslike plants? Botanically, true grasses are all members of one huge cosmopolitan family, Gramineae (or Poaceae). Other families embrace the grasslike plants; the sedges in the Cyperaceae and the rushes in the Juncaceae are the primary kin to the grasses. The grass family includes a rich variety of life forms, from the annual (for example, the diminutive alien June grass, *Poa annua*) to rhizomatous perennials like the invasive quack grass (*Agropyron repens*). For the gardener, the most desired life form is a tufted, clump-forming perennial such as Idaho fescue (*Festuca idahoensis*). Size of grasses runs the gamut from a few inches to the 4-to-6-foot-tall giant rye (*Elymus canadensis*). All Northwest natives are herbaceous and most die down

220

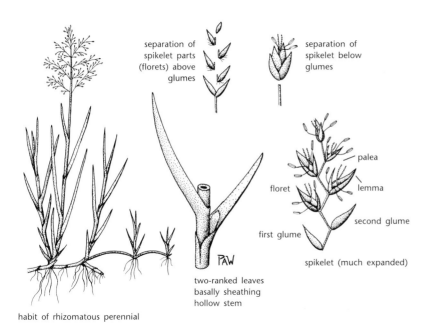

separation of spikelet parts (florets) above glumes

separation of spikelet below glumes

palea

floret

lemma

second glume

first glume

spikelet (much expanded)

two-ranked leaves basally sheathing hollow stem

habit of rhizomatous perennial

Vegetative and floral parts of a grass (bent grass, *Agrostis*)

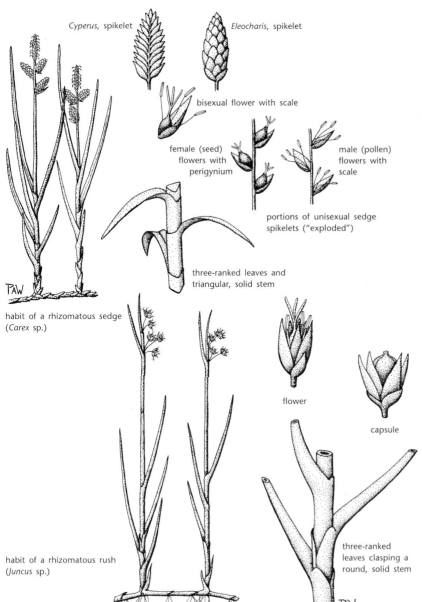

Cyperus, spikelet

Eleocharis, spikelet

bisexual flower with scale

female (seed) flowers with perigynium

male (pollen) flowers with scale

portions of unisexual sedge spikelets ("exploded")

three-ranked leaves and triangular, solid stem

habit of a rhizomatous sedge (*Carex* sp.)

Vegetative and floral parts of Cyperaceae (sedges and relatives)

flower

capsule

three-ranked leaves clasping a round, solid stem

habit of a rhizomatous rush (*Juncus* sp.)

Vegetative and floral parts of a rush (*Juncus* sp.)

Woodlands

3 cm

Semaphore grass (*Pleuropogon refractus*).
Infrequent in wet places west of the Cascades;
its distinctive "right-angled" spikelets on 18-
inch stems evoke the name "semaphore grass"

to their persisting root crown in winter; only in the tropics are there woody grasses: the bamboos.

The key features of grasses are the spikelet, the hollow stem or culm, and the grass leaf, which consists of the terminal blade and the proximal, clasping sheath. These features are illustrated on page 221. The spikelet is a compact cluster of tiny flowers (florets), each cluster or spikelet enveloped by two papery bracts (glumes). The one to several florets are stripped down to the bare essentials for seed production: three pollen-bearing stamens and one seed-bearing ovary topped by a feathery pollen-catching stigma. No petals or sepals, just two tiny scales called lemma and palea partially enclose the essential (sex) organs. At the peak of flowering, stamens protrude to shed pollen, carried by wind, to the exposed, feathery stigmas. Each floret develops a single seed (caryopsis or grain) that is dispersed by wind, gravity, or animals to secure the next generation. Many grass florets bear a projecting needle-like awn to aid in animal dispersal.

There are native grasses for nearly every garden setting. Their natural habitats range from woodland and wetland to prairies, dry steppe, and mountain meadow; they even venture into the treeless alpine. This diversity of natural habitats bodes well for matching a variety of garden settings, from full shade to full sun, with grasses. The focus here will be on perennial natives; there are very few annual grasses that are native and none is a worthy garden subject. A further caveat: the common grasses of cities, towns, suburbia, and farm lands are mostly not native, especially in cultivated or disturbed sites. Although some of these naturalized aliens are attractive, most are nuisances. The annual June grass, the common lawn grasses (mostly bent grasses of the genus *Agrostis*), and the rank grasses of wayside places—orchard grass (*Dactylis glomerata*), canary grass (*Phalaris* spp.), quack grass (*Agropyron repens*), and a variety of bromes and fescues—hardly merit cultivation. Furthermore, these aliens often insinuate themselves into a garden. Especially vexing is when they insinuate themselves in a clump of favored native grass or sedge.

Grasses for Woodland Settings

Though few in number the woodlanders are handsome with their tall, arching floral stems. A favorite of mine is nodding trisetum (*Trisetum cernuum*); its two to several erect spikelet-bearing stems reach up to three feet and bear copious pendant spikelets (the species name means "nodding"). It, like all grasses, is easily grown from seed. Another tall and graceful woodlander is Alaska or Sitka brome (*Bromus sitchensis*), which is not uncommon west of the Cascades, from the Puget trough to the seacoast. Slightly less tall is the remarkable semaphore grass (*Pleuropogon refractus*); its longish stems bear several large and showy spikelets horizontally—a railroad semaphore signal! This species is only occasional throughout western Oregon and Washington. Other woodland choices are listed in Appendix D.

Kin to grasses are the sedges and rushes. An elegant sedge for the open woodland is Merten's sedge (*Carex mertensii*). This 2-to-3-foot, tufted perennial displays large pendant spikelets on its several arching stems. Look for it in forest openings mid-montane in the Cascades and Olympics; it is also known from wetter areas in northern Idaho and western Montana. Though this is my favorite sedge, many others of this vast clan should be tried, and a number are now offered in the trade as seed or plants ("Hortus West" 1995).

The rushes come in at least two distinct patterns. While the round- and flat-stemmed species of *Juncus* are best for wetlands, the wood rushes of the genus *Luzula* are charming carpeters for the woodland garden. *Luzula campestris* is our most common wood rush. It naturalizes easily, seeding itself in almost any shady situation. Other wood rushes should be tried; *L. piperi* and *L. hitchcockii* are attractive montane species.

Grasses and Their Kin for Wetlands

Bogs, swamps, and the borders of lakes, ponds, and streams can either be shaded or in full sun. Their key habitat feature is freestanding water for at least part of the growing season. Although "wetland" is a slippery term, a good working definition, adopted by public agencies in Washington State, is "those areas that are inundated or saturated by surface or ground water at a frequency and duration to support . . . a prevalence of vegetation typically adapted for life in saturated soil conditions" (Kruckeberg 1991). Gardeners, let alone obligated developers and public trustees of wetlands, are faced with the same challenge: how to preserve, restore, or recreate a wetland. Far from being a biological wasteland, a wetland can evoke a watery charm all its own. The gardening potential of wetlands was memorialized by Gertrude Jeckyll, the eminent British garden sage. When asked by a client, "What can I do about the bog on my property?" Miss Jeckyll replied, "Get down on your knees and thank God for your bog!"

Grasslike plants (sedges and rushes) dominate the wetland habitat. Yet a few grass species inhabit wet areas. Manna grass (*Glyceria* species) frequents pools and slow-moving fresh water. *Glyceria elata*, the commonest species, has flowering culms up to three feet, tipped with many tiny spikelets; the overall effect is a graceful, misty look. Another common grass of wet places, tufted hair grass (*Deschampsia caespitosa*), is mostly one or two feet tall; its hair-thin leaves and many tiny spikelets impart a gossamer halo to its bright green basal tufts. Nearly every wetland from tidewater to the alpine features species of sedge (*Carex*). *Carex lyngbyi* and *C. obnupta* are widely used for wetland restoration and are available in the trade. Wetland species of *Juncus* (the rushes) also work well in wetlands. And for sheer wetland boldness, cattail (*Typhya latifolia*) takes the prize. All of the above species are grown readily from seed or offshoots.

Wetlands

Merten's sedge (*Carex mertensii*). Frequent in openings of montane forests; its attractive pendant floral spikes borne on 2-foot stems

4 cm

Green fescue (*Festuca viridula*). Common and widespread grass of open subalpine meadows; 18-24 inches tall, with distinctive bright green foliage

Meadow Grasses

Most of the woodland and wetland grasses are suited for meadows that retain moisture throughout the growing season. But meadow and prairie habitats that must endure summer drought call for other native species. Two fescues, *Festuca idahoensis* (Idaho fescue) and *F. californica,* are admirably suited for summer-dry prairie and meadow life. My wife and I have kept California fescue in a dry meadow for several years. The big, bold evergreen clumps send forth dozens of arching, flowering culms with copious drooping (lax) spikelets, creating a dramatic effect. Idaho fescue, rather smaller than *F. californica,* is frequent on both sides of the Cascades and is especially common in the Fort Lewis (Tacoma) prairie country. It is widely used for prairie and meadow restoration. At Mima Prairie (Thurston County) it is being used to restore the mounded prairies to their indigenous state, replacing the undesirable alien grasses (R. Schuller, personal communication). Among the several other dry meadow species (see Appendix D), I rank highest the perennial brome (*Bromus carinatus*), tall wild rye (*Elymus glaucus*), various of the onion grasses (*Melica* spp.), and the dramatic side-oats grama (*Bouteloua curtipendula*).

A final thought on the prairie environment. Remember that pristine—or even altered—prairies and meadows were, and shall become, a rich mixture of grasses *with* other herbaceous perennials. To recreate such a setting, one seeks beyond the grasses to plant "forbs," those flowering plants other than grasses and their kin. Camas, balsamroot, asters, fleabane, yarrow, cinquefoil, and others should be companions to grasses in prairie and meadow settings.

Grasses at the Seashore

The outer coast bordering the Pacific Ocean is far from a homogeneous habitat. Sites range from wet (marshes and wet meadows) to dry (dunes and stable, well-drained meadows). Sea beaches with strand vegetation can give way to steep, timbered bluffs and headlands. Such landscape diversity begets a variety of vegetation types, admirably described in detail in Franklin and Dyrness (1988). Grasses, sedges, and rushes often occupy dominant roles in certain of these habitats. Gardening along the outer coast presents special challenges: salt spray, sterile dune sands, brackish marshland, and the like. But, rather than despair, the coastal gardener should observe what Nature has used to clothe these habitats with flora, and then proceed to imitate Nature.

For dune habitats, try dune wild rye (*Elymus mollis*), red fescue (*Festuca rubra*), native bluegrass (*Poa macrantha*), and bighead sedge (*Carex macrocephala*). For wetter areas, the sedge *Carex obnupta,* the rush (*Juncus phaeocephala*), and tufted hair grass (*Deschampsia caespitosa*) should work well. Avoid at all costs introducing the two alien invaders that already have established a firm beachhead and are inundating native seashore vegetation: cord grass (*Spartina* spp.) has taken an aggressive dominion over natives in salt marshes, while European beach grass (*Ammophila arenaria*) can overrun dunes and strand. The native grasses and their kin are amiable companions to other coastal plants, which are listed in Appendix B.

Alpine and Low-growing Grasses for the Rock Garden

Native grasses abound in the meadowy parkland of the upper montane zones; most are blue grasses (*Poa*) and fescues (*Festuca*) of moderate stature. The low, tufted perennials, including grasses and sedges, predominate in the alpine zone. Several are suitable for the rock garden or low, sunny border bed. Three low-growing grasses with spikey flower heads merit cultivation: alpine timothy (*Phleum alpinum*), alpine trisetum (*Trisetum spicatum*), and prairie June grass (*Koehleria cristata*). Two parkland (upper montane) grasses can add charming contrast to the low heathery shrub borders of the rock garden: mountain bunchgrass (*Festuca viridula*), up to two feet tall, emits a bright viridescence (green) from its tufted basal herbage to the showy flower clusters. It is frequent in dryish nonforested openings east of the Cascade crest; it makes spectacular displays at Sunrise (Yakima Park) on the east side of Mount Rainier. Growing among mountain heathers and low huckleberry is a dainty charmer. A relative of the cosmopolitan tufted hairgrass, the more demure *Deschampsia atropurpurea*, not over 10 inches high, has erect stems tipped with nodding, reddish purple spikelets—a unique hallmark for a grass. Of the several sedges and rushes in the subalpine and the land above the trees, watch for the imposing *Carex spectabilis*, *Luzula piperi*, and two rushes, *Juncus drummondii* and *J. parryi*. Still other grasses and their kin of low stature are listed in Appendix D.

Grasses for East of the Cascades

Grasses truly come into their own on the dry side of the mountains. Especially rich and diverse are the grasslands of open, yellow pine woodlands and of sagebrush country. While gardeners west of the Cascades should yield to the temptation to try some of these dryland inhabitants in the driest of westside sites, the eastside gardens and open spaces can foster with ease a mix of dryland grasses with other hardy eastsiders. For starters, consider these three, each singular in habit and flower. The tallest native grass in the Pacific Northwest surely must be giant rye grass (*Elymus canadensis*); 4-to-6-foot stems, bearing stiffly erect spikes of flowers aloft over a "bed" of large, grey-green blades. A small rye-grass kin is the ubiquitous blue-bunch wheat grass (*Agropyron spicatum*); while it is sagebrush's most constant companion, it ventures up into the mid-montane of the interior mountains. Its steely blue-green clumps bear few to several floral spikes. Another spikey dryland grass is squirrel-tail grass (*Sitanion jubatum*). In sharp contrast to these rye-

Rock Gardens / East of the Cascades

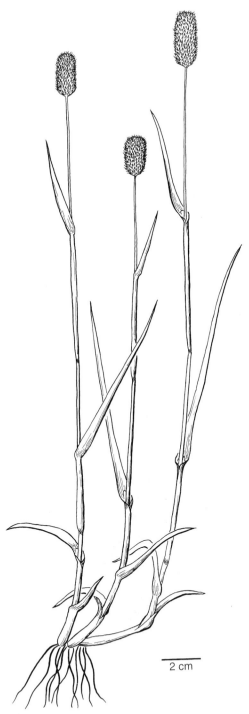

2 cm

Alpine timothy (*Phleum alpinum*). Widespread in montane meadows of the Old and New Worlds; its erect dense spikes borne on 8- to 12-inch stems

East of the Cascades

and wheat-grasses is the dryland Indian rice grass (*Oryzopsis hymenoides*). Its great appeal is the plant in full bloom. The tiny, single-floreted spikelets are borne profusely in a dichotomously branching, diffuse inflorescence. It is an especially choice grass for the dry bouquet—as are most grasses, except those that "shatter" when dry. Consult Appendix D for a roster of eastside grasses.

Squirrel-tail grass (*Sitanion jubatum*), a common perennial from sagebrush country to the subalpine

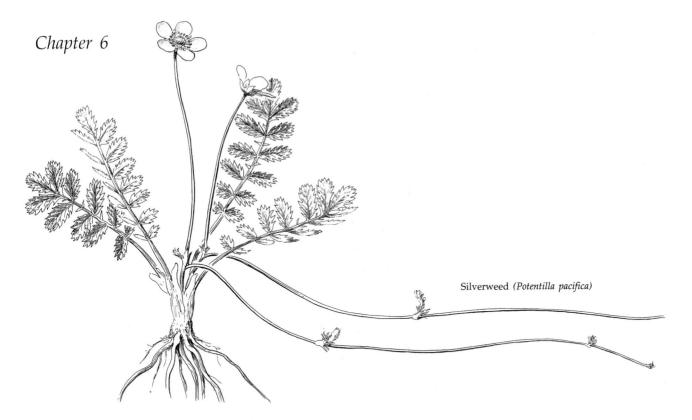

Chapter 6

Silverweed *(Potentilla pacifica)*

Supplement: More Native Plants for Garden and Habitat Reclamation

It is tempting to add to the rich palette of natives already described in the first edition of this book. Now that more and more native plants are offered commercially as plants or seeds, it is desirable to call attention to some natives not included in the 1982 edition. Grasses and grasslike plants get their own special niche in this revised edition (see chapter 5). Along with some noteworthy annuals that merit promotion, here I list in alphabetical order by botanical name herbaceous perennials and woody species that did not appear in the 1982 edition.

Annuals (usually easy from seed)

CLARKIAS *(Clarkia* species). Evening Primrose Family (Onagraceae). Several of these godetias, ragged-robins, farewell-to-spring clarkias make it into the Pacific Northwest from California. Their showy pink flowers are either open goblets or ribbony petalled. Seeds of *Clarkia amoena* and *C. pulchella* are available.

COLLINSIAS *(Collinsia* species). Snapdragon Family (Scrophulariaceae). Blue-eyed Mary *(Collinsia parviflora)* is the charming miniature, but several Oregon species have larger, showier flowers: lavender, splotched white, corollas shaped like penstemon or monkey flowers.

COLLOMIA *(Collomia grandiflora)*. Phlox Family (Polemoniaceae). "An attractive annual that readily maintains itself in the wild garden,"

Annuals

according to Hitchcock, and I agree. In nature, expect to find it blooming in late spring in open dry places in ponderosa pine country.

CALIFORNIA POPPY (*Eschscholzia californica*). Poppy Family (Papaveraceae). California poppy, so widely naturalized in the Pacific Northwest, is also native here from the Columbia Gorge south to California. Our most glamorous wildflower, parading its splashes of big, golden-yellow flowers on greyish foliage, is a familiar sight nearly everywhere in sunny places west of the Cascades. It can behave as a perennial.

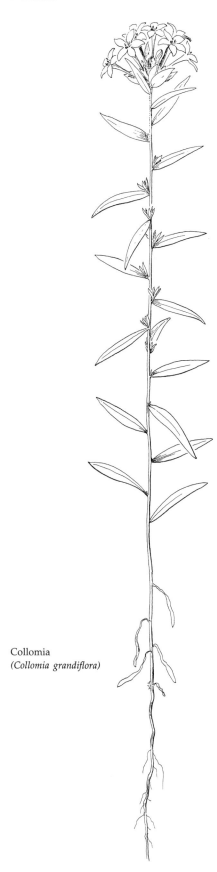

Collomia
(*Collomia grandiflora*)

California poppy (*Eschscholzia californica*)

GLOBE GILIA (*Gilia capitata*). Phlox Family (Polemoniaceae). The globe gilia is aptly named for its tightly clustered, lavender flowers at the tips of each lateral and terminal branchlet. The delicate filigreed compound leaves reminds one of yarrow foliage. It grows wild in dry, open places on both sides of the Cascades; commonest in the Columbia Gorge.

ROSY PLECTRITIS (*Plectritis congesta*). Valerian Family (Valerianaceae). The appearance of rosy plectritis in early spring signals the advent of the new year's floral season. Sheets of this delicate annual with rosy pink flowers carpet mossy open headlands in the San Juans and in coastal Puget country. Our local race is showy and readily maintains itself by seeding in the wild garden.

JEWEL FLOWER (*Streptanthus tortuosus*). Mustard Family (Brassicaceae). Our only common jewel flower occurs in dryish openings of woodlands and chaparral in southwestern Oregon; it can be gregarious on roadcuts. Its many smallish flowers on branching, 1-to-3-foot stems are yellow, streaked with purple, and shaped like delicate urns—little earrings!

Herbaceous Perennials

MAIDENHAIR FERNS (*Adiantum* species). The only one listed in the first edition was *Adiantum pedatum*, our commonest and choicest one. It has been renamed *A. aleuticum* to embrace both the widespread wetland form and the unusual serpentine race, as well as the dwarf (formerly var. *subpumilum*). The reader may add two others to a wish list of maidenhair ferns: *A. capillis-veneris*, the venus-hair fern, found mostly in alkaline hotsprings, and *A. jordanii*, which can be found in rocky places along Oregon's Rogue River.

Globe gilia *(Gilia capitata)*

Dwarf maidenhair fern (*Adiantum pedatum* var. *subpumilum*)

Herbaceous Perennials

Alpine aster *(Aster alpigenus)*

HORSE MINTS *(Agastache* species). Mint Family (Menthaceae). The horse mints, all from east of the Cascades, come in two sizes. The tall, coarse ones *(Agastache occidentalis* and *A. urticifolia)* are best for a prairie wildflower garden. The dwarf, *A. cusickii,* is a good subject for the rock garden. All have mint flowers (two-lipped corollas), white to pink, borne in dense terminal clusters.

SPREADING DOGBANE *(Apocynum androsaemifolium).* Dogbane Family (Apocynaceae). Common on both sides of the Cascades, this dogbane looks much like an herbaceous version of snowberry *(Symphoricarpos),* with its opposite leaves and dainty pink flowers. But the milky juice of a cut stem and its long pods with cottony seeds are telltale dogbane features. It prefers dry, sunny sites.

ROCK CRESSES *(Arabis* species). Mustard Family (Brassicaceae). From this vast clan of rock cresses, choose the dwarfs inhabiting talus and cliffs. A sampler includes white-flowered ones like *Arabis furcata, A. lyallii,* and *A. nuttallii.* Purple-flowered cresses, though less common, merit a place in the rock garden: *A. koehleri, A. breweri, A. serpentinicola, A. macdonaldiana.* All are easy from seed.

ALPINE ASTER *(Aster alpigenus).* Aster Family (Asteraceae). Suited to the rock garden or trough, this fine alpine aster has a compact rosette of narrow leaves that unfurls one to several short stems, each bearing a single showy lavender-flowered head. It makes its home at timberline and above in rocky openings in the Olympics, Cascades, and Wallowa Mountains.

BALSAMROOT *(Balsamorhiza hookeri).* Sunflower Family (Asteraceae). The bigger balsamroots meet this pygmy everywhere in sagebrush country. Its flat rosette of deeply cut leaves sends forth bronzy-golden flower heads, not over 6 to 10 inches high; it is happiest in well-drained stony ground. Watch for hybrids between it and the larger balsamroots (described on pp. 166-67).

CHICKWEED *(Cerastium arvense).* Chickweed Family (Caryophyllaceae). Other chickweeds are mostly weedy annuals. But this fine perennial of open sunny places from coastal bluffs to alpine screes merits a place in the garden. Its many large white flowers make it welcome in low borders or the rock garden.

SOAP LILY *(Chlorogalum pomeridianum).* Lily Family (Liliaceae). This bizarre kin of lilies and camas occurs in open woods and chaparral from southern Oregon into California. From a huge bulb emerge two to several ribbony, wavy-margined, straplike leaves. The leafless flower stalks, up to 5 feet tall, bear many tubular flowers, greenish-white to lilac, often with darker veins. The soap plant, in a hot, dry garden site, is sure to transfix the viewer.

Balsamroot *(Balsamorhiza hookeri)*

BUGBANE (*Cimicifuga elata*). Buttercup Family (Ranunculaceae). This bold, tall (3-to-6-foot) woodlander is infrequent in lowland westside forests. Thought to be effective against lice and certain other bugs, bugbane is not at all repellent to the eye. Its coarsely divided compound leaves give accent to the tall flowering stems; each bears many tiny white flowers with showy cream-colored stamens. It will remind one of goat's beard (*Aruncus sylvester*, p. 159).

HOUND'S TONGUE (*Cynoglossum* species). Forget-me-not Family (Boraginaceae). Kin to bluebells (*Mertensia*), hound's tongue is a robust, leafy perennial with many blue to violet flowers. *Cynoglossum grande* is the best of the three native species; it is occasional in open woods from British Columbia to California and extends through the Columbia Gorge. It gets its name from its rough-textured leaves and nutlets.

SEA-CLIFF STONECROP (*Dudleya farinosa*). Stonecrop Family (Crassulaceae). The fleshiest of the stonecrops, dudleyas are widespread in western California. Only one grows in the Pacific Northwest, the sea-cliff variety, from Bandon, Oregon, southward. These stout succulents are outsized sedums and require the same dry, sunny garden conditions (pp. 211-12). Flowers pale yellow on 6-to-18-inch stalks, fleshy like the rosette leaves at the base.

Pacific hound's tongue *(Cynoglossum grande)*

Herbaceous Perennials

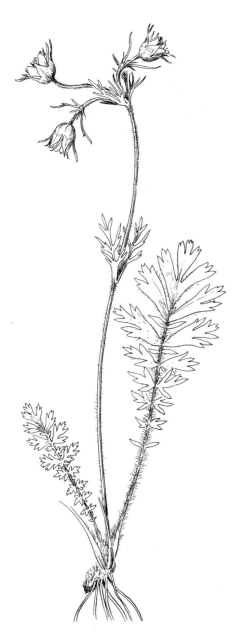

Prairie smoke *(Geum trifolium var. ciliatum)*

SEASIDE DAISY (*Erigeron glaucus*). Daisy Family (Asteraceae). The seaside daisy is one of the showiest of the genus. The thick, glossy foliage supports a multitude of large flower heads, lilac to white. This daisy has been in cultivation for years and is suitable for sunny borders. In the wild it is on cliffs above the sea, from northwest Oregon to California.

QUEEN-OF-THE-FOREST (*Filipendula occidentalis*). Rose Family (Rosaceae). This handsome 3-to-5-foot woodlander that looks like a *Spiraea* or *Astilbe* is waiting to be discovered by gardeners. It has many small white flowers atop a leafy stalk. Queen-of-the-forest occurs infrequently in northwest Oregon, in rock crevices just above high water along coastal rivers. It does best in moist areas with full sun or partial shade.

BLANKET-FLOWER (*Gaillardia aristata*). Daisy Family (Asteraceae). An old favorite for dry, sunny borders, the blanket-flower offers showy heads of large daisy flowers, yellow-suffused reddish-purple. Native to prairies and dryish meadows east of the Cascades.

BEDSTRAWS (*Galium* species). Madder Family (Rubiaceae). Perennial bedstraws remind one of woodruff: short stems with whorled linear leaves and clusters of small white flowers. While *Galium multiflorum* (pp. 194-95) is best for the rock garden, other bedstraws, like *G. boreale*, *G. verum*, and *G. oreganum*, are suited to the woodland garden.

GENTIAN (*Gentiana newberryi*). Gentian Family (Gentianaceae). Like *Gentiana calycosa* (p. 195) of the Cascades and Olympics, this Oregonian grows in wet meadows in the Klamath-Siskiyou Mountains. Suitable for damp woodland sites or the bog bed.

PRAIRIE SMOKE (*Geum triflorum* var. *ciliatum*). Rose Family (Rosaceae). Called prairie smoke or old man's whiskers, this charming ally of the garden geums and alpine avens boasts pink flowers followed by a fetching topknot of dusky plumed seeds. Mostly a yellow-pine associate, it does have a subalpine race, var. *campanulatum*, in the Olympics; 6-8 inches tall, with finely dissected foliage.

HEDYSARUMS (*Hedysarum* species). Legume or Pea Family (Fabaceae). Several sweet-vetches (or hedysarums) are native in the Pacific Northwest, but *Hedysarum occidentale* is the most accessible and easiest to grow. It is widespread in the subalpine meadows of the Olympic Mountains. Like many other legumes, it has compound leaves and purple, vetchlike pea flowers. But in fruit it is unique: each pod is a succession of rings or circles, like a multiple lorgnette. Try it in a sunny low border or the rock garden. It is also native throughout the Rocky Mountains of Idaho and Montana.

HELENIUMS (*Helenium* species). Sunflower Family (Compositae). All three of our native Heleniums (sneezeweeds, alas!) inhabit montane wet places in southern Oregon, so they should be suitable for dampish garden spots. *Helenium hoopsii, H. bigelovii,* and *H. bolanderi* all have showy yellow flowering heads.

HESPEROCHIRONS (*Hesperochiron* species). Waterleaf Family (Hydrophyllaceae). Both species (*Hesperochiron californicus* and *H. pumilus*) have been in cultivation in Britain, but they seem not to have appeared in Pacific Northwest gardens. Hitchcock says about them: "The species are tempting to native garden enthusiasts, and they might be coaxed into doing well east of the Cascades." Both occur in spring-wet places as delicate low perennials with fleshy basal leaves and large white, pink-veined flowers.

KELLOGGIA (*Kelloggia galioides*). Madder Family (Rubiaceae). This kin to our native bedstraws (*Galium* sp.) has larger, funnel-shaped flowers (white to pink) and opposite—not whorled—leaves. It is found in open rocky places mostly on the east slopes of the Cascades. It should be tried in the rock garden.

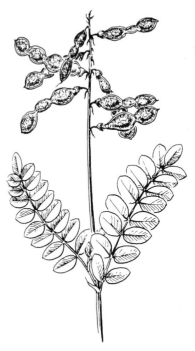

Sweet vetch (*Hedysarum occidentale*)

LESQUERELLAS (*Lesquerella* species). Mustard Family (Cruciferae). Along with the bladderpods in *Physaria* (p. 208), these ground-hugging crucifers like sunny, gritty root-runs in the rock garden. The Rocky Mountain species, *Lesquerella alpina* and *L. ludovicianna* of sagebrush country, merit trial.

SAND LILY (*Leucocrinum montanum*). Lily Family (Liliaceae). The low-growing sand lily puts forth many long-stalked white flowers from a rosette of narrow leaves; this eye-catching display arises from a deep underground rhizome. Seek seed of it in stony or clay soils east of the Cascades in Oregon (sagebrush to yellow pine country) and east to Idaho and Montana.

DESERT PARSLEYS (*Lomatium* species). Parsley Family (Apiaceae). Desert parsleys or biscuit-roots come in all sizes from the 3-foot tall *Lomatium dissectum* to ground-hugging species like *L. martindalei* and *L. watsonii*. The more than fifty Pacific Northwest species all have finely dissected leaves and yellow, white, or purplish tiny flowers in dense umbellate clusters—the family's key feature. Culture of desert parsleys is a real challenge; best grown from stratified seed and seedlings planted out in well-drained sunny sites.

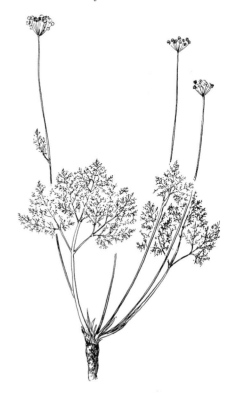

BLAZING STAR (*Mentzelia laevicaulis*). Blazing-star Family (Loasaceae). I usually see these showy herbs on roadcuts most places east of the Cascades. They can get up to two feet, tipped with the most glamorous golden-yellow flowers with showy stamens. Blazing-star behaves as a biennial or perennial, flowering the second year from seed sown

Desert parsley (*Lomatium dissectum*)

Herbaceous Perennials

Blazing star *(Mentzelia laevicaulis)*

outdoors in the fall. Curiosity will lead you to discover that the sandpapery foliage sticks to clothing.

MILKWORT *(Polygala californica)*. Milkwort Family (Polygalaceae). The rosy flowers of this milkwort imitate the lupine flower. This low-growing herb with a woody rootstalk is found in open stony ground and thickets in southwestern Oregon and on into California.

KNOTWEED *(Polygonum newberryi)*. Knotweed Family (Polygonaceae). Widely distributed throughout the volcanic Cascades, this eye-catching perennial likes unstable slopes of pumice; it is also at home on serpentine in the Wenatchee Mountains. Its many grey-green leafy shoots come from a thick rootstalk. The fleshy stems are tipped with many small greenish-yellow flowerlets, followed by copious three-angled fruits. Untried and possibly difficult; it should do best in gritty soil of the rock garden.

POTENTILLAS *(Potentilla* species). Rose Family (Rosaceae). Besides the cinquefoils offered on page 209, most potentillas are worthy of culture. *Potentilla anserina* and *P. pacifica*, two silverweeds of wet meadows and mudflats, are valuable in wetland restoration. *Potentilla drummondii, P. gracilis*, and *P. diversifolia* are montane plants and are suited to the sunny low border or rock garden. All have yellow flowers and compound, often dissected, leaves.

YELLOW BUTTERCUPS *(Ranunculus* species). Buttercup Family (Ranunculaceae). From a host of wet-meadow yellow buttercups, try *Ranunculus occidentalis* and its many varieties. For dampish cool sites in the rock garden, the alpine *R. eschscholtzii* and *R. suksdorfii* merit trial.

WATERLEAF *(Romanzoffia sitchensis)*. Waterleaf Family (Hydrophyllaceae). Looking like some saxifrages, these dainty herbs are at home on wet cliffs from nearly sea level to the montane. Largish white flowers, often with a yellow eye, over a loose rosette of roundish toothed leaves. Should be ideal bordering a garden pool or stream.

BRAMBLES *(Rubus* species). Rose Family (Rosaceae). The generous account of native brambles (pp. 125-26) can be supplemented by yet a few others. Though a bit invasive, the blackcap *(Rubus leucodermis)* redeems its rampant growth with luscious blackcap raspberries. It is easy from suckers or seeds; its tall bluish-grey stems are a give-away. Another native bramble, *R. ursinus*, can be a pest. But in wild lands its small sweet blackberries are unbeatable. Rare among brambles, *R. ursinus* has separate sexes, so not all plants bear fruits. Someday, *R. bartonianus*, the Snake River thimbleberry, will make its way into gardens; its large, single white flowers on tallish stems should make it a winner. It grows wild in places that are difficult of access in the Snake River Canyon.

WINGED DOCK (*Rumex venosus*). Knotweed Family (Polygonaceae). This is a striking plant, both for its tenacity on inland dunes and for its red foliage and flower stems. It increases by runners, sending up short (6-12-inch) shoots bearing large oval to lance-shaped leaves. In fruit the tassels of red achenes complete the crimson theme. Look for it along the Columbia River and in the nearby Juniper Dunes near Hanford, Washington.

BURNET (*Sanguisorba sitchensis*). Rose Family (Rosaceae). Wet meadows and stream banks in the high mountains favor this handsome native burnet. Greyish compound leaves cluster at the base of 1-to-2-foot flowering stalks, bearing smallish pink flowers in profusion. It should be happy in the bog garden.

RUSH LILIES (*Schoenolirion* species). Lily Family (Liliaceae). Two rush lilies, *Schoenolirion album* and *S. bracteosum*, tower over cobra lilies (*Darlingtonia*) and other bog-loving plants in southwestern Oregon seeps. From bulbs, tall leafless flower stems bear many small, white to purplish blooms. Try it in a bog garden from seed. Digging bulbs in the wild is a no-no! (See *Hastingsia* in Hickman 1993.)

SCULLCAPS (*Scutellaria* species). Mint Family (Menthaceae). Old-world skullcaps have been in gardens for years. It is time to give our Pacific Northwest natives a trial. Scullcap gets its name because of the unique floral device of a hat-shaped calyx, out of which emerges a typical mint flower: two-lipped and mostly blue. The taller *Scutellaria lateriflora* (mad dog skullcap) should do well in a dampish border. *S. angustifolia* (blue) and *S. nana* (yellow) are small enough for the rock garden. Propagate by seed or rhizomes.

MOUNTAIN GOLDENROD (*Solidago multiradiata* var. *scopulorum*). Aster Family (Asteraceae). Goldenrods are mostly tall plants of prairie and wayside waste places—fine for meadow restoration. But this mountain goldenrod is unique, both in its modest height (4-8 inches) and its wide occurrence in subalpine areas of the Cascades and Olympics. Easy from seed, it forms a well-behaved mat of basal leaves in the rock garden, to send up shafts of golden heads.

DESERT MALLOWS (*Sphaeralcea* species). Mallow Family (Malvaceae). Two desert mallows, *Sphaeralcea munroana* (bright pink) and *S. coccinea* (brick red), are show pieces for the dryland garden. Hitchcock says that *S. coccinea* has performed well in sunny, well-drained sites even in Puget Sound gardens. The leafy stems of desert mallows bear dusty roundish leaves, shallowly to deeply cleft. These two, and *S. grossularifolia*, all are from sagebrush country east to the Great Plains.

WESTERN STENANTHIUM (*Stenanthium occidentale*). Lily Family (Liliaceae). Along with *Narthecium* (bog asphodel) and *Tofieldia*, this

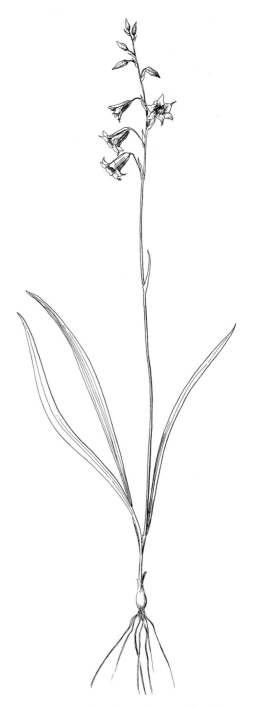

Western stenanthium (*Stenanthium occidentale*)

Trees

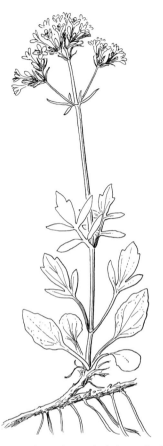

Wenatchee valerian (*Valeriana columbiana*)

wetlander is another charmer for the bog garden. All grow from spreading rootstalks, bearing grasslike leaves. *Tofieldia* and *Narthecium* have yellow flowers; those of *Stenanthium* are dark red. Native to montane seeps, bogs, and stream banks.

VALERIAN (*Valeriana columbiana*). Valerian Family (Valerianaceae). The mountain heliotrope or Sitka valerian graces page 180, but the smaller *V. columbiana* merits culture too. Wenatchee valerian is a diminutive version of *V. sitchensis*, only 3 to 6 inches high, bearing a showy stalk of white flowers. It is a most worthy addition to the native rock garden. Rare and local as it is in Kittitas and Chelan counties of Washington, it should be grown from sparingly collected seed.

Trees

Though Pacific Northwest native trees were generously covered in the original edition, some were slighted and are included here.

SHASTA RED FIR (*Abies magnifica* var. *shastensis*). Pine Family (Pinaceae). Shasta red fir is the northern race of that magnificent Sierran conifer, California red fir (*Abies magnifica*). Its grandeur can be witnessed in the wild in the high country just west of Mount Ashland, southern Oregon. Though it becomes a 150-to-200-foot tree in nature, young specimens (in our garden) are slow growing. So it should be suitable for large gardens and for public plantings west of the Cascades. Its foliage is like that of noble fir (*Abies procera*, p. 30).

WHITE ALDER (*Alnus rhombifolia*). Birch Family (Betulaceae). Forgive my nostalgic attraction for this grand alder. It was my constant companion when growing up botanically in California. Yet, white alder gets as far north as southern British Columbia, on both sides of the Cascades, mostly along streams. It is not easy to distinguish from red alder (*Alnus rubra*, p. 73). White alders' leaves are finely toothed, and the bark of mature specimens is whitish. It can get up to 60 feet tall, or can grow as a large shrub. If you are intimidated by the "weediness" of red alder, try *A. rhombifolia*. Handsome as a specimen tree for wet areas in the garden, it also merits use in wetland restoration projects.

WESTERN HACKBERRY (*Celtis douglasii*). Elm Family (Ulmaceae). This eastsider of sere habitats is most "unelmlike" in flower and fruit; yet its foliage is suggestive of small-leaved elms—obliquely (unevenly) tapered at the base of the ovate leaf and with an elm leaf's finely rough surface (like emery-paper). It is usually a large shrub or can be tree-like, up to 30 feet tall in favored sites. Its pea-sized pulpy berry is reddish brown and sweetish to the taste. It is occasional in dry rocky places above stream courses in the Snake and Columbia rivers country. We have had it in our westside garden for years; it has done well but never

Hawthorn *(Crataegus douglasii)*

flowered. It should be a worthy companion to hawthorns and choke-cherries and should be a promising woody addition to dryish habitats, especially east of the Cascades.

HAWTHORNS *(Crataegus* species). Rose Family (Rosaceae). These tall de-ciduous shrubs, or small trees, are easily identified as hawthorns, with their stout spines (actually short, spine-tipped lateral branches). Their rather showy white flowers, borne in terminal or lateral clusters give way to the crabapple-sized, dark red to purplish black fruits. Our two native hawthorns may be distinguished by differences in thorn length and fruit color. *Crataegus columbiana* has long slender thorns and reddish fruits; it occurs widely from moist to dry sites east of the Cascades. *Crataegus douglasii* has shorter, stouter thorns and blackish fruits; it can be found on both sides of the Cascades. Both hawthorns provide food and cover for wildlife and enjoy dryish sunny sites in the garden; stratified seed germinate well. Be aware of the two alien species, *C. monogyna* and *C. oxyacantha*; both have become naturalized west of the Cascade Range. They are readily recognized by their deeply (3-7) lobed leaves; our native hawthorns have entire or only faintly lobed, toothed leaves.

BAKER'S CYPRESS *(Cupressus bakeri)*. Cypress Family (Cupressaceae). Baker's cypress held the distinction of being the only one of its genus in the Pacific Northwest until the new *Jepson Flora of California* sunk both Pacific Northwest species of *Chamaecyparis* (Lawson cypress and Alaska cedar) into the genus *Cupressus*—a hard pill to swallow for both bota-nists and horticulturists! Species of *Cupressus* (of yore) are mostly small,

Trees

Western crabapple *(Malus fusca)*

shrubby trees of dry open habitats, quite unlike their grand forest kin in *Chamaecyparis*. *Cupressus bakeri*, like Sargent and Macnab cypresses, is a small tree, suitable for plantings west of the Cascades. It favors open woods on dry slopes in southern Oregon and northern California. Though Baker's cypress resembles Rocky Mountain juniper in habit and foliage (pp. 52-54), it has small, silvery, woody cones, not the "gin" berries of juniper.

WESTERN CRABAPPLE *(Malus fusca)*. Rose Family (Rosaceae). Our only native crabapple, a multistemmed large shrub or small tree, takes no great prizes in crabapple competition. But what it may lack in ornamental value is amply compensated for by its value as a wetlander. Just follow Hitchcock et al. into its damp home: "Moist woods, stream banks, swamps and bogs, to open canyons and foothills . . ."—a choice candidate for restoring or recreating wetland habitats, on the wet side of the mountains. Its narrowly ovate leaves are toothed and often shallowly lobed. The white to pink apple-blossom flowers are arrayed in clusters near the ends of leafy twigs; its smallish fruits may be yellow or purplish red. Western crabapple, though resembling the hawthorns in foliage, flower, and fruit, has no thorns. Propagation is by layering or from cleaned, stratified seed.

WILLOWS *(Salix* species). Willow Family (Salicaceae). The willows described in the first edition (p. 126) barely sampled the vast potential of this large clan. Besides the tall shrubs and the prostrate willows for the rock garden, there are tree species of handsome aspect. Scouler's willow *(Salix scouleriana)*, most often a largish multistemmed shrub (p. 126), can reach tree size (30-50 feet) and have but a single trunk. Red willow *(S. lasiandra)* and peach-leaved willow *(S. amygdaloides)* can get to 30 or 40 feet in height. Both have long, tapered leaves; they are found east of the Cascades, though one variant of red willow (var. *lasiandra)* occurs west of the Cascades and in moist regions of northern Idaho and northwestern Montana. Still other tree willows should tempt both gardeners and landscape restorers: Arroyo willow *(S. lasiolepis)*, valley willow *(S. hindsiana)*, and Bebb's willow *(S. bebbiana)*. All these tree willows prefer wet places—streamsides, edges of lakes, or borders of swamps and bogs. Propagate from cuttings.

WESTERN YEW *(Taxus brevifolia)*. Yew Family (Taxaceae). Like Cinderella, western yew was once disdained by foresters. But with its "magic slipper," its medicinal bark, our native yew has gained notoriety and favor, as well as a modicum of protection. Western yew is now the best source of *taxol*, a miracle drug for the treatment of certain cancers. For this reason alone, plants are now readily available commercially. As a garden subject, the text on pages 55 and 56 is still appropriate. I would underscore my earlier opinion that Wenatchee Mountain shrub forms are superior to the westside trees. With its new notoriety, western yew will be seen more in gardens and public plantings.

Shrubs

A few suitable garden subjects of shrub habit escaped the first edition.

Berberis piperiana. Barberry Family (Berberidaceae). We have grown this elegant kin to tall Oregon grape (*B. aquifolium*, pp. 100-102) for years in our garden. Its striking foliage—grey-green, heavily veined leaflets—is topped by a rich display of golden yellow flower clusters. The multi-branched plants reach 5 to 7 feet in cultivation. It is wild in southern Oregon from the Rogue River Valley to Klamath County and, as expected, south to northern California. A charming, low-growing barberry, *Berberis pumila* from serpentine habitats in Oregon, is well worth growing in a sunny rock garden.

MOUNTAIN HEATHS (*Cassiope* species). Heather Family (Ericaceae). Here are two more native mountain heaths to challenge and delight the connoisseur. While *C. mertensiana* is the showiest (p. 91), the following are choice subjects for the peaty areas of the rock garden. *Cassiope stelleriana* bears single, dainty, white bells on short lax stems; its tiny needle-leaves are reminiscent of crowberry (*Empetrum nigrum*, p. 91). It grows wild from Mount Rainier north to Alaska and on to northeast Asia. *Cassiope tetragona* is a shyer version of *C. mertensiana*; it has the same four-angled short stems with overlapping scale leaves, but smaller white flowers. It is known in our area as an alpine plant from the Rockies west to Okanogan County, Washington.

CEANOTHUS (*Ceanothus* species). Buckthorn Family (Rhmnaceae). *Ceanothus sanguineus*, though of lesser rank than its wild lilac kin (see pp. 103-4), is a winner for the wild garden or for wildlands restora-

Mountain heath *(Cassiope stelleriana)*

Berberis *(Berberis pumila)*

tion. Its somewhat tawny (off-white) flowers rate it a bit below its closest relative, *C. integerrimus* (deer brush). On both sides of the Cascades, buckbrush or Oregon tea-tree is a favorite browse-plant for deer and elk. It can get up to 8 or 10 feet high, sparingly clothed with deciduous foliage, much like deer brush (p. 103). Another wild lilac, *Ceanothus cordulatus* (snow brush Ceanothus), is purely first-class in the wild. Its low-growing, intricately branched form bears blue-grey (glaucous) leaves and tight clusters of white flowers. Look for it in southern Oregon, both in the Cascades and the Coast (Siskiyou) Mountains in fairly high-elevation, open, dryish woods. For gardens, alas, it is "planta incognita." I find no record of its being tried, even in California where it is widespread in the Sierras. So some skilled propagator should take it on; it may be fastidious, but will be a winner if it succeeds.

SQUAW APPLE (*Peraphyllum ramossissimum*). Rose Family (Rosaceae). Here is a shrub just made for the east-of-Cascades xeriscape (drought-tolerant) garden. Squaw apple, a kind of desert cherry or indeed a xeric crabapple, thrives in sagebrush country to yellow pine woodlands, from central Oregon into southern Idaho and on into the Intermountain West beyond. The single species is one of those desert marvels: intricately branched with small, fascicled (clustered) leaves; its flowers are small, pink to rose, that set small, bitter crabapples. Now available commercially (*vide* "Hortus West"), it is worthy of eastsiders' gardens and restoration projects.

Chokecherry *(Prunus virginiana)*

CHOKECHERRY *(Prunus virginiana)*. Rose Family (Rosaceae). This attractive large, deciduous shrub bears its cherry flowers profusely in terminal, elongate clusters, to be followed by spiky racemes of pea-sized, red or purple cherry fruits. It is common east of the Cascades, everywhere from open yellow pine and Douglas fir woods to stream banks in sagebrush country. Such a luxuriant producer of fruits is sure to attract wildlife in the garden. Despite the common name, chokecherry fruits can be cooked and made into jelly; the "choking" comes only when tasting fresh, uncooked cherries. Hitchcock et al. distinguish two forms: var. *melanocarpa*, a largish shrub (6-18 feet tall) with purplish black fruits, is widespread east of the Cascades but can also be found in coastal southern Oregon; var. *demissa*, a smaller (4-12 feet tall) version, can be found west of the Cascades from British Columbia to northwestern Oregon. Both varieties have broadly ovate leaves, somewhat leathery in texture, yet deciduous. Plant them in full sun from seedlings started by cold-stratification of cleaned seed collected in late summer.

SHRUBBY WILLOWS (*Salix* species). Willow Family (Salicaceae). It's high time we put more of our shrubby willows to the test of cultivation—and the resource is endless! Most of our many native willows are low- to medium-sized shrubs, growing in riparian habitats from sea level to nearly timberline. It is invidious to pick and choose, but let me suggest the following for trial: *Salix barclayi*, *S. cascadensis*, and *S. commutata*, all of montane wet meadows. Then there is *S. exigua*, the sand bar willow of creek bottoms in sagebrush country; *S. brachycarpa* is a gem of a small upright shrub, locally frequent around serpentine seeps in the Wenatchee Mountains of Washington. These shrubs propagate best from cuttings; if you are lucky, you can catch the airborne, gossamer seed.

GREASEWOOD (*Sarcobatus vermiculatus* and *Eurotia lanata*). Goosefoot Family (Chenopodiaceae). Most members of this family are weedy barnyard annuals. But watch for these two shrubs on the dry east side. My favorite spot for seeing greasewood is in lowlying alkaline areas of sagebrush territory along the lower reaches of Satus Creek, Yakima County, Washington. Here it is gregarious on alkaline soils at the base of sagebrush slopes. Greasewood is a tallish spiny shrub with fleshy, rounded leaves (hence the name "vermiculatus," like vermicelli or even worms). Its insignificant flowers yield intriguing, dry fruits, like miniature flying saucers. Best for alkaline (high pH) sites in the desert garden, greasewood should also be on the list of plants for mending degraded arid habitats. Seed is now available ("Hortus West"). A similar alkaline-tolerant desert shrub merits attention: *Eurotia lanata* (winter fat), also a chenopod of the Goosefoot family, is a wooly version of greasewood, with striking, fuzzy fruiting heads. Both shrubs are widespread in semi-desert areas east of the Cascades.

GROUSEBERRY (*Vaccinium scoparium*). Heather Family (Ericaceae). Grouseberry can be a gregarious ground cover in conifer woods east of the Cascades. I have seen it even as a monoculture, a sea of green under lodgepole pine. This low huckleberry (less than 2 feet tall) has angular stems and small leaves, with red fruits—looking like a dwarf version of the westside red huckleberry (*Vaccinium parvifolium*, pp. 115-16). It merits trial in dryish conifer woodland gardens on either side of the Cascades.

Shrubby willow (*Salix commutata*)

Collecting in the Wild

Throughout this book, the reader has been encouraged to collect native plants in the wild with the utmost regard for the conservation of the plants sought. The collecting of seeds or cuttings is to be preferred over the digging of whole plants. The latter can be condoned only under special circumstances: if the habitat is disturbed or under certain threat of destruction. Plants found in road cuts, borrow pits, logged or burned areas, or in sites under development, may be carefully dug, properly stored for transport, and then planted in a holding bed at home or in a nursery. Having condoned some digging of plants, I hasten to remind the collector that such plants are hardest to introduce successfully into the garden. So, again, be content with seeds, cuttings, or layerings as the primary modes of propagation.

Lands where one wants to collect invariably belong to someone else. Courtesy, and often the law, demands that ownership of the lands (public or private) be recognized by the collector. Whenever possible, permission of private owners should be sought before collecting. With regard to public lands, states differ on rules for collecting. California law prohibits the digging of wild plants. In other states and provinces collecting on public lands may be controlled by various rules, regulations, and statutes. No unauthorized collecting of any sort is allowed in national and state parks, or in specific "Natural Areas" (state, provincial or federal). A guide to rational collecting on Forest Service lands is published for Oregon and Washington in a pamphlet entitled "The National Forest Garden," available from Headquarters, Region 6, U.S. Forest Service, P.O. Box 3623, Portland, Oregon 97208. The pamphlet states that moderate collecting for personal use is permitted. Collection of rare plants on Forest Service land requires special permission of a forest officer (e.g., the District Ranger's office). Since the Forest Service recognizes the growing list of rare plants designated by the various natural heritage programs in the states, the list in the 1976 pamphlet needs to be updated. State and provincial departments of natural resources also have rules regarding plant collecting.

The careful, conscientious collector who seeks seeds or cuttings of plants on public lands (national parks, state or provincial parks, and specified natural areas excepted) should not find it necessary to seek permission. Particular regulations, mostly applying to commercial exploitation of native plants, may be found in:

—*U.S. Forest Service Manual,* Section Title 2400, Timber Management, subsection 2467.26

—*Lands in Washington State:*

Statutes

RCW 47.40.070 Damage to project unlawful

RCW 47.40.080 Penalty for destroying native flora on state lands or on adjoining highways and parks

RCW 64.12.020 Injury to or removing trees, etc.; damages

RCW 76.04.397 Cutting or destroying trees without authority; penalty

RCW 76.48.020–76.48.910 Specialized forest products

RCW 79.40.070 Cutting, breaking, removing Christmas trees; compensation

Rules and Regulations

WAC 332-52-040 (1) Public behavior—recreation sites

Lists of Native Plants for Particular Settings

A selection of the best of Pacific Northwest natives for particular garden habitats or unusual settings runs the risk of bias from one's personal tastes and experiences. Yet, there should be fair agreement among plantsmen that most of the following are meritorious and are placed in the proper categories. It should be remembered that many species have rather broad tolerance ranges for garden (and native) habitats; hence some plants may be accommodated in more than one of the environmental categories.

For those just beginning to garden with natives, these lists may be the best place to start. Since the plants in the lists are described in detail within the body of the text, the novice can make up a "shopping list" here, and then read up on the attributes of the plants selected.

Evergreen Trees

SUN

Abies lasiocarpa, Subalpine fir

Abies procera, Noble fir

Arbutus menziesii, Madrone

Calocedrus decurrens, Incense cedar

Chamaecyparis lawsoniana, Lawson
  cypress

Chamaecyparis nootkatensis, Alaska cedar

Juniperus scopulorum, Rocky Mountain
  juniper

Lithocarpus densiflorus, Tan oak

Quercus chrysolepis, Canyon live oak

Pinus contorta, Lodgepole pine

Pinus monticola, Western white pine

Pinus ponderosa, Yellow pine

Pseudotsuga menziesii, Douglas fir

Thuja plicata, Western red cedar

Tsuga mertensiana, Mountain hemlock

SHADE

Abies grandis, Grand fir

Chamaecyparis nootkatensis, Alaska cedar

Taxus brevifolia, Western yew

Tsuga heterophylla, Western hemlock

Thuja plicata, Western red cedar

Umbellularia californica, Bay laurel

Chrysolepis chrysophylla, Golden
  chinquapin

Deciduous Trees

SUN

Betula occidentalis, Water birch

Betula papyrifera, Paper birch

Larix occidentalis, Western larch

Populus tremuloides, Quaking aspen

Populus trichocarpa, Black cottonwood

Prunus virginiana var. *demissa,* Bitter
   cherry

Quercus garryana, Garry oak

Quercus kelloggii, California black oak

Sambucus cerulea, Blue elderberry

SHADE

Acer circinatum, Vine maple

Acer macrophyllum, Big-leaf maple

Acer glabrum, Douglas maple

Cornus nuttallii, Pacific flowering
   dogwood

Corylus cornuta, Hazel

Prunus emarginata var. *mollis,* Bitter
   cherry

Tall Evergreen Shrubs

SUN

Arctostaphylos columbiana, Hairy
   manzanita

Berberis aquifolium, Tall Oregon grape

Ceanothus thrysiflorus, Blue-blossom

Ceanothus velutinus, Mountain balm

Chrysolepis sempervirens, Shrubby
   chinquapin

Garrya elliptica, Silk-tassel bush

Lithocarpus densiflorus var. *echinoides,*
   Tan oak (shrubby form)

Myrica californica, California wax
   myrtle

Quercus vaccinifolia, Huckleberry oak

Taxus brevifolia, Western yew

SHADE

Garrya elliptica, Silk-tassel bush

Gaultheria shallon, Salal

Quercus sadleriana, Sadler's oak

Rhododendron macrophyllum, Rhododendron

Umbellularia californica, California bay
   laurel

Vaccinium ovatum, Evergreen huckleberry

Medium-to-Low Evergreen Shrubs

SUN	SHADE
Arctostaphylos X media, Media manzanita	*Berberis nervosa*, Low Oregon grape
Arctostaphylos nevadensis, Pine-mat manzanita	*Gaultheria shallon*, Salal
Gaultheria shallon, Salal	*Kalmiopsis leachiana*, Kalmiopsis
Juniperus communis, Common juniper	*Leucothoe davisiae*, Leucothoe
Ledum glandulosum, Trapper's tea	*Phyllodoce empetriformis*, Mountain heather
Ledum groenlandicum, Labrador tea	
Pachistima myrsinites, Oregon box	
Penstemon fruticosus, Shrubby penstemon	

Tall Deciduous Shrubs

SUN	SHADE
Amelanchier alnifolia, Serviceberry	*Acer circinatum*, Vine maple
Betula glandulosa, Swamp birch	*Cornus stolonifera*, Red-osier dogwood
Ceanothus integerrimus, Deer brush	*Lonicera involucrata*, Twinberry
Cornus stolonifera, Red-osier dogwood	*Menziesia ferruginea*, Fool's huckleberry
Holodiscus discolor, Oceanspray	*Osmaronia (Oemleria) cerasiformis*, Indian plum
Philadelphus lewisii, Mock-orange	*Oplopanax horridum*, Devil's club
Quercus garryana var. *breweri*, Brewer's oak	*Ribes sanguineum*, Red-flowering currant
Rhododendron occidentale, Western azalea	*Rosa* spp., Wild rose
Ribes lobbii, Gooseberry	*Rubus spectabilis*, Salmon berry
Ribes sanguineum, Red-flowering currant	*Vaccinium parvifolium*, Red huckleberry
Rosa nutkana, Wild rose	*Viburnum edule*, Squashberry
Sorbus sitchensis, Mountain ash	
Spiraea menziesii, Hardhack	

SUN

Betula glandulosa, Swamp birch

Myrica gale, Sweet gale

Potentilla fruticosa, Shrubby cinquefoil

Ribes lobbii, Gooseberry

Salix brachycarpa, Willow

Sheperdia canadensis, Buffalo berry

SHADE

Vaccinium deliciosum, Blue huckleberry

Vaccinium scoparium, Grouseberry

Medium-to-Low Deciduous Shrubs

SUN

Arctostaphylos media, Media manzanita

Arctostaphylos nevadensis, Pine-mat manzanita

Arctostaphylos uva-ursi, Kinnikinnik

Ceanothus prostratus, Mahala mat

Ceanothus pumilus, Squaw carpet

Fragaria chiloensis, Coastal strawberry

Juniperus communis, Common juniper

Luetkea pectinata, Alaska spirea

Vancouveria hexandra, Inside-out flower

SHADE

Achlys triphylla, Vanilla leaf

Anemone spp., Anemone

Asarum caudatum, Wild ginger

Asarum hartwegii, Wild ginger

Cornus canadensis, Bunchberry

Dicentra formosa, Bleeding heart

Fragaria vesca, Strawberry

Gaultheria ovatifolia, Wintergreen

Linnaea borealis, Twinflower

Maianthemum dilatatum, False lily-of-the-valley

Micromeria douglasii, Yerba buena

Oxalis oregona, Wood sorrel

Petasites frigidus, Coltsfoot

Rubus lasiococcus, Rubus

Rubus pedatus, Rubus

Tiarella trifoliata, Foam-flower

Trientalis arctica, Star flower

Whipplea modesta, Whipplea

Vancouveria hexandra, Inside-out flower

Ground Covers

Settings

Plants for Seaside Gardens

TREES

Arbutus menziesii, Madrone

Picea sitchensis, Sitka spruce

Pinus contorta, Beach pine

Pseudotsuga menziesii, Douglas fir

SHRUBS

Arctostaphylos uva-ursi, Kinnikinnik

Gaultheria shallon, Salal

Lupinus arboreus, Tree lupin

Myrica californica, California wax myrtle

Salix hookeriana, Beach willow

Vaccinium ovatum, Evergreen huckle-berry

HERBS

Abronia, Sand verbena

Carex macrocephala, Bighead sedge

Elymus mollis, American dunegrass

Fragaria chiloensis, Beach strawberry

Lupinus littoralis, Lupine

Polygonum paronychia, Black knotweed

(*Ammophila arenaria*, Beachgrass, should be avoided; it is of European introduction, very much a fire hazard.)

Plants for Land Reclamation

TREES

Acer macrophyllum, Big-leaf maple

Alnus rubra, Red alder

Fraxinus latifolius, Ash

Pinus contorta, Shore pine

Pseudotsuga menziesii, Douglas fir

Sambucus cerulea, Blue elderberry

SHRUBS

Amelanchier alnifolia, Serviceberry

Arctostaphylos columbiana, Hairy manzanita

Artemisia tridentata, Sagebrush

Ceanothus integerrimus, Deer brush

Gaultheria shallon, Salal

Holodiscus discolor, Ocean spray

Osmaronia cerasiformis, Indian plum

Purshia tridentata, Bitter brush

GROUND COVERS

Arctostaphylos uva-ursi, Kinnikinnik

Fragaria chiloensis, Beach strawberry

Maianthemum dilatatum, False lily-of-the-valley

Petasites frigidus, Coltsfoot

Vancouveria hexandra, Inside-out flower

Plants for Wet Places

TREES

Alnus rubra, Red alder

Fraxinus latifolius, Ash

Thuja plicata, Western red cedar

Umbellularia californica, California bay
  laurel

SHRUBS

Cornus stolonifera, Red-osier dogwood

Kalmia polifolia, Swamp laurel

Ledum glandulosum, Trapper's tea

Lonicera involucrata, Twinberry

Myrica gale, Sweet gale

Oplopanax horridum, Devil's club

Salix spp., Willow

Vaccinium oxycoccus, Cranberry

HERBS

Athyrium filix-femina, Lady fern

Carex spp., Sedge

Equisetum spp., Horse tail

Glyceria, Manna grass

Juncus spp., Rush

Lysichitum americanum, Skunk cabbage

Menyanthes trifoliata, Buckbean

Nephrophyllidium faurei, Deer cabbage

Peltiphyllum peltatum, Umbrella plant

Rorippa nasturtium-aquaticum, Water cress

Plants for the Rock Garden

Allium spp., Wild onion

Arabis, Rock cress

Arenaria capillaris, Sandwort

Arenaria obtusiloba, Sandwort

Aspidotis densa, Indian's dream

Aster alpigenus, Aster

Balsamorhiza hookeri, Balsamroot

Calochortus spp., Mariposa lily

Campanula rotundifolia, Harebell

Cheilanthes gracillima, Lip fern

Claytonia megarhiza var. *nivalis,*
  Claytonia

Cryptogramma crispa, Parsley fern

Dodecatheon pauciflorum, Shooting star

Douglasia dentata var. *nivalis,* Douglasia

Douglasia laevigata, Douglasia

Dryas octopetala, Mountain avens

Elmera racemosa, Alum root

Erigeron compositus, Fleabane

Eriogonum umbellatum, Wild buckwheat

Gilia aggregata, Scarlet bugler

Heuchera cylyndrica, Alum root

Horkelia fusca, Horkelia

Hulsea algida, Hulsea

Iris innominata, Iris

Ivesia tweedyi, Ivesia

Lewisia columbiana, Lewisia

Lewisia cotyledon, Lewisia

Lewisia leana, Lewisia

Lewisia tweedyi, Lewisia

Settings

Plants for the Rock Garden (continued)

Luetkea pectinata, Alaska spirea

Luina hypoleuca, Luina

Monardella odoratissima, Monardella

Pellaea bridgesii, Cliff break

Penstemon spp., Penstemon

Polypodium hesperium, Licorice fern

Petrophytum hendersonii, Rock spirea

Phacelia sericea, Fiddle-neck

Phlox diffusa, Phlox

Polemonium pulcherrimum, Jacob's ladder

Potentilla breweri, and other spp.,
   Cinquefoil

Raillardella argentea, Raillardella

Sedum spathulifolium, Stonecrop

Sedum obtusatum, Stonecrop

Silene acaulis, Moss campion

Silene californica, Catch fly

Silene hookeri, Catch-fly

Spraguea umbellata, Spraguea

Synthyris pinnatifida, Synthyris

Talinum okanoganense, Talinum

Townsendia spp., Townsendia

Viola spp., Violet

Zygadenus elegans, Death camas

Woodland Herbs

Aconitum columbianum, Monk's hood

Aquilegia formosa, Columbine

Adenocaulon bicolor, Trail-blazer

Arnica cordifolia, Arnica

Aruncus sylvester, Goat's beard

Blechnum spicant, Deer fern

Campanula rotundifolia, Harebell

Corydalis scouleri, Corydalis

Dicentra formosa, Bleeding heart

Disporum spp., Fairy bells

Dryopteris spp., Shield fern

Erythronium revolutum, Glacier lily

Erythronium oreganum, Fawn lily

Heuchera micrantha, Alum root

Iris tenax, Iris

Lilium columbianum, Tiger lily

Nephrophyllidium crista-galli, Deer
   cabbage

Nothochelone nemorosa, Woodland
   penstemon

Polystichum munitum, Sword fern

Smilacina racemosa, False Solomon's seal

Streptopus spp., Twisted-stalk

Synthyris reniformis, Synthyris

Synthyris missurica, Synthyris

Tellima grandiflora, Fringe-cup

Thalictrum spp., Meadow rue

Tiarella trifoliata, Foam-flower

Tolmiea menziesii, Youth-on-age

Trillium ovatum, Western wake-robin

Woodwardia fimbriata, Chain fern

When the written word is not enough, the seeker of information on Northwest native plants may want to contact various plant-oriented sources: societies, private and public organizations, or plant taxonomists and plant ecologists in departments of botany or biology at the various colleges and universities, who are often excellent sources of specific information. Also, staff horticulturists, plant pathologists, and entomologists with Cooperative Extension Service offices in most counties can be of help. Consult your local telephone directory for these.

Sources of Information on Native Plants

State and provincial offices of the Cooperative Extension Service:

Extension Ornamentals Specialist
Horticulture Dept.
Oregon State University
Corvallis, OR 97331

University of Idaho Extension
   Horticulturist
P.O. Box 300
Boise, ID 8370

Nursery and Seed Services
California Dept. of Food and
   Agriculture
1220 N. St.
Sacramento, CA 95814

WSU Extension Horticulturist
Western Washington Research &
   Extension Center
Puyallup, WA 98371

Nursery Horticulturist
B.C. Ministry of Agriculture
Box 1172, Station A
Surrey, B.C. V3S 4P9
Canada

Extension Horticulturist
Agricultural Extension Service
University of California
Davis, CA 95616

Clubs and societies that foster the enjoyment, study, and conservation of native plants:

California Native Plant Society
(many local chapters)
2330 Ellsworth Street, Suite D
Berkeley, CA 94704

Idaho Native Plant Society
   (Pahove Chapter)
c/o Harold M. Tucker, Herbarium
College of Idaho
Caldwell, ID 83605

Vancouver Natural History Society
[address varies with president]
Contact Univ. of British Columbia
   Botanical Garden
Vancouver, B.C. V6T 1W5
Canada

Vancouver Island Rock and Alpine
   Society
Ms. C. B. Caunt, Hon. Sec.
334 Niagara St.
Victoria, B.C. V8R 5Z9
Canada

The Arboretum Foundation
(annual plant sales)
c/o Univ. of Washington Arboretum
Seattle, WA 98195

Friends of the Berry Garden
Berry Botanical Garden
11505 SW Summerville Ave.
Portland, OR 97219

Native Plant Society of Oregon
c/o Dr. Frank Lan
Department of Biology
Southern Oregon State College
Ashland, OR 95720

Washington Native Plant Society
c/o A. R. Kruckeberg
Department of Botany
University of Washington
Seattle, WA 98195

Alpine Garden Club of B.C.
c/o Mrs. Josephine Bridge
1310 W. King Edward Ave.
Vancouver, B.C. V6H 1Z9
Canada

251

Sources

American Rock Garden Society
(annual seed exchange & plant sale)
Northwest Unit
c/o Univ. of Washington Arboretum
Seattle, WA 98195

Northwest Ornamental Horticultural
   Society (annual seed exchange &
   plant sales)
c/o Univ. of Washington Arboretum
Seattle, WA 98195

Saratoga Horticultural
   Foundation, Inc.*
20605 Verde Vista Lane
P.O. Box 308
Saratoga, CA 95070
*Publishers of *The Source: Selected
California Native Plants,* rev. ed.

Other sources of information on NW native plants:

Washington Natural Heritage Program
(inventories of rare plants)
3111 Seminar Bldg. (TA-00)
Evergreen State College
Olympia, WA 98505

California Natural Diversity Data Base
c/o Nature Conservancy
987 Jed Smith Drive
Sacramento, CA 95819

Idaho Nursery and Tree Association
2528 North Cloverdale Road
Boise, ID 83702

California Association of Nurserymen
Suite 303
1005 Eighth St.
Sacramento, CA 95814

Oregon Natural Heritage Program
(inventories of rare plants)
c/o Nature Conservancy
1234 NW 25th
Portland, OR 97210

Washington State Nurserymen's
   Assoc., Inc.
1202 25th Ave. Court, N.E.
Puyallup, WA 98371

Oregon Association of Nurserymen
12750 SW Pacific Highway
Suite 2C
Portland, OR 97223

Public collections of native plants often devote a section of their plantings to native plants. Arboreta and botanic gardens of the Pacific Northwest merit repeated visits, both to consult with their staffs and to see the natives under cultivation.

BRITISH COLUMBIA

Botanic Garden
University of British Columbia
Vancouver, B.C.
Canada

Van Dusen Gardens
38th and Granville St.
Vancouver, B.C.
Canada

CALIFORNIA (central & northern)

Regional Parks Botanic Garden (all native)
Tilden Regional Park
Berkeley, CA 94708

Strybing Arboretum and Botanical
   Gardens
Golden Gate Park
9th Avenue and Lincoln Way
San Francisco, CA 94122

Joseph McInnes Memorial Botanic
   Garden
Mills College
Seminary and MacArthur Blvd.
Oakland, CA 94613

Saratoga Horticultural
   Foundation, Inc.
20605 Verde Vista Lane
Box 308
Saratoga, CA 95070

University of California Botanical
   Garden
Strawberry Canyon
Berkeley, CA 94720

Rancho Santa Ana Botanic Garden
1500 North College Ave.
Claremont, CA 91711
(This world-famous garden is devoted
to native plants of the entire state)

IDAHO

Charles Huston Shattuck Arboretum
College of Forestry
University of Idaho
Moscow, ID 83843

OREGON

The Berry Botanic Garden
11505 SW Summerville Ave.
Portland, OR 97219

Peavy Arboretum
School of Forestry
Oregon State College
Corvallis, OR 97331

Hoyte Arboretum
4000 SW Fairview Blvd.
Portland, OR 97221

Leach Botanical Park
7604 SE 122nd Ave.
Portland, OR 97236

WASHINGTON

Finch Arboretum
W. 3404 Woodland Blvd.
Spokane, WA 99204

Point Defiance Park
5402 North Shirley
Tacoma, WA 98407

Carl S. English, Jr., Gardens
Hiram Chittenden Locks
NW 54th St. and 32nd Ave. NW
Seattle, WA

Silva Glen
Rt. 1, Box 402a
Mead, WA 99021

Washington Park Arboretum
Seattle, WA 98195

South King County Arboretum Foundation
Box 32
Kent, WA 98031

Wind River Arboretum
U.S. Forest Service
Carson, WA 98610

Sehome Hill Arboretum
Western Washington State University
Bellingham, WA 98225

Sources of Plants and Seeds

While a number of nurseries and seed dealers carry some of the more common native plants, there are only a few firms that sell natives in variety. The following list of some nurseries that specialize in natives is neither complete nor "cast in concrete." Dealers in native plants are springing up all over the place, some to survive and grow, others to wither and fade away. As this list becomes dated, it would be advisable to consult "Hortus West," a western North American native plant directory and journal. Published twice a year at $9.00 per year, this directory is "the last word" for sources of native plants. Available in some libraries or by subscription: P.O. Box 2870, Wilsonville, OR 97070-2890.

CALIFORNIA (see also source list in Schmidt, *Growing California Native Plants*)

California Nursery Company
P.O. Box 2278
Fremont, CA 94536

Environmental Seed Producers, Inc.
(bulk wildflower seeds)
P.O. Box 5904
El Monte, CA 91734

Native Plant Farm
3350 St. Helena Highway
St. Helena, CA 94574

Shop in the Sierra
P.O. Box 1
Midpines, CA 95345

Clyde Robin Seed Company, Inc.
P.O. Box 2855
Castro Valley, CA 94546

Forest Seeds of California
P.O. Box 561
Davis, CA 95616

Saratoga Horticultural Foundation
(wholesale)
15185 Murphy Avenue
San Martin, CA 95046

Western Hills Nursery
16250 Coleman Valley Road
Occidental, CA 95465

Sources

IDAHO

Fantasy Farm Nursery
Box 157
Peck, ID 83545

Northplan Seed Producers
N.A.P.G., Inc.
P.O. Box 9107
Moscow, ID 83843

Jacklin Seed Company
Route 2, Box 402
Post Falls, ID 83854

Clifty View Nursery
Rt. 1, Box 509
Bonners Ferry, ID 83805

MONTANA

Lawyer Nursery (Inc)
Route 2, Box 95
Plains, MT 59859

Valley Nursery
P.O. Box 4845
Helena, MT 59601

Four Winds Nursery
5853 East Shore Rt.
Polson, MT 59860

Mountain Home Nurseries
Box 26
DeBorgia, MT 59830

Bitterroot Restoration, Inc. (wholesale)
445 Quast Lane
Corvallis, MT 59828

OREGON

Oregon Desert Farms, Inc.
P.O. Box 709
Lakeview, OR 97630

Reforestation Services, Inc.
P.O. Box 3291
Salem, OR 97302

Woodsman Native Nursery
4221 Hwy. 101
Florence, OR 97439

Pacific Forest Seeds
P.O. Box 1363
Medford, OR 97501

Forest Farm
990 Tethernow Rd.
Williams, OR 97544

Siskiyou Rare Plant Nursery
2825 Cummings Road
Medford, OR 97501

Callahan Seeds
6045 Foley Lane
Central Point, OR 97502

BRITISH COLUMBIA

Alpenglow Gardens
13328 King George Hwy.
Surrey, B.C. V3T 2T6
Canada

WASHINGTON

Alpines West
Box 259, Route 2
Spokane, WA 99207

Specialty Nursery Association
11907 Nevers Road
Snohomish, WA 98290
(published *Specialty Nursery Guide 1989*)

MsK Rare Plant Nursery
20312 15th Ave. NW
Shoreline, WA 98177

Northwest Ground Covers and
  Nursery
14461 NE 190
P.O. Box 248
Woodinville, WA 98072

Gull Harbor Nursery
5304 Gull Harbor Rd.
Olympia, WA 98506

Plants of the Wild
P.O. Box 866
Tekoa, WA 99033

McLaughlin's Seeds
Buttercup's Acre
Mead, WA 99021

Native Grasses and Their Kin for Gardens and Parks and for Naturalizing

Woodland Habitats

Bromus sitchensis and *B. pacificus*, Alaska and Pacific brome   T

Carex deweyana, C. hendersonii, and C. mertensii, Sedges   M

Glyceria elata, Manna grass   T

Hierochloe odorata, Vanilla grass   M

Juncus spp., Rushes

Deschampsia caespitosa, Hair grass   M

Luzula campestris, L. parviflora, L. piperii, L. hitchcockii, Wood rushes   L

Pleuropogon refractus, Semaphore grass   M

Trisetum cernuum, Nodding trisetum   T

Wetlands

Carex aquatilis, C. lyngbyei, C. obnupta, and *C. stipitata,* Sedges   M

Deschampsia caespitosa, Hair grass   M

Glyceria elata, Manna grass   T

Juncus acuminatus, J. ensiformis, Rushes   M, T

Scirpus microcarpus and other species, Bulrushes   M, T

Typha latifolia, T. angustifolia, Cattails   T

Prairies and Meadows

Bromus carinatus and *B. marginatus,* Brome grasses   M

Calamagrostis nutkaensis, Pacific reedgrass   M

Elymus glaucus, Wild rye grass   T

Festuca idahoensis, Idaho fescue   M

F. californica, California fescue   T

Melica spp., Onion grasses   M

T = 3-5 feet tall; M = 2-3 feet tall; L = prostrate to 1 foot tall

Seashore

Calamagrostis nutkaensis, Pacific reedgrass M

Carex macrocephala, Big-head sedge L

Deschampsia caespitosa, Hair grass M

Elymus mollis, Dune ryegrass T

Festuca rubra, Red fescue M, T

Poa macrantha, Native bluegrass M

Rock Garden Grasses

Carex geyeri (and other low-growing sedges) L

Danthonia spicata, Oatgrass L, M

Festuca viridula, Green fescue M

Koehleria cristata, Prairie June grass L, M

Poa spp. (alpine spp.), Bluegrass L

P. curtifolia, Serpentine bluegrass L

Trisetum spicatum, Downy oat-grass L

Phleum alpinum, Alpine timothy L

East of the Cascades (drylands)

Agropyron spicatum, Blue-bunch wheat grass M

Buchloe dactyloides, Buffalo grass L

Bouteloua spp., Grama grasses L, M

Calamagrostis rubescens, Pinegrass T

Elymus canadensis, Giant ryegrass T

E. glaucus, Wild ryegrass M, T

Oryzopsis hymenoides, Indian rice grass M

Sitanion hystrix and *S. jubatum*, Squirrel-tail grasses L

Poa spp., several dryland bluegrasses L, M

Stipa spp., Needlegrasses M, T

T = 3-5 feet tall; M = 2-3 feet tall; L = prostrate to 1 foot tall

ACHENE. Small, nutlike, one-seeded fruit of the sunflower family and others
ALLELOPATHY. Adverse effect of chemicals from one plant on another plant
ALPINE. The land above tree-line
ALPINE (COOL) HOUSE. Unheated greenhouse, well ventilated, used for growing difficult alpine plants
ALTERNATE. Leaves borne singly along the stem
ANNUAL. Herbaceous plant of one year's duration
ARCUATE. Veins curving and parallel to leaf margin
BIENNIAL. Herbaceous plant flowering and dying in its second year
BINOMIAL. The combined genus- and species-name of plants and animals (e.g., *Alnus rubra*)
BLADE. Flat, usually expanded portion of a leaf
BRACT. Leaflike appendage, green or variously colored, larger or smaller
BULBLET. Specialized plantlet found in some flowers in place of seeds
CAESPITOSE. Low, compact growth form, usually of a perennial herb
CANOPY. The leafy, shade-producing tops of trees
CALLUS. Whitish tissue formed by wounding, as at the cut tip of a twig; first stage of root formation in a cutting
CAPSULE. A dry seed pod with regular openings
CARYOPSIS. Seed of a grass
CATKIN. Usually pendant flower cluster with tiny male or female flowers
CHAPARRAL. Vegetation type of drought-resistant, spiny shrubs
CLONE. Offspring derived from single parent; the progeny of vegetative (asexual) propagation
COMMUNITY. A grouping of many individuals, usually of two or more species
COPPICE. Practice of cutting trees or shrubs near ground, thus inducing re-growth of sucker shoots
COMPOST. Well-decomposed organic matter
COMPOUND LEAF. Leaf subdivided into leaflets
CORM. Compact, bulblike underground stem
CRUCIFER. Any member of the mustard family; alludes to the usual cross-shaped, four-parted flower
CULM. Stem of a grass
CULTIVAR. A variety of a species originating and perpetuated under cultivation
DAMPING-OFF. Death or injury to seedlings caused by molds
DECIDUOUS. Plants whose leaves last but one growing season; absence of leaves in winter
DENTATE. Right-angle teeth on edge of leaf
DICOT. For *Dicotyledoneae* one of two main divisions of flowering plants, usually with two seed leaves, flowers not three-parted, and net-veined leaves
DIGITATE. Divided into segments or leaflets, like the fingers of the hand
DISSECTED. Structure (leaf, petal, etc.) subdivided into finer segments, usually irregular
DORMANCY. State of rest; various processes of dormancy prevent germination of seed

Glossary
of Botanical,
Horticultural,
and Gardening
Terms

DRIFT. Plantings of a single species in indefinite, often large, numbers

ECOLOGICAL RESTORATION. Revegetation of degraded sites using ecological techniques

ENDANGERED SPECIES. Plant or animal species threatened by extinction

ERICAD. Any member of the heather family (Ericaceae); ericaceous (adj.)

EVERGREEN. Coniferous and broad-leafed species with leaves persisting through the winter

EXOTIC. Plant or animal not native to a region

FAMILY. Grouping of one to many related genera; family names mostly end in -aceae (thus, Rosaceae)

FISTULOSE. Having stout, hollow stems

FLORA. The plants of a region; also, book identifying same

FLORET. Small flower (flowerlet); of two types in sunflower family (Compositae): ray vs. disc florets; in grasses, the tiny flower of the spikelet (inflorescence)

FORMA. A local minor variant in nature

FRUIT. The ripened pistil (or ovary) of a flower, containing seeds

GEMMAE. Pieces of vegetative tissue that detach from parent plant to form an asexual offspring, as in some *Lycopodium* species

GENUS. Collective term for one to many species of close relationship; genera (plural), generic (adj.); particular genera have their own names (e.g., *Pinus, Lupinus, Rosa, Arbutus*)

GLAUCOUS. Bluish green or greenish blue; also, covered with a whitish bloom

GLUME. Scale at the base of a grass spikelet

GRAIN. Seed (caryopsis) of a grass

GRAMINOID. A grasslike plant

GRASS. Any member of the Grass Family (Gramineae or Poaceae)

GRASSLIKE PLANT. Sedges and rushes resembling grasses

HABITAT RESTORATION. Revegetation of degraded habitat

HEAD. Compact, usually flat-topped cluster of small flowerlets (florets), typical of the sunflower family (Compositae)

HEEL-CUTTING Branchlet detached at juncture of main branch; the "heel" when trimmed forms callus tissue and roots in proper soil

HIP. The smooth, often red fruit of members of the rose genus *Rosa*

IMBRICATE. Overlapping parts (leaves or bracts), like shingles of a roof

INFLORESCENCE. Any variety of flower clusters

INSECTIVOROUS. Insect-eating

INTERNODE. The length of stem, branch, or twig between leaves or buds

LANCEOLATE. In the shape of a lance or spear head

LAYERING. Rooting of an intact (undetached) lower branch of a tree, shrub, or herbaceous perennial

LEAFLET. Leaflike segment of a compound leaf

LEMMA. Larger of two scales of a grass floret

LINEAR. Narrow appendage (leaf, leaflet, or flower part) with parallel edges

MARGIN. Edge or border of leaf, bract, or flower part

MEADOW. Habitat, wet or dry, usually devoid of woody plants and rich with grasses and other herbs

MICROCLIMATE. The local climate near the ground

MICROHABITAT. The local "address" of an organism

MONOCARPIC. Herb that dies after blooming

MONOCOT. General term for the large group of plants (*Monocotyledoneae*) with parallel-veined leaves, flower parts in threes (e.g., lilies, grasses)

MIST SYSTEM. Mechanism for supplying constant or intermittent fog or mist to cuttings to aid rooting

MUTANT. Hereditary change with visible effect; a "sport" propagated by vegetative means

MYCORRHIZAE. The intimate association of fungus with roots, often changing the shape and quantity of the host root; the resulting union of root and fungus benefits the host plant

NODE. The point of departure, on a stem, of a lateral branch or leaf

OVATE. Oval outline, tapered at tip

p.p.m. Parts per million, measure of a substance placed in water or other solvent

pH. Degree of acidity/alkalinity: 0.0 to 6.9 is acidic; 7.0 to 14 is alkaline

PALEA. Smaller of two scales of a grass floret; may be rudimentary or missing altogether

PALMATE. Shaped like the palm and fingers of the hand

PANICULATE. Shape and branching pattern of a flower cluster, usually pyramidal in outline with flowers on lateral branches of flower-cluster axis

PARKLAND. Montane landscape with conifer tree clumps and open meadow

PEDICEL. The ultimate stalk of a flower in a flower cluster

PEDUNCLE. The main axis or stem of a flower cluster

PERENNIAL. Living for two or more years (woody or herbaceous)

PETIOLE. Leaf stalk

PINNA (AE). The leafy parts of a fern frond

PINNATE. Divisions of a compound leaf in the pattern of a feather

PINNULES. The ultimate leaflets of a divided (compound) fern frond

PISTIL. The seed-producing organ in the center of a flower

PRICKING-OUT. Spaced-out transplanting of young seedlings

POLSTER. Mosslike mound; a cushion-plant

PRAIRIE. Landscape usually devoid of trees or shrubs, with grasses and other herbs

PROPAGULE. Offspring (sexual or asexual) of a plant

PUBESCENCE. Hairiness of plant surfaces, especially of leaves and stems

PUMICE. Light, porous volcanic rock, ranging in size from sand grains to pebbles and even boulders

RACEME. Flower cluster (inflorescence), bearing several to many stalked flowers on a single axis

RETICULATION. Netlike surface (of an onion bulb)

REVOLUTE. Edge or margin of leaf inrolled

RHIZOME. Underground stem, usually horizontal

ROCKERY. Rock wall, usually built to stabilize a steep slope; a rock garden

ROOT CROWN. The summit of a thick taproot, crowned with leaves, and/or the base of the stem

ROSETTE. Basal cluster of leaves attached to root crown, usually the pre-flowering stage of an herbaceous perennial

RUSH. A grasslike plant of the genus *Juncus* (Juncaceae)

SCALE LEAVES. Tiny leaves usually closely beset on stem, as in juniper and western red cedar

SCAPE. Leafless, flower-bearing stalk

SCARIFICATION. Mechanical abrasion of seed coat by nicking, filing, etc.

SCREE. Small angular rock derived from rock outcroppings upslope

SEDGE. A grasslike plant of the genus *Carex* (Cyperaceae)

SEPAL Small, leaflike (usually green) appendages just outside petals of a flower

SERPENTINE. Rock (and soil derived therefrom) made up of silicates of iron and magnesium; infertile to most plants, but the home of a select few adapted to such stressful habitats

SERRATE. Incised or cut edge of leaf; saw-like teeth

SESSILE. Without a stalk (e.g., sessile flower or leaf)

SHEATH. Basal portion of grass leaf that envelops the stem (culm)

SIMPLE. An undivided leaf, though may be toothed or lobed

SORUS (SORI). Clusters of spore cases on fern frond

SPECIES. One consistent kind of plant, e.g., a species of strawberry or penstemon; population of interbreeding individuals that share common attributes

SPHAGNUM. The moss of peat bogs, often used in propagation

SPIKE. Elongate cluster of sessile (stalkless) flowers

SPIKELET. Basic inflorescence (flower cluster) unit of grasses; consists of basal pair of glumes and one or more florets

SPORE. Tiny, resistant cell that germinates to reproduce a stage of a fern

SOFTWOOD. Twigs of current season's growth

SPINOSE. Spiny; teeth of a leaf edge with a spiny tip

STAMEN. Erect, pollen-producing filaments of flower

STIGMA. Tip of the female pistil, often minutely feathery, where pollen lands

STOLON; Horizontal runner between plants at ground level

STRATIFICATION. Cold (or heat) treatment of seeds to break dormancy

STRATIFIED (COMMUNITY). Foliage layers from tree-top and shrub, to herb and moss cover at ground level

STYLE. Stalk perched atop ovary (seed-chamber) of a flower's pistil

SUBALPINE. Upper montane zone, often seen as parkland landscapes; just below timberline

SUCCULENT. Fleshy texture of the herbage or flower parts

TALUS. Loose boulders and rocks at base of montane slope

TEETH. Regular, toothlike indentations at edge of leaf

TESSELATED. Checkered patterning on surface of seeds

TRIDENTATE Three-toothed

TRIFOLIATE Three leaflets of a leaf of clover, strawberry, etc.

TIMBERLINE. Upper margin of forested regions, bordering the alpine in mountains

UMBEL. Flat-topped flower cluster with flower stalks (pedicels) from common origin; typical of parsley family (Umbelliferae)

VARIETY Named variant of a species, e.g., *Pinus contorta* var. *latifolia*

VEGETATION. The plant cover of an area

VEGETATIVE PROPAGATION. Production of offspring in the absence of flowers, such as, from cuttings or layerings, as well as from stolons or rhizomes

WETLAND. Any habitat where water stands for at least part of the season; usually consists of vegetation adapted to standing water; bogs, marshes, swamps, lake and stream margins, tideflats, etc.

Derivations
and Meanings
of Genus
and Species
Names Used
in the Text

(Words listed are derived from Latin unless otherwise stated; species names are in italics.)

Abies. Fir
acaulis. Stemless
Acer. Maple
Achlys. Greek goddess of night or obscurity
Aconitum. Monkshood; ancient Greek name used by Dioscorides and Theophrastus
Actaea. Elder tree (Greek)
acuminatum. Drawn out to a long narrow point
adamantina. Hard; diamondlike
Adenocaulon. Gland-stem (Greek)
Adiantum. Without moisture (Greek), for the rain-shredding property of the foliage
adsurgens. Rising erect
adunca. Hooked
affinis. Related or similar to
Agastache. Greek for much and grain, as in dense flower clusters
aggregata. Clustered
agrestis. Growing in fields
Agropyron. Greek for wild and wheat
Agrostis. Greek for a grass
alaskense. Alaskan
albicaulis. White-stemmed
albiflorum. White-flowered
album. White
algida. Cold (or, of high mountains)
Allium. Garlic
alnifolia. Alderlike foliage
Alnus. Alder
alpigenus. Of the alpine
alpina/alpestris. Alpine; of the mountains
amabilis. Pleasing, lovely
Amelanchier. Possibly French for a European species
americanum. American
amplexicaulis. Clasping the stem
amplexifolia. Clasping the leaf

amygdaloides. Leaves resembling the almond tree
Anaphalis. Greek name of possibly similar plant
andersonii. Possibly named for Dr. Rufus Anderson, correspondent of Asa Gray
andrewsiana. For Dr. Andrews, early California collector
Andromeda. Daughter of Cepheus and Cassiopeia in Greek mythology
androsaemifolium. Leaves with milky sap
Anemone. Wind (Greek); usage obscure
anglica. English
angustifolium. Narrow-leaved
annua. Annual; plant lasting a year
anserina. Of geese
Antennaria. Insect antennae
apiculatus. Ending in a short point
Apocynum. Greek for away from and dog; thus the common name, dogbane
aqua-gelidae. Of cold water
aquatilis. Aquatic; growing in water
aquifolium. From *aquila*, eagle; possibly refers to sharp-pointed leaf margin
Aquilegia. From *aquila*, eagle; petals likened to those of eagle's claws
Arabis. For Arabia
Aralia. According to Fernald, from *aralie* (French-Canadian)
arboreus. Treelike
arbuscula. A low shrub of treelike form
Arbutus. Name for one species of the genus; strawberry tree
arctica. Of the Arctic
Arctostaphylos. Bear + cluster of grapes (Greek); bearberry
Arenaria. From *arena* (sand) for the plant's habitat
arenicola. Of the sands
argentea. Silvery
arguta. Sharply notched or toothed

aristata. Having a sharp point or awn

aristatus. With bristles

Arnica. Derivation uncertain

Artemisia. Wife of Mausolus in Greek mythology

Aruncus. From *aryngos* (goat's beard; Greek), referring to flower clusters

arvensis. Of the fields

asarifolia. Having foliage like Asarum (wild ginger)

Asarum. Name for a European species (Greek)

asperum. Rough

Aspidotis. From *aspis* (shield; Greek), for the covering of spore clusters

Asplenium. Without spleen (Greek), for its supposed medical properties

Aster. Star (Greek), from the appearance of the "heads" of florets

Astragalus. Ankle bone (Greek), possibly because of shape of leaf or pod

Athyrium. Without shield (Greek), referring to covering of spore clusters

Atriplex. Name for plant

atropurpurea. Very purple

attenuata. Thin, weak

aucuparia. Referring to birds (?)

aurantiacus. Orange

aureum. Golden

Baccharis. Greek name from Bacchus; first applied to another shrub

bakeri. For Milo S. Baker, noted California botanist

balfouriana. For Sir Isaac B. Balfour, Scottish professor of botany

Balsamorhiza. Balsam root (Greek)

barclayi. For Charles Barkley, who collected the plant on Kodiak Island in about 1850

barrettiae. For Mrs. Barrett, early collector in Columbia Gorge country

bartonianus. For Mrs. R. Barton of Wallowa County, Oregon

bebbiana. For M. S. Bebb, student of willows

beckwithii. For Lt. E. G. Beckwith, leader of U.S. Army expedition from Salt Lake to California, 1854

bellum. Beautiful

Berberis. Arabic name for plant

berryi. For S. Lucien Berry, friend and field companion of Alice Eastwood, noted California botanist and author-collector of *Penstemon berryi*

Besseya. For Charles Bessey, 20th-century Nebraska botanist

Betula. Birch

betulifolia. Birch-leaved

bicolor. Two colors

biennis. Lasting two years

bigelovii. For Dr. John M. Bigelow, American pharmacologist and botanist

Blechnum. Ancient Greek name for another plant, adopted by Linneaus for this genus

bolanderi. For H. N. Bolander, 19th-century collector in California and Oregon

boreale. Of the north

Boykinia. For Samuel Boykin, early American naturalist

brachycarpa. Short pistil or fruit

bracteata/bracteosa. With bracts

brevifolia. Short-leaved

breweriana/breweri. For W. H. Brewer, botanist with Whitney's California surveying party, 1860-64

Brickellia. For John Brickell, physician and botanist in Georgia

bridgesii. For T. Bridges, collector in Northern California, 19th century

Brodiaea. For James Brodie, Scottish botanist

Bromus. Greek for the oat

bronchialis. Said to alleviate bronchitis

brownii. For Robert Brown, 19th-century English botanist

Buchloe. Greek for buffalo and grass

burkei. For a collector in Snake River country, early 19th century

caespitosa. Growing in low tufts

Calamagrostis. Greek for reed and grass

californicus. Of California

Calocedrus. Beautiful cedar

Calochortus. Beautiful grass (Greek)

Caltha. Ancient name for a yellow-flowered plant (Greek)

calycosus/calycina. Having a large calyx (outer whorl of floral parts)

Calypso. Greek sea nymph; *kalypso*, to hide from view (Greek)

Camassia. From Indian word *camas*, or *quamash*

Campanula. Little bell

campanulatus. Bell-shaped

campestris. Of the fields

camschatcensis. Of Kamchatka, Siberia

canadensis. Of Canada

canescens. Hoary surface

capillaris. Capillary; like a hair

capitata. Capitate; forming a dense headlike cluster

Cardamine. Ancient name for a species of this plant (Greek)

cardinalis. Scarlet

Carex. Classical Latin for sedge

careyana. For John Carey, friend of Asa Gray, who sent American plants to Kew, England

carneum. Flesh-colored

cardwellii. Unknown, though name was used by J. T. Howell in his *Flora of Northwestern North America*

carinatus. Keeled

carolinensis. Of the Carolinas, eastern U.S.

cascadensis. Of the Cascade Range

Cassiope. From Cassiopeia, wife of Cepheus and mother of Andromeda in Greek mythology

Castanopsis. Like Castanea, for its resemblance to chestnut

Castilleja. For Domingo Castillejo, Spanish botanist

caudatum. Tailed (or, having a tail)

caudicifera. Bearing a caudex, or stout stalk

caulescens. Of the stem (having a stem)

Ceanothus. Name of a Greek plant

Celtis. Name obscure, though used in Latin and Greek

cerasiformis. In the shape of a cherry

Cerastium. Greek for horn, as in the slender, curved capsule

Cercocarpus. Tail fruit (Greek), because of long tails on fruit

cereum. Waxy

cernuum. Drooping; nodding

cerulea. Blue

Chaenactis. Gape + ray (Greek), referring to ray flowers

Chamaebatiaria. Resembling Chamaebatia, another plant of the rose family

Chamaecyparis. Dwarf cypress; the genus somewhat resembles true cypresses

chamissonis. For Louis C. A. von Chamisso, 18th/19th-century naturalist who visited the North Coast region of America with Russians

Cheilanthes. Margin flower (Greek), for position of spore clusters *cheiranthoides.* Like Cheiranthus, the wall-flower

chilensis. Of Chile

chiloensis. Of the island Chiloe, off the coast of Chile

Chimaphila. Winter loving (Greek), because of evergreen habit

Chionophila. Snow loving (Greek), referring to alpine habitat

Chlorogalum. Greek for green and juice

chloropetalum. Green-petalled

chrysantha. Golden flower

Chrysothamnus. Golden bush (Greek)

ciliatum. With marginal hairs

ciliosa. Bearing cilia (marginal hairs)

Cimicifuga. Greek for bug and repel, thus the common name, bugbane

cinerascens. Becoming ash-colored

circinatum. Curled like a crook

Cirsium. From kirsos, a swollen vein (Greek), for which thistles were a reputed remedy

citrinum. Lemon-colored; citron-colored

Cladothamnus. Branch bush (Greek)

calvatum. Club-shaped

Clarkia. For Capt. William Clark of the Lewis and Clark expedition

Claytonia. For John Clayton, colonial Virginia botanist

Clematis. Greek name of obscure meaning

Clintonia. For DeWitt Clinton, naturalist and former governor of New York

coccinea. Red

Collinsia. For Z. Collins, American botanist

Collomia. From kolla, glue (Greek), for the seeds when wet

colubrina. Snakelike (or, of the Snake River)

columbiana. Of the Columbia River

columnaris. In the form of a column

communis. Common

commutata. Changed or altered

compositus. Forming aggregates or clusters

concolor. Uniform in tint

congesta. Congested; closely arranged

conjugialis/conjugens. Joined in pairs

contorta. Twisted

Coptis. To cut (Greek), for the dissected leaves

cordifolia. Heart-shaped leaf

cordulatus. Somewhat heart-shaped leaves

Cornus. Horn or leather, probably referring to hard wood

cornuta. Horned (or, hornlike)

coronaria. Forming a crown

Corydalis. Greek name for the crested lark, for likeness to the spurred upper petal

Corylus. Hazelnut

cotyledon. Cavity (Greek), for the cup-shaped form

crassicaulis. Thick-stemmed

crassifolius. Thick-leaved

Crataegus. Greek for strength, for its strong wood

crenulatum. Scalloped or blunt-toothed margin

crinita. Furnished with tuft of long, weak hairs

crista-galli. Cockscomb

cristata. Crested or tufted, for the dense clusters of flowers

Cryptantha. Hidden flower (Greek), because some species have tiny flowers

Cryptogramma. Hidden line (Greek), for linear, marginal covering of spore clusters

cucullaria. Hoodlike

cuneatus. Wedge-shaped

Cupressus. Classical name for cypress

curtifolia. Having short leaves

cusickii. For W. C. Cusick, Oregon botanist

cyaneus. Blue

cylindrica. Cylindrical

Cynoglossum. Greek for dog and tongue, thus the common name, hound's tooth

Cypripedium. Venus foot (Greek), for the slipperlike lip

Dactylis. For fingerlike clusters of spikelets

dactyloides. Like the fingers of the hand

Danthonia. For E. Danthoine, French botanist

Darlingtonia. For W. Darlington, Philadelphia botanist

davidsonii. For Anstruther Davidson, California botanist

davisiae. For N. J. Davis, who first collected Leucothoe, her namesake, in Nevada County, Calif., 19th century

decurrens. Decurrent; running parallel to

deliciosum. Of pleasant flavor

Delphinium. Latin form of *delphinion* (Greek), for the larkspur

deltoidea. Deltoid; shaped like a triangle; Greek letter "delta"

demissa. Hang down; pendant

densa. Dense

densiflora/densifolia. Dense flowers/leaves

dentatum. Dentate; toothed

Deschampsia. For L. A. Deschamps, French botanist

detonsa. Bare

deweyana. For Rev. C. Dewey, specialist in sedges (Carex)

Dicentra. Double spurred (Greek), for the spur of outer petals

diffusa. Diffuse; spreading

digyna. Having two female parts (carpels)

dilatata. Dilated; widened

Diplacus. Double cake (Greek), referring to the placentae

discolor. Of different colors

Disporum. Double seed (Greek); seeds are often two per fruit chamber

dissectum. Finely divided

distentifolium. Separated (or, swollen?) leaves

divergens. Spreading outward; divergent

diversifolia. With different-shaped leaves

Dodecatheon. Twelve gods (Greek); plants protected by the gods

Douglasia/*douglasii.* For David Douglas, Scottish botanist in Pacific Northwest

Draba. Wood nymph (Greek); name used by Dioscorides for a member of the mustard family

Drosera. Dewy (Greek), for the gland-tipped hairs of the leaves

drummondii. For Thomas Drummond, early North American collector chiefly in Canada and Texas

Dryas. A wood nymph

Dryopteris/*dryopteris.* Oak fern (Greek)

Dudleya. For W. R. Dudley, Stanford University botanist

dumosus. Compact; bushy

durata. Hard

echinoides. Prickly

edule. Edible; article of food

elatum. Tall

elegans. Graceful

elliptica. Elliptical

Elmera. For A. D. Elmer, a collector in the West

Elymus. Greek for a grain grass

emarginata. Having a small notch at the tip

empetriformis. With Empetrum-like leaves

Empetrum. Upon a rock (Greek)

ensiformis. Sword-shaped, as with leaves of iris and rushes

Ephedra. Possibly meaning horsetail (Greek)

Epilobium. Upon a pod (Greek), because flower parts are on top of the capsules

Epipactis. Ancient name for the hellebore (Greek)

Equisetum. Horse bristle, for fancied likeness of some species to horse's tail

Erigeron. Early old man (Greek), for early flowering

Eriogonum. Woolly knee (Greek), referring to woolly nodes and stem

Eriophyllum. Woolly leaf (Greek)

Eritrichium. Woolly hair (Greek), for the woolly pubescence of *Eritrichium nanum*

Erysimum. From *erusimon* (Greek), for its use as a mustard to cause blistering

Erythronium. Red (Greek), for the pink or red flowers of some species

erythrosepala. Red sepals

Eschscholtzia/eschscholtzii. For J. F. S. Eschscholitz, Russian scientist who, with Capt. Kotzebue, visited California in 1816

Euonymus. Good name (Greek)

Eurotia. Mold (Greek), for grayish moldlike surface

eurycarpus. Broad carpel or fruit

exigua. Very small

falcifolium. Sickle-shaped leaf

farinosa. Mealy or powdery

feei. For A. L. A. Fee, botanist of Strasbourg

fendleri. For August Fendler, early collector in New Mexico

ferruginea. Rust-colored

Festuca. Ancient Latin for a grass

Filipendula. Latin for thread and hanging, as in the pendant tubers of one species

filix-femina. Lady-fern

fimbriata. Fimbriate or fringed

flavescens/flavum. Yellowish

flettii. Named for a plant collector of Olympic Peninsula and other western Washington areas, early 20th century

flexilis. Capable of being bent

floribunda. Flowering freely

florifer. Producing many flowers

fluviatilis. Growing in a stream

foliosus/foliaceus. Leafy

formosa. Beautiful

Fragaria. Strawberry

fragilis. Brittle

franklinii. For Capt. John Franklin, leader of trans-Canada expedition in early 19th century

Frasera. For John Fraser, English nurseryman, late 18th century

Fraxinus. Ash (tree)

fremontii. For John Fremont, famous western explorer

frigida. Cold

Fritillaria. Dice box, for the likeness to the capsule

frutescens. Shrubby

furcata. Forked

fusca. Dark-colored.

gale. From the English common name for wax myrtle or sweet gale

Gaillardia. For Gaillard de Marentoneau, French botanist

galioides. Like Galium, the bedstraw genus

Galium. From *gala*, milk (Greek), because of the use of *Galium verum* for curdling

gambelii. Named for a 19th-century ornithologist whose California plant collection was described by Nuttall

Garrya/garryana. For Nicholas Garry, of the Hudson's Bay Company, who aided David Douglas on his expeditions

Gaultheria. For Dr. Gaulthier, a Quebec physician, ca. 1750

Gentiana. For King Gentius of Illyris, who knew of the medicinal properties of the plant

Geranium. Crane (Greek), in reference to long-beaked capsules

Geum. Old Latin for one species

geyeri. Named for a German botanist who collected extensively in eastern Washington and Idaho, early 19th century

gigantea. Unusually tall or large

Gilia. For Spanish botanist Felipe Luis Gil

glabella. Somewhat smooth

glabrum. Smooth

glanduliflora. Glandular flowers

glandulosa. Glandular; with glands

glareosum. Of gravelly places

glauca. With grey or bluish waxy bloom

glomerata. Flowers in tight clusters

Glyceria. Greek for sweet grain

glycyrhiza. Sweet root

Goodyera. For John Goodyer, 17th-century English botanist

gordonii. For George Gordon, British gardener

gormanii. Named for a late-19th-century collector in Oregon and southern Washington

gracilis. Dainty

gracillima. Very slender

graminifolia. With grasslike leaves

grandis. Large (*grandi-* as prefix)

Grayia. For Asa Gray, 18th-century American botanist

Grindelia. For D. H. Grindel, Russian botanist

groenlandicum. Of Greenland

grossulariifolia. With gooseberrylike leaves

guttatus. Covered with small dots as if sprinkled

Gymnocarpium. Naked fruit (Greek), for lack of covering of spore clusters

Habenaria. Rein (or, strap), for narrow lip of some species

Hackelia. For Joseph Hackel, 19th-century Czech botanist

hallii. For H. M. Hall, California botanist

Haplopappus. Simple seed-down (pappus) (Greek)

hartwegii. For T. Hartweg, British collector

hastata. Shaped like the head of a spear

heckneri. For John Heckner, who first collected this Lewisia species

Hedysarum. Greek, though meaning obscure

Helenium. For Helen of Troy

helianthoides. Like Helianthus, the sunflower

hendersonii. For the noted Oregon

botanist and collector of many
Northwest plants
Heracleum. From Hercules
hesperium. Evening (or, western)
Hesperochiron. Greek word for
evening and centaur
heterophylla. With leaves of different
shapes
Heuchera. For J. H. von Heucher,
18th-century German professor of
medicine
hexandra. Six-parted flower
Hierochloe. Greek word for holy and
grass
hindsiana. Possibly for W. Hinds, British
botanist
hirsutissimus. Very hairy
hirta. Hairy
hispidula. Somewhat bristly
hitchcockii. For C. Leo Hitchcock,
Northwest botanist and senior
author of the region's major flora
Holodiscus. Whole disk (Greek) for the
unlobed floral disk
hoodii. Possibly named for Sir Samuel
Hood; also used by Capt. Vancouver
for Oregon's Mt. Hood
hookeri. For British father-son botanists,
J. D. Hooker and W. J. Hooker
hoopesii. For T. Hoopes, who botanized
on Pike's Peak
Horkelia. For Johan Horkel, 18th-
century German physiologist
horridus. Very thorny
howardii. For Winslow J. Howard, 19th-
century collector in Rocky Mountains
howellii. For T. J. Howell, noted Oregon
botanist, author of state's first flora
Hulsea. For C. W. Hulse, U.S. Army
humifusa. Spreading over the ground
Hydrophyllum. Water leaf (Greek)
hyemale. Of the winter (also spelled
hiemale)
hymenoides. Membranous
hypoleuca. Whitish beneath

idahoensis. Of Idaho
ida-maia. For Ida May Burke, daughter
of discoverer of this unusual *Brodiaea*
in California
Iliamna. After mythical Alaska Indian
princess; also lake in Alaska
imbricans. With parts (usually leaves or
leaflets) overlapping like tiles
incana. Quite greyish in hue
incerta. Uncertain

incisum. Incised; having margins
deeply and sharply cut
ingramii. For Douglas C. Ingram,
Northwest forester and naturalist
innominata. Unnamed
insolitum. Unusual or uncommon;
strange
integerrimus. Undivided; without teeth
integrifolia. Undivided leaf
intermedia. Between extremes
interrupta. Interrupted; not continuous
involucrata. Having an involucre, a
membranous covering
Iris. Rainbow (Greek)
Ivesia. For Eli Ives, 19th-century
American botanist/physician

japonicus. Of Japan
jeffreyi. For John Jeffrey, Scottish
gardener who collected in California
in mid-19th century
jessicae. Named by E. A. McGregor for
his sister who assisted him in the
field
jonesii. For Marcus E. Jones, prodigious
western botanist
Juncus. Greek for rush
Juniperus. Juniper

Kalmiopsis. Like Kalmia, a related
ericaceous shrub; for Peter Kalm, a
student of Linneaus
Kelloggia/*kelloggii.* For A. Kellogg,
botanist and collector, central
California, 19th century
kellyanum. Named by J. G. Lemmon
Kelseya. For Rev. F. D. Kelsey who
first collected it
kentrophyta. Prickle-plant, owing to
spinescent leaves
klamathensis. Of the Klamath Mountains
(or River) in Oregon and California
Koehleria/*koehleri.* For G. L. Koeler,
German botanist
kruckebergii. For Arthur Kruckeberg,
Washington botanist and author

lacustre. Living in lakes or ponds
laetus. Pleasing
laevicaulis. Smooth-stemmed
laevigatus. Smooth; polished
lambertiana. Named for author of early
work on pines
lanatum. Woolly; soft, hairy
lanceolata. Lance-shaped; spear-shaped
lanuginosa. Woolly or cottony
Larix. Larch

lasiandra. Woolly flowers
lasiocarpa. Woolly fruit
lasiococcus. Woolly berries
lasiolepis. Woolly scales
lateriflorus. Flowers attached on side
Lathyrus. Ancient Greek name for this
or related plant
latifolia. Broad-leafed
lawsoniana. For P. Lawson, 19th century
Scottish nurseryman
laxiflorus. Flowers lax or loose (not
compact)
leachiana. For 20th-century husband-
wife botanist team in Oregon
leana. For 19th-century Portland, OR,
florist L. W. Lee
ledifolius. Foliage like Ledum (Labrador
tea)
Ledum. From *ledon,* meaning mastic
(Greek), originally used for another
genus, Cistus, from which aromatic
resin was obtained
leichtlinii. For Max Leichtlin, German
botanist
lemmonii. For J. G. Lemmon, early
California botanist
lepidus. Charming or elegant
Leptarrhena. Slender male (Greek), for
the slender staminal filaments
Leptodactylon. Thin-fingered (Greek),
for the narrow leaf segments
leptosepala. Thin sepals
Lesquerella. For Leo Lesquereaux,
American moss specialist
leucodermis. White skin
leucophaea. Dusky-white
leucophylla. White or silvery leaf
Leucotohe. In Greek mythology,
daughter of King Orchamus
Lewisia/*lewisii.* For Meriwether Lewis,
of Lewis and Clark Expedition
Lilium. Latin form of *Leirion,* classical
Greek name
limbosperma. Fringed seed or spore
linearis. Narrow; linear
Linnaea. For Carolus Linnaeus, 18th-
century botanist
Linum. Flax
Lithocarpus. Stone fruit
Lithophragma. Stone wall (Greek), for
the plant's habitat
Lithospermum. Stone seed (Greek), for
the bony seeds
littoralis. Growing on the seashore

lobbii. For William Lobb, 19th-century explorer-botanist

Loiseleuria. Named for a French botanist

Lomatium. Greek for border; some species with winged fruits

lonchitis. Pointed, like a lance

lonchocarpa. Lance-shaped pods

longaeva. Long-lived

longiflora. Elongate flower

longifolia. Long-leaved

longisepala. Elongate sepal

Lonicera. For A. Lonitzer, 16th-century German herbalist

lucida. Clear; shiny

ludoviciana. Of Louisiana

Luetkea. For Count F. P. Luetke, 19th-century Russian explorer

Luina. Anagram of Inula, another composite

Lupinus. From lupus, wolf; uncertain meaning

luteum. Yellow

Luzula. Latin for grass of light (shining when dewey)

lyallii. For David Lyall, 19th-century botanist

Lycopodium. Wolf foot (Greek), for likeness of branched tips to wolf's paw

lyngbyi. For H. C. Lyngbye, a Dane who collected this sedge on the Faeroe Islands

Lysichitum. Loose tunic (Greek), for the large spathe enveloping flower stalk

macdonaldiana. For Capt. J. M. McDonald, patron of California botany

macloskyi. Named for a Princeton University professor, early 20th century

macrantha. Large-flowered

macrocarpa. Large fruit

macrophyllum. Large leaf

macrum. Large

madidum. Moist

Maianthemum. May flower (Greek), for time of blooming

major. Larger

Malus. Apple

malvaceus. Like the mallow

margaritacea. Pearly

marginatus. Distinctly margined

maritimum. Growing by the sea

marmoratum. Marbled or streaked with irregular veins

marshallii. For William Marshall, British horticulturalist

martindalei. For I. C. Martindale, American botanist

media. Middle or intermediate

megarhiza. Large root

melanocarpa. Black-fruited

Melica. Possibly ancient name for a grass

membranaceum. Membranous (or, skinlike)

Mentzelia. For C. Mentzel, German botanist

Menyanthes. Monthly flower (Greek)

Menziesia/menziesii. For Archibald Menzies, surgeon-naturalist on expedition of Capt. Vancouver

Mertensia/mertensiana. For F. C. Mertens, 18th/19th-century German botanist

micrantha. Small flowered

microcarpus. Small fruit

microphylla. With small leaves

millefolium. Thousand-leaved; finely divided leaves

Mimulus. Diminutive of mimus, a mimic

missouriensis/missurica. Of the Missouri River

Mitella. Turban (or, cap), for shape of fruit

modesta. Modest; unassuming

mollis. Soft

Monardella. Diminutive of Monarda

monogyna. Single pistil

montanus. Of the mountains

monticola. Mountain-loving

multiflora. Many-flowered

multiplex. Manifold; many

multiradiata. With many ray florets

munitum. Armed

munroana. Possibly for W. Munro, English general and grass specialist

Myrica. Old Greek name, possibly applied to another plant

myrsinites. Resembling myrtle

nanum. Small; dwarf

nardosmia. Generic name of member of aster family; fragrant

Narthecium. Narthex, Greek name

nauseosus. Nauseating

nemorosa. Inhabiting shady places

neowebsteri. For E. B. Webster of Port Angeles, collector in Olympics; neo = renamed

Nephrophyllidium. Like Nephrophyllum (Greek), another plant with kidney-shaped leaves

nevadensis. Of the Sierra Nevada (California or Spain)

newberryi. Named for a 19th-century western collector

nigrum. Black

nivalis. Of the snow

nootkatensis. Of Nootka Sound, Vancouver Island

norvegica. Of Norway

Nothochelone. False (Greek) + Chelone, another genus

nubigena. Born among the clouds

nuda. Naked

nuttallianum/nuttallii. For Thomas Nuttall, early North American collector

obcordatum. Heart-shaped at free end

oblongifolia. Oblong, elliptical leaf

obnupta. Greek for without and wife

obtusatum. Blunt; rounded end

occidentalis. Western (or, of the West)

octopetala. Eight-petalled

odorata. Having an odor; sweet-smelling

odoratissima. Very fragrant

Oemleria. Named for a Confederate officer and first American to discover nitrogen-fixation

Oenothera. Greek name used by Theophrastus; said to mean wine-scented

okanoganense. Of Okanogan country of British Columbia and Washington

oligosperma. Few-seeded

Oplopanax. Tool or weapon (Greek) + Panax, another genus

oppositifolia. Opposite-leaved

opulus. Rich (or, referring to a kind of maple)

Opuntia. Derivation uncertain

orbiculata. Round

oregonense/oreganum. Of Oregon

ornithorynchya. Shape of a bird's beak

Oryzopsis. Greek for ricelike

Osmaronia. Smell (Greek) + Aronia, another genus; see Oemleria

Osmorhiza. Odorous root (Greek), for pleasant odor of original species

ovalifolia/ovatifolia. Oval leaf

ovatum/ovalis. Oval

ovina. Pertaining to sheep

Oxalis. Sharp or sour (Greek), for the acid taste of many species

oxyacantha. Sharp-spined

oxycoccus. Sharp-pointed (or sour) berry

Oxyria. Sharp (Greek), for acid taste of leaves

Oxytropis. Sharp keel (Greek), because of beaked flower keel

Pachystima. *See* Paxistima

pacificus. Of the Pacific Coast

Paeonia. Greek word commemorating Paeon, physician of the gods

pallidipes. Pale at base; pale or gray stalk

palustris. Growing in marshy ground

paniculatus. Flowers in a panicle (branched inflorescence)

papyrifera. Paper-bearing

pardalinum. Marked like a panther

Parnassia. For Mt. Parnassus, Greece

parryi. For C. C. Parry, western botanist

parvi-. Small (as prefix)

patula. Standing open, or spreading

pauciflorum. Few-flowered

Paxistima. Thick stigma (Greek)

pectinata. With numerous closely spaced leaves, like teeth of a comb

pedatus. Palmately lobed or parted; resembling a bird's foot

Pedicularis. Referring to lice, for the superstition that lice infestation followed ingestion of this plant

Pediocactus. Field cactus (Greek)

Pellaea. Dark (Greek), referring to leaf stalks

peltatum. Shieldlike; having the petiole attached to the lower leaf surface rather than at margin

Peltiphyllum. Shield-leaf (Greek)

Penstemon. Five threads (Greek), for the stamens

pentandra. Having five stamens

Peraphyllum. Greek for leather pouch and leaf

peregrinus. Wandering

perennis. Perennial

Petasites. Broad-brimmed hat (Greek), for the large leaves

petiolatum. With a petiole or leaf-stalk

Petrophytum. Rock plant (Greek), for rock crevice habitat of plant

Phacelia. Bundle or fascicle (Greek), for congested flower cluster

Phalaris. Greek for a grass

phegopteris. Former generic name of a fern

Philadelphus. Love + brother (Greek), for Ptolemy Philadelphus, an Egyptian king

Phleum. Greek for some reedy grass

Phlox. Flame (Greek), alluding to the bright flowers

Phoenicaulis. Shiny stem (Greek)

Phyllodoce. Greek sea nymph

Physaria. Bellows (Greek), for inflated pods

Physocarpus. Bladder fruit (Greek)

Picea. Derived from Latin *pix*, pitch

picta. Painted or etched with more than one color

pilularis. Bearing little balls, like pills

pinnatifida. Pinnately divided

Pinus. Pine

piperi. For C. V. Piper, author of first flora of Washington

Pityrogramma. Bran + line (Greek), for branlike coating along the lines of spore cases

planipetala. With flat petals

platyphylla. Broad-leaved

Plectritis. Greek for plaited, as in the complex flower heads of the genus

plicata. Folded; pleated

Pleuropogon. Greek for side and beard, as in laterally attached awn

Poa. Greek for a grass

Polemonium. Said to be named for Polemon, Greek philosopher; strife (Greek)

polifolia. Having narrow leaves like the mint Teucrium

polyacantha. Having many spines

Polygala. Greek for much and milk (some species aid flow of milk)

Polygonum. Greek for many and knee (some species have swollen joints)

polyphylla. Many-leaved

Polypodium. Many feet (Greek), referring to branching underground stem

Polystichum. Many rows (Greek), for uniform rows of spore clusters

pomeridianum. Of the afternoon

ponderosa. Large and heavy

Populus. Poplar

porteri. For C. L. Porter, Wyoming botanist

Potentilla. Powerful, for drug properties of some species

praemorsa. Appearing as though bitten off

prenanthoides. Like the genus Prenanthes, member of chicory tribe

Primula. Early (or, first), for early flowering species

procera. Very tall

procumbens. Lying flat on the ground

propria. One's own; singular, unique

prostratus. Prostrate

Prunus. Plum

Pseudotsuga. False hemlock

Pteridium. Fern (Greek)

pudica. Bashful; modest

pulchellus. Pretty

pulcherrima. Very beautiful

pulverulenta. As though dusted with powder

pumilus. Low (or, small)

pungens. Sharp-pointed

purdyi. For Carl Purdy, California native plant nurseryman

Purshia/*purshiana/purshii*. For F. T. Pursh, colonial botanist and author of early American flora

pyramidata. Pyramidal

Pyrola. Diminutive of *pyrus*, pear, for pear-shaped leaves of some species

pyrolaeflorus/pyrolaefolius. Flowers (leaf) like pyrola (wintergreen)

Pyrus. Latin for pear

Quercus. Oak

racemosus. Flowers arranged in a raceme, borne singly along a stem

radulinus. Rough or rasping surface

Raillardella. Named for its similarity to Raillardia

ramosa. Branching

ramosissimum. Diffusely branched

Ranunculus. From *rana*, frog, for the plant's aquatic habitat

Ratibida. Name unexplained

recurva. Curved backwards

rediviva. Renewed; rebirth

refractus. Bent

reniformis. Kidney-shaped

repens. Prostrate; creeping

reticulata. Net-veined

revolutum. Rolled back, as for edge of leaf

Rhamnus. Greek name for the plant

Rhododendron. Rose tree, ancient Greek name for the oleander

Ribes. Arabic name for these plants

richardsonii. For John Richardson, botanist associated with Franklin expedition across Canada

rigidus. Rigid or stiff

rivale/rivularis. Growing by streams

robinsonii. Named for early 20th-century botanist at Gray Herbarium, Harvard

Romanzoffia. For Count Romanzoff, sponsor of Kotzebue's voyage to the Pacific Coast of North America

Rosa. Classical Latin name

roseus. Rose-colored

rotundifolia. Leaf round in outline

ruaxes. Volcano (Greek); H. St. John found *Draba ruaxes* on Glacier Peak, a North Cascades volcanic peak

rubescens. Reddish; turning red

rubra. Red

Rubus. Bramble

Rudbeckia. For Olaf Rudbeck, father and son, who preceded Linneaus at Uppsala

ruderale. Of waste places and vacant lots

Rumex. Latin for this plant

rupicola. Growing in rocky places

sabinii. For Joseph Sabine, founder of Horticultural Society, London

sadleriana. For Joseph Sadler, botanist at Budapest

saggitata. Arrow-shaped

Salix. Willow

Salvia. Name of cultivated sage

Sambucus. Name for a European species in the genus

sanguineum. Blood-red

Sanguisorba. Latin for blood and absorb, for blood-quenching properties of some species

Satureja. Name of a species in the genus

Saxifraga. Breaks rock, for many species that inhabit rock crevices

scabrella. Somewhat rough

schizantha. Split flower, for the deeply cut petals

Schoenolirion. Greek for rush and lily

scirpoides. Rushlike

Scirpus. Latin for some bulrushes

Scoliopus. Crooked foot (Greek), for the recurved stalks

scoparium. Broomlike

scopulorum/scopulina. Of the rocks or cliffs

scouleri/scouleriana. For John Scouler, who collected with David Douglas in the Northwest, 1825

Scrophularia. Named for its reputed value in treating scrofula

Scutellaria. Latin for tray, as in the appendages to the calyx

Sedum. Perhaps from *sedeo*, I sit, for the squatty habit of the plants

selago. An old Latin name used by Pliny for a ceremonial plant of the Druids

sempervirens. Evergreen

Senecio. Old man, possibly for the white pappus or pubescence of some species

Sequoia. Name of an Indian chief

serpentinicola. Living on serpentine rock/soil

serra/serrulatus. Saw-toothed leaf margin

shallon. Latinized Indian name for salal (*sallal* in Chinook Jargon)

sheltonii. Presumably a member of Captain Whipple's party in the Pacific Railroad Survey, 1850s

Shepherdia. For John Shephard, English botanist

Sibbaldia. For Sir Robert Sibbald, 17th/18th-century professor of medicine at Edinburgh

Sidalcea. Sida + Alcea, both names of other genera in mallow family

Silene. Possibly from *sialon*, saliva (Greek), for the sticky stems

simpsonii. Possibly for Sir George Simpson of the Hudson's Bay Company, Fort Vancouver

sinuata. With a wavy or undulate margin

Sisyrinchium. Name used by Theophrastus for an irislike plant

Sitanion. Greek for grain

sitchensis. Named for Sitka, Alaska

Smelowskia. For T. Smelowsky, 18th/19th-century Russian botanist

Smilacina. Diminutive of *smilax*, a liliaceous vine

Solidago. To make whole, referring to its healing properties

Sorbus. Latin for one of the species of the genus

spathulata/spathulifolium. In the shape of a spatula; a leaf of this form

speciosa. Good-looking; showy

spectabilis. Admirable; spectacular

Sphaeralcea. Greek for sphere and mallow; referring to spherical fruits

sphaerocephalum. With a round head (or flowers)

spicant. From ancient German name

spicata/spicatum. Flowers sessile (not stalked)

spinescens. Spiny

Spiraea. From *speira*, coil or wreath (Greek); obscure meaning

Spraguea. For Isaac Sprague, 19th-century botanical artist

stanfordiana. For Leland Stanford, founder of Stanford University

stauropetala. Petal in the form of a cross

stellata. Starlike (usually referring to hairs)

stelleriana. For G. W. Steller, German naturalist who traveled widely in Russia and visited Alaska on Bering's expedition

Stenanthium. Greek for narrow and flower, as in the narrow petals (tepals)

stenopetalum. Narrow petal

Stipa. Greek for tow or oakum, for the often feathery awns

stipitata. Stalked

stolonifera. Producing runners (stolons)

Streptanthus. Greek for twisted and flower

streptopoides. Referring to similarity to Streptopus (twisted stalk)

Streptopus. Twisted foot (Greek), for the bent or twisted flower stalks

subpumilum. Somewhat dwarfed

suecica. Swedish (or, Sweden)

suendermannii. For F. Suendermann, Lindau nurseryman, student of alpine plants

suffrutescens. Somewhat woody or shrubby

Suksdorfia. For Wilhelm Suksdorf, 19th/20th-century botanist who labored in the Columbia Gorge region

Sullivantia. For W. S. Sullivant, 19th-century moss specialist

Swertia. For E. Sweert, 19th-century Dutch botanist

sylvester. Of the woods or forest; also, growing wild rather than as a cultivated species

Symphoricarpos. Fruit borne in clusters (Greek)

Synthyris. United door (Greek), for the capsule apertures

Talinum. Possibly a native African name; of uncertain meaning

Taxus. Yew (Greek); believed to have been derived from *taxon*, a bow, made from the yew from antiquity

Tellima. Anagram of Mitella

tenax. Tough, firm; matted

tenuipes. Slender-stalked

tenuis/tenuissima. Thin, slender; diminutive form

tetragona. Four-angled

Thalictrum. Dioscorides' name for some unknown plant

Thelypteris. Female fern (Greek)

Thermopsis. Lupinelike (Greek)

Thlaspi. Old Greek name for some plant of this family

thompsonii. For J. W. Thompson, 20th-century plant collector in Pacific Northwest

Thuja. Evergreen tree (Greek), possibly a juniper

thymoides. Like thyme

thyrsiflorus. With flowers in clusters called a thyrse

Tiarella. From tiara (Greek), ancient Persian headdress, which the fruit resembles

tilingii. For H. S. T. Tiling of Nevada

Tofieldia. For T. Tofield, British botanist

Tolmiea/*tolmiei.* For W. F. Tolmie, surgeon-naturalist with Hudson's Bay Company at Fort Vancouver and first white man to ascend Mt. Rainier

tomentella. Somewhat hairy

tortuosus. Twisted

Townsendia. For David Townsend, 19th-century American amateur botanist

Trisetum. Greek for three and bristle

Trautvetteria. For van Trautvetter, 19th-century Russian botanist

tremuloides. Like European quaking aspen (*Populus tremula*)

triangularis. Shaped like a triangle

trichocarpa. Hairy-fruited

tridentata. Three-pronged (or, trident), especially leaves

Trientalis. Measure of 1/3 of a foot, referring to plant's height

trifida. Divided in threes

trifoliata. With three leaflets

Trifolium. Three-leaved

trifurcata. Three-pronged at tip

Trillium. From *tres*, three, for the three leaves

trinervata. Three-nerved

trolliifolium. Leaves like those of trollius, globe flower

Trollius. Latin rendering of German *Trollblume*

Tsuga. Hemlock (Japanese)

tweedyi. For Frank Tweedy, member of North Transcontinental Survey (Northern Pacific Railway), 19th century

umbellatum. Arranged in, or resembling, umbels (flower clusters of parsley family)

Umbellularia. Little umbel, referring to the flower cluster

uniflora. Single-flowered

ursinus. Linked with bears

urticifolia. Nettlelike leaves

utahensis. Of the state of Utah

uva ursi. Literally, berry of the bear

vaccinifolia. Foliage like Vaccinium, the huckleberry genus

Vaccinium. Blueberry

Valeriana. Possibly from *valere*, to be strong

validum. Strong; well-developed

Vancouveria. For Capt. George Vancouver, 18th-century Pacific Northwest explorer

velutinus. Velvety; covered with fine, soft down

venenosus. Poisonous

venosus. With conspicuous veins

ventosa. Pertaining to the wind (?); inflated (?)

venustus. Lovely; graceful

Veratrum. Hellebore; true black

vermiculatus. Wormlike

Veronica. Perhaps named for St. Veronica

verum. True, real

vesca. Small, fine; feeble

Viburnum. Classical name of a European species

Viola. Violet

virginiana. Of the state of Virginia, where much of early North American botany began

viridis/viridescens. Green; becoming green

viscida/viscidiflorus. Sticky; sticky-flowered

viridula. Distinctly green

viscosum/viscossisimum. Clammy, sticky; superlative form

Vitis. Grape

vollmeri. For L. Vollmer, student and grower of California lilies

vulgare. Common

wallacei. For W. A. Wallace, collector in Los Angeles region, from 1854

wallowensis. Pertaining to the Wallowa Mountains of N.E. Oregon

washingtonianum. Of the state of Washington

Whipplea. For A. W. Whipple, 19th-century leader of U.S. Railroad Exploring Expedition

whitneyi. For J. D. Whitney, leader of California Geological Survey, mid-19th century

wigginsii. For Ira Wiggins, noted California botanist

Woodsia. For Joseph Woods, 19th-century English architect and botanist

Woodwardia. For T. J. Woodward, 18th/19th-century English botanist

wormskjoldii. Named for a 19th-century Danish botanist with Russians at Kamchatka

Wyethia. For Nathaniel Wyeth, 19th-century explorer, first collector of the plant

xantholeucum. Yellowish-white

Xerophyllum. Dry leaf (Greek), for the dry and rough leaves

Zygadenus. Yoke gland (Greek), for the paired glands of a species of death camas

Selected Bibliography

Literature Cited

Bean, W. J. *Trees and Shrubs Hardy in the British Isles.* 8th ed. London: John Murray, 1970.

Clarke, C. B. *Edible and Useful Plants of California.* Berkeley: University of California Press, 1977.

Cooperative Extension Service. *Plant Materials for Landscaping.* Bulletin 592. Pullman, WA, 1969.

Dallimore, W., and A. B. Jackson. *A Handbook of Coniferae and Ginkoaceae.* New York: St. Martin's Press, 1967.

Fernald, M. L. "Some Historical Aspects of Plant Taxonomy," *Rhodora* 44 (1942):21-43.

Franklin, J. F., and C. T. Dyrness. *Natural Vegetation of Oregon and Washington.* Corvallis: Oregon State University Press, 1988. (Originally published as USDA Forest Service General Technical Report PNW-8, U.S. Government Printing Office, Washington, D.C., 1973.)

Grant, J. A., and C. L. Grant. *Trees and Shrubs for Pacific Northwest Gardens.* Palo Alto, CA: Pacific Books, 1974. (See page 272 for new edition.)

Greenlee, John. *The Encyclopedia of Ornamental Grasses.* Emmaus, PA: Rodale Press, 1992.

Hardy, G. A. *Fifty Edible Plants of British Columbia.* British Columbia Provincial Museum Handbook no. 1, 1942.

Hitchcock, C. L., and A. Cronquist. *Flora of the Pacific Northwest.* Seattle and London: University of Washington Press, 1973. (A very useful condensation of the five-volume work, *Vascular Plants of the Pacific Northwest,* by Hitchcock et al.; the pictured "keys" are especially novel and useful. Both the condensed edition and volume 1 of the five-volume edition are essential references for grasses and their kin.)

Hitchcock, C. L.; A. Cronquist; M. Ownbey; and J. W. Thompson. *Vascular Plants of the Pacific Northwest.* 5 vols. Seattle and London: University of Washington Press, 1955-69. (Without this masterly treatment of our native flora, the present book could not have been written. The student of our native plants, the gardener of wild plants, and the itinerant naturalist will make constant reference to this detailed treatise, so skillfully illustrated by Jeanne Janish and John Rumely. Many of the plants of garden potential were singled out for pithy comment by Hitchcock, aided by Carl S. English, Jr., and Brian O. Mulligan.)

Hortus West. Issue no. 6, 1995. (A native plant directory and journal, Wilsonville, OR.)

Hoshizaki, B. J. *Fern Grower's Manual.* New York: Alfred A. Knopf, 1975. (Excellent book on fern culture, from spore to adult.)

Kruckeberg, A. R. *The Natural History of Puget Sound Country.* Seattle and London: University of Washington Press, 1991.

Kruckeberg, A. R. "Plant Life on Serpentine and Other Ferro-Magnesian Rocks in Northwestern North America," *Syesis* 2 (1970):15-144.

Munz, P. A., and D. D. Keck. *A California Flora.* Berkeley: University of California Press, 1959 (reprinted, 1973).

Oakes, A. J. *Ornamental Grasses and Grasslike Plants.* New York: Van Nostrand Reinhold, 1990.

Peattie, D. C. *A Natural History of Western Trees*. New York: Houghton Mifflin Co., 1953.

Peck, M. E. *A Manual of the Higher Plants of Oregon*. 2d ed. Portland, OR: Binsford and Mort, 1961. (Especially useful for Siskiyou Mountain plants and others south of the range of the Hitchcock books.)

Proctor, J., and S. R. J. Woodell. "The Ecology of Serpentine Soils," *Advances in Ecological Research* 9 (1975):255-366.

Rehder, A. *Manual of Cultivated Trees and Shrubs Hardy in North America*. New York: Macmillan, 1956.

Shank, D., ed. *See Hortus West*.

Sudworth, G. B. *Forest Trees of the Pacific Slope*. Washington, D.C.: U.S. Government Printing Office, 1908.

Whittaker, R. H. "Vegetation of the Siskiyou Mountains, Oregon, and California," *Ecological Monographs* 30 (1960):279-338.

Willis, A. R. *The Pacific Gardener*. 6th ed. Sydney, B.C.: Grays Publishing Ltd., 1973.

Wolf, Carl. *Rancho Santa Ana Botanic Garden Leaflets of Popular Information* 41 (1941):2.

Other Useful References

Arno, S. F., and R. P. Hammerly. *Northwest Trees*. Seattle: Mountaineers, 1977. (This and the work by Taylor and Douglas, cited below, are handy and accurate field guides to some of our more common Northwest plants, and the illustrations in each are a treat.)

Art, H. W. *A Garden of Wildflowers: 101 Native Species and How to Grow Them*. Pownal, VT: Garden Way Publications, 1986. (Several Pacific Northwest natives are included in this national coverage.)

Art, H. W. *The Wildflower Gardener's Guide*. Pacific Northwest, Rocky Mountain, and Western Canada Edition. Pownal, VT: Storey/Garden Way Publishing, Inc., 1986. (Text and fine illustrations of many natives; includes annuals and herbaceous perennials.)

Benoliel, D. *Northwest Foraging: A Guide to Edible Plants of the Pacific Northwest*. Seattle, WA: Signpost Publications, 1974. (Reprinted, 1988.)

Bradshaw, A. D., and M. J. Chadwick, *The Restoration of the Land*. Berkeley: University of California Press, 1980. (This landmark book by noted ecologists laid the groundwork for habitat restoration.)

Brough, S. G. *Wild Trees of British Columbia*. Vancouver, B.C.: Pacific Educational Press, 1990. (This compact handbook features an illustrated key, good line drawings, and notes on habitat and Indian uses.)

Burns, R. M, and B. H. Honkala. *Silvics of North America*. Vol. 1: *Conifers*; vol. 2: *Hardwoods*. Washington Agricultural Handbook 654. Washington, D.C.: Forest Service, USDA, 1990. (Encyclopedic work on trees of North America: ecology, life-history, reproduction, and diseases.)

Clay, S. *The Present-day Rock Garden*. London: Thomas Nelson and Sons, 1954. (A compendious supplement to R. Farrer's classic *The English Rock-Garden*; contains many Western natives omitted by Farrer.)

Cox, J. *Landscaping with Nature*. Emmaus, PA: Rodale Press, 1991. (The theme is "design with nature.")

Dirr, M. A. *Manual of Woody Landscape Plants*. Champaign, IL: Stipes Publishing Co., 1990. (Includes several Pacific Northwest natives, covering their attributes and propagation.)

Douglas, D. *Douglas of the Forests: The North American Journals of David Douglas*. Edited by John Davies. Seattle: University of Washington Press; Vancouver, B.C.: Douglas and McIntyre, 1980.

Douglas, D. "Journal Kept by David Douglas During His Travels in North America, 1823-1829." Reprinted in *The Quarterly of the Oregon Historical Society* 5(3). (Two biographies of Douglas are available: *Douglas of the Fir*, by A. G.

Harvey [Cambridge, MA: Harvard University Press, 1947] and *Traveler in a Vanished Landscape*, by W. Morwood [New York: Crown, 1973].)

Durand, H. *Taming the Wildings*. New York and London: G. P. Putnam's Sons, 1923. (Though mostly for the eastern United States, Durand's book is a gold mine of information about species that span our continent.)

Elias, T. S. *The Complete Trees of North America: Field Guide and Natural History*. New York: Van Nostrand Reinhold, 1980.

Farrer, R. *The English Rock-Garden*. 2 vols. London: T. C. and E. C. Jack, Ltd., 1930. (The "bible" for the rock gardener, though many of the species names have changed over the years. Farrer's style delights and entertains, even when one may disagree with him.)

Foster, H. L. *Rock Gardening: A Guide to Growing Alpines and Other Wildflowers in the American Garden*. New York: Bonanza Books, 1968. (Foster gives generous space to the garden attributes and culture of many Northwest native plants.)

Grant, J. A., and C. L. Grant. *Trees and Shrubs for Pacific Northwest Gardens*. Portland, OR: Timber Press, 1990. (This standard work, revised by Marvin Black, Brian Mulligan, Jean Witt, and Joe Witt, includes many native ornamental woody plants.)

Griffiths, A. J. F., and F. R. Ganders. *Wildflower Genetics: A Field Guide for British Columbia and the Pacific Northwest*. Vancouver, B.C.: Flight Press, 1983. (A paperback account of inheritance in Pacific Northwest native plants and common weeds.)

Harker, D. F., et al. *Landscape Restoration Handbook*. Boca Raton, FL: Lewis Publishers, 1993.

Hartzell, Hal, Jr. *The Yew Tree: A Thousand Whispers*. Eugene, OR: Hulogosi, 1991. (Social, cultural, and botanical history of the genus *Taxus* [Yew species], including the Pacific Northwest native.)

Hickman, J. C., ed. *Jepson Manual of Higher Plants of California*. Berkeley: University of California Press, 1993. (Many California plants range into the Pacific Northwest, especially Klamath-Siskiyou country; this flora is unique in that it gives horticultural notes on many of the native plants.)

Hunn, E. S. (with James Selam and Family). *Nch'i-Wana, "The Big River": Mid-Columbia Indians and Their Land*. Seattle and London: University of Washington Press, 1990. (This fine book on the ethnobiology of mid-Columbia Indians, as well as Moore 1979 and Kuhnlein and Turner 1991, gives the many uses made by Indians of our Pacific Northwest native plants.)

Kozloff, E. N. *Plants and Animals of the Pacific Northwest: An Illustrated Guide to the Natural History of Western Oregon, Washington, and British Columbia*. Seattle and London: University of Washington Press, 1976. (A fine naturalist's guide for the lowland west side; beautiful illustrations in color.)

Kruckeberg, A. R. *The Natural History of Puget Sound Country*. Seattle and London: University of Washington Press, 1991. (Discusses the ecological setting for growing natives on the "wet" side of the mountains; gives habitats of many natives.)

Kuhnlein, H. V., and N. J. Turner. *Traditional Plant Foods of Canadian Indigenous Peoples: Nutrition, Botany, and Use*. Philadelphia: Gordon and Breach, 1991. (This encyclopedic work does well for us south of the border, too.)

Lenz, L. W. *Native Plants for California Gardens*. Rancho Santa Ana Botanic Garden, 1956.

Liberty Hyde Bailey Hortorium. *Hortus Third. A Concise Dictionary of Plants Cultivated in the United States and Canada*. New York: Macmillan, 1976. (An essential reference book for the serious gardener.)

Martin, L. C. *The Wildflower Meadow Book: A Gardener's Guide*. Charlotte, NC: East Woods Press Books, 1986. (Meadow plantings for the Northwest region in chapter 11.)

Moore, M. *Medicinal Plants of the Mountain West*. Santa Fe: Museum of New Mexico Press, 1979.

Pojar, J., and A. MacKinnon. *Plants of the Pacific Northwest Coast*. Redmond, WA: Lone Pine Publishing Co., 1994. (The most thorough of the field guides for areas west of the Cascades.)

Rowntree, L. *Hardy Californians*. New York: Macmillan, 1939.

Royal Horticultural Society. *Dictionary of Gardening*. 4 vols. Oxford: Clarendon Press, 1951. Rev. ed., 1992. (Standard reference for cultivated plants worldwide; both editions give Pacific Northwest natives the English gardener's touch.)

Schenk, G. *How to Plan, Establish, and Maintain Rock Gardens*. Menlo Park, CA: Lane Publishing Co., 1964. (A skillful and sensitive artist with plants and rocks makes the fine art of rock gardening readable and attainable; superb black-and-white photographs by Don Normark.)

Schmidt, M. G. *Growing California Native Plants*. Berkeley and London:University of California Press, 1980. (Treats a number of natives suitable to the Northwest; complements this volume.)

Schopmeyer, C. S. *Seeds of Woody Plants in the United States*. Dept. of Agriculture Handbook 450. Washington, D.C.: USDA, 1974. (Valuable reference on collecting, storing, and propagating native woody plants.)

Sperka, M. *Growing Wildflowers: A Gardener's Guide*. New York: Harper and Row, 1973. (Though mainly for eastern North American plants, many of our Northwest genera appear here; good hints on propagation and culture.)

Spurr, J. *Wild Shrubs: Finding and Growing Your Own*. Seattle: Pacific Search Press, 1978.

Sunset New Western Garden Book. Menlo Park, CA: Lane Publishing Co., 1979. (Contains Pacific Coast hardiness maps. A fifth edition [1988], expanded and updated, contains many plants native to the Pacific Northwest.)

Taylor, R. J. *Northwest Weeds*. Missoula, MT: Mountain Press Publishing Co., 1990. (Indispensable reference for telling weeds from natives.)

Taylor, R. J. *Sagebrush Country*. Missoula, MT: Mountain Press Publishing Co., 1992. (A fully revised version of Taylor and Valum's 1974 handbook of the same title; superb photographs, keys to families, and valuable ecological notes.)

Taylor, R. J., and G. W. Douglas. *Mountain Plants of the Pacific Northwest: A Field Guide to Washington, Western British Columbia, and Southeastern Alaska*. Missoula, MT: Mountain Press Publishing Co., 1995. (This field guide with its superb colored photographs, pithy text, and usable keys covers trees, shrubs, and herbs from Washington to southeastern Alaska.)

Wali, M. K., ed. *Ecosystem Rehabilitation*. Vol. 1: *Policy Issues*; vol. 2: *Case Studies*. The Hague: SPB Academic Publishing, 1992.

Wilson, J. *Landscaping with Wildflowers: An Environmental Approach to Gardening*. Boston: Houghton Mifflin, 1992. (How to create natural habitats with native plants; habitats and plants by regions, including the Pacific Northwest.)

Young, J. A., and C. Y. Young. *Seeds of Woody Plants in North America*. Rev. and enlarged ed. Portland, OR: Dioscorides Press, 1992. (A fine successor to Schopmeyer's 1974 work on seeds of woody plants, cited above.)

Journals/Periodicals

(available at libraries of major Northwest colleges and universities)

Hortus West (native plant directory and journal)

Restoration Ecology (Society for Ecological Restoration)

Reclamation and Revegetation Research

Reclamation Review

Restoration and Management Notes

Land and Water

Wetland Journal: Research, Restoration, Education

Index

Bold-face numerals refer to pages on which a plant is discussed in detail. (For the most part, a plant's illustration appears on the same page as its description.)

Abies, 28–31
  amabilis, **31**
  concolor, **28**
  grandis, **28–29**
  lasiocarpa, **29–30**
  magnifica, 236
  magnifica shastensis, 236
  procera, **30–31,** 236
  procera forma *glauca,* 31
  procera forma *prostrata,* 31
Acer, 69–73
  circinatum, **69–70**
  glabrum, 69, **70–71**
  macrophyllum, 69, **71–72**
  palmatum, 70
Aceraceae, 69
Achillea, 193
Achlys triphylla, **163–64**
Aconitum columbianum, **158**
Actaea rubra, **165**
Adder's tongue, fetid, **146–47**
Adenocaulon bicolor, **164**
Adiantum pedatum, **132,** 229
  Aleutian Island form, 132
  aleuticum, 229
  capillis-veneris, 229
  'Dyce's Dwarf,' 132
  forma *imbricans,* 132
  Japanese form, 132
  jordanii, 229
  pedatum var. *aleuticum,* 132
  pedatum var. *minor,* 132
  pedatum var. *subpumilum,* 132, **229**
Agrostis, 221, 222
Agropyron spicatum, 225
Alder, 15, 16, 17, **73,** 76
  mountain, **73**
  red, **73,** 236
  Sitka, **73**
  white, 236
Alder family, 73, 236
Alkaline soils, 241
Allium acuminatum, **150**
  cernuum, **150**
  crenulatum, **150**
  douglasii, **150**
  falcifolium, **151**
  macrum, **151**
  robinsonii, **150**
  validum, **150**
Alnus rhombifolia, 236
  rubra, **73,** 236
  sinuata, **73**
Alpine fir. *See* Fir, subalpine
Alum root, **170–71,** 190, 196
Alyssum, 213
Amelanchier, 4, **107–8**
  alnifolia, **107–8**
  alnifolia var. *cusickii,* 108
Ammophila arenaria, 225

Anacardiaceae, 122
Anaphalis margaritacea, **165,** 182
Andromeda polifolia, **87**
  polifolia var. *compacta alba,* 87
  polifolia var. *congesta,* 87
  polifolia var. *grandiflora compacta,* 87
Anemone, **181–82**
Anemone cylindrica, **182**
  drummondii, **182**
  lyallii, **182**
  multifida, **182**
  nuttallii, **181**
  occidentalis, **181–82**
  oregana, **182**
  piperi, **182**
Antelope brush, **120–21**
Antennaria alpina, **182**
  microphylla, **182**
  parvifolia, **182**
  racemosa, **182**
  suffrutescens, **182**
Apiaceae, 233
Apocynaceae, 230
Apocynum androsaemifolium, 230
Apple, western crab, **238**
  squaw, 240
Aquilegia, 23, **165–66**
  coerulea, **166**
  flavescens, **165–66**
  formosa, 22, **165–66**
  jonesii, 166
Arabis breweri, 230
  furcata, 230
  koehleri, 230
  lyallii, 230
  macdonaldiana, 230
  nuttallii, 230
  serpentinicola, 230
Araceae, 148
Aralia, western, **158–59**
Aralia californica, **158–59**
Araliaceae, 118, 158
Arbute-tree, 57
Arbutus menziesii, **57–60**
  unedo, 3, **60**
Arctostaphylos, **83–87,** 95, 96
  canescens, 87
  columbiana, 23, 84, **85–86**
  nevadensis, 83, **84,** 86
  parvifolia, 87
  patula, 83, **87**
  stanfordiana var. *hispidula,* 87
  uva-ursi, **83–85**
  viscida, 87
  X *media,* 84, **86**
  X *media* var. *grandiflora,* 86
Arenaria capillaris, **182**
  congesta, **182**
  franklinii, **182**
  obtusiloba, **182**
Aristolochiaceae, 182–83

Arnica, **166**
Arnica amplexicaulis, **166**
  cernua, **166**
  chamissonis, **166**
  cordifolia, **166**
Artemisia, **93–94, 166,** 210
  frigida, **166**
  norvegica, **166**
  tridentata, **93–94,** 166
  trifurcata, **166**
Aruncus sylvester, **159,** 180
Asarum caudatum, 19, **183**
  hartwegii, **183**
  marmoratum, **183**
Ash, mountain, 20
  Oregon, **78–79**
  Sitka mountain, 20
Ash family, 78–79
Aspen, quaking, **77**
  western trembling, **77**
Aspidotis densa, 131, **133**
Asplenium trichomanes, 133
Aster, **166,** 192
  alpine, 230
Asteraceae, 230, 232, 235
Aster alpigenus, **230**
  foliaceus, 166
  ledophyllus, 166
  radulinus, 166
Aster family, 93–94, 116, 159, 161–66, 169, 172, 176, 181, 182, 186, 192, 193, 195, 196, 210, 212, 214, 235
Astilbe, 232
Astragalus, 177, **183,** 204
  agrestis, **183**
  kentrophyta, **183**
  newberryi, **183**
  purshii, **183**
  whitneyi, **183**
Athyrium, **134,** 141
  distentifolium, **134**
  filix-femina, **134**
Atriplex spinosa, **117**
Avens, mountain, **190**
Awn, 222
Azalea, Cascade, **122**
  dwarf, **91**
  Kurume, 88
  mock-, 118
  western, 20, **114**

Baccharis pilularis, **94**
  pilularis var. *consanguinea,* 94
Balm, mountain, 103
  western, **203**
Balsamorhiza careyana, **167**
  deltoidea, **167**
  hookeri, 230, **231**
  macrophylla, **167**
  sagittata, **166–67**
Balsamroot, **166–67,** 181, 230, 231
  hybrids, 230
Bamboos, 222
Baneberry, **165**

Barberry, 180
Barberry family, **100–102,** 163, 180, 239
Bayberry, 93
Bay tree, California, 66
  green, 66
Beadlily, **144,** 146
Bearberry, 85
Bear grass, **149**
Beard-tongue, **175, 205–6**
  woodland, **173–74**
Beckwithia, 210
Bedstraw, **194–95,** 232
Beech, 61
Bellflower, **184–85**
  Scotch, 184
Berberidaceae, **100–102,** 163, 180, 239
Berberis aquifolium, 5, **100–102,** 239
  nervosa, **102**
  piperiana, 239
  pumila, **102, 239**
  repens, **102**
Berry, buffalo, **123**
  grouse, **128,** 241
  snow, 24
  squash, 20
Besseya, 183, 214
  rubra, **183**
  rubra X *Synthyris missurica,* 183
Betulaceae, 73, 75, 236
Betula glandulosa, 73, **116**
  occidentalis, **73**
  papyrifera, 73
Birch, 16, 23, **73**
  bog, **116**
  paper, 20, **73**
  scrub, **116**
  swamp, 73
  water, 20, **73**
Birch family, 73, 75, 236
Bird's beak, **204**
Birthwort family, 182–83
Bishop's cap, **202**
Bitterbrush **120–21**
Bitterroot, **198–99**
Blackcap, 234
Black-eyed Susan, **162–63**
Bladder-pod, **208,** 233
Blade, 222
Blanket flower, 232
Blazing star, 233, **234**
Blazing star family, 233
Blechnum spicant, **134**
Bleeding heart, **169**
Bleeding-heart family, 159–69
Bluebell, **172,** 231
Blueblossom, 8, **103**
Blue bunch wheat grass, 225
Blue dicks, **151**
Blue-eyed Mary, 227
Bluegrass, 224
Bog, 223
Bog asphodel, 235
Borage family, 171

Boraginaceae, 171
Bouteloua curtipendula, 224
Boykinia, **167**, 214
  elata, 167
  major, **167**
Box, Oregon, 20, 24, **95**, 99
Boxwood, myrtle, **95**
Brake, cliff, **136–37**
  rock, **133**
Bramble, 234
  dwarf, **126**
  strawberry, 125, **126**
Brassicaceae, 229, 230
Brickellia grandiflora, **167**
Brodiaea, fire-cracker, **151**
Brodiaea coronaria, **151**
  elegans, **151**
  hendersonii, **151**
  ida-maia, **151**
Brome, Alaska (Sitka), 222
  perennial, 224
Bromus carinatus, 224
  sitchensis, 222
Brush, coyote, **94**
Buckbean, **178–79**
  bog, **179**
Buckbean family, 172
Buckbrush, **103–4**, 239-40
Buckthorn family, 79, 99,
  103, 108, 239
Buckwheat, rush, **160**
  tall, **160**
  wild, 5, **192–93**, 214
Buckwheat family, 160,
  192–93, 203
Buffalo berry, russet-
  leaved, **123**
  silver-leaved, **123**
Bugbane, 231
  false, **179–80**
Bull bay, 58
Bunchberry, 92, **187–88**
Bunchgrass, 26, 122, 170,
  171
  mountain, 225
Burnet, 235
Burning bush, **117**
Buttercup, marsh, **183–84**
  sagebrush, **210**
Buttercup family, 117, 158,
  165, 167-68, 181, 183,
  187, 210, 231, 234
Buxus sempervirens, 90, 95

Cabbage, skunk, **149**
  deer, **172**
Cactus, hedge-hog, **106–7**
California poppy, **228**
Calluna vulgaris, 91
Calocedrus decurrens, 50–52
  decurrens cv. 'Com-
    pacta,' 51
Calochortus, **151–52**, 153
  apiculatus, **152**
  eurycarpus, **152**

  purdyi, **152**
  tolmiei, **152**
  uniflorus, **152**
Caltha, **183–84**, **217**
  asarifolia, **184**
  biflora, **184**
  leptosepala, **184**
Calypso bulbosa, **143**
Camas, 150, **153**
  death, **154**
  great, **153**
Camassia, 150, **153**
  cusickii, **153**
  leichtlinii, **153**
  quamash, **153**
Camellia, 62
Campanula, 23, 24, **184–85**
  lasiocarpa, 184, 185
  parryi, 185
  piperi, 184, **185**
  prenanthoides, **184–85**
  rotundifolia, **184**
  scabrella, 185
  scouleri, **184–85**
Campanulaceae, 184–85
Campion, 177, **212–13**
  moss, **213**
Candy-tuft, alpine, 213,
  215
Caprifoliaceae, 79–92, 124,
  127, 128
Cardamine integrifolia, **185**
  pulcherrima, **185**
Carex, 221, 224
  lyngbyi, 223
  macrocephala, 224
  mertensii, **223**
  obnupta, 223, 224
  spectabilis, 225
Carnation family, 182
Caryophyllaceae, 177, 182,
  212–13, 230
Caryopsis, 222
Cascades, 235
Cascara, **79**
  shrub, **121–22**
Cassiope mertensiana, 91, 239
  stelleriana, **239**
  tetragona, 239
Castanopsis. See *Chrysolepis*
Castilleja, **185**, 204
Catch-fly, 177, **212–13**
Cattail, 223
Ceanothus cordulatus, 240
  cuneatus, **104**
  gloriosus, **104**
  integerrimus, **108–9**, 240
  prostratus, **104**
  pumilus, **104**
  sanguineus, 240
  thrysiflorus, **103**
  thrysiflorus var. *griseus*,
    103
  velutinus, **103**
  velutinus var. *laevigatus*,
    103
Cedar, Alaska, 237
  western red, **45–46**
  giant canoe, **45**

Port Orford, **46–48**
  incense, **50–52**
Celastraceae, 95, 117
Celtis douglasii, 236
Cerastium arvense, 230
Cercocarpus ledifolius, **96**
  montanus, **96**
  montanus var. *glaber*, **96**
Chaenactis alpina, **186**
  douglasii, **186**
  ramosa, **186**
  thompsonii, **186**
Chamaebatiaria millefolium,
  116
Chamaecyparis lawsoniana,
  46–48, 237
  lawsoniana cv.
    'Allumii,' 47
  nootkatensis, 48–49, 237
  nootkatensis cv.
    'Compacta,' 49
  nootkatensis var.
    'Lutea,' 49
  nootkatensis var.
    'Pendula,' 49
Checker-mallow, **177**
Chenopodiaceae, 241
Chickweed, 230
Chickweed family, 230
Cheilanthes feei, **134**
  gracillima, **134**
  lanosa, **134**
Chimaphila umbellata, **90–91**
  menziesii, **91**
Chinquapin, golden, **60–61**
  shrub, **94–95**
  Sierra, **94–95**
Chionophila tweedyi, **186**
Chlorogalum pomeridianum,
  230
Chokecherry, **240**
Chrysolepis chrysophylla,
  60–61
  sempervirens, **94–95**
Chrysothamnus nauseosus,
  116–17
  viscidiflorus, **116–17**
Cicely, sweet, **174**
Cimicifuga elata, 231
Cinquefoil, **209**, 212
  shrubby, **112–13**, 212,
    234
Cirsium arvense, 159
  edule, **159**
  foliosum, **159**
  vulgare, 159
Cistus, 59
Cladothamnus pyroliflorus,
  116
Clarkia amoena, 227
  pulchella, 227
Claytonia, **186**, 198, 214
  lanceolata, **186**
  megarhiza, **186**, 198
  megarhiza var. *nivalis*,
    186
Clematis columbiana, **117**
  hirsutissima, **167**
Clematis, rock, **117**

Clintonia andrewsiana, **144**
  uniflora, **144**, 146
Clover, big-head, **217**
Coast redwood, 24, 25,
  56–57, 144
Cobra plant, **167–68**
Coffeeberry, **99**
Collinsia parviflora, 227
Collomia, alpine, **186–87**
Collomia debilis, **186–87**
  grandiflora, **227**, **228**
Coltsfoot, **176**
  yellow pine, **161–62**,
    176
Columbia Gorge, 228
  River, 236
Columbine, 22, **165–66**
Compositae, 93–94, 116,
  159, 161-66, 169, 172,
  176, 181-82, 186, 192,
  193, 195-96, 210, 212,
  214, 233
Convallaria majalis, 147
Copper bush, **116**
Coptis asplenifolia, **187**
  laciniata, **187**
Cornaceae, 67, 110, 187
Cornel, dwarf, **187–88**
Cornus, 67–69, 110, 187–88
  canadensis, 92, **187–88**
  cv. 'Eddie's White
    Wonder,' 68
  florida, 68, 69
  glabrata, 110
  nuttallii, **67–69**, 110
  nuttallii cv. 'Colrigo
    Giant,' 68
  nuttallii cv. 'Eddiei,' 68
  nuttallii cv. 'Gold Spot,'
    68
  occidentalis, 110
  pubescens, 110
  stolonifera, **110**
  stolonifera cv.
    'Flaviramea,' 110
  stolonifera cv. 'Kelseyi,'
    110
  stolonifera var.
    occidentalis, 110
  suecica, 188
Corydalis, coldwater, **159**
  fitweed, **159**
Corydalis aqua-gelidae, **159**
  cusickii, **159**
  scouleri, **159**
Corylus cornuta, **75–76**
Cotoneaster, 59
Cottonwood, black, **76–77**
Crabapple, 240
Cranberry, high-bush, **128**
Crane's bill, **170**
Crassulaceae, 211–12, 231
Crataegus columbiana, 237
  douglasii, 237
  monogyna, 237
  oxyacantha, 237
Creambush, **110–11**
Cress, bitter, **185**
  rock, 230

Crowberry, **91**, 239
Cruciferae, 185, 189, 194,
  208, 213, 215–16, 233
Cryptantha, **187**
Cryptantha leucophaea, **187**
  nubigena, **187**
  propria, **187**
  thompsonii, **187**
Cryptogramma crispa, **135**
  densa, 133
Culm, 220
Cupressocyparis leylandii,
  49–50
Cupressus, 95
  bakeri, 237
  macrocarpa, 49
Currant, 35
  blood, **113–14**
  golden, 114
  red-flowering, **113–14**
  squaw, 113, 114
  sticky, 114
  swamp, 114
  winter, **113–14**
  yellow, 113
Cynoglossom grande, **231**
Cyperaceae, 220
Cypress, Alaska, **48–49**
  Baker's, 238
  Lawson, **46–48**, 237
  Leyland, **49–50**
  Macnab, 238
  Monterey, 49
  Sargent, 238
  Sitka, 48
Cypress family, 238
Cypripedium californicum,
  143
  montanum, **143**
Cystopteris fragilis, **136**

Dactylis glomerata, 222
Dagger-pod, **208**
Daisy, 166
  cut-leaved, **192**
  Michaelmas, 166
  seaside, 232
  subalpine, **192**
Daisy family, 232
Darlingtonia californica,
  167–68, 235
Deer brush, **108–9**, 240
Deer cabbage, **172**
Deer's tongue, **160–61**,
  178
Delphinium, **168–69**
Delphinium burkeii, **169**
  glareosum, **169**
  glaucum, **169**
  multiplex, **169**
  nuttallianum, **169**
  trolliifolium, **169**
  viridescens, **169**
  xantholeucum, **169**
Dentaria, 185
Deschampsia atropurpurea,
  225
  caespitosa, 223, 224

Desert parsley, **233**
    sweet, **116**
Devil's club, 19, **118–19**,
    158
Dicentra cucullaria, **169**
    formosa, **169**
    formosa var. *oregona*, **169**
    uniflora, **169**
Diplacus. See *Mimulus*
Disporum smithii, **144–45**
Dock, winged, 235
Dodecatheon conjugens, **188**
    dentatum, **188**
    hendersonii, **188**
    jeffreyi, **188**
    pauciflorum, **188**
Dogbane, spreading, 230
Dogbane family, 230
Dogwood, 69
    creek, 20, **110**
    dwarf, **187–88**
    eastern flowering, 68
    Pacific flowering, **67–69**,
        110
    red osier, **110**
    western flowering, **67–69**
Dogwood family, 67, 110,
    187
Douglas fir. *See* Fir,
    Douglas
Douglasia, **188–89**
Douglasia laevigata, **189**
    nivalis var. *dentata*, **189**
    nivalis var. *nivalis*, **189**
Draba, **189–90**
Draba aureola, **189**
    densifolia, **189**
    douglasii, **189**
    lemmonii, **189**
    lonchocarpa, **189**
    oligosperma, **189**
    paysonii, **189**
    ventosa var. *ruaxes*, 189
Drosera anglica, **190**
    rotundifolia, **190**
Droseraceae, 190
Dryas drummondii, **190**
    octopetala, **190**
    X *suendermannii*, **190**
Dryopteris, **136**, 141
    austriaca, **136**
    expansa, **136**
Dudleya farinosa, **231**
Dunes, 224
Dutchman's breeches, **169**

Elderberry, blue, **79**
    red, **79**
Eleagnaceae, 123
Eleagnus angustifolia, **123**
Elephant's head, **204**
Elm family, 236
Elmera racemosa, 3, 139,
    190–91, 196
Elymus canadensis, 220, 225
    glaucus, 224
    mollis, 224
Empetraceae, 91

Empetrum nigrum, **91**, 239
Ephedraceae, 117
Ephedra family, 117
Ephedra nevadensis, **117**
    viridis, **117**
Epilobium, 160, **191**, 219
    angustifolium, **160**
    latifolium, **191**
    luteum, **191**
    obcordatum, **191**
    rigidum, **191**
Epimedium, 180
Epipactis gigantea, **143**
Equisetaceae, 142
Equisetum, 117, **142**
    hyemale, **142**
    scirpoides, **142**
Erica, 91
Ericaceae, 5, 57, 61–91,
    114, 115, 116, 122, 128,
    209, 241
Erigeron, **169–70**, 192
    aureus, **192**
    compositus, **192**
    glaucus, 232
    linearis, **192**
    peregrinus, **170**, 216
    poliospermus, **192**
Eriogonum, 5, **192–93**, 214
    compositum, **192**
    douglasii, **193**
    elatum, **160**
    flavum, **193**
    ovalifolium, **193**
    pyrolaefolium, **192–93**
    sphaerocephalum, **193**
    thymoides, **193**
    umbellatum, **192**
Eriophyllum lanatum, **193**
Eritrichium nanum, **193–94**
    howardii, **194**
Erysimum, 23, **194**
    arenicola, **194**
    asperum, **194**
Erythronium, 146, 154
    citrinum, **146**
    grandiflorum, **146**
    hendersonii, **146**
    howellii, **146**
    montanum, **146**
    oreganum, **146**
    revolutum, **146**
Eschscholtzia californica,
    228
Euonymus, 95, 117
    occidentalis, **117**
Eurotia lanata, **117**, 241
Evening primrose, desert,
    203
Evening primrose family,
    160
Everlasting, 182
    pearly, 165, 182
Exochorda, 108

Fagaceae, 60, 61, 63, 73–
    75, 94–95, 98, 104–6
Fairy bell, **144–45**

Farewell-to-spring, 227
Fern, Anderson's sword,
    139
    beech, **141**
    bladder, **136**
    chain, **141–12**
    deer, 131, **134**
    goldback, **137**
    holly, **138–40**
    Kruckeberg's sword,
        139, 140
    lace, 134, 135
    lady-, **134**
    licorice, **137–38**
    maidenhair, **132**, 229
    mountain holly, **139–40**
    oak, 19, 131, **136**
    parsley, **135**
    pod-, **133**
    rock sword, **140**
    serpentine, **140**
    Shasta, **140**
    shield, **136**
    sword, 72, 131, **138–40**
    Venus-hair, **229**
Fescue, green, 220, 225
    Idaho, 220, 224
Fescues, 222
Festuca californica, 224
    idahoensis, 224
    viridula, 220, 224, 225
Festuca spp., 225
Fiddleneck, **207**
Figwort, **163**
Figwort family, 96–97, 99,
    163, 173, 175, 183, 185,
    186, 202, 204–6, 214–15,
    217
Filipendula occidentalis, 232
Fir, Douglas, 5, 16–19, 23,
    26–27, 30, 32, 34, 41,
    43, 45, 55, 59, 61, 70,
    76, 85, 106, 110, 155
    California red, 236
    grand, 26, **28–29**, 43, 59
    noble, **30–31**, 236
    Pacific silver, 30, **31**, 38
    Shasta red, 41, 236
    subalpine, **29–30**, 38,
        48, 114, 122
    white, **28**
Fireweed, **160**
Firs, true, **28**
Flax, wild blue, **171, 201**
Flax family, 11
Fleabane, **169–70**, 192
    desert, **192**
Floret, **221**, 222
Foam flower, **216**
Forbs, prairie/meadow,
    224
Forget-me-not, alpine,
    193–94
    white, **187**
    wild, **170**
Forget-me-not family,
    171, 231
Fort Lewis, 224
Foxglove family, 96–97,

    99, 163, 173, 175, 183,
    185, 186, 202, 204–6,
    214–15, 217
Fragaria chiloensis, **194**
    vesca, **194**
    vesca var. *bracteata*, 194
    vesca var. *crinita*, 194
    virginiana, **194**
Frasera, giant, **160–61**
Frasera albicaulis, **178**
    montana, 178
    speciosa, **160–61**, 178
Fraxinus latifolia, **78–79**
Fringe cup, 178
Fritillaria, 146, **153–54**
    adamantina, **154**
    atropurpurea, **154**
    camschatcensis, **153**
    glauca, **154**
    lanceolata, 4, **153**
    pudica, **153–54**
    recurva, **154**
Fritillary, **153–54**
Fuchsia, California, **219**
Fumariaceae, 159, 169
Fumitory family, 169

Gaillardia aristata, 232
Galium, **194–95**
    boreale, 232
    multiflorum, 195, 232
    oreganum, 232
    verum, 232
Garrya, **97–98**
    buxifolia, 97
    cv. 'James Roof,' 98
    cv. 'Pat Ballard,' 98
    elliptica, 6, **97–98**
    fremontii, 97
Garryaceae, **97–98**
Gaulnettya 'Wisley Pearl,'
    82–83
Gaultheria humifusa, **82**
    ovatifolia, 17, **82**
    shallon, **81–83**, 142
Gentian, 195, 232
Gentiana affinis, 195
    calycosa, 195
    detonsa, 195
    newberryi, 232
Gentianaceae, 195, 232
Gentian family, 195, 232
Geranium, wild, **170**
Geranium oreganum, 170
    richardsonii, 170
    viscosissimum, **170**
Geum ciliatum, **232**
    var. *campanulatum*, 232
    triflorum, 232
Gilia, **195**
    granite, **197–98**
    scarlet, 195
Gilia aggregata, **195**
    capitata, **229**
    congesta, **195**
Ginger, wild, 19, **182–83**
Ginseng family, 118, 158
Globe flower, **217**

Globe gilia, **229**
Glume, **221, 222**
Glyceria elata, 223
Goat's beard, **159**, 179
Goldenrod, **163, 214**
    mountain, 235
Gold thread, **187**
Goodyera oblongifolia, **143**
Gooseberry, 35
    Menzies', **114**
    prickly, **114**
Gooseberry family, 113
Goosefoot family, 117,
    241
Grain, 222
Grama, side-oats, 224
Gramineae, 220
Grape, Oregon, 15, 24,
    59, 72, **100–102**
    western wild, **123**
Grape family, 123
Grass, annual, 220
    bear, **149**
    blue-eyed, 5, **157**
    canary, 222, 224
    cord, 225
    European beach, 225
    Indian basket, **149**
    Indian rice, 226
    June, 220
    manna, 223
    onion, 224
    orchard, 222
    prairie June, 225
    quack, 220, 222
    semaphore, **222**
    squirrel-tail, 225, **226**
    tufted-hair, 223
    Whitlow, 189
Grasses, alpine and low-
    growing, 224
    companion species, 224
    east of the Cascades,
        225
    introduced, 224
    meadow, 224
    rock garden, 225
    seashore, 224
    wetland, 223
    woodland, 222, 223
    woody, 222
Grass-of-Parnassus, **204**
Grayia spinosa, 117
Greasewood, 241
Grindelia integrifolia var.
    macrophylla, **99**
Gromwell, **171**
Grossulariaceae, 113
Groundsel, 212
    arrowleaf, **163**
Grouseberry, 241
Gum plant, **99**
Gymnocarpium dryopteris,
    19, **136**

Habenaria dilatata, **143**
    orbiculata, **143**
Hackberry, western, 236
Hackelia arida, **170**
    davisii, **170**
    floribunda, **170**
    jessicae, **170**
    venusta, **170**
Haplopappus, **195**
Haplopappus acaulis, **195**
    lyallii, **195**
    uniflorus, **195**
    uniflorus var. *howellii,*
        195
Harebell, Alaskan, **184**
    Olympic, **184**
    Piper's, **185**
Harebell family, 184–85
Hastingsia, 235
Hawthorns, **237**
Hazel, 20, **75–76**
Heath, 91
    mountain, **239**
Heather, alpine, **91**
    mountain, **91**
Heather family, 5, 18 57,
    81–91, 114–16, 122, 128,
    209, 239, 241
Hedysarum occidentale, 232,
    233
Helenium bigelovii, 233
    bolanderi, 233
    hoopsii, 233
Heliotrope, mountain,
    180, 236
Hellebore, false, **148**
Helleborine, **143**
Hemlock, mountain, **38–
    40,** 114, 122
    western, 19, 30, 32, **37–
        38,** 39, 40, 45, 55, 56,
        106
    western cv. 'Iron
        Springs,' 24, 38, 106
Hens-and-chickens, **211–12**
Heracleum lanatum, **161**
Hesperochiron, **195–96**
Hesperochiron californicus,
    196, 233
    pumilus, **196,** 233
Heuchera, 23, **170–71,** 190,
    196
    cylindrica, **196**
    glabra, **170–71**
    grossulariifolia, **196**
    micrantha, **170–71**
Holly, English, 64
    Japanese, 90, 95
Holodiscus discolor, **110–11**
    dumosus, **111**
Honeysuckle, California,
    124
    chaparral, **124**
    hairy, **124**
    trailing, **124**
Honeysuckle family, 79,

92, 124, 127, 128
Hopsage, spiny, **117**
Horkelia, **196**
Horkelia congesta, **196**
    fusca, **196**
Horse mint, 230
Horsetail, 117, **142**
Hound's tongue, Pacific,
    231
Huckleberry, 14, 18, 20,
    128
    evergreen, 20, 39, 81,
        89–90
    fool's, **118**
    red, 20, **115–16,** 241
Hulsea, **196**
Hulsea algida, **196**
    nana, **196**
Hyacinth, Indian, **153**
Hydrangeaceae, 111, 123
Hydrangea family, 111, 123
Hydrophyllum, 195, **196–97**
    capitatum, **197**
    fendleri, **197**
    occidentalis, **197**
    tenuipes, **197**
Hydro phyllaceae, 195, 196-
    97, 233, 234

Idaho, 232
Ilex crenata, 90, 95
Illiamna longisepala, **161**
    rivularis, **161**
Indian paintbrush, 185
Indian plum, 24
Indian rice grass, 226
Indian's dream, 133
Indian tobacco, 103
Inside-out flower, **180–81,**
    188
Iridaceae, 143
Iris, golden, **155**
    grass, **154–57**
    Oregon, **155**
    Siskiyou, **155**
    western, **156–57**
Iris, 143, 150, **154–57**
    bracteata, **155**
    chrysophylla, **156**
    cristata, **156**
    douglasiana, **155**
    innominata, **155**
    missouriensis, **156–57**
    purdyi, **156**
    section Californicae,
        155–57
    section Evansia, 156
    tenax, **155**
    tenax var. *gormanii,* 155
    tenax var. *klamathensis,*
        156
    tenuis, **156**
    tenuissima, 156
Ivesia, 197
Ivesia baileyi, **197**
    gordonii, **197**
    tweedyi, **197**
Ivy, poison, 122

Jacob's ladder, **208–9**
Jeckyl, Gertrude, 223
Jepson Flora of California,
    237
Jewel flower, 229
Juncaceae, 220
Juncus, 221, 223, 224
    phaeocephalus, 224
    drummondii, 225
    parryi, 225
June grass, prairie, 225
Juniper, 24, 44, **52–55**
    common, **54–55,** 84
    dunes, 235
    dwarf, **54–55**
    Pfitzer, 59
    Rocky Mountain, **52–54,**
        238
    Sierra, **54**
    'Tam,' 55
    western, **54**
Juniperus communis, **54–55,**
    84
    communis var. *depressa,*
        54
    communis var. *jackii,* 55
    communis var. *montana,*
        54
    occidentalis, **54**
    sabina var. *tamariscifolia,*
        55
    scopulorum, **52–54**
    scopulorum cv.
        'Argentea,' 53
    scopulorum cv.
        'Columnaris,' 53
    scopulorum cv.
        'Horizontalis,' 53
    scopulorum cv.
        'Viridiflora,' 53

Kalmia microphylla, **88**
    occidentalis, **88**
    polifolia, **88**
Kalmiopsis, 81, **88**
    leachiana, **88**
    'LePiniec' form, 88
    'Umpqua River' form,
        88
Kelloggia galioides, 233
Kelseya, **197**
Kelseya uniflora, **197**
Kinnikinnik, 16, 18, 24,
    83–85
Kittentail, 183, **214–15**
    lowland, 214
    mountain, 129
Knotweed, 234
Knotweed family, 234, 235
Koehleria cristata, 225

Labiatae, 203
Lady-fern, **134**
    alpine, **134**
Lady's slipper, **143**
Lady's thimble, **184**
Larch, **42–44**

Lyall, **44**
    western, 26, **42–43**
Larix gmelinii, 43
    lyallii, **44**
    occidentalis, **42–43**
Larkspur, **168–69**
Lathyrus japonicus, **171**
    latifolius, **171**
    littoralis, **171**
    nevadensis, **171**
    polyphyllus, **171**
    rigidus, **171**
    sylvestris, **171**
Lauraceae, 64
Laurel, bog, **88**
    California bay, **64–66,**
        105, 106
    mountain, 66
    sticky, **103**
Laurel family, 64
Laurus nobilis, 66
Leather flower, **167**
Ledum glandulosum, **87**
    glandulosum var.
        columbianum, 87
    glandulosum var.
        glandulosum, 87
    groenlandicum, 87
Leguminosae, 98, 162,
    171, 177, 178, 183, 201–
    2, 217, 232
Lemma, 221, 222
Leptarrhena pyrolaefolia,
    198
Leptodactylon, 195, **197–98**
    pungens, **197–98**
Lesquerella alpina, 233
    ludoviciana, 233
Leucocrinum montanum,
    233
Leucothoe, western, **88**
Leucothoe davisiae, **88**
Lewisia, **198–200**
Lewisia, **198–200,** 214, 215
    columbiana, 186, **199,**
        200, 215
    columbiana var. *rupicola,*
        199
    columbiana var.
        wallowensis, 199
    cotyledon, 186, **198–99**
    cotyledon 'Insriach,' 199
    cotyledon var. *cotyledon,*
        199
    cotyledon var. *fimbriata,*
        199
    cotyledon var *heckneri,*
        199
    cotyledon var. *howellii,*
        199
    cotyledon var. *purdyi,*
        198–99
    leana, **199,** 215
    rediviva, **198,** 200
    tweedyi, **200**
Libocedrus decurrens, **50–
    52**
Lilac, wild, 8, 20, **103–4,**
    109

Liliaceae, 4, 143–54, 230,
    233, 235, 236
Lilium, **143–44,** 146, 154
    bolanderi, **154**
    columbianum, **143**
    kelloggii, **144**
    kellyanum, **144**
    maritimum, **144**
    occidentale, **143**
    pardalinum, **144**
    parvum, **143**
    rubescens, **143**
    vollmeri, **144**
    washingtonianum, **144**
    wigginsii, **143–44**
Lily, alpine, **143**
    avalanche, 146
    Bolander's, **154**
    checker, 4, **153–54**
    chocolate, **153–54**
    corn, 148
    fawn, 146
    glacier, 146
    leopard, **144**
    lilac, **143**
    mariposa, **151–52**
    redwood, **143**
    rush, 235
    sego, **151–52**
    slink, 146
    soap, 230
    small tiger, **143**
    tiger, **143**
    western, **143**
    Wiggins, **143–44**
Lily family, 143–45, 230,
    233, 235, 236
Lily-of-the-valley, false,
    147
Linaceae, 171
Linanthastrum, 195
Linnaea borealis, 24, **92,**
    123
Linum perenne var. *lewisii,*
    171, 201
Lion's beard, **167**
Lithocarpus densiflorus, **61–
    63,** 105, 106
    densiflorus forma *attenu-
        atodentatus,* 63
    densiflorus var. *echi-
        noides,* 62, 98, 106
Lithophragma parviflora,
    201
Lithospermum incisum, **171**
    ruderale, **171**
Loasaceae, 233
Locoweed, 177, **183**
Loiseleuria procumbens, **91**
Lomatium dissectum, **233**
    martindalei, 233
    watsonii, 233
Lonicera caerulea, **124**
    ciliosa, **124**
    conjugialis, **124**
    hispidula, **124**
    interrupta, **124**
    involucrata, **124**
    utahensis, **124**

Lousewort, **204**
Luetkea pectinata, **201**
Luina, silverback, **172**
Luina hypoleuca, **172**
    nardosmia, 161–62, 176
Lupine, Russell, 162
Lupine, 158, **201–2**
    big-leaf, **162**
    Sabin's, **162**
    tree, 162
Lupinus, 192, 201
    arboreus, 98, 162
    laxiflorus, 162
    lepidus var. *lobbii,* **201–2**
    leucophyllus, **162**
    polyphyllus, **162**
    polyphyllus var.
        pallidipes, 162
    sabinii, **162**
Luzula campestris, 223
    hitchcockii, 223
    piperi, 223, 225
Lycopodiaceae, 142
Lycopodium clavatum, **142**
    selago, **142**
Lysichitum americanum,
    149

Madder family, 194, 232,
    233
Madroña, 57
Madrone, Pacific, 14, 15,
    18, 19, 20, **57–60,** 110
Madrone-tree, 57
Madroño, coast, 57
Mahala mat, **104**
Mahoberberis, 100
Mahogany, mountain, **96**
Mahonia aquifolium, 5, 100
Maianthemum dilatatum,
    147
Maidenhair fern, 132, **229**
Mallow, desert, 235
    globe, **161**
Mallow family, 161, 177,
    235
Malus fusca, **238**
Malvaceae, 161, 177, 235
Manzanita, 20, 39, 81, **83–
    87**
    green, **87**
    hairy, 23, 84, **85–86,** 87
    media, 86
    pinemat, **83–85,** 86
    rough, 87
    small-leaved, 87
    white-leaved, 87
Maple, 15, 23, **69–73**
    big-leaf, 16, 20, 43, 69,
        71–72
    Douglas', **70–71**
    Japanese, 70
    mountain, 69, **70–71**
    Rocky Mountain, 70
    Sierra, **70**
    vine, 15, 16, 20, **69–70,**
        75
Maple family, 69–73

Marigold, bog, **184**
    marsh, **183–84,** 217
Meadow rue, **178**
Meadowsweet, **110–11**
Melica, 224
Menthaceae, 230
Mentzelia laevicaulis, 233,
    234
Menyanthaceae, 172
Menyanthes trifoliata, 172
Menziesia ferruginea, **118**
    glabella, 118
    pilosa, 118
Mertensia, 231
    bella, **172**
    longiflora, **172**
    oblongifolia, **172**
    paniculata, **172**
    platyphylla, **172**
Mespilus, snowy, 4
Milkwort, **234**
Milkwort family, 234
Mima prairie, 224
Mimulus aurantiacus, **96–97**
    cardinalis, **173**
    guttatus, **173,** 202
    lewisii, **173,** 204
    tilingii, **202,** 204
Mint, horse, 230
Mint family, 203, 230, 234
Mitella breweri, **202**
    caulescens, **202**
    diversifolia, **202**
    nuda, **202**
    ovalis, **202**
    pentandra, **202**
    stauropetala, **202**
    trifida, **202**
Mitrewort, **202**
Mock-orange, 23, 108,
    111–12
    western, **111–12**
Monardella, mountain,
    203
Monardella odoratissima,
    203
Monkey flower, **173**
    alpine, **202**
    shrubby, **96–97**
Monkshood, **158**
Montana, 232
Moss, club, **142**
    little club, **142**
Mountain ash, European,
    114
    Sitka, 20, **114–15**
Mountain balm, **103**
Mountain lover, **95**
Mount Ashland, 236
Mule's ear, **181**
Mustard family, 185, 189,
    194, 208, 213, 215–16,
    229, 230, 233
Myosotis, 170
Myrica californica, **92–93**
    gale, 93, **118**
Myricaceae, 118
Myrtle, California wax,
    20, **92–93**

Oregon, 20, 22, **64–66,**
    105, 106
Myrtlewood, 66

Narthecium, 235-36
*Nephrophyllidium crista-
    galli,* 172
Ninebark, **120,** 121
Nothochelone nemorosa,
    173–74

Oak, 23, 155
    Brewer's, 74, **121**
    California black, 73, **74,**
        75
    canyon live, 20, **63–64,**
        104
    deer, **104**
    English, 74
    evergreen, 6
    Gambel's, 121
    Garry, 4, 43, 73, **74–75**
    huckleberry, 20, **104–5**
    leather, 20, **105**
    Oregon post, **73–75**
    poison, **122**
    red, 3, 74
    Sadler's, 20, **104**
    shrub tan, **98**
    tan (tanbark), 20, **61–63,**
        104
    white, 75
Oak family, 60, 61, 63,
    73–75, 94–95, 98, 104–6
Oceanspray, 14, **110–11,**
    120
    desert, **111**
Oemleria cerasiformis, **119**
Oenothera biennis, 162
    caespitosa, 203
    erythrosepala, 162
    hookeri, 162
Old man's whiskers, **232**
Oleaceae, 78–79
Oleaster family, 123
Olive, California, **66**
    Russian, 123
Olympics, 232
Onagraceae, 160
Onion, nodding, **150**
    Pacific, **150**
    scalloped, **150**
    sickle-leaf, **151**
    swamp, **150**
    tapertip, **150**
    wild, **150–51**
Onion grass, 224
Oplopanax horridum, 19,
    118–19
Opuntia fragilis, **106**
    polyacantha, **106**
Orange, mock-, 23, **111–12**
Orchid, native ground,
    142–43
Orchidaceae, 142–43
Orchid family, 142–43
Oregon, southwestern,
    229

Oregon grape, 15, 24, 59,
    72, 100–102
    Cascade, 5, **102**
    creeping, **102**
    low, 17, **102**
    tall, 17, **100**-102, 180,
        239
Oregon sunshine, 193
Oregon tea-tree, 239-40
Oryzopsis hymenoides, 226
Osmanthus delavayi, 90
Osmaronia cerasiformis,
    119–20
Osmorhiza chilensis, **174**
    occidentalis, **174**
Oso berry, **119–20**
Oxalidaceae, 203
Oxalis, 203
Oxalis family, 203
Oxalis oregana, **203**
    suksdorfii, **203**
Oxyria digyna, **203**
Oxytropis, 204
    campestris, **183**
    sericea, **183**

Pachystima myrsinites, **95–
    96,** 99
Paeonia brownii, **174**
Paeoniaceae, 174
Paintbrush, Indian, **185**
Palea, **221,** 222
Parnassia fimbriata, **204**
Parrya menziesii, **203**
Parsley family, 161, 174,
    233
Parsnip, cow, **161**
Partridge foot, **201**
Pasque flower, 181–82
Pathfinder, **164**
Pea, golden, **178–79**
Pea family, 98, 162, 171,
    177, 178, 183, 201–2,
    217, 232
Pearlbush, 108
Pedicularis bracteosa, **204**
    contorta, **204**
    groenlandica, **204**
    ornithorhynchia, **204**
    racemosa, **204**
Pediocactus, 106
    simpsonii, **107**
Pellaea breweri, **137**
    bridgesii, **137**
    glabella, **137**
Peltiphyllum peltatum,
    174–75
Penny-cress, alpine, **215–
    16**
Penstemon, Barrett's, **205**
    shrubby, **99**
    woodland, **173**-4
Penstemon, 23, 24, **175,**
    205
    acuminatus, **175**
    barrettiae, 99, **205**
    cardwellii, 24, **205–6**
    cyaneus, **175**

Dasanthera section, 99,
    206
    davidsonii, 99,199, **205**
    fruticosus, 24, 75, **99,** 205
    laetus, **175**
    lyallii, **175**
    newberryi var. *berryi,* **206**
    procerus var. *tolmiei,* **206**
    richardsonii, **175**
    rupicola, 24, 99, **205**
    serrulatus, **175**
    speciosus, **175**
    tolmiei, **206**
    venustus, **175**
Peony, western, **174**
Peony family, 174
Pepperwood, 66
Perigynium, **221**
Pernettya mucronata, 82
Petasites frigidus, 161, **176**
    frigidus var. *nivalis,* 176
    frigidus var. *palmatus,*
        176
    japonica, 176
    sagittatus, 176
Petrophytum, **206–7,** 213
Petrophytum caespitosum,
    207
    cinerascens, **207**
    hendersonii, **207**
Phacelia, 195, 197
    hastata, **207**
    lyallii, **207**
    sericea, **207**
Phalaris, 222
Philadelphus, 108
Philadelphus lewisii, **111–12**
Phleum alpinum, 220, **225**
Phlox, prickly, **197–98**
    shrubby, **197–98**
Phlox, 182, **207–8**
Phlox adsurgens, **208**
    colubrina, **208**
    diffusa, **208**
    hendersonii, **208**
    hoodii, **208**
    longifolia, **208**
    speciosa, **208**
Phlox family, 186, 195,
    197, 207–8, 229
Phoenicaulis cheiranthoides,
    208
Phyllodoce empetriformis, **91**
    glanduliflora, **91**
    X *intermedia,* **91**
Physaria alpestris, **208**
    geyeri, **208,** 233
Physocarpus capitatus, **120,**
    121
    malvaceus, **120**
Picea, 41
    breweriana, 41
    engelmannii, **41**–42
    pungens, 42
    sitchensis, 40, **41**–42
Piggyback plant, **179**

Pine, 23, **31–36**
Pine, bristle-cone, 32–33
  eastern white, 32
  five-needled, **31–33**
  foxtail, 33
  ground, 142
  jack, 35
  Japanese red, 36
  Jeffrey, **34**
  knobcone, **34–35**
  limber, **32**
  lodgepole, 26, 31, **35–36**
  ponderosa, **34**, 166, 170.
  shore, **35–36**, 52
  sugar, 31, **32**
  three-needled, **34–35**
  two-needled, **35–36**
  western white, **31–32**,
    41, 106
  white-bark, **33**
  yellow, 3, **34**, 43, 74,
    120, 155, 171, 172,
    174, 183, 199, 201,
    208, 210, 212, 218
  yellow Scot's, 36
Pine family, 177, 182, 212–
  13, 236
Pinus, **31–36**
Pinus albicaulis, 31, **33**
  aristata, **32**
  attenuata, **34**
  balfouriana, 33
  banksiana, **35**
  contorta, **35–36**
  contorta var. *contorta*, 35
  contorta var. *latifolia*, 35
  flexilis, **32**
  jeffreyi, **34**
  lambertiana, **32**
  monticola, **31–32**
  ponderosa, 3, **34**
  strobus, 32
Pipsissewa, **90–91**, 116
Pitcher-plant, California,
  167–68
Pitcher-plant family, 167–
  68
Pityrogramma triangularis,
  137
Plantain, rattlesnake, 143
Plectritis, rosy, 229
Plectritis congesta, 229
Pleuropogon refractus, **222**
Plum, Indian, 24, **119**
Poa, 225
  macrantha, 224
Poison oak, 122
Polemoniaceae, 186, 195,
  197, 207–8, 229
Polemonium carneum, 208,
  209
  elegans, **209**
  pulcherrimum, 208
  viscosum, **209**
Polygala californica, 234

Polygalacene, 234
Polygonaceae, 160, 234,
  235
Polygonum newberryi, 234
Polypodiaceae, 131
Polypody, **137–38**
Polypodium glycyrrhiza,
  137–38
  hesperium, **138**
  scouleri, **137**
Polystichum, 132, **138–40**
  andersonii, **139**
  imbricans, **139**
  kruckebergii, 139, **140**
  lemmonii, **140**
  lonchitis, **139–40**
  mohrioides var. *lemmonii*,
    140
  munitum, **138–39**
  munitum var. *imbricans*,
    139
  scopulinum, **140**
Populus acuminata, **76**
  angustifolia, **76**
  deltoidea, **76**
  tremuloides, 77
  trichocarpa, **76–77**
Portulacaceae, 186, 198–
  200, 214, 215
Potentilla, 24, 112, 196,
  209, 212
  anserina, 234
  brevifolia, **209**
  breweri, **209**
  diversifolia, 234
  fruticosa, **112–13**
  gracilis, 234
  ovina, **209**
  pacifica, 227, 234
Prairie smoke, **232**
  star, **201**
Primrose, evening, 162
Primrose family, 176–77,
  188, 216–17
Primula, **176–77**
Primulaceae, 176–77, 188,
  216–17
Primula cusickiana, **177**
  incana, **177**
  japanica, 176
  nivalis, 176
  parryi, **176–77**
Prunus emarginata var.
  mollis, **78**
  virginia vars. *demissa*,
    melanocarpa, **240**
Pseudotsuga menziesii, **26–
  28**
  cv. 'Brevifolia,' 27
  cv. 'Fletcheri,' 27
  var. *glauca*, 27
Puccoon, **171**
Pulsatilla, **181**
Purshia tridentata, **120–21**
Purslane family, 186, 198–
  200, 214, 215
Pussypaws, **214**
Pussy-toes, **182**

Pyrola, 209
Pyrola, 116, **209**
  asarifolia, **209**
  dentata, **209**
  picta, **209**

Queen's cup, **144**
Queen-of-the-forest, 232
Quercus, 5, 61, 63
Quercus breweri, **74**
  chrysolepis, 5, 6, **63–64**,
    104–5
  durata, **105**
  gambellii, 121
  garryana, 4, 5, **73–75**
  garryana var. *breweri*,
    74, **121**
  kelloggii, **73–74**
  oerstediana, 74
  robur, 74
  rubra, 3, 74
  sadleriana, 6, **104**
  vaccinifolia, 6, **104**
  velutina, **74**

Rabbitbrush, 116–17
  sticky, **117**
Raillardella, silvery, 210
Raillardella argenta, **210**
Ranunculaceae, 117, 158,
  165, 167, 168, 181, 183,
  187, 210, 231
Ranunculus andersonii, **210**
  eschscholtzii, 234
  occidentalis, 234
  suksdorfii, 234
Ratibida columnaris, **162**
Rattle-pod, **153–54**, 183
Redwood, coast, 24, 25,
  56–57, 144
Rein-orchid, 143
Resinweed, 99
Rhamnaceae, 79, 99, 103,
  108, 240
Rhamnus californica var.
  crassifolia, **99**
  californica var.
    occidentalis, **99**
  californica var.
    tomentella, **99**
  purshiana, **79**, 106
  purshiana var.
    "arbuscula," 121–22
Rhododendron, Pacific,
  88–89
Rhododendron, 58, 62, 81,
  82, **88–89**, 93
  albiflorum, **122**
  Fortunei series, 89
  Lapponicum series, 68
  macrophyllum, **88–89**
  occidentale, **122**
  Ponticum series, 89
Rhubarb, Indian, **174–75**
Rhus diversiloba, **122**
  glabra, **122**

glabra cv. 'Laciniata,'
  122
  radicans, **122**
  trilobata, **122**
  typhina, 122
Ribes, 35
Ribesaceae, 113
Ribes aureum, 113, **114**
  cereum, 113, **114**
  lacustre, **114**
  lobbii, **114**
  menziesii, **114**
  sanguineum, **113–14**
  viscossisimum, **114**
Rock brake, **132**
Rockmat, Olympic
  Mountain, **206**
Rockrose, 59
Romanzoffia sitchensis, 234
Rosaceae, 78, 96, 107, 110,
  112, 114, 116, 119, 120,
  125–26, 159, 190, 194,
  196, 197, 201, 206–7,
  209, 212, 232, 234, 238,
  240
Rosa gymnocarpa, **125**
  nutkana, **125**
  woodsii, **125**
Rose, bald-hip, **125**
  Nootka, **125**
  wild, 24, **125**
  wild guelder, **128**
  Wood's, **125**
Rose family, 78, 96, 107,
  110, 112, 114, 116, 119-
  20, 125–26, 159, 190,
  194, 196, 197, 201, 206–
  7, 209, 212, 227, 232,
  234, 238, 240
Rosemary, bog, **87**
Rubiaceae, 194, 232, 233
Rubus bartonianus, 234
  lasiococcus, **126**
  leucodermis, 234
  parviflorus, **125**
  pedatus, 125, **126**
  spectabilis, **125–26**
  ursinus, 234
Rudbeckia hirta, **162**
  occidentalis, **162**
Rue, meadow, **178**
Rush, scouring, **142**
Rushes, 220, 221, 224
  wood, 223
Rusty leaf, **117**
Rye, giant, 220, 225

Sage, **210–11**
  spiny hop, **117**
Sagebrush, 19, 26, 54, **93–
  94**, 116, 122, 166, 170-
  72, 174, 182, 185, 192,
  201, 202, 208, 210-12,
  216-18
Sagebrush country, 230
Salal, 14, 15, 18, 23, 24,
  39, 59, 72, **81–83**, 100,
  142

little, **17**
Salicaceae, 70–71, 238, 241
Salix amygdaloides, 238
  arctica, **126**
  bebbiana, 238
  cascadensis, **126**
  exigua, **126**
  fluviatilis, **126**
  hindsiana, 238
  hookeriana, **126**
  lasiandra, 238
  lasiolepis, 238
  nivalis, **126**
  scouleriana, **126**, 238
Salmonberry, **125–26**
Salt marsh, 224, 225
Salt spray, 224
Salvia dorrii, **210**
  dorrii var. *carnosa*, 210
  sonomensis, **210–11**
Sambucus cerulea, **79**
  racemosa, **79**
Sand lily, 233
Sandwort, **182**
Sanguisorba sitchensis, 235
Sarcobatus vermiculatus, 241
Sarraceniaceae, 167–68
Sassafras, California, 66
Satureja douglasii, 123
Saxifraga, 211, 214
  arguta, **211**
  bronchialis, **211**
  caespitosa, **211**
  marshalii, **211**
  mertensii, **211**
  oppositifolia, **211**
  tolmiei, **211**
Saxifragaceae, 167, 170,
  175, 179, 190, 196, 198,
  201, 202, 204, 211, 214,
  216
Saxifrage, **211**
  false, **198**
  leatherleaf, **198**
Saxifrage family, 167, 170,
  175, 179, 190, 196, 198,
  201, 202, 204, 211, 214,
  216
Schoenolirion album,
  bracteosum, 235
Scoliopus bigelovii, **147**
  hallii, **146**
Scrophulariaceae, 96–97,
  99, 163, 173, 175, 183,
  185, 186, 202, 204–6,
  214–15, 217
Scrophularia californica, **163**
  lanceolata, **163**
Scutellaria angustifolia, 235
  lateriflora, 235
  nana, 235
Sedge, big-head, 224
  Merten's, **223**
Sedges, 220, 224
  rhizomatous, **221**
Sedum, broad-leaf, **212**
Sedum, 23, **211–12**
  divergens, **212**

lanceolatum, **212**
lanceolatum var. *rupicolum*, 212
laxum, **212**
obtusatum, **212**
oregonense, **212**
spathulifolium, **212**
stenopetalum, **212**
Selaginella densa, **142**
douglasii, **142**
oregana, **142**
wallacei, **142**
Senecio crassicaulis, **163**
flettii, **212**
integerrimus, **163**
neowebsteri, **212**
porteri, **212**
serra, **163**
triangularis, **163**
Sequoia sempervirens, 26, **56–57**
cv. 'Cantabrica,' 57
cv. 'Nana Pendula,' 56
cv. 'Prostrata,' 56
Serviceberry, 4, 20, **107–8**
Shadberry, 4
Shadbush, 4
Sheath, **221**, 222
Shepherdia argentea, **123**
canadensis, **123**
Shieldleaf, **174–75**
Shooting star, **188**
Sibbaldia procumbens, **212**
Sidalcea hendersonii, **177**
malvaeflora, **177**
oregana, **177**
Silene acaulis, **213**
californica, **213**
campanulata, **213**
douglasii, **177**
hookeri, **212–13**
ingrahamii, **213**
lemmonii, **213**
oregana, **177**
parryi, **177**
pulverulenta, **213**
scouleri, **177**
scouleri var scouleri, 177
Silk-tassel bush, **97–98**
Silk-tassel family, 97–98
Silverweed, **227**
Sisyrinchium, 5, **157–58**
bellum, **157**
californicum, **157**
hitchcockii, **157**
douglasii, **157–58**
Sitanion jubatum, 225, **226**
Skullcap, **235**
Sky pilot, **208–9**
Slink pod, **146**
Slipper, fairy, **143**
lady's, **143**
Smelowskia, **211**
Smelowskia calycina, **213**
ovalis, **213**
Smilacina, **144**
racemosa, **145**
stellata, **145**
Snapdragon family, 96–97,

99, 163, 173, 175, 183, 185, 186, 202, 204–6, 214–15, 217
Snake River, 234, 236
Snowball bush, **120**, 128
Snowberry, 24, 59, **127**, 128, 230
Snowbrush ceanothus, 240
Solidago canadensis, **163**
graminifolia, **163**
multiradiata scopulorum, 235
occidentalis, **163**
spathulata var. nana, **214**
Solomon's seal, false, **145**
Sophora, western, **177–78**
Sophora leachiana, **177–78**
Sorbus aucuparia, **114**
scopulina, **115**
sitchensis, **114–15**
Sorrel, mountain, **203**
wood, **203**
Spartina, **225**
Speedwell, **217**
Sphaeralcea coccinea, **235**
grossularifolia, **235**
munroana, **235**
Spice tree, **66**
Spikelet, **221**, 222
Spikenard, **158–59**
Spindlebush, western, **117**
Spindlebush family, 95, 117
Spiraea, 23, 120, **126–27**, 207, 232
Spiraea betulifolia var. lucida, **126–27**
densiflora, **127**
douglasii, **126**
X pyramidata, **127**, 128
Spirea, **126–27**
Spirea, Alaska, **201**
dwarf, **206**
hardhack, **126**, 127
pyramid, **127**
shiny-leaved, **126–27**
subalpine, **127**
Spleenwort, **133**
Spraguea umbellata, **214**
var. caudicifera, **214**
var. umbellata, **214**
Spring-beauty, **186**
Spruce, **41**
Spruce, Brewer's, 17, **41**
Colorado blue, **42**
Engelmann, **41–42**
Sitka, 40, **41–42**
weeping, **41**
Squashberry, 20, **128**
Squawbush, **122**
Squaw carpet, **104**
Squirrel-tail grass, 225, **226**
Staff-tree family, **95–96**
Star flower, **216–17**
Steer's head, **169**
Stenanthium occidentale, 236

Stenanthium, western, 235, 236
Stick-tight, **164**
Stonecrop, **211–12**
sea-cliff, **231**
Stonecrop family, 211–12, 231
Stoneseed, **171**
Strawberry, wild, **194**
Strawberry tree, 3
Streptanthus tortuosus, **229**
Streptopus, 144, 145
amplexifolius, **145**
roseus, **145**
streptopoides, **145**
Sugarbowls, **167**
Suksdorfia, **214**
Sullivantia, **214**
Sumac, **122**
Sumac family, 122
Sundew, **190**
Sundew family, 190
Sunflower, desert, **166–67**
Sunflower family, 230
Sunrise (Mount Rainier), 225
Sweet-after-death, **163–64**
Sweet cicely, **174**
Sweet gale, **118**
Sweet gale family, 118
Sweet pea, wild, **171**
Sweet William, wild, **207–8**
Swertia, 161, **178**
perennis, **178**
Symphoricarpos, **127**, 230
mollis var. hesperius, 128
Synthyris, 183, **214–15**
missurica, 129, **214–15**
missurica var. stellata, **215**
pinnatifida var. lanuginosa, **215**
reniformis, **214**
schizantha, **215**
Syringa, **111–12**

Talinum, **215**
Talinum okanoganense, **215**
spinescens, **215**
Tamarack, **42**
Tanbark, dwarf, **98**
Tan oak, shrub, **98**
Taxaceae, 55-56, 105-6, 238
Taxol, **238**
Taxus baccata, 56
brevifolia, **55–56, 105–6,** 238
Tea, Labrador, **87,** 118
Mormon, **117**
Tellima grandiflora, 23, **178**
Thalictrum, **178**
Thelypteris limbosperma, **141**
nevadensis, **141**
phegopteris, **141**
Thermopsis montana, **178–79**

Thimbleberry, **125, 126**
Snake River, 234
Thistle, Canada, **159**
horse, **159**
Indian, **159**
Thlaspi, 213, **215–16**
fendleri, **215–16**
Thousand mothers, **179**
Thuja, 44, 45–46
Thuja plicata, **45–46**
cv. 'Atrovirens,' 46
cv. 'Aurea,' 46
cv. 'Aureovariegata,' 46
cv. 'Cuprea,' 46
cv. 'Hogan,' 46
cv. 'Pumilio,' 46
Tiarella trifoliata, 214, **216**
Timothy, alpine, **220, 225**
Tobacco, Indian, **103**
Tolmiea menziesii, **179**
Toothwort, **185**
Townsendia, **216**
Townsendia florifer, **216**
montanum, **216**
parryi, **216**
Trailblazer, **164**
Trautvetteria caroliniensis, **179–80**
Trisetum alpine, **225**
nodding, **222**
Trisetum alpinum, **225**
cernuum, **222**
Trientalis arctica, **217**
latifolia, 216, **217**
Trifolium macrocephalum, **217**
thompsonii, **217**
Trillium, 147–48, **216**
giant, **148**
round leaved, **148**
Trillium chloropetalum, **148**
ovatum, **147**
petiolatum, **148**
rivale, **148**
Trollius laxus, **207**
Tsuga, 36–40
heterophylla, 28, **37–38,** 40
heterophylla cv. 'Conica,' 38
heterophylla cv. 'Iron Springs,' 38, 106
mertensiana, **38–40**
mertensiana cv. 'Argentea,' 39
mertensiana cv. 'Glauca,' 39
X jeffreyi, 40
Twinberry, **124**
Twinflower, 24, **92**
Twisted-stalk, **145**
Typha angustifolia, **223**
latifolia, **223**

Ulmaceae, **236**
Umbelliferae, 161, 174
Umbellularia californica, **64–66,** 106
Umbrella plant, **174–75**

Vaccinium alaskense, **128**
deliciosum, **128**
macrocarpon, **128**
membranaceum, **128**
ovatum, **89–90**
oxycoccus, **128**
parvifolium, **115–16,** 241
scoparium, **241**
Valerian, **236**
Sitka, **180**
Valerianaceae, 180, 229, 236
Valeriana columbiana, **236**
sitchensis, **180,** 236
Valerian family, 180, 229
Vancouveria, **180–81**
Vancouveria, **180–81,** 188
chrysantha, **180**
hexandra, **180,** 181
planipetala, **180–81**
Vanilla leaf, **163–64**
Vase flower, **167**
Venus-hair fern, **229**
Veratrum californicum, **148**
insolitum, **148**
viride, **148**
Veronica, 183, **217**
cusickii, **217**
wormskjoldii, **217**
Vetch, milk, **183, 204**
sweet, **233**
Viburnum, moosewood, **128**
Oregon, **128**
oval-leaved, **128**
Viburnum edule, 20, **128**
ellipticum, **128**
opulus, 120, **128**
Vine, whipple, **123**
Viola, **217–19**
adunca, **218**
beckwithii, **218**
canadensis, **218**
flettii, **219**
glabella, **218**
mackloskyi, **218**
nuttallii, **218**
nuttallii var. praemorsa, **218**
palustris, **218**
sempervirens, **218**
sheltonii, **218**
trinervata, **218**
Violaceae, 217–19
Violet, 24, 158, **217–19**
dog's tooth, **146**
Violet family, 217–19
Vitaceae, **123**
Vitis californica, **123**

Wahoo, western, **117**
Wake-robin, **147**
western, **147**

Wallflower, 23, **194**
Waterleaf, **196–97**
Waterleaf family, 196–97, 207, 233, 234
Wax myrtle, California, 20, **92–93**, 118
    Pacific, 93
Wetland, defined, 223
Whipplea modesta, **123**
Whitlow grass, 189

Whortleberry, red, **115–16,** 118, 128
Willow, 15, 20, 76, **126**
    Arroyo, 238
    Bebb's, 238
    Hooker's, **126**
    peach-leaved, 238
    red, 238
    Scouler's, **126,** 238
    shrub, 240–41
    tree, 238
Willow family, 70–71, 126, 233, 240–41

Willow-herb, alpine, **191**
    fuchsia-flowered, 219
Windflower, **181–82**
Winter fat, **117,** 241
Wintergreen, 116, **209**
Woodland star, **201**
Woodsia, **141**
Woodsia oregana, 131, **141**
    scopulina, **141**
Woodwardia fimbriata, 132, **141–42**
Wormwood, **166**
Wyethia helianthoides, **181**

Xerophyllum tenax, **149**

Yakima Park (Sunrise, Mount Rainier National Park), 225
Yarrow, 116
    common, 193
    false, **186**
    golden, **193**
Yerba buena, 123
Yerba de selva, **123**
Yew, 24

English, 56
    western, 20, **55–56,** 105–6, 238
Youth-on-age, **179**

Zauschneria californica, **219**
    latifolia, 219
Zygadenus elegans, **154**
    venenosus, **154**

About the Author

Arthur R. Kruckeberg, a Northwest naturalist for more than forty years, is professor emeritus of botany at the University of Washington. Since 1950, when he began teaching at the University, he has lectured widely to both scholarly and lay audiences on horticulture, conservation, and environmental ethics; and has led hundreds of students, of all ages, on field trips to the region's mountains, lakes, meadows, and sagebrush country. His wife Mareen's rare plant nursery, which specializes in Northwest natives and which he helps to run, provided a living source for this book. He is also the author of numerous other books on the region, including *The Natural History of Puget Sound Country* (University of Washington Press, 1991). In 1976 he cofounded the Washington Native Plant Society.

Library of Congress Cataloging-in-Publication Data

Kruckeberg, Arthur R.
    Gardening with native plants of the Pacific Northwest / Arthur R. Kruckeberg. —Rev. ed.
        p.   cm.
    Includes bibliographical references (p.   ) and index.
    ISBN 0-295-97476-1 (pbk. : alk. paper)
    1. Native plant gardening—Northwest, Pacific. 2. Native plants for cultivation—Northwest, Pacific. 3. Plants, Ornamental—Northwest, Pacific. I. Title.
SB439.K78   1995   95-10553
635.9'5179-dc20   CIP